Of Siblings

THE TWENTIETH CENTURY RECOLLECTIONS OF AN EVERYDAY WOMAN, 1933 – 2016

by Molly Poulter

© Molly C Poulter
First published 2016
Second edition 2017
Third edition 2018

Published by Oast Publishing, The Old Dairy, Street Farm,
Ulcombe, Near Maidstone, Kent ME17 1DP

Tel: 01622 842988

ISBN 9 780995 689503

Designed by Alexandra Hawes, Ampersand.
Email: *alexandra.hawes@btopenworld.com*

Contents

CHAPTER 1	Early Years – My Home and Relatives, 1933 – 1939	7
CHAPTER 2	The War Years, 1939 – 1945	24
CHAPTER 3	The Post War Years, Education and the Baptist Church, 1945 – 1952	37
CHAPTER 4	University, 1952 – 1956	48
CHAPTER 5	The India Office Library and Marriage, 1956 – 1963	55
CHAPTER 6	Life in Chislehurst, 1960 – 1966	73
CHAPTER 7	We Bought The Oast, May 1966	80
CHAPTER 8	Preparations, 1965 – 1966	86
CHAPTER 9	We Take Up Residence, September 1966	90
CHAPTER 10	Adjustments	95
CHAPTER 11	The Playgroup Venture, January 1967	103
CHAPTER 12	The Baby Sitting Club, 1968 onwards	118
CHAPTER 13	The Oast Garden, 1967 – 1999	120
CHAPTER 14	Pre School Playgroup Association and Adult Education, 1970 – 1973	129
CHAPTER 15	Community Activities, 1966 – 2016	133
CHAPTER 16	Sharing a Car, 1973 – 1975	154
CHAPTER 17	The French Connection, 1952 to the present	157
CHAPTER 18	The Swimming Pool and the Guest House Venture, 1982 – 1985	164
CHAPTER 19	Back to School, 1973 – 1986	182
CHAPTER 20	Culture Shock	188
CHAPTER 21	Curriculum Innovations	207
CHAPTER 22	English and Social Studies	215
CHAPTER 23	Reflections on my Teaching Experience	238
CHAPTER 24	The Hospice Charity, 1985 – 1993	255
CHAPTER 25	Fund Raising for the Maidstone Hospice Appeal	281
CHAPTER 26	The Hospice is Built, October 1991	309
CHAPTER 27	My Christian Journey	327
CHAPTER 28	Of Such Things	341

CHAPTER 1

Early Years – My Home and Relatives, 1933 – 1939

'You must be mad,' say my friends, when I tell them about the fifteen packing cases of my personal papers in the attic. My family are more understanding, accepting wryly my idiosyncrasies and eccentricities, knowing that as an archivist I have been incapable throughout my life of throwing anything written away.

They know I have left the papers in my will to the local record office which, some years before, expressed an interest in having them. Whether this interest will be maintained after my death or whether the packing cases will be consigned to the fire is, fortunately, something beyond my control and which will no longer be of concern to me.

But I do believe that the papers would be of interest to future social historians and that is one of the reasons I have kept them. I always feel distressed when I read of famous people whose relatives have destroyed their papers after their death – Lord Byron, Jane Austen, T. E. Lawrence to name but a few. Henry James in his book, *The Aspern Papers,* leaves one with a feeling of desolation when, after much heart-searching, the manuscripts are consigned to the fire.

As an archivist, I always rejoiced when families preserved their manuscripts through generations, and enabled one to feel the past come alive in a vibrant way.

I am not vain enough to think that my life has had any special significance. But my life has been varied and interesting. I have followed several different careers – archivist, lecturer, teacher and charity fund raiser, as well as being involved in a great many community activities, both local, medical and ecclesiastical. My papers record the experience of living through the Second World War in a heavily bombed area, education just before and after the 1944 Education Act, the conversion of a derelict oast house on a shoe-string, and the building of a hospice. I have also kept all my financial files which record the huge changes that have taken place in the cost of living in the second half of the twentieth century. As my papers are comprehensive, the social historian of the future could trace the changing value of money, the changing life styles, and the sort of activities in which middle class educated women of the twentieth century indulged.

I cannot deny that there is an element of vanity in wanting to publish my Memoirs. People write their memoirs to enlighten their children and descendants about their inheritance. Others, living in the public domain, record their memoirs because they know they will be of interest to the public (and also, let it be said, because they will bring in financial reward).

In writing my Memoirs I have relived my past and realised how fortunate I have been in my marriage, my wonderfully caring son and daughter and their spouses, and now, in my beautiful six grandchildren (three boys and three girls) whom I adore, my sister and husband and their three boys, my caring foster son and his baby daughter. I feel fulfilled in that I have tried to use all the talents I have been blessed with, and have few regrets except for the inevitability of widowhood when one has a much older husband.

As I said I have left my papers in my will to the local archive office. Making a will is an event that has all the elements of trauma – that is why so many people put off making one. However simple the will, it forces one into an awareness that life is transitory, and that at some point in time, all one's earthly possessions will come into the hands of someone else.

Remaking a will is, if anything, an even more traumatic experience because it is then that the passing of time is made more apparent. Or so it seemed to us, I remember, when, at the period when our two children had reached their late teens and were about to embark on higher education, we decided our previous wills were out of date.

When we had made our first wills under the guidance of our bank manager, we had been forced to consider the awesome prospect of our whole family being wiped out in one fell swoop. "You often travel together as a family in one car ... what," said our friendly bank manager, "would you want to happen to all your possessions in that event?" Deaf to our protestations that we didn't care what happened once we were dead and buried, he insisted we made adequate provision for the disposal of our property, and we found ourselves making detailed lists of bequests, both pecuniary and material, to an assortment of relatives and friends.

The rewriting of our wills in the 1980s was imperative. But it forced us to think very carefully about our lives, both past and present. Changes of a more positive nature than death had taken place. We had a foster 'nephew' whom we wished to include in our wills – and I had become a Christian.

Now, forty years on, once again thinking about my will, it is painful to note the many gaps in that list. My husband died nine years ago, my parents on both sides are no longer with me, my sister-in-law and three brothers-in-law have died, a much loved friend is missing. And our two children, for whom we had made detailed provision in the event of both our deaths, are now perfectly capable of taking care of themselves, each having three children of their own.

Molly aged 50

It was in moving to The Oast in 1966 that our lives began to depart from the conventional path that we had followed up to that point, and I, at least, began to find myself. Our lives and characters are shaped very much by our upbringing and by the expectations of our families. And for me, those expectations had been of a very conventional nature once it had been established that I was 'clever' and capable of obtaining a degree. A degree, in my father's eyes, led to the taking up of a profession such as teaching or librarianship. Archive work, once

Wedding of Lin Mountfort and Rene Mortimer in 1931

my father understood what it entailed, was an acceptable alternative. And, of course, marriage was followed by child bearing and giving up work altogether, and when it came to housing, the expectation was that one would buy a modern house that accorded with one's income.

But for us, such was not to be. For, as I was to discover when we purchased the Oast, our lives are also shaped by a great variety of unexpected events and encounters. Our years at the Oast were a voyage of exploration and discovery – for me, an exploration of my own strengths and weaknesses, a development of talents I was not aware I possessed, and a discovery of the complexity of human relationships and behaviour. The voyage has been exciting and demanding, often joyful, sometimes painful. And as the years have gone by, I have come to believe that there has been a divine purpose throughout my life which I had refused to accept in earlier years, and I have come also to realise that of such 'trivial' things is the kingdom of heaven.

But I had better start at the beginning. My childhood was very conventional – although we had all the traumas of living through the Second World War. We lived in a terraced house on a suburban estate in Bromley which was built in 1931. When my mother was a child, Bromley was 'the country' and they used to go there on outings, but by 1931 it was covered with an urban sprawl of suburban terraced houses.

My parents paid £750 for their house – and needed a mortgage to pay for it. They chose a house in the middle of a terrace of five houses, thinking it would be warmer and easier to heat!

40 Bishops Avenue purchased for £750 in 1931

It was a well-built house. It had a lounge at the front with large windows, and a dining room at the back with French doors leading onto the garden. Both the dining room and the lounge had open fires, and there was a gas pipe leading to them to which we attached a poker which we lit to ignite the coal. I can still hear the hissing sound it made for about twenty minutes as it slowly warmed up the coal. There was a long narrow kitchen with a stove at one end which heated the water and the kitchen, and built in cupboards at the other end which housed all our crockery and cooking utensils. Near the back door was a stone sink with a wooden draining board. There was also a substantial sized pantry. We had no refrigerator or washing machine. These came much later. Up against the ceiling was a long rack which one could pull down and drape all the wet washing over it. I always hated Mondays because the kitchen was full of damp condensation from the drying clothes.

Upstairs were two good sized double bedrooms and a small box room which just took a single bed and a dressing table. My mother made a hanging wardrobe across one corner with a curtain. The bathroom was all in one – but was always nice and warm because it had an airing cupboard with the hot water tank in it.

We had an outside lavatory attached to the back of the pantry. The garden was long and narrow – just the width of the house. But it was very attractive as my mother was a keen gardener and landscaped it beautifully with stone edged flowerbeds, a rockery, and shrubs and roses climbing up both fences.

Bishops Avenue garden early days

We had a garden shed two thirds of the way down the garden which was hidden from the house by shrubs. There was a vegetable garden at the end and a garage which one approached down an alley at the side of the end house.

My father worked in Shell and my mother remained at home as did most newly-weds at the time. I was born in June 1933, and apparently my mother was three days in labour. When I eventually arrived I was paralysed down the right side of my face. I had a mass of straight black hair and cannot have been a pretty sight! I was given to understand that my father was horrified when he first saw me – a piece of information that stayed with me for years and didn't give me much self confidence!

Two and a half years after I was born my sister Barbara arrived. When my mother went into labour my mother's sister, who was my godmother, came and collected me. Her husband came from a rich family and they had a beautiful detached house in Petts Wood. But she and her husband couldn't have children, so they apparently idolised me as a proxy child, and over the years I spent a lot of time with them.

Me as a toddler

But on this occasion I think I stayed too long. It was not until years later that research at the Tavistock Clinic revealed what a severe effect separation from the mother for a lengthy period had on a young child. For me the separation was compounded by the fact that when I got home, there was this little baby whom my mother spent ages trying to feed every day because she wouldn't take milk. I think these factors accounted for the intense jealousy I felt of my little sister. Apparently I took my jealousy out on the dog, a black spaniel, and my parents had to part with it!

My sister was a beautiful baby and as she grew older, had lovely blond ringlets (my hair was nearly black and dead straight) and people made a great fuss of her.

I have comparatively few very early memories, but I remember the clothing we used to wear. Throughout the winter, we were buttoned into Liberty bodices – padded vest-like garments which were not very comfortable. We also used to wear leggings – again buttoned up, which we had to put on when we went out. I can also remember particular family gatherings – especially those where one's memory is enhanced by photographs taken at the time.

Barbara

Our house was at the bottom of a fairly steep hill. At the top of the hill were 'superior' houses which were owned by people who were rather better off than we were. But most of the people our end of the road were of very similar background – what would probably have been classified as middle class (and we felt ourselves very superior to the people who lived in Canon Road – a row of Victorian artisan houses half a mile away).

We didn't think much of one family who lived opposite us. They had five sons who were a bit wild and they didn't look after their house very well. Instead of curtains, they had whitewash over the windows! Ironically, at the top of the hill was a well-to-do builder who had five daughters. We always said the two families should have done a swop!

We were very fortunate in having children all round us to play with. Our particular playmates lived next door but one – Geoffrey six months younger than me, and Myrtle, a year younger than my sister – but we were inseparable. Then, when I was nine, another family moved in opposite with three children, one of whom, Pam, was my age, and her brother Alan was my sister's age. Pam became my best friend. Living immediately opposite, from time to time we would rig up a string telephone across the road from her bedroom to mine. Later in the War, she lived with us for six months when we were evacuated.

My parents were the poorest of both sides of the family. My mother's sister had married a rich man as did my father's sister. My father's mother died giving birth to him – or rather I should say that she died trying to give birth to a twin which she didn't know she was carrying. His grandmother was devastated at losing their only daughter and blamed my father for her death, so he was farmed out to poor relations while his sister, Audrey, two years older, was taken in by her grandmother and her mother's sister, Auntie Mab, and brought up in considerable luxury.

When his father married again, he took my father back – but he wasn't happy as his stepmother didn't like him – devoting all her attention to her own sons, Dudley and Eric. My father didn't stay with his father for long, and moved around a bit – spending some very happy years with a cousin, Nellie, and more years with his paternal grandmother. She was obsessed with the idea that her son should be the Marquis of Townsend, and my father had vivid recollections of being taken round by her in a carriage trying to unearth the relevant records. Nothing came of it – and we always wondered where all her research material went to. The only curious part about it was that both my father and his sister carried the unusual name of Woolfield. Recently my nephew, Rupert, discovered on the internet a nineteenth century architect in New Zealand with the name Thomas Woolfield Mountfort who must almost surely have been a relative.

My mother's parents, to begin with, had a smallholding at High Beach on the edge of Epping Forest. My mother and aunt always used to talk about it nostalgically, but my grandmother didn't enjoy country life and persuaded our grandfather to return to the London area. They purchased a substantial house in Brockley, and when my grandfather died, my grandmother divided it into flats, keeping the flat on the main floor for herself. In the large sitting room was an old fashioned chaise long, a beautiful bureau, and a round inlaid dining table. Her bedroom was equally large and abutted onto a conservatory which was full of plants – some of which I am sure were aspidistras. Around the walls in the hall were huge portraits of her ancestors. There was a small kitchen which had a curious smell, and an extraordinary bathroom with an old-fashioned toilet mounted on a step, and a bath on legs. The whole flat had a very different smell to our own house – not unpleasant, but somehow the aroma of a different age.

My grandparents' garden

The garden was a delight. My grandfather, being a stonemason, had all sorts of raised beds, arches and pergolas made of stone. It also had a couple of pear trees that had the most delicious fruit I have ever tasted. We asked our neighbour who worked in Covent Garden fruit market to identify it for us – but he was unable to do so. Never, anywhere, have we been able to find similar pears.

Barbara and I only had the one grandparent. My mother's father died before I was born, and, as I said, my father's mother died giving birth to him. His father died before my parents were married.

We were very fond of our grandmother. She had iron-grey hair which she wore in a bun. My recollection of her was that most of her clothes were grey, but I may be mistaken. She wore rimless glasses – and I don't think, she had much of a sense of humour. She was one of six sisters and I have wonderful photographs of them all together – looking buxom and wearing elaborate and close fitting Victoria garments. She was a devout Christian and would take herself off to church when she was staying with us.

House at Brockley sold for £1,700 in 1954

I loved her dearly but at seventy, she seemed an old lady, and looking back, my aunts, too, seemed old and set in their ways. But at eighty, I don't feel (nor, I believe, do I look) old and am still involved in numerous activities – as are most of my friends of the same age. One wonders what it is that has so altered the aging process. I think it is the affluent and easier life which we all live, coupled with great advances in medicine. One only has to look at people in the third world to realise that poverty and ill health lead to a much reduced life expectancy. I wonder, do we always realise our good fortune in living in a civilised country?

When our grandmother died in 1954, this substantial four storey Victorian house sold for £1,700 – and this was considered a good price. Years later, after both our grandmother and our mother had died, my sister and I sneaked into the garden and were devastated to see that the house had an air of decay, the garden was a jungle, all the stonework had gone, and the pear trees had been cut down.

Our grandmother, Cecilia Mortimer, aged c. 70

As I said, my parents were the poor relations of the family, although they didn't feel sorry for themselves, nor did they ever express any jealousy of their wealthier sisters, and maintained close relations with both of them throughout their lives. The only thing they did envy was the cars both sisters had. Visits to them often entailed going on lots of different buses and carrying heavy luggage. We had to take two different buses to our grandmother in Brockley with no easy connections, but my mother made the trip every Thursday for years. My aunt, with a car, was a less frequent visitor!

Similarly, visits to my mother's sister in Petts Wood involved taking two buses, while visits to my father's sister in Ashtead involved three buses with long waits at Croydon for the connection. Neither of the sisters nor their husbands ever offered to collect us. Looking back, it is amazing that my mother never expressed any resentment.

Buses at this time always had both a driver and a conductor – and we were issued with coloured bus tickets according to the amount we had to pay. The bus conductor used to clip the tickets with a machine that gave out a nice bell-like pinging sound. We

My 21st birthday – family group with my father's and my mother's sisters

enjoyed the shorter journeys, but I often felt very sick on the longer journeys, so my mother always carried acid drops with her which I sucked to ward off the sickness.

My aunt and uncle in Petts Wood lived in a lovely mock Tudor house, with a garden at the back big enough for a tennis court. It was beautifully landscaped by my stone mason grandfather. He built a lovely stone sunken garden full of roses. There were rockeries, lots of shrubs, places to hide and a swinging hammock which was bliss to lie in and read.

My Aunt and Uncles' house at Petts Wood

We approached the house along a path with lavender bushes on either side – and the scent was intoxicating. The smell inside the house was equally pleasurable for my aunt always had bowls of lavender and pot pourri scattered round the house. She was very house proud and all the furniture gleamed – the wooden panels in the hall, the brass ornaments hanging on the walls, and the lovely oak chests. She was also a very good cook, so we always enjoyed our meals.

Until a year into the Second World War, she and my uncle had a gardener whom they always referred to as Pullen to denote his status. They also had a live-in maid called Betty. She had one of the smaller bedrooms upstairs, and when not working, would sit in the kitchen which was square and comfortable with a warm stove, but I think she must have been very lonely. She always wore a little white and black lace cap and a short white apron over a black dress. She served all the meals and cleared the table afterwards. We never had to help with the washing up! We became very fond of Betty who was a Welsh lass from a mining village, and felt very sad when she had to go back to Wales to look after her parents.

Stella came next – then a succession of maids. During the early years of the War one of them transgressed badly – or so my uncle thought. She brought back a soldier and took him up to her bedroom. My uncle must have heard them because he went into the bedroom, confiscated the man's trousers and threw him out of the house. I think the maid left the next day! But the days of maids for middle class families was soon to come to an end because the girls who had fulfilled this role were needed for war work – either in factories or the armed forces.

Afternoon tea was always a ritual. Betty would bring into the lounge a large tray with silver teapot and milk jug and china teacups, and place it on an occasional table in front of my aunt. Then she would bring in a dumb waiter piled high with cucumber and egg sandwiches, scones and an assortment of cakes which my aunt had baked herself. Tea plates and linen table napkins were handed round – and then we would fall on the repast. While we were children, we enjoyed our Aunt's teas, but when we got older, we found it all too much, especially if we were staying there and knew that dinner would follow on three hours later!

My aunt and uncle had a dog called Judy. She was a black and golden cross between a collie and a spaniel. She had a lovely temperament and I loved her dearly. We used to enjoy taking her for walks with my uncle. There were bluebell woods at the bottom of the garden, and in the autumn acorns to collect, which we made into doll's house furniture. My aunt rarely walked. She much preferred staying at home.

One thing we could never get away from was my aunt's deafness. As an adolescent, she'd had measles very badly, and it had taken away most of her hearing. She wore a hearing aid that was attached to a large black box, which hung from her neck. It used to whistle incessantly which was a great irritant to us all, including my uncle. It was caused by feedback from the earpiece to the amplifier.

Conversation with my aunt always entailed looking directly at her and mouthing our words very carefully, She was a good lip reader – but much depended on who was talking and the shape of their mouths. She used to be able to read my lips and my mother's very well, so over the years, we used to find ourselves in the role of interpreters. Provided Auntie could grasp the key word of a topic of conversation, she managed quite well. But it was tiring for people like my mother and myself on whom she relied so much for interpretation.

My uncle was also deaf – but not nearly so acutely. He too wore a hearing aid. He wasn't a very fit man, and had a lot of chest infections. Over 6 ft tall, he suffered with back problems and sciatica which at times made him both irritable and sarcastic. My parents thought it was because he was a disappointed man. He worked part-time as a self-employed accountant because he had never passed his accountancy exams.

My uncle inherited money from his family and by our standards was rich. He had a car well before the War, and they went on many exciting holidays – something my parents could rarely afford. It always amazed me that my mother was not jealous of her older sister – but then, my mother was a lovely lady.

My aunt and uncle had a piano which my sister and I used to bang on, but we never produced anything musical. They also had a wonderful dressing up box which we used to enjoy playing with – and a bagatelle board which kept us occupied. She also had a blue enamel cooking set – saucepans and teapots – which my grand children enjoyed playing with, and were it in good condition, would be worth quite a bit of money.

I was very fond of my aunt and uncle, and over the years spent a lot of time with them. They could be irritating, but they were very kind and very fond of me. The house was always warm and cosy, and I would love the winter evenings, having a light supper of soup and sandwiches in their lounge, and then reading curled up on the sofa. They had no radio or television!

My mother had another sister, Gladys who was tall and lanky. But we rarely saw her standing up because she had disseminated sclerosis and spent most of her time in a wheelchair. She lived with her husband, and her daughter Glenda in a bungalow at Hayes. It was just opposite a small park in which red squirrels abounded, and we had many happy picnics watching the squirrels and playing hide and seek. Glenda was just six months younger than I was. The most I can remember of her is that she had dark hair and a fringe, and my most vivid recollections of Auntie Gladys were the delicious coconut ice sweets she made. We always came home with a box of pink and white goodies, but she never divulged the recipe to anyone.

Soon after the War began, while we were evacuated, Auntie Gladys died. Her husband took Glenda to Bath and not long after married again. I only saw Glenda once after that – just after our grandmother died.

As well as Gladys and Marie, my mother had a brother called Frank who lived in Brockley. He was married to Mill – a very thin lady who always wore dark glasses and drab clothes. She was an accomplished artist and a scientologist. Apparently the marriage caused a certain amount of upset in the family because my grandparents though Frank was much too young to marry at the age of twenty-one.

They had two daughters – Jean and Freda, who were ten year older than Barbara and I. Though they lived in the same road as my grandmother, I can only remember visiting them on a few occasions, and I suspect this was because my mother and Auntie Mill were not all that fond of each other.

Their house was similar in size and age to our grandmother's – and the garden was equally attractive as Uncle Frank was also a stonemason.

On my father's side of the family was the formidable Auntie Mab – a maiden lady who was very stately and well covered. She was not a pretty woman, and always wore heavy glasses. We were fond of her but rather in awe. She apparently had a beautiful singing voice, and we were told that, had she been more attractive, she might have become an opera singer. What amused us children was her snoring. It was so loud that the noise reverberated through the house, and sounded a bit like a cow in pain.

My father's other relatives – Uncle Frank Sleat, Auntie Bertha and Alan and Tony, who were a bit older than Barbara and me – lived in Bickley, not far from us, and we saw them occasionally, Uncle Frank Sleat died early on in the War – contracting meningitis when they were sheltering in the caves at Chislehurst during the bombing. Later, they all moved to Bath and worked for the admiralty. Alan's son, Neil Sleat, is now heard almost daily on Radio 4's *Today* programme.

Another family we had contact with as children was the family of Bert Sleat. He had been a manager of Shell in Hong Kong. We never met him, but when his wife died, we had contact with two of the five children, Margaret and Muriel, who lived with us for a time during the War.

My father' sister, Audrey, and her family figured largely in our lives. She and my uncle had three sons of whom we were very fond – two being the same age as my sister and I. My only recollection of early visits to their first house in Shirley was one Christmas when my cousin and I hid under the bed and he cut off my fringe. The grown ups were not amused, and my poor cousin was sent to bed.

Auntie Audrey was a real character even in those days. She was larger than life – in shape as well as in character. She had one glass eye which she had had since childhood – the result of an accident with a paper knife – but it didn't stop her from driving. In later years we were to develop the phrase 'an Auntie Audreyism' to indicate gross exaggeration. For our aunt used to regale us with stories and anecdotes which were always wildly exaggerated. She was good tempered and humorous, loved animals, especially dogs, and was outrageously lazy – more so as the years went by. Yet her three sons adored her and her husband waited on her hand and foot.

My Uncle Stan was a delightful character in later years, though when the boys were young he was going through an irritable phase and we used to keep out of his way as much as possible. I think some of it was caused by his extreme deafness which made it difficult for him to communicate with his lively and boisterous sons.

The family moved to a large house in Ashtead a year or two before the War – a wonderful Edwardian house with five bedrooms and all sorts of nooks and crannies to hide in. It seemed like a palace to us after our own little suburban terraced house with its long narrow garden and small rooms. The one-acre garden was perfect for playing hide and seek. There was a huge herbaceous border filled with a myriad of brightly coloured flowers, and a vegetable garden screened off by a line of espalier apple trees. Gravelled paths separated the flower and vegetable beds, and these were wonderful for riding bicycles along. (I remember vividly the day I learnt to ride a bicycle on the lawn – and my terrific sense of achievement.) At the side of the house was a garden enclosed by a yew hedge, which might once had been a bowling green, and at the far end of the garden was a huge beech tree with a swing hanging from one of the branches and a tree house which you reached via a rope ladder. There was also a magnificent magnolia tree just outside the kitchen window which had a mass of large pink blossoms in the spring. It was a house we loved visiting.

Where my mother's sister's house was immaculately clean and tidy, Auntie Audrey's house was shambolic – despite the fact that she too had a live-in maid, Freda. She always had a couple of dogs, a cat, and chickens while the boys kept rabbits and guinea pigs.

The house was comfortably furnished – though you often had to clear away papers and oddments of clothing before you could find a chair to sit on. My aunt loved bone china, but though she kept buying sets of china, it was rarely possible to find more than three cups, saucers and plates of the same set. I'm not sure who was responsible for all the breakages, but breakages there were in large numbers.

Like my mother's sister, my father's sister, Auntie Audrey was well off. Her husband, Uncle Stan, had inherited quite a lot of property from his father which he rented out at fairly lucrative rents. They too had a car. My mother always happily accepted this disparity in circumstances – despite the fact that Auntie Audrey was wildly extravagant and would go off to auction sales and come back with all sorts of unsuitable items. She and Uncle Stan were my sister's godparents

We loved being with our cousins – Neil my age and Ivor just six months older than Barbara. Neil was a rogue and a rebel but the most captivating and likeable person you could imagine. He had pale blue eyes, curly hair, and a most engaging smile. He was always, even at an early age, into wild adventures and daring enterprises, and was constantly in trouble with his father. On one occasion he rode a cart horse across the school playing fields and was suspended from school for a time. But he had a way of disarming criticism and had our maiden aunt, Aunt Mabel Lucy, who lived with them, eating out of his hand.

Ivor, the youngest was quieter than the other two. He was Neil's shadow, idolising him and following him everywhere, doing exactly what Neil asked him to do – as in fact, did my sister and I. We roamed the garden, played hide and seek in the large house, played

Monopoly and other board games, and spent a lot of time thinking how we could plague our cousin Colin who was seven years older than Neil and me, and a terrible tease

We did our best to keep out of the way of Uncle Stan, particularly on Saturday mornings, when Neil and Ivor failed to complete their pocket money chores satisfactorily. Uncle Stan's special part of the garden was an area screened off with lattice fencing where he tended his compost heap with great diligence and pride. It was a part of the garden we all hated and avoided as much as possible – especially the boys who knew they would be dragooned into 'turning' the compost if they drew too much attention to themselves.

Christmas was always a time for a large family gathering and we went to either Aunt Marie at Petts Wood or Aunt Audrey at Ashtead. They were magical times for my sister and me – even during the War when everything, including money, was in very short supply. Only in 1944 did we not get together. One of the great joys was that we would stay for several days. All we children would sleep on the floor on makeshift beds and our grandmother would often come too – though quite where all the adults slept I can't remember.

Christmas followed a similar pattern wherever we were. There was the magic of decorating the Christmas tree – though we couldn't afford lights, and the tree was much smaller than most of today's. As we got older, a group of us, before Christmas, would go carol singing round the roads and collect money for charity. Come Christmas Eve, there was the excitement of meeting up with our relatives, and the anticipation of Father Christmas's visit that night. Our Christmas stockings were one of our fathers' socks – not the large stockings that most children have nowadays. We believed in Father Christmas till we were about seven – but continued hanging up our stockings well into our teens. It's difficult to forget the magic of the early hours of Christmas morning when one could feel the heavy bulge lying at the foot of the bedclothes. We would secretly look at the contents, knowing that in the toe there would always be a tangerine, some nuts, a half crown piece (as we got older) and three or four little bits and pieces. We would wait till dawn before taking our stockings to our parents' beds and opening them all over again. We had to wait until after lunch before opening our main presents – usually only a few.

Though the pattern was the same wherever we were, it was at Petts Wood that we had the most elegant Christmases. The house was beautifully decorated and for the Christmas dinner, the table was elegantly laid with white linen tablecloth and table napkins, a tasteful Christmas decoration in the middle of the table, crackers, gleaming cutlery, and silver salt cellars and sugar sifters. Speciality of the house were the little glasses with handles full of cold custard – something my uncle was partial to.

The food was always superbly cooked. My uncle would carve the turkey ceremoniously at table, and as the meal progressed there was the fun of pulling the wish-bone, and wishing, and searching for the silver three-penny bit in the Christmas pudding.

Auntie Audrey's cooking was more slapdash – but she often had even larger numbers to cope with because her husband's brother Chris, and her Jewish friends, Jack and Jesse, would join us. We five children sat on a separate table. I remember we not only ate everything put before us, but went back for second and even third helpings. After the privations of the War, I think we enjoyed our food much more than children do today. Whereas chicken is a commonplace part of the diet today, chicken was a tremendous treat – something we had at most two or three times a year. During the War, rabbit was often our Christmas fare. It was not till after the War that we were able to get turkeys. I remember Daddy's cousins from Ireland sending over a turkey one Christmas during the War, but by the time it arrived, it was rotten and had to be thrown away, much to everyone's disappointment.

Wherever we were, at the end of the meal, we would repair to the lounge and sit solemnly to hear the King's speech. George VI had a terrible stutter, and we all felt sorry for him as he tried to get out his words. When the National Anthem was played at the end of the speech, we would all stand quietly to attention. Everyone felt very patriotic during the War and in the years after. It was not until we'd heard the speech that we opened our Christmas presents – which were usually distributed by one of the fathers. We opened the presents in rotation – eldest first and youngest last. Looking back, this was a great ploy for keeping the children in check.

Then would follow tea with Christmas cake. The adults would have a little rest while we played with our presents – and then started the fun and games in which everyone joined. We children were allowed to stay up all evening, and about 10 o'clock would sit down to a supper of cold turkey.

Boxing Day, all a bit jaded, we would go for a walk, eat turkey soup and a cold collation. If we were spending Christmas in Bromley, all the neighbours would join us in the evening and we would play party games – silhouettes, Pitt, charades, pelminism, murder in the dark, and so on. The next day, we would sometimes go up to London for a pantomime.

How things have changed over the century. Now, for many families, television dominates Christmas Day. Few people stand to attention in their own homes before the Queen's speech, and an evening at the cinema no longer ends with the National Anthem. Pillow cases are filled with sophisticated toys rather than socks with small bits and pieces. Computers are to be found in most homes, and children as young as four and five play with what seems to my generation to be complicated computer games. You can speak to people from all over the world on the telephone – and with a mobile phone you can keep in touch wherever you are. Change is inevitable and in all probability our sons and daughters will feel equally out of touch when they reach their seventies – though here again, with some 30,000 now reaching the age of a hundred, people at seventy may well feel themselves to be middle aged. It is changes such as these which, I hope, will make these Memoirs of interest to the next generation.

CHAPTER 2
The War Years, 1939 – 1945

We were all at Ashtead for the outbreak of the Second World War. I am sure I am not alone in remembering that day vividly. I was then six years of age. My father and uncle both worked for Shell, and when war broke out they were told they would have to move to Swansea. It was agreed that my mother, sister and I would join our Aunt in Ashtead as it was further away from London.

War broke out on a sunny September morning. It was one of those bright clear days and the blue of the sky seemed particularly deep, stretching out to infinity. It was a Sunday – mid morning. We were not churchgoers and everyone was in the house. But instead of the usual bustle and busyness, all the grown-ups were sitting solemnly in the lounge, speaking in hushed voices, with their attention focused on the large upright wireless-set in the corner. My uncle, who usually at this time of day would be pottering round his compost heap, was sitting in his large leather armchair with headphones on his head. My aunt, mother and father sat expectantly and tense in the other chair and we were all told to sit on the floor and be quiet. The tone of their voices and the look on their faces was such that not even my cousin Neil demurred at an order that demanded behaviour so contrary to the norm.

We heard the chimes of Big Ben and then a solemn voice started talking. I was too young to understand what he was saying but it was clear from the gravity of his tone, and the expression on the grown up's faces, that what he had to say was very important and very sad. When he had finished speaking I seem to remember the National Anthem was played and then silence descended on the room – to be broken by a frightening wailing sound that still, to this day, affects my spirits.

We children were instantly rushed out of the sitting room into the large kitchen where we were pushed under the heavy pine kitchen table and told to stay. The curtains in the kitchen were drawn and the adults sat around looking forlorn. Neil started crying and said he wanted to go into the garden. Despite his father's stern denial of his request, Neil dashed out from under the table and rushed out, returning a few minutes later clutching his pet rabbit which he cradled in his arms under the table throughout the "air raid". We then heard the wailing sound which we were later to welcome with such relief throughout the War as it signalled for us the safe end of an air raid. So our War began.

During the War we always seemed to have people living or staying with us. That, perhaps, is why I am so gregarious now! There were two cousins, Margaret and Muriel, in their late teens. They stayed with us until they were called up. Our neighbours shared our reinforced shelter in the dining room. At one point, we had two training college tutors living with us in turn as company for my mother.

Vicarage at South Stoke 1940

To go back to the War! After the declaration of war, we went back to Bromley, and soon after, because my father was in Swansea with Shell, my mother took us off to South Stoke, a pretty Berkshire village. We stayed in a flat on the top floor of the vicarage which was a very attractive stone house with a huge garden. I'm not quite sure how she got to know of the flat – but we spent a very happy three months there.

It was the period of the 'false' war with no raids at all on London, so our mother decided that as nothing was happening, we would return to Bromley. As we walked down the garden path to the front door, the first air raid siren for three months started wailing, and the bombing began in earnest.

Large bombs fell at both the top and the bottom of our road, leaving huge craters right across the road. My father had a lucky escape. He was by then back in London and in the Home Guard. He was walking up the hill when he heard the bomb falling. He flung himself to the ground – just below the brow of the hill, and the blast passed over him. He stood up to see this enormous crater in front of him.

The gas and water mains were both cut off, so Auntie Audrey came to the rescue. She couldn't get her car up to the house because we lived half way between the two bomb craters. So we lugged our suitcases to the bottom of the road where Auntie Audrey was parked, and went off to Ashtead for several months.

While we were there, my mother got me into my cousins' little private school. I was very unhappy there because the teachers tried to force me to write with my right hand. Being seriously left handed, it was a traumatic experience and my mother insisted they stopped. Such a thing would be unheard of today. But it was not long before our mother wanted to get back to Bromley, and from that point on, we stayed put till the doodlebugs started falling all round us.

To start with, we didn't have a shelter in the house, so, whenever the air raid siren went, my mother would get us up, dress us in warm clothes, and march us up the hill to an Anderson shelter in the back garden of one of the bigger houses at the top of the hill. The family didn't need the shelter because the owner, a builder, had fortified his house. We shared the shelter with one of the Bromley County School teachers. As the weather got colder, my mother decided we would be better sleeping under the stairs. So she emptied out the cupboard and made up beds on the floor where we spent many a night during the air raids.

Later, Mr Wilson the builder fortified our house. The back room, which had French windows leading onto the garden, was barricaded with a brick wall just outside the windows, a false ceiling held up by huge beams was installed, and a Morrison table erected inside the room. This is where my sister and I slept for the rest of the War. Later, we were joined by our neighbour's two children, Geoffrey and Myrtle.

Being on the outskirts of London we were caught up in very heavy bombing throughout the whole of the War. I shall always remember one raid which demolished four houses opposite us and left a huge bomb crater in the road. My father was in the Home Guard and went across to help rescue people. One family had been killed outright – but he brought back to the house a Jewish family – mother, father and two daughters. We already had our neighbour's family with us, and a couple of friends who had not been able to get home because of the bombing. So the room was very crowded. The father was in a state of shock and spent the rest of the night sitting upright on a chair in our fortified room, with a big cut on his forehead and a little black skull cap on his head. Gallons of tea were brewed during the night as the raid lasted for hours and I seem to remember we got no sleep at all.

It's difficult to imagine, if you haven't experienced it, what it was like living during the War. There was the awful

Daddy in the army

feeling of fear when you heard the wailing of the air raid warning and knew you had to get to a shelter as soon as possible. There was always a little lull, and then you would hear the sound of aeroplanes approaching, and the guns would start booming out – and then would come the sounds of bombs exploding – and all the time, you were hoping they were not going to fall on you. There was often a lull for a time as the planes went on to London. Then you would hear the planes returning, the guns would open fire again, and the Germans would drop any bombs they still had with them. Then, after a time, there was the blessed sound of the All Clear – a long drawn out wailing sound.

Most of the air raids were at night, and at times, there were air raids night after night – so we got very little uninterrupted sleep.

I felt fear from an early age – hearing my father, on his return from Home Guard duty, tell a very sad story about the death of a little girl of seven, no older than me. She had apparently been very unwell, and when the air raid warning went, her parents decided to let her sleep on instead of taking her down to the air raid shelter. But a bomb fell nearby, and the bedroom wall collapsed on her, killing her outright. It was, for me, a story that made me even more afraid.

My sister was far braver than I was – perhaps because she was younger. I would never go out and watch the dog fights during the day, but she would happily peep out behind the brick wall in front of the former dining room, and watch.

Hovering overhead in the sky were the great air balloons – menacing looking grey elongated balloons tethered to the ground in the hopes of intercepting German aeroplanes. After an air raid, we would go out and look for shrapnel – pieces of ammunition from the guns. These we would collect and place in rows on the mantelpiece. At one point in the War, we were warned not to pick up anything that looked like sweets or cardboard boxes, because the Germans were dropping bombs disguised as sweet packets.

My father was a bomb instructor in the Home Guard – somewhat surprising as he was not the most practical of men. He used to bring home boxes of bombs (minus detonators) and put them under their bed. My mother was, understandably, not too happy about that – and directly an air raid siren went, despite my father's protestations that they were quite safe, would pick up the box and take it to the bottom of the garden

For a while my father was billeted near Epsom – so we all went to stay in Ashtead in order to see him. I have a memory of a very happy and very sunny day spent at Boxhill when my father and three of his army friend joined us for the climb to the top of the hill where we had a picnic. One of the soldiers, Chalky White, became a family friend and I was to encounter him again, by an incredible coincidence, years later.

Another memory of Daddy in uniform was of my mother, sister and I going up to Victoria Station in London to meet him. The station was crowded with people in every sort of uniform. I was told to stick close to him and remember he was in army uniform. I did dutifully as I was told – but suddenly realised the soldier I was following was not my father. Panic set in before we were all reunited.

As more and more men were called up, a deep camaraderie was established between the women left behind, despite the fear, the privation, and the devastation all around. My father and our neighbour's husbands both got called up in 1943. This was unexpected as both men thought they would be too old for call-up. They were, in fact, the oldest age group to be called up during the War.

This brought my mother and our neighbour, Mrs Groom, close together. She and her children slept in our house to share the nights of bombing, and for over a year we shared a bed under the Morrison shelter with our neighbour's two children. Women didn't have an easy time, but I remember a lot of laughter. I shall never forget the night when Mrs Groom, who was a rather large lady, after a particularly loud explosion, dived head first for the Morrison shelter and got wedged between the edge of the shelter and a large beam that propped up the ceiling. You can imagine the sight! It took some time to extricate her.

Later, with my father away in the army, my mother decided to take in a lodger and Miss Edmundson came to live with us. She was a lecturer at Avery Hill Training College which had been, by some strange logic, evacuated from London to Bromley. She was a lovely lady in her fifties, I think, with silver hair and a very gracious manner. She introduced us to a number of interesting books. For some reason, she left the college and moved away and we were heartbroken. Then Miss Millican came to live with us. She was younger but was an equally delightful person. I remember she gave me a complete book of the Flower Fairies for my birthday. We kept up with both of them for a long time, and with Miss Millican right up to my going to university.

During the first part of the War, I went to Nettlestone School. This was a private school run by Miss Wells and Miss Randall in a large Victorian house. It's curious the incidents one remembers. My first day at school was one of these. The uniform was royal blue, but for some reason, my mother had not been able to buy my uniform before I started school, and I turned up in a mustard yellow cardigan. Children are cruel and I can still remember the jeers of the other children that first day.

But I enjoyed school. I remember making plasticine figures, painting flowers on parchment lampshades, playing singing games in the big empty room that doubled as a playroom, and being looked after by the nice boy who lived up the road from us.

We never went anywhere without our gas masks – packed in brown hessian boxes which we carried over our shoulders. People's recollection of the effects of gas in the First World War gave everyone a terrible fear of gas attacks, and we used to have gas mask practice once a week. Our little school was in a Victorian house with a cellar. Once a week we would descend into the damp cellar and sit for about twenty minutes wearing our gas masks. I hated them. They would very quickly fill with condensation so you could scarcely see out of the 'window' in the front, and there was a horrid smell of rubber as one breathed in and out raising and lowering the bottom half of the mask.

When she was old enough, my sister came to the school as well. We used to walk to school accompanied by two sisters who lived down the road from us. If the air raid siren went during our journey, we would knock on the nearest house and ask if we could shelter. It was a very different life.

I got very good reports at the school – except for music. Miss Randall wrote on the report for music, "Very poor. No voice at all". From that time on, everyone was very rude about my singing. I had a rather powerful voice, but enjoyed singing, so exercised it quite frequently, much to the dismay of the family. It was all rather sad!

From Nettlestone, I went to the County School. This was a four-form entry school, which took children in at eleven. But for some reason, there was a Lower Third form with just twenty-five pupils. I had to take an entrance exam for it. At that time, I used to suffer from 'acidosis' – an ailment which struck me down every five or six weeks. I would wake up with a terrible headache and be sick throughout the day. It usually lasted a couple of days, and on the third day I would slowly recover.

My mother believed that it was caused by anxiety. Come the day of the entrance exam, she may well have been right – for I woke up with the usual headache and sickness. Keen to see me accepted at the County School, she telephoned the teacher from the school with whom we had shared the Anderson shelter. She said to bring me along and she would arrange for a camp bed and a sick bowl outside the exam room, so that I could do as much of the exam as possible between bouts of sickness. So off we toddled to the school – which was only five minutes walk away – and I spent the morning alternating between writing the exam paper and dashing out to be sick.

Looking back, I feel very sorry for the other candidates! But I managed to pass and duly entered the Lower Third. I remember well the awe I felt that first day with all the prefects from the sixth form looking so tall and imposing. We all wore the same uniform – white blouses, navy blue gym slip, red ties with a stripey pattern, white socks and black shoes. Outside the school, we wore navy raincoats and hats with a red ribbon round it. Woe betide anyone who was found without a hat on their way home.

For gym, we wore white tea shirts and baggy navy blue serge bloomers – something the youngsters of today wouldn't be seen dead in!

Everyone was put into a house named after a famous Kentish man, and we all wore a shield shaped badge in the colour of the house we were in. I was in Darwin (orange). The other houses were Chaucer (pink), Harvey (blue), Sidney (Green), Wolf (yellow), and Pitt (dark blue). I always felt very sad that the new headmistress, Miss Smith, abolished houses soon after she took over from Miss Whiting.

Miss Whiting was a formidable lady. She was tall and slim, and wore her hair in a bun which was silver grey. We all had great respect for her. I remember three personal encounters with her: once when I went for the interview for the Lower Third, once when she taught our class and tried to get us to understand the concept of infinity, and once when I was sent out of the class for chatting – and Miss Whiting happened to be walking past and gave me a huge wigging.

I made friends with the Royan twins – Audrey and Sheila. We were very close – especially Audrey and I – and we used to sit in the school grounds writing stories. I didn't realise it at the time, but I put the nose out of joint of a girl called Gillian who had been their friend from primary school days.

Our year was at the very forefront of the educational revolution that was taking place. With the Education Act of 1944 the government had decided to set up the tripartite system of grammar School, Technical School and Secondary Modern Schools, They were all supposed to provide equally good educational experiences – but were designed to suit the aptitudes of the pupils who were assigned to them. In order to decide who went where, the first Eleven Plus exam took place in 1944 – an exam which comprised English, Maths, and the newly devised IQ test. Every child took the exam. Those who did well academically, then had to go for an interview at the newly named Grammar Schools before they were offered a place.

I still remember the story I wrote in the English exam – about a huge storm and a tree falling on a child! A few weeks later, I learnt that, not only had I passed the exam but that I was awarded a scholarship. This was a great relief to my parents, because at that time, one still had to pay fees at the County School. But when the time came, the following year, to take up my place, the County School had been renamed Bromley County Grammar School, and all the places were free.

By the May of my time in the Lower Third, the doodle bugs were falling all round us, followed by the V2s. I remember vividly the impact made by the first doodlebug. My parents had friends whom we called Uncle Andrew and Auntie Jean – a Scottish couple who had no children. We were very fond of them. Auntie Jean was dumpy and jolly, and had straight hair with a fringe. She made the most delicious scotch pancakes. Uncle Andrew was very tall, with a long face and grey hair and was the most morally upright man I have ever met – but there was always a twinkle in his eye. They lived

Uncle Andrew and Auntie Jean

about a mile away from us, and on this particular occasion, after a fairly quiet air raid the night before, we went round to see them. Uncle Andrew and my mother spent the time talking in hushed whispers about the very curious aeroplane they had seen the evening before. 'I watched the plane and there was something very sinister about it,' said my uncle. 'It made a funny noise, not like the usual German aeroplane. It was almost as though there was no pilot on board. It travelled in a dead straight line, then suddenly, the engine cut out, and the plane fell straight down to the ground and exploded.'

This, of course, was a classic description of a V1. They really were terrifying – largely because you could hear them coming with a sort of *zzx zzz* sound. Then the engine would cut out, and you would hold your breath waiting to know whether they were going to fall on you. The silence after the engines cut out probably lasted only a minute – but it seemed an eternity. Later on, after my mother had taken us away, a doodlebug fell at the bottom of the garden, flattening four houses in the adjacent road and seriously damaging our house.

The V2s were not quite so frightening as you didn't hear them coming – only a terrific explosion when they landed.

With doodlebugs dropping all around us, my mother decided it was time to take us away again. To begin with, she found us accommodation in a comfortable Victorian house in South Stoke in Oxfordshire owned by an elderly spinster, Miss Bullock. But then, when our house was devastated by a doodle bug, my mother went back to Bromley to sort out the mess. The family of my friend Pam, who lived opposite, had been sleeping in our house because they had no air raid shelter of their own, so my mother brought Pam back with her. Miss Bullock, who had no real idea of what the War was like near London, decided that enough was enough and asked my mother to find alternative accommodation. Three little girls were too much for her – and in that village, she was so isolated from the effects of war that she could not really comprehend my mother's need for sympathy and understanding at a time when she had lost everything but her family.

My mother, desperate to keep us all together, found lodgings in a small farm labourer's cottage belonging to Mr and Mrs Butler about a mile and a half outside the village. Mrs Butler did all her cooking on the kitchen range in the back room. We had the parlour in the front – quite cosily furnished and with a mass of geraniums in pots along the window-cil. The stairs led out of this room and were boxed in. Upstairs were two bedrooms – one for the Butlers and one, which the four of us shared. My mother and Barbara shared the double bed while my friend and I slept top-to-tail in the single bed. I often wonder how we all managed when our father came home on embarkation leave.

We were happy. Our only anxiety was having to go to the lavatory at the top of the garden. It was spidery and dark and didn't smell particularly pleasant – and one had to pass Nip, the less than friendly of the two sheep dogs. Once a week, Mr Butler would carry the heavy Elsan bucket half way down the hill and empty it into the little copse that we passed every time we went to the village.

Life was not so easy for my mother. For a start the conditions were primitive. She had to wait till Mrs Butler had fed her man before she was able to go into the kitchen, which was the Butler's sitting room, and cook our meal. While we were cavorting around the countryside, she was left alone, worrying about our father who was by then in France, and finding little real companionship with the Butlers, however kind. At night, once we went to bed, she had only a flickering oil lamp to read by, no electric fire to warm her and no radio to listen to. It must have been a very dreary time for her – but being so young, we had little understanding of her situation

When it came to bath time, my mother had to heat water in the

Mr and Mrs Butler (when we visited them after the War)

copper and then fill up an old tin tub which was placed in front of the Butler's range. Needless to say, we didn't bathe all that often. How my mother managed we shall never know.

For us children, life was idyllic. The long summer had started and the weather was perfect. There were rolling fields and meadows all round. There were two sheep dogs, one of whom, Jamie, we adored (the other was rather fierce), and the farm labourer, Mr Butler, was a wonderful character with a great sense of humour and a love of children which we instantly recognised. He and his wife, who was beautiful and aristocratic looking, and kind though strict, had no children and clearly enjoyed the presence in their home of three lively girls then aged nine and eleven.

We roamed the countryside, helped with the harvest, had a stable of imaginary horses, and galloped miles across the fields. We went down to the river and learnt to swim (my mother, a non swimmer, teaching us by holding us up in the water with a rope attached to a strong canvas band tied round our waists). It was not long before we were swimming across to the other side of the river with enormous confidence while my mother sat taut with anxiety till we returned.

Learning to swim in the Thames

We made ink from oak apples, picked mushrooms from the meadows behind the house and brought them back and fried them for breakfast, careered around on our bikes which my mother had managed to salvage from the wreckage, and played endless card and table games with an insatiable appetite. The cottage had a wonderful bookcase full of late Victorian children's novels and I remember weeping buckets over *The Wide Wide World, Uncle Tom's Cabin, The Children of the New Forest* and a whole host of others whose titles I cannot now remember.

Mr Butler was a shepherd though the War had forced him into other duties on the farm as well. Not long before we arrived he had had all his teeth extracted and was still struggling with the new dentures. Before every meal he would solemnly remove them and put them in a glass above the mantelpiece before sitting down to eat. Needless to say we were fascinated by this operation and made every excuse to be in the room when it took place.

We loved the cottage which was set on a hill and looked across rolling fields and down to the village and river below and the hills beyond. We would often walk along the tow path to the nearby town of Goring which was on the river and had a lock, and a fascinating mill wheel.

For some of the time we were at South Stoke, our grandmother stayed in lodgings in Goring because the bombing was so fierce in Brockley – but she soon went back to London.

In later years I came across a piece of writing I did while at the village school and for which I won a very special prize of two shillings and sixpence. Having just won a scholarship to Bromley County School (as it was then called) I was considered a clever little girl. But in the village school I was treated as something of a prodigy and made much of. There was an Essay Competition at the school, but we, as evacuees, were not considered eligible. I was so enraptured with country life that I had written a long essay about the idylls of the country and showed it to the schoolmistress. She kept it to read and must have shown it to the judges because they decided to make a special award. I was delighted. 2/6d represented a lot of purchasing power at that time.

In the autumn, we very sadly said farewell to the Butlers because there was no means of heating the parlour during the winter, and moved to a village four miles away – Woodcote. There we moved into the house of Dr Croucher – a retired doctor in his eighties. He lived with his unmarried daughter, a housekeeper, and a young Jewish girl, Irene.

Only ten at the time, I did not realise the significance of her presence. As children we hated the Germans. We could not but be aware of the War and knew the Germans were responsible. Our own lives were disrupted – by the air raids, the fact that we had to leave our homes, that our fathers were away in the forces, that everywhere you looked men and women were in uniform, and that food was rationed – but we had no idea of the horrors of the persecution of the Jews. Nor do I know how much people like my mother, an ordinary English housewife, knew about the Jewish situation. She almost certainly discussed Irene's presence with the housekeeper, Mrs Williams, but whether Dr Croucher ever explained to her how he had come to take in a Jewish girl we never knew.

Irene was about eighteen – tall with dark curly hair. We enjoyed her company but after a few months she went away and we never saw her again. Looking back, I would love to have heard her story.

Dr Croucher lived in a large Victoria house with a huge garden and wonderful orchard. Though over eighty, he had resumed his medical career as a GP because so many doctors had been called up. One of the large front rooms was a surgery. He and his daughter lived in the large drawing room and dining room, while the rest of us huddled in a small morning room at the back of the house.

My main memory of Dr Croucher was his feeding of the chaffinches. He had a battered old silver snuff box and would go out into the garden, open the lid and call, 'Mr Pinkie, Mrs Pinkie'. Within a few minutes he had four or five beautiful chaffinches sitting on his hand and pecking away at the nuts in the box.

His daughter, Miss Croucher, was a very large and very strange lady. She worked for the WRVS and was usually to be seen in her green uniform. She bred Irish wolfhounds for the Irish Guards. These lived in a stable behind the house which abutted on to a yard surrounded on all sides by high brick walls. They were lovely dogs – but they hated cats, and woe betide any cat that jumped into the yard, because the wolfhounds would tear it to pieces. I can still hear the horrific cries of the cats as they were torn limb from limb.

Mrs Williams, the housekeeper, was a warm and kindly soul. She had had a tragic life losing both her husband and only son in the 1918 flu epidemic. Forced to find a living, she had taken on the job of housekeeper to Dr Croucher and had been with him for many years.

It is curious how memories of the same events and times can differ. For me, again, it was a very happy period and I looked back on it with nostalgia. For Pam it was different. She was homesick – though I did not know this for many years, and I am not sure my mother did either. So, after a couple of months, Pam returned to her family and the bombing. We missed her – but then got on with our happy lives

We went to the local school where I shone academically. We roamed the garden, played endless games of cards, drew pictures, and made a lot of leather goods with a hole punch and thread. Food was, of course, a problem for the womenfolk because of rationing which limited the amount and variety of food available. We each had a ration book containing coupons for all the different foodstuffs that were on ration – meat, butter, sugar, eggs, preserves, and a huge variety of other foods. Vegetables were not rationed nor was bread so that became our staple diet. Fruit was limited to native fruits such as apples, pears, plums, and cherries. We didn't see a banana until after the War, and oranges, as I recall, were rationed. Children were given concentrated orange juice in half-pint bottles which we diluted with water. Because our butter and sugar rations were so limited, we each had our own pots, carefully labelled. Barbara's pot, I remember, was labelled 'Sugger fer piknik'. She loved sugar, I loved butter, so sometimes we did a swop.

Though food was rationed, I don't remember going hungry. My mother was a dab hand at making food interesting and stretching the rations. We ate lots of rabbit because that was, for some reason, off ration – so we had rabbit pie, rabbit stew and roast rabbit – all delicious.

I always remember the occasion when my mother was offered a rabbit by the cleaning lady, Mrs Bum (yes, Mrs Bum!). She accepted the offer with alacrity. But imagine her horror when she, a townswoman, was handed a complete rabbit – innards and all! Mrs Bum, seeing her consternation, said she would show her how to deal with it this time, but if she wanted any more she would have to deal with it herself.

My mother soon became a dab hand at gutting and skinning rabbits, and she used the fur to good effect. She would stretch out the skins on a board, rub them with salt petre and leave them to dry. Then we would make them into fur slipper and mittens for ourselves and for Christmas presents.

Sweets and clothing were also rationed, and I can remember the excitement of going to the village shop to buy our meagre 2ozs of sweets each week. At one point it went down to 1oz a week. I also remember the baker's shop at Woodcote which we passed on our way back from school. We would go in and buy a newly baked 'white' loaf (usually a grey sort of colour) and go home and tear off the crusts and eat them with jam – some of which had come over in large tins from Australia.

A lot of swapping round of clothes went on as new clothes were difficult to come by. To help out, the WRVS ran a sort of second hand clothing warehouse with clothes and bedding that came from Canada. I remember Miss Croucher taking us along once or twice, and we sifted through the clothes hanging on the rails. They smelt musty and were of a drab colouring, but we usually came home with one or two items. After the War was over, when my parents were friendly with a wealthy family called Duke (relatives of the famous war time pilot) my mother used to exchange her clothing coupons for the beautiful expensive clothes their three daughters had grown out of.

Christmas 1944 at Dr Croucher's house was magical. We had spent week's making presents out of rabbit skins, bits of leather, wool and cards. Come Christmas Day there was a huge snowfall and we imagined Father Christmas coming across the large lawn in his sledge to deliver our Christmas stockings which my mother had somehow managed to fill.

That day we were all invited to have lunch with Dr Croucher and his daughter in their elegant dining room. It was quite an experience.

The war dragged on till the spring. I recall vividly the days leading up to D-Day – though we children didn't really understand what was going on. The road immediately outside the doctor's house was obviously en route to some transit area because, for what must have been two weeks, a non-stop succession of tanks and lorries carrying troops filed past the house. The soldiers all seemed very cheerful and waved and cheered us as they passed.

As the War neared its end, my mother felt I ought to start getting a grammar school education, so I went to Henley grammar School – a mixed school. To get there, I had to cycle four miles to Checkenden, park my bicycle in the garden of a house, and then take the bus to Henley. I didn't enjoy the journey as I had to stand all the way to Henley – the older boys and girls occupying the seats.

The end of the War in Europe was celebrated with a huge bonfire on the green, and food, which the locals had magicked out of somewhere. For me, that was a memorable occasion because a boy I fancied, Donald Clinch, took my sister aside and said, 'Tell Molly I likes her'. That made my day!

A few weeks later my mother sent me back to my aunt in Petts Wood so that I could start back at Bromley Grammar School. She was worried that if I didn't take up my place, it would be taken by the hundreds of returning evacuees.

CHAPTER 3
The Post War Years, Education and the Baptist Church, 1945 – 1952

My return to the Grammar school in 1945 was the start of a rather unhappy time. I was very fond of my aunt and uncle, but they didn't really understand children. Returning to the school I expected to be welcomed back by the twins with whom I had corresponded while I was away. Instead, they and their friend Gillian (whom I never liked and who had been, I suspect, jealous of me) turned on me and rushed round the school saying 'That dreadful Molly Mountfort is back'. I was ostracised by a great many of the Third Formers (how cruel children can be), and didn't feel understood by my aunt and uncle. Moreover, I was travelling daily to Petts Wood which was outside the catchment area of the school, so had no travelling companions.

School netball team, me bottom right

I suspect that bullying in schools was never discussed at that period, and I'm not sure whether the teaching staff knew about the bullying. If they did, they certainly didn't do anything about it. I suspect they were all weary with trying to sort out the aftermath of the War years – trying to cope with all the returning evacuees who came back at different times and who had had very varying educational experiences during the War. Even today, bullying doesn't always seem to be taken seriously enough, though the effects of bullying on young children can scar them for many years, if not for life.

One exciting thing that happened to mitigate my unhappiness was that I was chosen for the school's Junior Netball Team, and had the excitement of visiting other schools for matches. Later, I graduated to the senior team. In the summer I played for the Cricket Team – but never shone at school as much as I did playing cricket on the bombsite!

The school had two excellent orchestras and two choirs led by our very talented music teacher, Miss Collins. Sadly, I belonged to neither. I failed the choir audition (what a surprise), and somehow, it never occurred to me or my parents to learn an instrument other than the piano which we didn't possess – something I very much regret.

It was a great relief when my mother and Barbara returned and we took up residence again in our house in Bromley. Though a flying bomb had fallen at the bottom of the garden, the powers that be decided the house was worth repairing. In many ways, that was sad because those houses that were rebuilt in their entirety had all sorts of modern innovations which made them more attractive.

I can't remember the exact date when my father was demobbed – but it was great to have him home again. But, looking back, I think my parents had problems of re-adjusting to shared responsibilities, for I remember quite a few fierce arguments, while my sister and I sat on the stairs feeling anxious. I think it was difficult for many couples after the war. The women had got used to organising everything without the support of husbands who were away in the forces. Many of them went out to work for the first time in their lives – and relished their changed status. But many of the men, returning from the horrors and privations of service life, were unaware of the changes that had taken place on the domestic front, and found it hard to adjust. A film that encapsulated this beautifully was *Perfect Strangers*, with Leslie Howard and Deborah Kerr, in which a rather slovenly and down at heel couple were both called up, and both blossomed and became officers. They dreaded going back to their spouses and had a difficult period of re-adjustment – until they realised that each had changed for the better.

That period was, in fact, the only time we ever heard raised voices in our family or among our friends – and we children were never shouted at or had voices raised to us in anger. I am very grateful for that, for I believe that shouting and screaming at children is a violent assault on their sensibilities, and is nearly as bad as a physical

Barbara, Pam, Geoffrey, me and Myrtle

assault. My mother's disciplinary method was amazing. She would stare at us across a room with her green eyes as hard and as cold as stones. When she put on her 'look' we stopped immediately whatever transgression we were involved in. It was very effective, because, usually, only my sister and I knew she was cross, so we were not shamed in front of others. I think I tried 'the look' with my own children – but have a suspicion it was not nearly so effective because they often laughed about it later.

About a year after the War we had our first family holiday – at Westgate. We stayed in a boarding house together with the Ashtead family, and a family called Nugent who had a daughter, Anne, a year or two younger than my sister. The Nugents became long standing family friends – and my mother and Sylvia Nugent were so close they were like sisters. I recall happy days on the beach, swimming alongside our cousins, and evenings playing games in the guest house. I remember, too, the day when my father beckoned us to go with him, and took us off to buy our very first ice cream. Not long after, we tasted our first bananas!

We never had foreign holidays – my parents couldn't afford them. Nor, to my disappointment, could they afford the school trips abroad. The only school trip I ever went on was to the Lake District and that was magical – seeing mountains for the first time. My first trip abroad was just after I had taken A' levels when I worked for six weeks in a Colonie de Vacance near Chambery in France.

The next few years were busy and active ones. Pam was living opposite with her brothers, and Myrtle and Geoffrey next door. We played cricket, first in the alley way which was lined with hollyhocks, but we lost so many balls over the fences that we gravitated to the bomb site at the back of our garden where four houses had been

Guide Camp

demolished. For the next few summers, a gang of us played cricket most evenings. Looking back, I'm not quite sure how the others tolerated me, because I always bowled underarm – very fast – and quickly got the others out, with the result that I think I hogged the batting.

We cycled everywhere without anxiety because there was so little traffic on the roads, and our parents didn't seem to be obsessed with a fear of who might attack or abduct us. How very different today!

Geoffrey and Myrtle's parents were devout Salvation Army people, and Mr Groom, Geoffrey, and their eldest son, Jameson, all played in the band. We could hear their band practice from our house – cornets and trombones. Myrtle had a lovely voice and used to sing solos. I wanted to learn to play the piano but we didn't have a piano at home, and although the Grooms offered to let me practise on their piano, my mother thought it would be too much of an imposition, and said no.

My sister Barbara, Pam, Myrtle and I decided to join the Girl Guides, but the first company we joined had rather dreary leaders – so we left. Then, one of the teachers at the school, Miss Mackenzie, a charismatic teacher of German, set up a new company, and we decided to join. It was a good decision because she was a superb leader, and we all adored her. We had wonderful times – camping at Whitsun and in the summer, going on hikes, and meeting regularly on a Friday evening. It says much for the quality of her leadership that we all remained as guides until we were sixteen. I went in for lots of badges and ended up with a whole armful, finally becoming a *Queens Guide*.

After the Guide meeting we would go along to the fish and chip shop and buy a pennyworth of chips – a good sized bag full to the brim.

At home, I organised a little local club which I called The Happy Club. We made dozens of little badges – painting each of them individually.

In fact, from early on, I was labelled as an organiser (or a bossy boots)! One day, Mrs Groom and a neighbour were walking along, and the neighbour asked where the children were. 'Oh,' said Mrs Groom, 'they're with Rene' and Molly is organising them as usual!'

It was not long after our return from Woodcote that Mrs Collison who lived a few doors away, started taking us to the Baptist Sunday School. Neither of my parents were religious, although I was christened at the parish church. My grandmother always went to church when she stayed with us, and my aunt and uncle at Petts Wood were

Molly a Queen's Guide

Congregationalists – though they seldom went to church because, being very deaf, they found it difficult to hear.

The Baptist Sunday school was my first real introduction to Christianity. I remember my first afternoon at the Sunday School very clearly. We did a drawing of sheep and a shepherd, and read Psalm 23 – and when I left I was given a little bookmark, which I still have, with the text "He leadeth me." Over the next weeks and months, we did a lot of drawing and we had to learn verses from the Bible – the 23rd Psalm, that lovely verse from St John's Gospel, "For God so loved the World that He gave His only begotten son that whosoever believeth in him should not perish but have everlasting life", and a little later, the whole of the passage from 1 Corinthians 13 beginning "Though I speak with the tongues of men and of angels and have not charity, it profiteth me nothing"

We had excellent instruction and were encouraged each year to take the Scripture Union exam based on a number of set books of the Bible. I always did well and won several prizes – sometimes getting a hundred per cent in the exam.

At about the age of thirteen, we graduated to the Young People's Fellowship. There were a number of girls in our group from school, and we had a very good group leader called Mrs Pipkin. I started going to church on a Sunday evening – when all the young people used to sit up in the gallery.

The YPF was great fun. There were plenty of social activities – a tennis club in the summer, social evenings on a Saturday in the Church hall once a month, and many outings. And while this was going on, there was good Christian teaching. The YPF was also a great marriage market – for the Baptists were eager to ensure that their young people married within the Christian faith.

For several years I had a terrible crush on a boy called Alan. He was tall with dark curly hair, and I thought he was wonderful. He knew I had a crush on him because my sister let the cat out of the bag when, one afternoon, he phoned to ask me to play tennis with him. Barbara picked up the phone, and hearing it was Alan, shouted out in an excited voice, 'Molly, it's Alan, it's Alan!' giving the game away completely. But he was not interested in me – though he did agree to come with me as my partner to the 'coming out' Fifth Year Dance in the Summer.

We had ballroom dancing lessons at school before the dance – the waltz, the foxtrot, the tango and the samba. The dance was a very formal occasion and we had to introduce our partners to the headmistress! We all purchased special new dresses for the occasion and I had a very pretty three-quarter length silky dress with a white background patterned with large pastel flowers. I was thrilled with my new dress, but was mortified when I got to the dance because a girl I didn't like at all arrived wearing an identical dress to mine!

Years later, when I was in my fifties, I met Alan again at a YPF Reunion. I didn't recognise this balding, very unattractive man who said, as I walked in, 'Hello Molly,' and I felt what a lucky thing it was that Alan hadn't fancied me!

As we got older a number of my friends at YPF went forward for Believer's Baptism. This is a very moving service in which the whole congregation shares. Those being baptised are dressed in white and they go down into the baptismal pool and are totally immersed by the minister as a symbol of being washed clean and then born again into a new life.

I knew that those who were being baptised had found something that I hadn't – and I envied them. I had no problem intellectually with the concept of Christianity – but it meant nothing to me personally. "Jesus my friend? Jesus my Saviour – dying for my sins?" What did this mean? I didn't really have any sins! I was a good girl. I worked hard, was conscientious, obedient to my parents, and I hadn't really done anything wrong that I could think of. My sister was a pain – but then that was her fault! And as for telling people that Jesus was my friend and Saviour, as we were urged to, well, that was the most embarrassing thing ever!

I think that, even had I wanted to, my father would have been dead against my being baptised. He believed that, though he didn't go to church himself, if you wanted to get on in life, you needed to belong to the Church of England. When I brought The Pledge home to sign (to abstain altogether from alcoholic drink) my father tore it up in anger – saying it would ruin my future social life. In that respect I think he was a very wise man! I must confess I'm glad he did!

In the fifties I was taken by the YPF to the Billy Graham Crusade at the Albert Hall in London. It was an amazing occasion – very emotional and compelling. I could feel my YPF leaders around me praying for me to go forward and make a public commitment to Jesus Christ. I felt myself being called out, but I was embarrassed and fearful – and stayed firmly in my seat.

Not long after this, my church going came to an end. I left home and spent six months working in a Workers Travel Association hotel on the Isle of Wight before going on to University.

During all these years, I was working hard at school. I was one of the brightest in the class – though by no means the top. I was good at the arts subject – English, History, RE and Latin. French was a problem because, coming back after the War at nearly the end of the Third year, I missed all the basics. But doing quite well, I was quickly promoted to one of the top sets – and never did catch up on the basics.

At the age of fourteen, those of us who were arts orientated dropped science altogether – a shameful decision by the school. I was good at maths until the time when the top group, which I was in, started working on calculus and logarithms. These meant absolutely nothing to me. I couldn't understand what was being calculated – and I got into such a tizzy that my parents had to pay for maths coaching for me when it came to matriculation.

At that time we took the General Certificate of Education, and if you passed well enough you got Matriculation Exemption. (Matriculation was a pre-requisite for going to university.) To get matriculation exemption, you had to pass at least seven subjects with a credit or distinction – and these subjects had to include English, Maths and a modern language. I passed with distinctions in English, History and Religious Instruction, and failed Latin – together with 30 others in my class! We had a very poor Latin mistress. For me, this was a very serious failure because, in order to get to University and read for an arts degree, you had to have Latin at Matriculation and Higher School Certificate level. So, immediately I entered the Sixth form, I had to start studying Latin in earnest – and managed to get a distinction at the end of the first term in the Sixth form.

A guinea pig with the IQ test at eleven, we were once again guinea pigs when the Higher School Certificate was abolished, and A' levels were introduced. I am not sure that there was a great deal of difference other than the fact that you could take subjects individually rather than as a package. I studied History, English, Latin and French at A' level – dropping French at the end of the first year Sixth. I obtained an

Sixth form friends – still in touch at 80

A in History, and a B in English and Latin – though I learnt this secretly because, initially, it was decided that pupils would not be told what grades they had achieved. I like to think that the marking was much more stringent then than it is today!

I felt a little isolated in the sixth form because I knew I would have to work very hard to get to university, while most of the girls who stayed on seemed to have no real academic ambitions. In the Upper Sixth, we acquired a board game which was rather like an enlarged shove-halfpenny board, and most of their free time was spent playing with it. None of them seemed to want to go on to university, and I felt I was regarded as a bit of a swot and rather dull!

Our year was very different to the year above when no less than twelve people got university places – including several to Oxford and Cambridge. I felt at the time that I would have been happier with the group in the year above. This could well have been a legacy from the bullying I received in the third year!

Later, several of my classmates went on to university – and a number of us still meet up once a year.

Had the year above and the staff had their way, I would have been head girl – but my own classmates preferred someone more-light hearted. That was a disappointment – one of many at the time.

At the time I entered the Sixth form, we had a very frequent visitor to the house – John Macnamara. He had digs nearby and his parents knew my father. John used to be round most weekends and we did a lot of things together, playing tennis and walking. He was short with fair curly hair and bright blue eyes – and I thought he was lovely. He came as my partner to the Sixth Form dance. But he was considerably older than I was, and soon met and married someone nearer his age. I was heartbroken for a while.

At that time my ambition was to be a teacher. Looking back, I think we had very poor careers advice. No one ever mentioned the possibility of going into law or journalism – two options that, with hindsight, I would have enjoyed. As these two careers were right outside the experience of my parents and relatives, (and I suspect, the staff) the idea was never mooted.

I was desperately keen to go to Oxford, so I stayed on in the Third year Sixth, the only girl to stay on from my year. In those days you had to sit a very stiff entrance exam for both Oxford and Cambridge. There were papers in History, English, Latin and French. I took the exam for St Hugh's College in Oxford, and later for St Anne's. Again, I think I was badly advised. My History teacher, Miss Mabbs, had been at St Hilda's, Oxford – but advised me to try for St Hugh's because she thought I was too timid to stand up to the dragon who was in charge of History at St Hilda's! But, of course, she overlooked the value of her connection with the college which might have stood me in good stead.

I was called for an interview at St Hugh's and was very excited. I remember going there in a dark blue high-necked dress and wearing a black hat! It was quite a gruelling interview. A number of the girls who went there wore their Cheltenham Ladies' College uniform – and it was obvious they would get preferential treatment over a mere grammar school girl.

But again, I was badly advised by my school. The tutor asked me if I would like to read PPE instead of History (politics, philosophy and economics). I didn't know what that was, and said 'no'. I am sure, looking back, that if I had said, 'yes', I would have been given a place.

Another mistake I made was not to stay the night in the college which I could have done. But I was desperately keen to go and visit the Butlers at South Stoke whom I hadn't seen since we left in 1944. Money was tight and South Stoke was on the rail line from Oxford to London. So I left after the interviews were over. I had a joyful reunion with the Butlers and stayed the night.

But my disappointment was great when the rejection letter arrived. Very nicely worded, it said I was up to standard but there were just not enough places. Sixteen of us had been interviewed and they took eight!

Similar disappointment followed with the St Anne's interview. One must remember that at that time only 2% of women went to university. All the Oxford and Cambridge Colleges were single sex – and there were just two colleges for women at Cambridge and five at Oxford. I took the Cambridge exams but they were even more difficult and I did not get an interview. However, after Christmas I sat an equally rigorous exam for Bedford College, London, and was told at my interview that I had definitely got a place. (Most people had to wait till well after the interviews were over to be told – so that did my ego no end of good!)

Workers Travel Association hotel at East Dene, Bonchurch 1953

There were six months to fill in before going to University – so I took a job in a WTA (Workers Travel Association) Hotel at Bonchurch on the Isle of Wight. My official title was Assistant Hostess and I had a wonderful time. I helped with reception, did the wages account each week (working out the tax to be deducted), helped arrange the flowers, and organised walks and outings for the visitors and games for the children. In the evenings, I assisted with the social events – dances, whist drives, beetle drives and concerts.

The hotel was in a beautiful house with gardens leading down to its own private beach. The house had belonged to the poet, Swinburne, and was spacious with over thirty bedrooms. Guests would book in for either a week or a fortnight – arriving and leaving on a Saturday. Saturday mornings were hectic. We all had to muck in and change beds, clean the bathrooms, re-do all the flowers, organise table seating – and be ready by 3 o'clock, all washed and spruced up to receive visitors.

We had eighty visitors when the house was full – which it usually was – and I made it my business to know everyone by name by the Sunday evening when we had a social gathering. It was an accomplishment that came in useful in later years.

We had some interesting visitors. Herbert Morrison, the then Foreign Secretary in the Labour Government came incognito with his wife. He joined in all the activities, and, because he had a very distinctive coif, told us that a number of the other visitors said they had nicknamed him 'Herbie' because he looked so like Herbert Morrison. He didn't let on! He used to come swimming with us on the beach, and I have a lovely photograph of him sitting between me and my friend Pam who had come down to visit. He made us promise we wouldn't send it to the press!

I had a whale of a time, and met my first real boyfriend, a young architect called Wilson who lived in Birmingham. It was a romance that lasted about nine months

– but Wilson then decided that his former girl friend in Birmingham was more accessible! I often wonder whether or not he became a successful architect.

Leaving Bonchurch, I was not at all certain I wanted to go to university. I loved the hotel life and was less than enthusiastic about my impending degree course at Bedford College. When our distinguished second cousin from New Zealand, Professor Anschutz, came to visit my parents, I think he was a bit shocked by my cavalier attitude to university. He was the son of my grandmother's sister, Auntie Rosie, who had gone to New Zealand as a young bride.

Pam and Molly on the beach with Herbert Morrison, the Foreign Secretary

CHAPTER 4
University, 1952 – 1956

However, come the end of September 1952 I set off for Bedford College quite happily. My parents had purchased a big black trunk for me which was sent on in advance. I took the train to London carrying a case with my new undergraduate gown which we were told we would have to wear for all lectures, seminars and tutorials, and for dinner in hall.

I had been given a place in a hall of residence called Lindsell Hall at Swiss Cottage. The hall consisted of four large Victorian terrace houses in Lindsell Road, and a further two houses in the parallel road. The two blocks of houses were joined by a garden. We had a common room, a dining hall, and a library. All the Freshers (first year students) had to share a room – and I found my room-mate was Cynthia, a tall girl from up north who was studying Classics. We had a very large room overlooking the garden which was very pleasant. The first thing Cynthia did was to put up a model of Blackpool Tower, and I learnt she was a keen horse rider. As my parents had never been able to afford to let us go riding, that was an immediate barrier.

Bedford College

We arrived in the afternoon, and all met up in the common room to have a little pep talk from the Warden. Obviously, some of the freshers were sizing us all up because when we went down to dinner, I found myself being grabbed and asked by Pat and Gill who shared a room, to sit at a particular table. It appeared that they had looked round and handpicked the other six people they wanted to sit at their table. My room mate was one of them, then there were Diana reading Geography and Jane, reading French, plus two science students, Liz and Val. From that point on we became known as The Eight – and still remain in contact although Jane died of cancer a few years ago.

The Eight

Everyone thought I was very mature because, not only had I been out in the working world for six months, I also had a boyfriend! Liz became my special friend, and we spent hours in discussion, and developing what we considered our wider education. Our room pairings – me with Cynthia and Liz's with Val – were not ideal. Val and Cynthia were both highly organised. They went to bed early, worked very hard to strict timetables, and got up early – and both ended up with Firsts. Liz and I were late birds – late to bed and late risers. I think we were all relieved when, in our second year, we had our own rooms.

Liz also had a boyfriend, Jim, who was at St Johns College in Cambridge. Jim wrote to Liz every single day. Liz took me up to Cambridge on a visit and there I met John who was reading history. He invited me to the May Ball – a fantastic occasion when we danced the night out and ate swan at supper (a special dispensation for St Johns). Both John and Jim got firsts. Jim went into the civil service and John became an academic. He later married the well known novelist, Penelope Lively. He died in about 1999 – so had I married him, I would have been a widow for much longer! Curious thought.

While at Bedford College, I made two special friends in the History Department. They both became academics. Margaret went to Waikato University in New Zealand and ended up as Head of the History Department there. We saw her quite regularly

Bedford College Summer Ball with Liz and Jim and John Lively

as she came back to England every five years on sabbatical leave, and used to spend Christmases with us. She was a heavy smoker and because she was very hard-up while at college, she always cut her cigarettes in half and used a cigarette holder. She lived at Ongar in Essex in a lovely old house – and I used to stay there from time to time.
In her fifties, she 'came out' as a lesbian which was rather a shock to us. She brought her partner over to stay with us – but sadly, none of us liked her, nor did her sister and friends in New Zealand. Margaret died of lung cancer in the 1980s – not a surprise to us as she never gave up her heavy smoking.

Alison studied Renaissance History and ended up as a Professor at Royal Holloway College. She lived in Norfolk and had a rather 'posh' family whom we met at her wedding. Two other friends from the History Department were Dorothy and Shirley – both of whom died young.

Shirley was a miner's daughter and was the only one in her family to go to university. Her brothers still worked down the mines. She married a doctor, and they lived quite near us at Sheerness. They had four children under six – and when Shirley contacted ovarian cancer and was having chemotherapy, my husband and I went over to stay in order to look after the children for two weeks. It was hard going as our two children were then only two and four.

Bedford College had several halls of residence and one got to know girls from other departments via a sort of network. Hence I became friendly with Alison's room-mate, Susan, and with Margaret's room mate. Doreen.

I also knew Doreen through rowing. I joined the College rowing club, and spent every Saturday morning on the River Thames rowing in an eight. It was the most strenuous sport I have every indulged in. Even when exhausted, you couldn't let up otherwise you would rock the boat. We rowed on the same course as the Oxford and Cambridge Boat Race – but rowed only half the course – two miles, not four. I became Captain of the Boat Club at the end of the second year, but gave up at Christmas in the third year in order to prepare for finals.

Diana, Doreen, Margaret and Alison

We had a fairly cushy time reading History. We only had to write eight essays a term and had no exams at all until finals. Not a good thing! We all studied European History, English History and Political Theory. Then you specialised. I studied 'The Reign of Henry II' and 'Ecclesiastical Institutions'. This necessitated the reading

Rowing Club – Molly in the middle as Captain

of Latin texts – which was not that easy. We had tutorials once a fortnight, and various seminars. As well as our lectures in college, we also went to the University of London's Senate House for University lectures. In our first year, we had to study an optional subject and I did Italian. I quite liked it – but gave up in the second year which, looking back, was a pity.

I don't remember doing too much studying during that first year – but I certainly enjoyed theatre life seeing such plays as *The Boy Friend, Look back in Anger* by John Osborne, and *The Love of Four Colonels* with Peter Ustinov – all quite avant garde at the time. For *The love of four Colonels*, we were unable to get 'proper' tickets, but had tickets which allowed us to stand at the back of the circle for one shilling and sixpence. We also explored the picture galleries and museums, and went to a number of concerts. It was a time when I believe our real education took place, expanding our knowledge of culture, and exploring the meaning of life. We did find time to talk about history and I recall heated discussion in the early hours about the relative merits of Plato and Aristotle.

We seldom went to pubs but went instead to Coffee Bars which were the in-thing then. We had very little money, but, looking back, I think we were a very fortunate generation. All our tuition fees were paid by the state, and we had what I now think were generous maintenance grants – based on our parents' income. I had a nearly a full maintenance grant – about £220 a year. Very few of us ended up in debt – but I think our expectations were lower. I also think we felt we were a bit of an elite generation, as only about 2% of women went to university at that period.

There were the Saturday night dances in Herringham Hall, and the even more exciting Summer Balls when we spent hours beforehand discussing who we would invite – and organising partners for those who didn't have a boy friend at the time. A few of our group met their future husbands during this period. I took John to two balls, and at one of them my cousin Neil came along too.

Highlight of our first year was the Coronation. Like so many others, we decided we would get a front row view of the Coronation procession by spending the night on the Mall. We arrived there about three o'clock in the afternoon armed with warm clothes, blankets, a large supply of food, thermos flasks of coffee, playing cards and games to while away the time.

Although we were among the earlier arrivals, it was not long before there were similar groups squatting along the Mall. The weather was warm and balmy, the sky blue, and it was a happy laughing crowd who sat waiting for the big event next day. My sister, then seventeen, persuaded our parents to let her join us on the Mall. The condition was that our parents would accompany her on the train to London, and try to find us, but if they didn't succeed, she would go back with them to Bromley.

Fortunately for Barbara, they found us. Many years later, at one of the Royal celebrations, a London magazine brought out some old photographs – and among them was one of my sister, me and some college friends sitting on the edge of the pavement in the Mall!

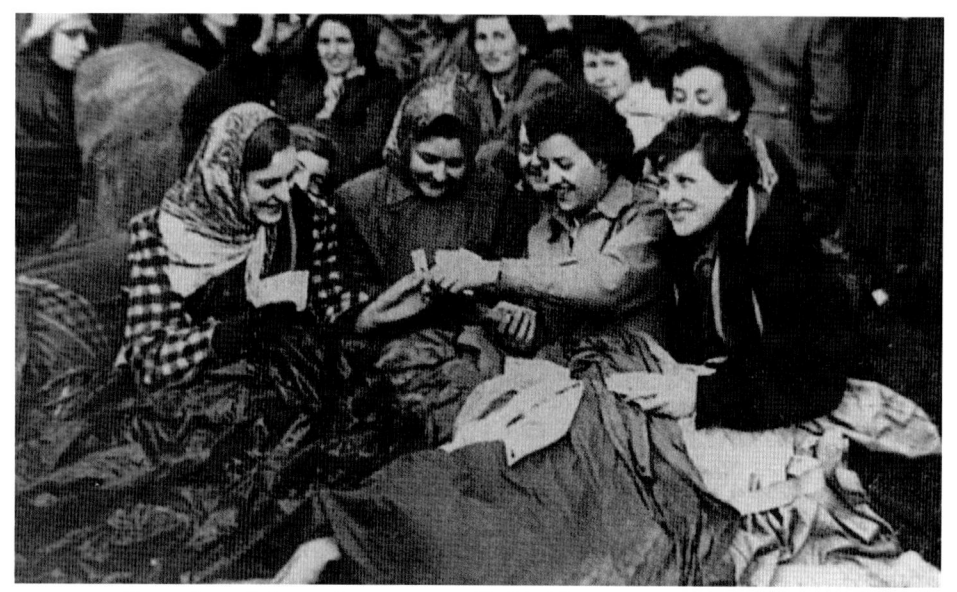

Coronation – sitting on the pavement on The Mall (Picture Post picture), June 1953

It was a magical night. As dusk fell, more and more people joined us. The atmosphere was electric. Vendors of food, drink, balloons, hats and flags, marched up and down selling their wares, while parties of soldiers, sailors and airmen, and people from all over the Commonwealth wandered down the Mall in a heart warming mingling of nationalities.

Favourite of the crowd was Queen Salote – a large lady with a shiny black face, an infectious grin and brilliantly coloured attire, who processed in her open carriage at frequent intervals up and down the Mall, bowing and waving to the crowds as if determined to grasp her share of the crowd's adulation.

The high point of the night came at about 2 am when a whisper rippled down the Mall that something was about to happen. Suddenly, the newspaper vendors came marching down shouting 'Everest Conquered! Hilary and Tensing reach the summit.' It is difficult now to understand quite how momentous that announcement was! The news had been held back for that very moment and we all rushed to buy newspapers.

We dozed for a few hours, but at 6 am the police made us all stand, and from then until the Queen's return at noon from the Abbey, we stood in serried rows at the edge of the pavement.

The Coronation procession was amazing with an endless procession of carriages and service people from all over the Commonwealth. For me, the criss-crossing of the marching legs was so mesmeric that I passed out and joined the procession by being marched to the First Aid tent. But I was soon back with my friends and remained there until the evening's appearance of the Queen and Royal Family on the Balcony. It was an unforgettable experience.

A less happy memory was the Great Smog in our second year at college. We had to keep windows tightly shut otherwise the smog came rolling in. We were advised only to go out if absolutely necessary, as there was a great danger of getting lost. Even if we stayed indoors our petticoats were grey up to the waist, and we breathed in acrid air from morning till night.

Then came Finals – in a heat wave. For those of us studying History it was traumatic. We had not had a single examination throughout our three years of study, and it meant that for most of us, it had been nearly four years since we had written from memory and under pressure. I hope that today's history students have a more rigorous timetable.

Not long after Finals came the visit of the Queen Mother to Bedford College. She was very gracious and wandered round the gardens at the college chatting easily to groups of students as she walked round with the Principal.

In my third year at Bedford I applied for a research scholarship – and was awarded one. But it was dependent on my getting an Upper Second, and as I only got a Lower Second, I had to give it up. Dame Lilian Penson, head of the History Department (and also Vice Chancellor of the University of London) suggested that, instead, I should do an Academic Postgraduate Diploma in Archive Administration at University College, London and become an archivist.

CHAPTER 5
The India Office Library and Marriage, 1956 – 1963

When I finished at Bedford in the June, I got another job with the WTA – this time at Bournemouth. It was the same job as at Bonchurch, but the house was not so nice. Again, I had a lovely time with all the visitors, and just two weeks before I had to leave to start my archive course, two young men came to stay – Leslie Grant and Bill Poulter. I spent a lot of my free time with them, and persuaded them to organise the concert that was put on each week. To Bill's chagrin, I did not, for some reason, go to the concert and see all the effort they had put into it!

A day or two before I left, my sister Barbara and her boy friend, James, came down to stay and bring me and all my luggage back. James had a car – quite unusual in those days. He was rather snobbish at that time and looked a bit askance at Bill who lived on a council estate – but later, they became very close friends.

I nearly didn't get a grant for my archive course. I was called for interview in Maidstone the same day as the wedding in Leeds of Jane. She was the first of our group to get married and I was desperate to get there. Kent County Council Education Committee's grant interview was scheduled for 2 pm. and I thought there would be plenty of time to catch the train to London to connect with the train to Leeds. But the Education Committee kept me waiting for two hours till 4pm and I knew

Bill, Les Grant and me

the time for the last train was fast running out. I was both angry and very anxious, and when I finally got to the interview, I was in quite a state. The Committee misconstrued my irritable mood as indifference, and a week or two later I received a letter saying that as I didn't seem very enthusiastic about doing the archive course, they had decided not to give me a grant! It was only through the help of one of the guests I had become friendly with at Bournemouth that the Education Committee was finally persuaded to give me a grant.

I managed by the skin of my teeth to get the last train to Leeds – arriving just before midnight and causing all sorts of difficulties in getting to Jane's house where I was to stay. (Jane's mother was a widow and had an unusual ailment – one huge elephantine sized leg – something she had contracted when abroad.)

When I left Bedford College, I returned home. But home was a different place, for my parents had purchased the ground floor flat in a large Victorian house in Bromley with a lovely garden. I started on the archive course in October 1955, travelling from home to London every day. Many of our lectures were in the evenings because most of our lecturers worked at the Public Record Office. The course was rather dreary, and so was the building where the lectures were held, but we learnt a lot. We studied palaeography, constitutional history, mediaeval Latin, Anglo Norman French, and the Preservation and Conservation of documents. At the end of the year we had written exams, and a year later had to present a thesis based on the archives we were working with.

During the course we had two weeks practical work – firstly at Essex County Record Office at Chelmsford, and then at Kent County Record Office in Maidstone. I also spent a wonderful fortnight at Burnt Norton, home of the Earl of Harrowby, listing his archives. The Public Record Office archivists had discovered that Lord Harrowby kept his priceless family archives on iron bed frames in a leaking attic. They persuaded him to let some archivists come down and sort them out – and I was invited to be one of them.

The Harrowby's main residence was Sandon Hall in Staffordshire, but they lived most of the time at Burnt Norton which was not quite so large. There I had a taste of the high life – with a butler to serve dinner (for which we wore evening dress), maids to turn down the beds, a nanny to look after the grandchildren, and a chauffeur to drive us around.

Lord Harrowby was a delightful eccentric – careless about his appearance but interested in everyone and everything. From that visit on, he wrote to me regularly in an angular and almost indecipherable hand. In eighteenth century fashion, he wrote over vertically what he had already written horizontally, and then, to add confusion even further, wrote in all the margins. It used to take me a fortnight to decipher his letters. (Years later, after he was widowed, Bill, our son Justin, and I visited him at Sandon Hall. There, to my amazement, he opened a filing cabinet and took out all the letters I had written to him over the years!)

While I was at Burnt Norton, Lord Harrowby wanted to know all about Bill, and when a year later we got married he sent us a telegram and a piece of silver as a wedding present. I met up with him in London once or twice after that, by which time he was wearing a hearing aid in each ear.

When it came to getting a job at the end of the archive course, I applied for, and got, a post in the India Office Library in London which was part of the Commonwealth Relations Office in King Charles Street, just off Whitehall. My job was Archivist in charge of the European Manuscript Collection – a collection of manuscripts relating to the British in India from 1603 to Indian independence in 1947

The collection was, in many ways, very different from the sort of collections we had learnt about on the archive course. The records only dated back to 1599 so there were few Latin documents to look after, and none in Anglo Norman French! But the collection was of endless fascination and it was a wonderful job which I only gave up very regretfully seven years later, when I became pregnant. It was a civil service appointment, and in those days, there was no maternity leave. If you had a baby, you had to go straight back to work after just a few weeks, so, unless you could afford to have a nanny, you had to give up work. Things have progressed (some may say regressed) since then!

Starting work at the India Office Library, I was assailed by tradition. On entry, you were greeted by a Messenger in uniform who conducted you to an ancient lift where you were greeted by another Messenger, Jim. He was a relic from the First World War. He had only one leg, but was very dignified and courteous and always cheerful. He had an old brown leather chair with a huge canopy over it at the side of the lift on which he used to sit while waiting for the next passenger. He told me later that he could still feel pain in his absent leg.

My room overlooked St James Park and the Clive steps. I had an enormous four pedestal desk. Soon after I arrived, I was informed with sadistic glee by one of the Paper Keepers, that Lord Ismay had died while sitting at it!

Coming straight from the archive course, with its emphasis on the proper care and control of manuscripts, the avoidance of fire hazards, careful shelving, and the right humidity levels etc, I was horrified to find that my room had an open fire without a fire guard, and that in the bookcases on the wall was a vast collection of manuscripts which had belonged to Robert Lord Clive which, even then, would have been worth thousands of pounds on the open market. Moreover, the door to my room was never locked!

The manuscripts in my care dated back to the time just after the defeat of the Spanish Armada in 1588. Queen Elizabeth granted a Charter to 'The Governor and Company of Merchants of London trading into the East Indies' to encourage them to compete in the lucrative trade in the east. These merchants in London got together and financed and fitted out five ships and sent them off to the East laden with European merchandise, and they returned with eastern goods – spices and materials of all kinds

Thus begun the British connection with India. Over the next two centuries, the

Stanley Sutton, the Director, and me

East India Company built up a huge Indian empire which they governed through a Governor-General, administrators, collectors, magistrates, and a large army. The Library was established by the Directors of the Honourable East India Company in 1801 in Leadenhall Street. In 1858, when the power of the East India Company was transferred to the Crown, the Library moved to Kings Charles Street, and when India became independent in 1947, the Library came under the control of the Commonwealth Relations Office. Shortly after I left, it moved to Blackfriars Road, and then, in the 1990s, it became part of the British Library.

The manuscripts I was appointed to look after comprised what was called the European Manuscripts Collection. The collection extended to half a mile of shelving. Many of the manuscripts had never been catalogued but had been dumped in various cupboards and nooks and crannies all over the library which extended across the whole of the top floor of the Commonwealth Office building.

Moreover, just before and during the first years of my appointment, the collection was being added to by a deliberate policy of acquiring on permanent loan the private papers of former Viceroys, Secretaries of State for India, and Governors of provinces. This policy was the brainchild of the Librarian, Stanley Sutton – a lovely man of whom I was very fond.

The Viceroys and Secretaries of State and Governors carried out both an official and an unofficial correspondence. The official correspondence was preserved in the India Office Records, but the private correspondence was taken home at the end of their term of office. As most of these holders of high office came from the ranks of the aristocracy, vast collections of papers were preserved in stately homes all over the country. For example, Lord Harrowby, whom I mentioned earlier, had two collections of papers relating to India because one of his ancestors was a Governor, and the other a Secretary of State for India.

The papers were of enormous interest to historians because the correspondence was uninhibited, and these great administrators revealed what they really thought about what was going on. Some of the collections were 'closed' because of the fifty year rule.

From time to time I was sent to look at collections before the owner agreed to let them come to the Library. One visit will always stick in my mind. It was to Kedleston Hall in Derbyshire, home of Lord Curzon who had been Viceroy of India at the turn of the century. I went to sort out his Indian papers which were stored in the vast basements which extended the whole length of Kedleston Hall. The basement was very cold and gloomy, but I was consoled by the fact that I was invited to join the family for lunch. When I went up to the beautiful dining room, my eyes lit up because the table was beautifully laid up with enough cutlery for a seven course meal and sufficient glasses for a different wine with each course. The butler, with his white gloves, was standing ready to serve us, and I sat down with eager anticipation. But I think that was one of the great disappointments of my life, for the meal consisted of mince, mashed potatoes and carrots, and our lovely wine glasses were filled with water. To add insult to injury, this was followed by rice pudding and prunes!

The collection of manuscripts I looked after related not only to the great officials but also to the ordinary men and women who were in India as merchants, officials soldiers – or just wives and families. I had many fascinating diaries in my care which

The India Office Library Reading Room

were kept by both men and women. Photography did not come in till the middle of the nineteenth century, and many of the diarists filled their volumes with sketches of the people of India and their fascinating costumes. They also painted pictures of the places they visited. Others kept what are known as Commonplace Books – a sort of scrap book of reminiscences. Particularly fascinating were the diaries kept during the Indian Mutiny, some of which described the terrible siege conditions, and the privations suffered by the women and children.

Life was not easy for the women. Death in childbirth was common – and so too was the death of young children. The climate was difficult and disease was rampant, and the European graveyards are full of monuments recording the death of child after child of the same parents.

Just as harrowing was the separation of parents and children. For at about the age of six, the children were shipped back to England to be educated – and parents frequently never saw their children again, and certainly not for many years.

For me it was a fascinating life. The Library was used by scholars and postgraduate students from all over the world. If you walked into the Reading Room you would see men and women from India and Pakistan, Burma and Nepal – many, especially the women, wearing their native costumes. We also had numerous American students, as well as a few from other parts of the world. It was a cosmopolitan environment and I made some wonderful friends. I was invited to join in the fortnightly postgraduate seminars at the School of Oriental and African Studies (where the author of *White Swans* is now a Lecturer) and I actually embarked on a PhD – but had to abandon it when I became pregnant.

We had a fascinating collection of Readers. We had the illegitimate daughter of the King of Nepal, who was writing a history of her country; the gorgeously handsome Dr Gopal who was the son of the President of India (he took me out for the best Indian meal I have ever had). The Indian women were very sophisticated and independent – and often incredibly beautiful. Many of them were married and had left their children back in India with ayahs while they did their PhDs. I still correspond with some of them.

One interesting reader was President Nasser's tutor. He took me to lunch at the National Liberal Club in Whitehall on the day that President Kennedy was assassinated. I remember the occasion vividly because during lunch we had been wondering what Kennedy would do once his Presidency was over as he was still so young. It seemed ironic that the question was answered so quickly.

I found the Indians both interesting and different. They were intensely curious and would think nothing of asking detailed personal questions about one's family, and financial situation and life style. Bill and I enjoyed many an Indian meal with them, and began to understand what the word curry really meant. One of the readers, Dr Bish Pandey, became one of our closest friends. He wrote a biography of Nehru. He was married to Valerie, and had two daughters, Nina and Tara who were later to be our daughter, Alex's, bridesmaids. Sadly he died on the evening of the day he chaired a symposium with the Attenboroughs on the *Gandhi* film. Valerie later married Guy, a lovely man, who also became one of our closest friends.

We also had a number of American friends – Dr Frykenberg who was a Baptist minister as well as a historian; Jock Mclane, Brit Martin – to name but a few. When Bill and I were married, we used to entertain and be entertained by a number of readers – and had a very interesting time. We kept up with them for many years.

When I had been in the Library for five years, the Director decided I needed an assistant and a young woman named Stella Whitehouse, who had done the archive course in Liverpool and had spent two years at Worcester County Record Office, was appointed. She worked on

Dr Bish Pandey

A visit by Stella and John Rimington when Justin was a toddler

the other side of my huge four pedestal desk. We went to her wedding and when I retired to have a baby, she was appointed in my place. She later became, as Stella Rimington, the Head of M15!

Bill and I met, as I said before, at the WTA hotel in Southborne. He was then working for an insurance firm in London – which he hated. I always remember the first day he came to our home in Bromley. He arrived dressed in his Sunday best – but he had only been there a short time when my father got him helping with a bonfire!

During the next few months, Bill showered me with presents – two lovely green umbrellas (I left the first on the train), a small portable gramophone, and innumerable other bits and pieces. He was doing quite well at his job and had more money to play with at that time than he ever had afterwards!

Bill lived in a rather different house to our spacious ground floor flat in a large Victorian house in Bromley with its lovely garden. He spent Christmas Day with us and then on Boxing Day took me for my first visit to his family. For me, it was a bit of an eye opener. They lived in a council house in East Ham – a dreary place even then. The house had an outside loo, a very primitive kitchen, one sitting room and three bedrooms. All Bill's sisters and their husbands and boy friends assembled during the afternoon to see Bill's girl friend. Although Bill was then twenty-nine, he had never brought a girl home before so they were all curious!

Bill had two brothers and five sisters. Nellie was the oldest. She was married to George and had a son who was the same age as Bill's youngest sister – mother and daughter being pregnant at about the same time! During the War Nellie and her husband had lived in a pre-fab house, and Nellie developed TB. In those days, radical surgery was often the way TB was treated, and Nellie had had one lung

Bill

Bill's mother, five sisters and sister-in-law, Bill's niece, Alex and me

removed, so she was always short of breath. Her husband, George, was a banana and tomato salesmen. He used to say how naïve people were. The traders would buy one box of tomatoes, divide them in half, and sell one half as top quality and therefore more expensive!

Next came Arthur (whom I didn't meet till later). He was married to Betty and had two sons and a daughter. Arthur had been captured in Crete right at the beginning of the War and had spent the rest of the War in a prisoner of war camp in Poland. It was not until years later, when he came over from Australia for a visit, that he opened up and told us about his prison camp experiences. Within a month of demob he married his childhood sweetheart, and, soon after I met Bill, he and his family went off to Australia on the £10 assisted passage scheme.

Next came Albert who was quite a character. His wife was called Betty, as was Arthur's wife and Bill's younger sister so I found it all quite confusing. Albert had

Bill's elder brother, Albert in his Merchant Navy uniform

Bill's oldest brother, Arthur, with Betty and children – John, Hilary and Stephen

served in the navy during the War and was torpedoed three times – the third time near the Greek island of Leros. This was a significant occasion in Albert's life. For years, his wife said he would wake screaming in the middle of the night from remembering the horrors of that event. At the Millennium, when the Government gave grants to ex-servicemen to go back to their wartime locations, Albert and his wife went back to Leros. There he discovered that, though there were memorials to the dead of the Italians, the Greeks and the Germans, there was nothing for the British. Albert decided something had to be done and set about raising money for a memorial to the British dead, and in 2006, a memorial was built, and he and Betty went over for the unveiling. It was a wonderful occasion – but the significant thing about the story is that from that day onwards, Albert's nightmares ceased.

After Bill came Lily who married Benny, Albert's best friend. They had a tragedy in their life which probably would not have happened with today's medical knowledge. Their second son, Gordon, was brain damaged at birth from lack of oxygen. They began to be suspicious when, at three years of age, their son had still not started talking. Today they would have sued for compensation, but then they had to struggle to get help. Despite this Gordon has developed into a lovely, caring man.

The youngest sister, married to Derek, together with their three children, followed their brother Arthur to Australia on the £10 assisted passage scheme, and it was not long before another sister, Ivy, also married to a Derek, followed. Only Betty, the younger sister, who was engaged, stayed put in East Ham until they got a council house near Brentwood.

So, on that first visit, Bill and I arrived in time for lunch, and at that stage only Betty and Lyn and their fiancés were present. There was an unease at the lunch table on both sides. Bill's family thought I was posh, and were on their best behaviour, while I was feeling a bit snobbish about the council house and the table-ware – just one knife, fork and spoon! After lunch, the rest of the family arrived unexpectedly and the sitting room and kitchen became very crowded. By the evening George became outrageous – drinking beer from a huge flower vase! There was a lot of singing and laughter – and it was all rather bewildering. I stayed the night (I think poor Bill slept on the sofa) and I spent the next day there before returning home in the evening.

It was quite a journey from Bromley to East Ham, but Bill came over to Bromley often. He used to phone me from a telephone box, as there wasn't a phone at his house. One day, he was talking on the phone when he suddenly exclaimed 'Good heavens, there's an elephant walking past' It was a circus elephant making his way to the show ground.

We got engaged in 1956 and went up to London to buy a ring. We agreed I wouldn't have a new ring but would go for a second hand ring because they were then free of purchase tax. It meant I could have a much better ring for the money. We chose a ring with a sapphire in the centre surrounded by diamonds. It cost all of £45 – a lot of money at the time.

Our wedding with both sets of parents, bridesmaids, best man and ushers

Our wedding, 20 July 1957

We got married on the 20th of July 1957 at the parish church in Bromley. The church had been badly bombed during the War, but restoration work was going apace. I had hoped that it would be finished by the time of our wedding – but it was not to be. When I went down the aisle, huge green tarpaulins still closed off the east end of the Church. My sister and my friend Pam were the bridesmaids. The bridesmaids dresses were an unusual bluey-green colour, and Barbara and Pam carried yellow roses as did I. The vicar was Canon the Rev'd Murray Walton. Bill's brother-in-law and my sister's boy friend were the ushers.

We had the reception at home in Bromley and a local bakery firm did the catering – a buffet lunch at three shillings and sixpence a head! All my college friends came to the wedding, as did all our relatives on both sides of the family, and old family friends. I think we had about eighty people there.

My wedding album lists all the guests and the presents we received which, as was the custom, were put on show on tables in one of the bedrooms.

Weddings didn't go on like they do nowadays. At 6 o'clock we left the reception and were taken up to London by a business friend of my father. He took us to a restaurant in Soho, and I think paid in advance for our meal. We then went to the station and took the train for Southampton where we embarked on a boat to Guernsey. From there we took a smaller boat across to Sark.

Sark was beautiful. We arrived in the little harbour, and were taken by horse and cart up the steep hill to our hotel about a mile away. There were no cars on the island and you had to travel everywhere on foot, by horse and cart or by bicycle. There were only three hotels on the island and one big house called the Seigneurie – owned by the Lady of the Manor. It had the most beautiful walled garden.

The island was very small – about four miles long – but was indented with dozens of very different beaches – some sandy, some rocky, some with fascinating caves to explore. We did a lot of swimming – though the water was very cold and I got cramp in my wrists. We explored the caves, and did a lot of walking. The weather was glorious so we were very lucky

We stayed in a lovely hotel where we had wonderful food – with salmon, crab and lobster on the menu every day. There were several honeymoon couples in the hotel – but we had fun pretending we were an old married couple and no one found out! Staying in the hotel with us was Julian Slade who had written a West End hit called *Salad Days*. While he was at the hotel he was busy writing *Free as Air*, and would sit on the rocks on the beach composing, and in the evenings would play several of his new songs to us. It was a blissful time – and the year after our fortieth wedding anniversary we went back to Sark. We were not disappointed.

Our first home was a flat in Masons Hill, Bromley, over a hairdresser's shop. At the time, flats were very hard to come by and we were very fortunate in finding this one. We had a large bedroom, a large sitting room, a rather pokey kitchen and a bathroom. The toilet, which was separate, we had to share with the hairdresser below.

Our first home in Mason's Hill

    There was another big room on our floor – but it was full of the landlord's furniture. He wasn't supposed to let out the premises as he himself was a tenant, but he let us have the place for thirteen pounds, ten shillings a month. This included telephone and electricity!! We were very lucky. We also had a small square garden at the back where I tried my hand for the first time at gardening. There was also a basement – under water most of the time and full of fungus. We never went down there except to read the meter.

    We decorated the whole flat and made it very presentable. The one problem was the staircase. We tried to paint the railings white – but the black paint kept oozing through. Eventually James, my sister's fiancé by then, got us some special silver barge-paint to put on as an undercoat – and then we were able to paint the banisters white.

    My parents gave us two beds from home, and the landlord had left behind an old wardrobe. We purchased two armchairs @ £5 each and a small sofa that converted into a single bed. Our aunt gave us a gate-legged table, and we purchased six Ercol dining chairs second hand. Much of the rest of our furniture was improvised, Our only real extravagance was the purchase of a refrigerator which cost about £85 – a lot of money in those days. There was a filthy gas cooker in the kitchen, but through the help of a colleague of Bill, the gas board agreed to exchange it for a more modern one.

The flat was half way up a hill overlooking the garden of the hospital. Our bedroom and lounge were on the front of the house. For the first year or two, we were not worried about the noise, but as the ownership of cars increased, the noise became more and more intrusive, and we used to try and escape to the country at weekends or go round to my parents' house. We also had Bill's parents and all Bill's brothers and sisters to visit as well as my sister who married two years after us and lived in a bungalow near Cudham..

For a short while, Bill had a Vespa which he purchased from his brother-in-law, but it didn't work very well so we seldom used it. Then one day, coming down the hill Bill skidded badly on black ice and did a complete U-turn. He decided Vespas were not for him, and offered it to a colleague – first warning him of its imperfections. The colleague had a friend who knew all about Vespas and quickly discovered that one of the cogs had been put on the wrong way round!

In our early days of marriage, I experimented with all sorts of cooking. My father, who was somewhat conservative about his food, decided to keep a little black book and record his comments about the meals we gave him. The comments were quite amusing. I had quite a few disasters – tipping spagetti down the sink when trying to strain it, leaving eggs on to boil and forgetting them so that they exploded all over the ceiling (while I was thinking that the noise was someone knocking at the door). One very lively incident occurred on a Saturday morning when I planned to cook fish and chips. I put some oil in the frying pan and asked Bill to watch it and call me when the oil was hot enough to fry the fish in. He asked me how he would know – and I told him it would be ready when blue smoke started rising. I left the kitchen to do something – and returned to find the room full of smoke – and Bill sitting calmly on the window-cil drinking a glass of beer. I was so angry I threw a piece of battered fish at him. He ducked – so I threw the second. The fish went out of the window – much to the delight of a dog below – and we were left without food for our lunch!

We had not been married all that long when the Lewisham Train Disaster occurred. Bill was commuting to the City, and on that evening had still not returned at 9 o'clock. I phoned my parents to tell them how worried I was – and said I would put on the wireless. They tried to persuade me not to, and said they would come straight round. Of course, I did put on the wireless and heard about this terrible crash with dozens killed – and realised it was a train that Bill could well have been on. The next three hours were acutely tense as we waited and waited. About midnight, Bill returned. He had walked most of the way from London, trying to telephone whenever he passed a telephone box. But they were all full, with queues of people waiting to use them – so he decided the best thing was to walk home as quickly as possible. The relief when he walked in was indescribable.

Bill had had very little education due both to the War and to his parent's poverty. He had passed the exam to the grammar school, but his parents couldn't afford the uniform and the books, so he had gone to the local elementary school. Then came the

My sister, Barbara's wedding to James in 1959

war, and many of the schools in East Ham were shut down and the pupils evacuated. After the age of thirteen, Bill had almost no education,

But Bill was very clever and creative and used to write a lot of poetry. When he was in the army just before the end of the War, he did some studying preparatory to taking some pre-university exams. Sadly, the day before he was due to sit the exams, he was posted away. When he was demobbed, he felt needed at home and his brother found him a job in the City. He gave up all thoughts of further education – that is, until he met me.

We discussed it a lot. Bill was not happy doing insurance work, and I suggested he could still go to university. I was earning quite a good salary, and I knew he could get a grant. So Bill embarked on evening classes – taking O' level Maths and English and A' level Constitutional History, Economic History and English. He did all this from scratch in two years. He then applied for a place at University and was offered a place at my old college, Bedford, to read Sociology. Sadly, Kent Education Committee would not give him a grant – but said that if he studied to be a teacher, he could have one. So he applied to and got a place at Goldsmith's College in New Cross.

He started there in 1959 and much enjoyed it. Often he would travel to London with James, my sister's fiancé. He did well at college. He wrote a most interesting thesis entitled 'A study of astronomy in English poetry of the seventeenth century' for which he got a distinction.

When he finished, he got his first job at Raglan School – a very scruffy and difficult secondary modern school in the poorer end of Bromley. They had a number of gypsy children there – some of whom were sewn into their clothes for the winter so it was not the most salubrious of environments.

During this time we constantly seemed to be going to weddings, mostly of university friends.

Gill and Trevor Warren

Pat and Clive Minton

Liz and Jim Benton

In 1960 we started thinking about trying to buy our own flat. We really wanted to live in London and found a nice flat in Hampstead, but my father, who was lending us the deposit, was against the idea of London. Eventually, he and my mother, out walking one day, found a nice development of flats in Chislehurst, and persuaded us to go and see it. The builders had pulled down an old house in three acres of grounds, and had built three blocks with six flats each – all nicely spaced out. We went to look at them and decided to purchase a top floor flat. It had a large lounge, two bedrooms, a bathroom and a kitchen – and quite reasonable cupboard space. The view from the lounge and kitchen was lovely – looking over a wooded area with a few houses dotted here and there. Below, were two rows of garages. The flat in 1962 cost £3,400!

CHAPTER 6
Life in Chislehurst, 1960 – 1966

We were very happy in our flat at Chislehurst. There were a lot of young couples of our age living there which enabled us to enjoy a very pleasant social life.

But we hadn't been long at Hatton Court when Bill's father was taken ill, diagnosed with bowel cancer, and died soon after. Bill's mother went to live with her eldest daughter, Nellie and her husband George.

Working among Indians as I did, I was delighted to meet up with Singh, a Sikh, and very surprised to find his wife Betty had been at the same school as me – albeit in the year above. We struck up a friendship and decided we would make an overland trip to India together. We spent many happy evenings planning our route, but before we had made any concrete plans, we thought we ought to do a trial run together. It was a good thing we did. We decided to go to Italy. At that stage Bill and I didn't have a car, but Betty and Singh owned a small Mini. It was a tight squeeze getting everything into the Mini. We had the camping equipment on the roof, the cooking equipment in the small boot, and our clothes and toilet accessories in the very small compartments on either side of the seats. As you can imagine, we took only a very limited supply of food and clothing. We also took with us (or so we thought) just the limited amount of currency allowed at the time – £50. Later, we discovered Singh had secreted away quite a lot more. This had implications for the trip as they were able to eat out from time to time while Bill and I found ourselves eating somewhat insipid dishes of rice and spaghetti.

However, we set off with a good heart – Bill and I sitting in the back and Betty and Singh sharing the driving. Once in France, we quickly realised our overland trip was in jeopardy when we discovered that our companions both had explosive tempers. They would spend a lot of time arguing and then the one driving would slam on the brakes, fling open the door and stalk off. The other would similarly open the passenger door and go off in the opposite direction. Bill and I would sit like nanas in the back waiting for their tempers to cool down and return to the car.

Although it was late summer, we encountered snow in Austria and instead of camping, spent the night in an Austrian inn – a very pleasant experience as there was music in the bar after we had eaten.

We camped in Italy where Bill grew a beard. Though he had brown hair, the beard was orange and he quickly shaved if off, never to grow a beard again.

Italy was lovely. We camped outside Venice, visited Pisa and Florence, and vowed to come back again when we had a little more money.

But the experiences on the trip put paid to the idea of an overland trip to India.

Instead, we decided the time had come to start a family. I conceived almost immediately and was three months pregnant when we were invited to my aunt and uncle's Silver Wedding party. By then my parents, and my two aunts (father's and mother's sisters) and their husbands, were all living at Bexhill.

We were to stay with my aunt and uncle, and found my aunt in a terrible state when we arrived as a squirrel had come down the chimney into the lounge and created havoc. As I said before, my aunt was extremely house-proud, and Bill and I had to work very hard to get the room back in order ready for the party. The party was a great success, but whether or not it was the squirrel incident, I don't know, but the next day I threatened to miscarry.

The doctor advised bed rest if I wanted to keep the baby – so I moved in with my parents rather than risk the journey back to Chislehurst. Two and a half months later, I was still there, and miscarried in the October. It would have been a little girl.

The miscarriage was traumatic – made worse by the fact that at the hospital the nurses put my dead baby in a basin at the foot of my bed and left her there for several hours for me to look at. As the ward was full of happily pregnant women, it caused me deep depression for several months after.

It was during the period I was threatening to miscarry that we purchased our first car – a grey Standard 8. That was a very exciting moment for, up to that time, we had struggled with public transport – buses and trains. Now, at last, we were independent. It was great.

Just before Christmas I went back to work, and in the March became pregnant again. The baby was expected on the 11th of December, exactly the same date on which both my sister's first baby and my cousin Neil's out in Uganda were expected – an amazing coincidence. Neil's son Christopher arrived on the 28th of November, my sister's son Rupert arrived on the 10th of December, while Justin stayed firmly put. My sister and I were booked into the same hospital, and each morning she asked whether I had come in during the night. She went home, and I was still waiting.

On the 20th of December, my parents came up to stay with us – planning to go and see Barbara and her new baby the next morning. Because of the earlier miscarriage, I hadn't touched alcohol throughout my pregnancy – but that night my father persuaded me to have a glass of wine with dinner, and a night-cap of whisky on going to bed. That must have persuaded Justin to start making his appearance because at 2 am my waters broke, and Bill took me off to Farnborough Hospital. He went home but came back next morning just in time to be masked and gowned and, to his amazement, pushed into the labour room, and was there to see Justin born. It is now quite commonplace for fathers to be present at the birth, but at this time, it was almost unknown. For Bill, it was a wonderful experience which he wouldn't have missed for the worlds.

So, on the 21st of December 1963, my dear parents had the joy of visiting their first two grandchildren on the same day!

In those days you spent ten days in hospital after giving birth, so Justin and I spent Christmas at the hospital. It was in many ways a great experience. The doctors and nurses did their best to make the occasion festive. The wards were all decorated (Bill helped with this when he came to visit), and the nurses prepared little stockings in blue or pink to put on each baby's cot, containing useful little presents. On Christmas Eve, the wards were darkened and the nurses and doctors came round carrying lanterns, wearing their red cloaks and singing carols. It was quite magical.

On Christmas Day itself, we all sat down at a long table for our Christmas dinner with two of the doctors, wearing chefs' hats, carving the turkey.

It saddens me that today young mothers giving birth are sent home almost immediately. They have no time to adjust to the new situation and get some much needed rest and sleep. We were given the opportunity to have a night's sleep at the hospital as the nurses took care of the night feeds. As a result we went home refreshed and ready for what is often an exhausting experience during those first few months. I think this is why so many young woman experience post natal depression – a depression I believe to be very often caused by simple tiredness.

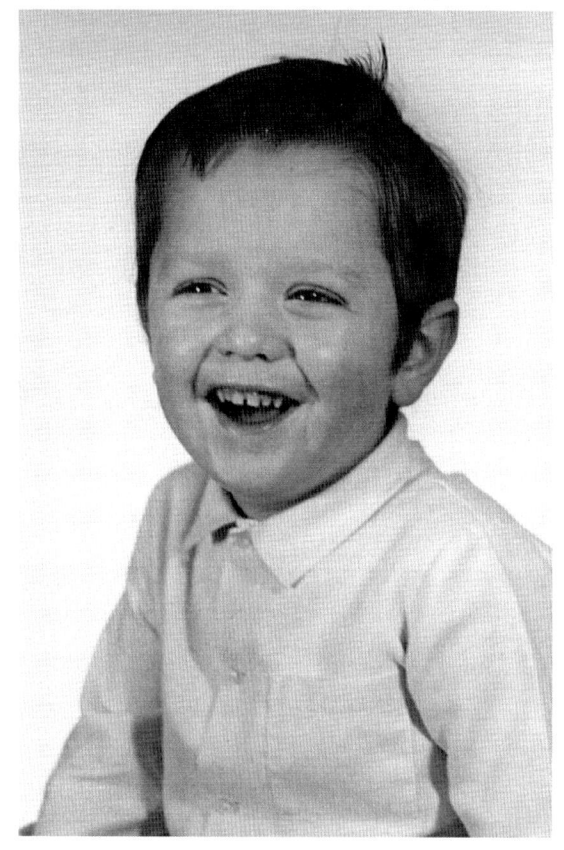

Justin

Before Justin's birth I had had very little contact with babies and young children. Although Bill's brothers and sisters were reproducing in all directions, they all lived at a distance and we only saw them occasionally. So it was that when Justin was born and we were handed this little scrap of humanity to take home and care for, I really had little idea of what we had let ourselves in for. One of the first things we did on returning from the hospital was to rush to the book shop and buy as many books on baby and child care as we could find. We very soon discovered that the sanest and most practical guide was Doctor Benjamin Spock's *Baby and Child Care*, a book to which I shall ever remain deeply indebted.

About a fortnight before Justin was born, I met a girl from the adjacent staircase, a doctor, who had just had her first baby, a little boy called Ian.

I was deeply fortunate in having Barbara as a neighbour and friend. She had specialised in paediatrics. We spent an enormous amount of time together (as did our husbands) and when the babes were about ten months old, each looked after the other's baby for a day a week, she doing a day's GP locum work, and I doing a day's archive work. Though the babes were so young, they played with each other – crawling after each other round the flat, and bouncing in opposite doorways in their baby bouncers.

In January 1965, I had my tonsils out at Farnborough Hospital – not a pleasant experience, but it did reduce the number of severe colds that I got each winter. Justin was just over a year, and Bill had looked after him while I was in hospital, and we

Sister Barbara and Dr Barbara in Hatton Court garden with our three babies

then went down to Bexhill to my parents to recuperate. We had only been home a few days when Justin became very ill with gastro-enteritis. I was very ignorant about baby's illnesses and the potentially lethal nature of gastro-enteritis. Justin was vomiting with severe diarrhoea for a couple of days and I was desperately trying to keep pace with the nappies and sheets and worrying about his progress – especially when on the second day he had a febrile convulsion. But the doctor allayed my fears, so I continued the treatment of regular small sips of water and the medicine. The crisis occurred about five o'clock in the afternoon on the fourth day. Justin had been whimpering virtually all day, standing up in his cot and crying 'ga ga' – his word for water. Then he suddenly lay down and fell into a deep sleep. I was relieved and felt that at last he was feeling a little better and able to rest. Had my friend Barbara not called then, Justin might not have lived. As it was, she took one look at him and said, 'He's very ill. We must get him to hospital immediately'. I, in my ignorance, had not realised that Justin was now in an extreme stage of dehydration.

We wrapped him in a blanket, slipped down to the flat below where another friend, Judy, was in bed trying to prevent a miscarriage, dumped Barbara's baby in bed with her, rushed down to the car, and drove furiously to the hospital where Barbara had worked before her son's birth. The hospital refused to admit us as we were infectious, so we then raced back to the car and drove up to the Brook hospital at Blackheath where Barbara's husband was a consultant.

There, Justin was admitted and put on a drip immediately. X-rays showed he had developed a paralytic ileas and we were warned that Justin was very seriously ill. The hospital allowed me to stay (the campaign to admit mothers with toddlers was only just beginning and the Brook Hospital was one of the more forward looking hospitals at the time) and I spent an uneasy night dozing and looking at Justin as he lay in a troubled sleep.

Early next morning, I was summoned by the Matron who looked very grave. She warned me that Justin was not likely to live, and pointed out that his notes showed that Justin had not been christened. She said that many parents whose children died felt even more deeply distressed if they had not been christened, and asked whether we would like her to call the chaplain and have a bedside christening.

We were not churchgoers and called ourselves agnostics. We had contemplated having Justin christened, but when we had asked my oldest friend to be his Godmother, she had declined, saying she could not, in all conscience, accept the role as she no longer went to church. This moral stand left us feeling uncertain, and we had put the whole matter in abeyance.

Now, presented with a crisis of this magnitude, moral considerations seemed insignificant. It was our son's life and our son's soul that was at issue. We said 'yes'. The matron phoned Bill's school, and Bill was summoned by the headmaster and told to go straight to the hospital – a moment he did not forget in a hurry. When he arrived, the Chaplain was called, and we had a brief discussion with him, and decided

My friend Pam with Justin and me

to ask our friend Barbara to stand as godmother. John, who was at the hospital and had been a great support, telephoned Barbara to get her consent. Then we all assembled at Justin's bedside and he was christened.

I think we must both have prayed – I know I did – and we used God in the same way that a pilot uses a parachute – useful in an emergency! Our son, to our great joy, and the doctor's amazement, recovered. And yet I still continued to run away from God. It was not for many years, until 1982, that the effect of this event on my own spiritual life manifested itself, and I became a Christian and was confirmed.

I stayed in the hospital with Justin, and to our immense joy he began, bit by bit, to recover. After three days we were told he would live. But I was not to have the joy of being with him as he slowly made progress, for on the third day, I went down with gastro-enteritis myself and the hospital turned me out immediately.

I was not to see Justin for the next two weeks while he was in hospital. My parents came up and visited him daily, and Bill spent every minute of the day with him after his lessons were finished. So Justin was not without close family contact. But when, eventually, Bill brought him home from hospital and I rushed to greet him, Justin rejected me!

It was a heartbreaking moment, and I suffered deeply as I slowly tried to regain his trust and confidence. In his little mind, I am sure he felt his mother had abandoned him in his hour of need. He was far too young to understand that I too had been ill. In my heart of hearts, I am convinced that that episode had an effect on our relationship. Justin and I have often talked about it, and he is aware of what happened and understands. But I know that in a time of real stress, it was to my husband and not to me that Justin would have turned for support.

Research done later at the Tavistock Institute revealed that separation of a young child from its mother, even for a short period of a week or two, could have a traumatic effect on the mother and child relationship, and that small children separated in this way often rejected their mothers when first reunited.

We enjoyed living in Chislehurst and made a lot of friends. It was an attractive place with a lovely garden all round which was maintained for us out of the maintenance charge. But it wasn't really suitable for a growing toddler who was ready to play outside on his own. Being on the top floor flat, and with a large unfenced garden, there was no way we could let Justin go in the garden alone. So we started on our quest for a new home.

Hatton Court Garden from the Dining Room

CHAPTER 7
We Bought The Oast, May 1966

Bill and I wanted to live in the country, and, because Bill was very practical, the idea of buying up an old house and converting it appealed to both of us. Our family was dispersed fairly widely throughout the southern counties so we felt we could move anywhere in the south. In the 1960s, teachers were in short supply and could be sure of finding a job wherever they were. Bill therefore started his search for an old house by contacting estate agents in Kent, Surrey, Sussex, Hampshire and Wiltshire.

Estate agents' blurbs began to flood through our letter box – most of which we discarded immediately. But some seemed promising and Bill embarked on a series of goose chases throughout the southern counties – returning time and again dispirited and disillusioned.

He visited houses that were too vast, too small, too derelict, too remote, too expensive. He saw cowsheds, abandoned churches, barns and stations. Some were ideal but badly situated – others ideally situated but impossible.

But, one day, details of what seemed the perfect property dropped through the door. It was a Tudor cottage in Wiltshire which had a stream through the garden. The word stream was like a magnet to Bill whose passion in life was fly fishing.

He immediately made contact with an old army friend he had not seen for years and set off in high hopes to renew old friendships and see his dream house – a "delightful rural Tudor cottage with oak beams, quarry tiles on the floor, a large garden with orchard, and a stream."

The cottage was as described – absolutely charming. But the 'stream at the bottom of the garden' turned out to be a ditch full of rubble, old prams and bicycles, and the 'rural' situation was marred by a huge electricity pylon station immediately opposite the cottage.

It was a very dispirited Bill who returned home from Wiltshire. Two years had elapsed since our search began, and at two, our son was nearing the age when he very much needed a garden to play in. Our flat on the top floor made it impossible for our son to play in the garden on his own – something which we felt was restrictive for his development.

We therefore agreed to abandon our search for an old property and take the conventional path and buy a modern house. But, determined that this would be in a rural area, we narrowed our search to Kentish villages around Maidstone.

It didn't take us long to track down suitable properties and we settled on a beautiful village where a small estate of ten modern houses was being built. It seemed ideal. There was every possibility that some of the other houses would be purchased

Of Such Things

by couples with young families, there was a village school near by, a flourishing playgroup, several village shops and a good bus service into Maidstone. It seemed the ideal compromise.

We put down a deposit, contacted our solicitor and set about planning our new life. Now seemed the right time to have a second child – and I conceived almost immediately. But, a few week's pregnant, the bombshell dropped. Our solicitor was a close friend, and phoned advising us strongly against the purchase. He said the builder absolutely refused to incorporate any maintenance clause in the contract, and David felt that we would leave ourselves wide open to major financial problems if anything went wrong with the building. We accepted his advice, and sadly withdrew our deposit.

Was it providence or blind chance that was guiding our lives at that stage? I often wonder what David's thoughts were later when he saw what his advice led us into. For a few days after we had taken his advice and abandoned the modern house, an unassuming envelope which was to change our lives dropped through our letterbox. It contained details of an oast house in the centre of a small village south of Maidstone.

It happened to be polling day for local elections and my husband's college was closed for the day. It was also the day when I left my son with Dr Barbara. As Bill and I were both free, we thought we would have a day out together and drive down to look at The Oast. The weather was dreary and damp and it was only the thought of a day out together without the demands of a toddler that made us feel enthusiastic.

The village had an unusual name and it took us quite a time to find it on the map. It was in a part of Kent we had not explored before, and as we drove off the main road and started our trek down wooded and winding country lanes, we felt as though we were driving into the back of beyond.

Ulcombe and The Oast from the Church

The oast from the front after the coal heap was cleared away

The approach to the village was down a steep and gloomy hill, so overhung with trees that it felt as though we were travelling through a dark tunnel. The road was pitted and muddy and The Oast itself was up a little dirt track on the edge of the village street. As we drove up the track our hearts sank. Here we were on another wild goose chas!

We picked our way over rubble and huge piles of ash and broken bottles, and came to what we supposed was the front door. The place looked uninhabited although the agent had assured us there were people in residence.

We knocked and the door was opened by a down-at-heel sad looking woman. She asked us in. The inside was no better than the outside. She pointed us upstairs, saying her husband was still asleep downstairs and she did not want to disturb him.

The stairs were crude and quite bare – up against the wall on one side and enclosed on the other by hardboard panels. Upstairs the floors were bare, the boards badly pitted and worn away. There were three rooms. The end one was very large and spanned the width of the barn. It had windows on three sides and looked up to the Church which nestled at the top of the hill. The room had no furniture and no curtains but contained what must have been over three hundred empty bottles and jars of assorted shapes and sizes.

The other two rooms were bedrooms – primitive in the extreme. Each contained two iron beds but there was no carpeting on the floor and one could see through the gaps in the floor boards to the barn below which was open to the elements.

Old sheets nailed to the windows served as curtains and on the beds were ancient pillows and blankets which had clearly not seen a wash tub for years. The rooms were indescribably desolate and I wanted to get out of the house as quickly as possible.

But I was curious to see the bathroom before leaving. It had an old bath, free standing with claw feet, with huge red rust marks extending from the plug hole across the whole of the surface, and a washbasin that was very badly cracked. There was no toilet. I turned to make my way to the stairs and as I did so I looked across to the window on the other side of the corridor and saw the most beautiful view across rolling fields and trees for miles and miles. The sun came out momentarily and I was lost. I wanted this house desperately.

The squalor that met us downstairs did not alter my feelings. The view was sufficiently attractive to drive from my mind the sight of the filthy lavatory by the front door, and the primitive kitchen with nothing more than an old stone sink, ancient wooden draining board, table cluttered with unwashed dishes, and two battered free standing cupboards.

The lady of the house was reluctant to show us any more of the house, but we insisted and she pointed us into two oasts which led one into the other. The far oast was divided into two bedrooms and we could understand the woman's embarrassment when we walked in and found the large double bed occupied, and stentorian snores emanating from the mouth of an unkempt looking man lying in the bed. We beat a hasty retreat, but not before we had taken in the curious shape of the two rooms, like two half dinner plates wedged together with a little entrance hall carved out of the rooms at the point where the two oasts were joined like an egg timer.

The other oast was a sitting room dominated by a crude fireplace with hideous mustard coloured tiles, a cupboard at the side, and peeling wallpaper. This completed the 'converted' part of the house and I felt sorry for the woman who had to live in such squalor and try and bring up what seemed like a large family from the number of beds I had seen in the two bedrooms.

But I was still undaunted and we explored the rest of the building. The barn below the three upstairs rooms was mud floored with huge doors at one end, and had clearly once housed farm machinery. There was an unconverted roundel with a brick kiln which contained another vast assortment of empty bottles. Outside were outhouses and a stone building which had once been a milking parlour.

The land around The Oast was totally uncultivated. It would have been difficult to grow anything as it was quite clearly the village dump. Huge pieces of corrugated iron, telegraph poles, an assortment of metal objects, including water tanks, aircraft landing strips and rusty farm machinery lay strewn over the ground intertwined with giant nettles and other weeds. It was a depressing sight. But the view was wonderful.

We drove home in silence – each contemplating both the possibilities of the place and the herculean task that would be involved in making the place habitable.

The view won and by the time we reached our flat we had decided to make an offer.

Early picture of the Oast

The asking price was £5,000 and we offered £4,500 that same day. Next morning, the estate agent came back to us and said the owner was not prepared to drop the price as he had a number of people who were interested in the property. A night's sleep had confirmed us both in our desire to have the place, and in a realisation that we were mad to contemplate it with so few financial resources to hand. But the desire overcame the madness and we made a full offer which was accepted.

The next move was to ask our friend Ray, a surveyor, to look at it. I think we secretly hoped he would reject it out of hand and so control what we recognised to be madness. But, to our amazement, he was enthusiastic and encouraged us to go ahead.

So we then enlisted the opinion of another friend Peter, an architect, who was far more cautious than Ray. Peter examined the place with scrupulous care and thoroughness, realising what was involved in his verdict. He jumped on floors, crawled over the roof space, poured coloured water down the drains, prodded and probed – and came up with the opinion that the place was sound and was a good buy provided we were prepared for a lot of hard work.

We often wondered later whether it was the double privy that had convinced Peter. His excitement was intense when he came upon it hidden in the bushes, and Bill had great difficulty prizing him away. For months after, his wife told us it was his main topic of conversation at dinner parties.

For us, our fate was sealed. With both Ray and Peter enthusiastic, we could only go ahead. But we did not realise what headaches were ahead as we tried to persuade building society after building society to give us a mortgage.

When I think that we sold our oast in 1999 for £376,000, and two year's later it was on the market for, £980.000, I smile when I think of the building societies' reluctance to lend us £4,000. They were convinced that the building was overpriced. Several societies were prepared to lend us 50% but that would have left us with no money at all for the conversion, for we had absolutely no capital other than what was tied up in our flat at Chislehurst.

It seems incredible, looking back, to think of how prices have escalated over what seems a comparatively short space of time. In 1966 we sold our modern well appointed two bedroomed flat set in three acres of garden for £5,400. We had purchased it in 1960 for £3,400. My husband's salary in 1966 as a lecturer in a College of Further Education was £1,500 per annum.

We knew that if we were to have The Oast we needed the maximum mortgage available. It was clear from the beginning that we would have to rewire the whole place, construct a complete new bathroom and kitchen, and repair all the flooring upstairs before we could even begin to think about converting the barn downstairs. Moreover, it was obvious we would have to do something about the woodworm which both Ray and Peter had identified in the roof.

There were also legal conveyancing fees to think about, removal expenses and a host of sundry items involved in any move, however straightforward, which this would certainly not be.

We calculated that, with a £4,000 mortgage, we would have £1,600 left to cover all these expenses including the £600 needed to 'do' the conversion. We were sufficiently naive and trusting in our own abilities and staying power to face this prospect with equanimity. It was as well, at this stage, that we decided not to let my parents see the house. My father's pessimism and lack of ability to see potential in anything, would have killed the project stone dead.

As it was, we spent the next six months touting our mortgage request round all the major building societies – while the farmer who owned The Oast got increasingly restless and even at one point offered to lend us part of the money.

Then quite by chance we heard of a small London building society which specialised in conversions. We wrote and were amazed and delighted to find that the Secretary of the Society was none other than the brother of my oldest friend – a lad who had lived in the house opposite for the greater part of my childhood. We got our mortgage – but the price was high. We had to pay 1% more than the current mortgage rate – a factor that put a heavy burden on our finances for years ahead.

CHAPTER 8
Preparations, 1965 – 1966

We'd started our quest for a mortgage the first week in September 1965 and we finally obtained one in April 1966. I was by then eight months pregnant. On receiving the good news of the mortgage we set in train immediately the work on the woodworm as we knew that to be a major operation which would leave a most unpleasant smell for weeks afterwards. But we had planned without thought because it coincided with our decision that the time had come to relent and let my parents see the house.

The day we selected for The Visit was a Good Friday. Over the years, that day has, quite by chance, proved to be an especially significant one in the history of The Oast. My parents were to be driven over by old friends – and we arranged to go on to a local pub for lunch afterwards.

As we drove down the hill to the village, the sun was shining and the day seemed auspicious. For some reason I have a very vivid memory of a little scene at the end of the lane that led up to the Church – a group of men standing round the Rector, all robed in elaborate clerical vestments, and all smoking. We were puzzled by the sight until we remembered it was Good Friday and that the group must have been resting between services. We had not so far visited the Church but it looked attractive and interesting, standing proudly at the top of the hill overlooking the village. I little realised then what an important a part of my life the Church was to become.

We arrived at The Oast just a little before my parents. We hadn't been down to the house for some weeks, and it seemed to have deteriorated considerably since our last visit. The tenants had moved out (evicted, we later discovered, after a court order) and had demonstrated their anger by breaking a number of windows round the house.

On entering the house we were dismayed to find that the woodworm people had started work and the whole place reeked of cuprinol – an unpleasant smell at the best of times but overpowering when sprayed throughout an entire house. Walking first into the sitting room we found that the tenants had left behind a filthy broken-down sofa which reposed in the centre of the room. But this was not the worst. Looking up to the ceiling we saw a gaping black hole through which protruded a quantity of old sacking. The woodworm control men had fallen through the ceiling. The smell was indescribable – and at that moment, the sun disappeared and a car tooted outside to signal the arrival of my parents.

Never an optimist at the best of times, my father's face expressed horror and dismay as he faced the desolation before him. The vision needed to see the potential of the place was quite beyond him, and after an hour touring the house and prodding and poking at the beams, he declared the house unfit for habitation (which it was) and beyond all hope of repair (which it was not).

The tour ended, his face settled into an expression of deep gloom and he declared solemnly '"You are both stark staring mad" and stomped off to the car. Even his friends' guarded enthusiasm failed to dissipate his gloom or give him any reassurance, and my mother told me later that he spent a number of sleepless nights worrying about his daughter, and reviling his crazy son-son-law who was leading her astray.

Years later, when he would phone up and say he was bringing friends down to show them our 'lovely' oast, it was with great difficulty I refrained from reminding him of his earlier reactions to the house.

Being by then eight months pregnant, with our flat sold and the moving date fixed for the end of April, it was quite clear that the Oast as it stood was not suitable for a two year old toddler nor for a home confinement. So my father's gloom was confirmed when it was decided we should have to move in with my widowed aunt at Bexhill, and have the home confinement at my parents' house.

We said farewell to our comfortable flat on the 30th of April and moved in with my aunt – with Bill commuting every day from Bexhill to Chatham. We were young and enthusiastic, and gave no thought to the strain such a journey each day would put on Bill. But Colleges of Further Education, fortunately, ground to a halt in late June, and Bill had the prospect of the long summer ahead of him to get on with the work of putting The Oast into a semblance of order.

I was soon immersed in breast feeding, nappies and coping with the twin demands of baby and toddler. The birth had gone very well despite the gloomy prognostications of my father who, it seemed, had been brought up on a diet of horror stories about childbirth. Alex arrived on a Sunday. I had started labour in the early hours, had got up and sorted out all the washing at my aunt's house (she being stone deaf and very house proud) before getting Bill to drive me round to my parents' house a mile away. We arrived, had breakfast and I walked round the garden while waiting for the midwife to arrive. Around lunch time I was put to bed and the house was quiet for the next two hours while Alex decided to make her appearance. Apparently, my father was utterly astounded when he heard her first cry – he had been waiting for the screams of childbirth which he had been fearfully expecting all day. It took him a long time to recover from the surprise of an easy and orderly birth.

Bill, with the birth safely over and the end of term in sight, began planning his work on the house. He felt the first imperative was to get a floor laid in the barn and replace the garage doors with a wall and windows. Nothing, as he was soon to discover, was simple. He found that it would be necessary to lower the floor of the barn in order to provide sufficient head room. He purchased a large fork and spade

The digger starts excavating

and started work. He had reckoned without the passage of time. The barn floor, though made of mud, was so impacted that it was harder than concrete. A hundred years and more of feet and machinery traversing the barn floor had impacted it so firmly that it was not even possible to pierce it with a pick axe. We were forced to hire a digger and operator from our local farmer to excavate the floor.

The digger had a big impact not only on our limited financial resources but also on our son's imagination. We made a visit to The Oast while the digger was working and he was mesmerised by the sight of a such a large machine inside the house. From that time on, whenever we went for a walk, his main objective was to find another digger. We spent hours standing by road works in Bexhill watching the 'roadies' and diggers at work – while he remained totally oblivious of the accompanying noise of pneumatic drills.

Once the digger had done its work the time came to lay a cement floor and build in wall and windows. Bill was fortunate in that a colleague and his teenage son lived in the next village and offered to help. So, for the months of July and August, they worked mixing up and laying cement and building brick walls, while the electrician and plumber re-wired and re-plumbed the whole house.

Meanwhile I was being comfortably looked after by my parents and was not exactly eager to leave the luxury of my parents' house for the privations of the Oast. But come the middle of September, Bill had to return to college, and it did not seem fair to impose that long journey each day on him. So I reluctantly agreed a date to move in.

Molly with Justin and Alex, 1966

CHAPTER 9
We Take Up Residence
September 1966

The great day came when we took up residence. Our furniture had been stored in the roundels, and we had both been too preoccupied to lift the covers and inspect it. This was a mistake for we'd overlooked the depredations made by damp, and when we came to move in, we found all our furniture covered by a fine layer of mould. That was a good start.

We next discovered that, though most of the plumbing had been done, the water to the new bathroom had not been connected. Our only source of hot water was the washing machine. We had to fill it with cold water, heat up the water, and then siphon it off. This was not exactly the easiest way to deal with a new baby and a toddler, particularly when the toddler was finding it difficult to settle into a new environment which was far from comfortable. I think back with horror to one evening when I'd siphoned the water off into a baby bath on the floor of the kitchen, and our son was being particularly energetic with his bathing. I suddenly noticed that the floor was awash with water which was trickling round the electric wires connecting the washing machine to the plug – and the plug was still switched on! I still go cold when I think what might have happened.

Life was far from easy those first few months. The place was cold and inhospitable. The weather suddenly changed and was wet and windy. The pace of work was slow as Bill was back at college and I could do little with two such young children to care for.

We decided we would live upstairs in the two bedrooms to start with while we made one of the oasts habitable. Bill had already torn down the curious artificial partition in the far oast – but that in some ways created more problems than it solved. For the floors of the two half-dinner-plate shaped rooms had been covered with cheap Marley tiles which had become very brittle. Where the partitions had stood, there were of course, no tiles at all, and in many parts of the floor the tiles had lifted. As the room was also filthy, we decided that that room would have to remain out of action for some time to come.

So we concentrated attention on the outer oast. The first priority as I saw it was to tear out the fireplace. I have a thing about fireplaces as the family will testify. When travelling and booking into strange hotels, I always check the lounge fireplace before deciding whether or not to stay! It seems to me an eminently logical thing to do. If the fireplace is not aesthetically pleasing, what chance is there of relaxing in the room? And as relaxation and tranquillity is the essence of a holiday, fireplaces in strange hotels seem to me to be of great importance. Sad to say it is not a view that is always shared by my travelling companions!

New fireplace

It was with great satisfaction, therefore, that I helped Bill tear down the hideous yellow fireplace in the outer oast. Then arose the problem of what to do with the hole we had created. Bill, romantic as ever, thought it would be nice to make the fireplace larger and more impressive. So, he set to, with a variety of masonry tools, to enlarge the opening. But this achieved, there was absolutely no question of buying a fireplace as our meagre funds were rapidly becoming depleted. However, we had, in what we euphemistically termed 'our garden', a vast quantity of rag stone and the idea of a stone fireplace appealed. I sat down to design what I thought would be a suitable fireplace for the room – one that went right across the end of the room and included two sitting areas and a space for logs. Needless to say we didn't get the design right the first time round, and poor Bill had several sessions tearing down and improving the fireplace over the years – but we were happy with the basic concept and delighted at the appearance.

But we had not bargained for the ensuing problems. Come the day when we were ready to light our first fire, our excitement quickly turned to dismay as smoke poured into the room and we had to put the fire out as quickly as we could.

In the next months, we tried every device we and our various friends and acquaintances were able to suggest. We put a cowl on the chimney – no success. We took that down (no easy job climbing to the top of a chimney stack). We put up another, of a different shape – and another, and another – but without success. We then took out a brick from the chimney stack. The smoke was worse than ever.

We put the brick back. We put a hood over the fireplace. The smoke still curled out, though not quite so badly. Here was the solution – a hood, but projecting more. We made another, larger, hood. The smoke was worse than ever.

After one of these 'adjustments' I had just lit the fire to see whether it would work when the Health Visitor arrived on a routine visit. I sat her down in an armchair and proudly brought in Alex, now six months old and very bonny and healthy. I sat down in an armchair across the room, Alex on my lap and beamed at the Health Visitor – but within a few minutes, she was no longer visible through the haze of smoke. We made a quick getaway into our primitive kitchen which I did not feel would recommend me to the Health Visitor as a proud housewife. The old stone sink and wooden draining board were still in use, and as a temporary measure we had purchased a couple of broken down sideboards to store our kitchen equipment in. Bill had removed the drawers from one of the sideboards and screwed them to the wall with curtains across as temporary storage space. We had stripped the broken Marley tiles from the floor and walked on bare concrete.

Fortunately the Health Visitor was understanding about our situation and became a good friend later when, together, we started planning a playgroup for the village.

The fireplace we were reluctant to abandon in the interests, by now, of warmth as much as appearance. For the weather was getting colder and we were discovering how cold the house was. In the daytime I was wearing two pairs of stockings if trousers were not in order. And in bed, we were so cold with the wind howling through the floorboards that we had more layers of blankets on our beds than I would ever have believed possible.

The Oast during the War before the black kiln was knocked down

The front garden!

One evening my sister and brother-in-law braved a visit. We advised them to dress warmly which they did. But on arrival, my brother-in-law, having divested himself of his overcoat, hastily put it back on again and refused to be parted from it all evening. At one point after dinner, which we had eaten in a corner of the lounge, he lit a candle and walked round the room with it, noting the many places where the draught was so strong the candle blew out. It was a long time before we could persuade them to visit again!

Apart from the fact that the house was still unfinished and there were gaping holes all over the place through which the wind howled, there was also the problem of electricity. Despite putting on all the bars of the electric fires available, very little warmth seemed to emanate from them. The lights were never very bright and from time to time they dipped even lower. On enquiry, we were told that our house was 'at the end of the line' and that the power lines were overloaded. Although the explanation did not seem to be very scientific, there is no denying that when, a few years later, a new electricity sub station was put in, our fires were hotter and our lights brighter.

It was not till the spring that we finally solved the problem. Just as we were about to brick up the fireplace and invest in a decent electric fire, someone told us about the Coal Utilisation Council and we wrote to them a despairing letter. A reply came back promptly with a leaflet and the suggestion that our problem was caused by the lack of a 'whiff'. Apparently, in enlarging the fireplace, Bill had made a straight opening up the chimney when he should have made it S shaped so that the smoke was pulled up round a bend.

It seemed complicated but worth a try. Bill decided to respond to the challenge, donned a mob cap, and spent the next three days (it was the Easter holiday) with his head up the chimney, building a whiff. After a week, during which we left the concrete to dry, we lit the fire and to our joy and delight the smoke went up the chimney rather than into the room. We had conquered the problem.

One of our visitors to The Oast at this time was my aunt and godmother. She had been widowed the year before and had always spent a lot of time with us. Stone deaf and in her mid seventies, she was a great trouper and often came to stay. She climbed ladders and wielded scrubbing brushes and paint brushes with the rest of us. It was all the more amazing because, while my uncle was alive, he had done absolutely everything for her. Until his death, she had never polished her own shoes, cleaned windows, or been on a bus. At the age of seventy-three she embarked on all these activities with great determination and enterprise.

Staying at The Oast during a particularly cold spell she was alerted to how inhospitable the place was in cold weather. She decided to do something to help, and offered us an 'advance on our legacy'. She had always told me I was to be one of her main legatees and she now suggested that we should have £500 of our legacy in advance in order to install central heating. She was quite insistent about it and toddled off to her solicitor on her own to make the necessary alteration to her will.

So, by the second winter of our residence at The Oast, we were the proud owners of a centrally heated house.

Alex in the front garden, 1968

CHAPTER 10
Adjustments

Those early months at The Oast, after Bill had returned to college and I was left alone with the two small children, miles from friends and family, were very difficult ones and I think that had it not been for our friend, the postman, I would have been very miserable indeed.

Postmen are my favourite people. I think my liking began when I was at school in the sixth form and later at university, and used to spend my Christmas holidays working in the Post Office.

I was lonely. Ulcombe was in many ways a typical rural village, but the local inhabitants were nowhere near as friendly as those we had met in Oxfordshire during the War. Then, evacuated from the horrors of bombings and doodle bugs, my mother, sister and I were heartened by the warmth of the local people who always greeted us cheerily when we met them in the village street or along the country lanes, and would stand and chat with us without any consideration of the passing of time.

But in this remote Kentish village, we were regarded not exactly with hostility but certainly with indifference. No neighbours called to welcome us, and when we walked down to the local shop, we received no smiles or greetings from those we met.

Looking back, this seems curious as now there is no absence of warmth, nor do people avoid us when we meet them in and around the village. We are now accepted and a part of the village scene.

But when we first arrived in 1966, we came at a time of quite significant change in village life not only here but throughout the country. It was the period when commuters were beginning to invade the rural areas and there was a large influx of middle class professional people whose experience of life and whose expectations were completely different from those of the rural community.

In our village, there were many, still middle aged, who only a few years before had been doing their washing in the stream that ran through the centre of the village. Many of the farm labourers' cottages still lacked internal lavatories and bathrooms, and main drainage was only that year being put through the village street.

Other changes were comparatively recent. The farm encircling our house which once employed a hundred labourers now had only three agricultural workers. The secondary school age children were now bussed out of the village instead of spending all their school life at the local school.

To those who had lived all their lives in the village, the arrival of newcomers was inevitably regarded with fear and suspicion. We were, after all, buying houses which in former days would have been kept in the family. Isolation, to begin with, was almost inevitable.

So, I felt lonely and more than a little depressed. The house was in a terrible state with little hope of speedy completion, the children were young and demanding, and Bill was out from before eight in the morning – sometimes not returning until 10 o'clock at night when he had evening classes. The milk lady delivered at 5am and there were no other regular callers – except for the postman.

He used to arrive about tea time in the afternoon (we had second deliveries then) and I always had a kettle on the boil in time for his arrival. He was a lovely man – small and wizened but with a keen sense of humour, a fund of stories and a warm smile. He had been a gardener for many years at Leeds Castle before taking up the job of a postman. He loved his job, knew everything about everyone, and not only cheered me up but also gave me a good basis for getting to know the village.

Hall before

Hall after

He remained our friend for years. Our daughter had a special affinity with him. He had known her as a three month old baby and saw her grow up. She used to send him postcards when we were on holiday (and in doing so, joined a real fan club as we later learnt from his son who took over the round when his father retired).

He must have been widely loved for, in later years, he and his wife (even smaller than Albert) were left a house by a couple he had done gardening for in his spare time.

Not so long ago, when visiting a friend in hospital just before Christmas, I happened to glance at the next bed and there was my old friend recovering from a heart attack. He was very indignant at what had happened. Then seventy-eight, he had never had a day's illness in his life and didn't believe what was happening to him. He had been looking forward to doing his Christmas round of the village as a temporary postman – something he had been doing every year since his retirement and was deeply frustrated that the doctors had told him it would not be possible.

Alex on her birthday

His son was as small as his father and every bit as kind. We never had to take our letters to the post-box but always left them sticking out of the letterbox ready to be collected by the postman. When I was working and used to leave home just before

Christmas musical evening

the post arrived, I would draw up my car alongside the post van and we would exchange letters – mine to be posted and his to be delivered. It was a very happy arrangement even if it did occasionally hold up the traffic!

As I said, my friendship with Albert and his son was not my first contact with postman. I had spent five Christmas vacations working with postmen and my memories of those times were all happy ones.

I quickly learnt in my first Christmas at the Post Office that the best place to be was inside. You earned much more because the shifts were longer and you had all the fun of the tea and coffee breaks, and the repartee with the regular postmen who tended to stay in over the pre-Christmas period, leaving the temporary postmen to brave the cold and tramp the rounds.

If you were accepted by the postmen, they would initiate you into all the ruses enabling you to stay on for the very late night shifts which were better paid. There were particular times when it was essential to stay on in the canteen or disappear to 'repair one's toilette'. Once the danger points had passed when one could have been signed off, one was sure of work until the shift ended.

The postmen were very protective of their 'young ladies', making sure we were not given sorting that was too difficult or heavy. We never had to cope with parcels but were placed alongside the regular postmen in the rows of sorting racks.

There was a very happy atmosphere – music blaring out throughout the day and night but at a level that was pleasant and conducive to good spirits and hard work. One of the things that I really liked about the postmen was that their language was never coarse and their humour always funny, but never smutty. It may have been the presence of us young students, but I have always suspected that it is a characteristic of the sort of person who takes on the job of postman. They seem to be people with a kindness and warmth that makes it easy to establish a rapport with others, and prevents them from doing or saying things which would offend and hurt.

Certainly, over the years, the postmen and postwomen I have met have all fallen into the same sort of category and I place them right at the top of my list of 'good' people.

Nowadays it is difficult to understand what a culture shock it was for me to move into such a rural environment. I had always loved the country, had enjoyed our frequent visits to our two aunts and uncles with their big houses and gardens in the country. And, as I have described above, we had the opportunity during the War of sampling life in the country for a long period – but I was then a child.

Now I was an adult who had spent most of her life in urban surroundings – working in London and living in Bromley and then in Chislehurst. One had all the amenities of civilised living – street lights, frequent transport, daily milk deliveries, easily accessible shops, pavements to walk on, and people all around.

Here in the village, it seemed as though we were cut off from civilisation. The mere approach to the village through a tunnel of thick woods and down and down into the village through more tunnels of trees gave a feeling of entering a strange new world. We had no friendly neighbours on either side. Instead, broken down outhouses and field upon field were all we could see from the windows – and of course, the view which by this time was shadowed in mist and rain as the weather became drearier. Our nearest neighbour was too far away to hear if one shouted out for help – and as we had no telephone to start with, I felt that I might indeed have to resort at some time to shouting for help.

I was, in fact, afraid at times of the environment especially at night when Bill was taking evening classes. One night in particular sticks vividly in my memory. I had just bathed the children (by then, we at least had all the basics in operation) and was sitting with them in front of the fire, Alex having her last feed and Justin sitting against my knee as I read a bedtime story.

Suddenly, I heard a ghostly wailing – the sound difficult to reproduce but chilling in the extreme. I froze. The wailing started again and the hair at the back of my neck stood on edge. There was no phone, no-one near at hand, and I was too frightened even to leave the sitting room. For at this time, although we had window frames in the openings we had knocked into the barn, we had not had time to put in any glass. The only barrier, therefore, between the habitable and inhabitable part of the house was a flimsy door with a tiny bolt.

It was getting on for eight o'clock and the ghostly wailing continued intermittently for the next two hours. I could not force myself to leave the room even though I was by now desperate to go to the toilet. The two children had fallen asleep uncomfortably on the sofa but my maternal instincts were not strong enough to overcome my fear of the Oast Ghost as I now positively believed it to be, and put the children to bed. And when at last, I heard Bill's footsteps outside, I was too frightened to go and greet him in case it was not him but the ghost!

With what relief I fell into Bill's arms I cannot describe. Needless to say, he dismissed immediately my contention that there was a Ghost at the Oast, insisted we put the children into their beds first, and then investigated the phenomena. For, the wailing which had ceased momentarily on Bill's return, to my relief resumed again, as I knew that had he not heard the sound for himself, he was such a sceptic that he would have put it down to my imagination.

Anyhow, children safely tucked in bed, we set out to trace the ghost. It was not long before Bill discovered what it was. There was a door from the kitchen leading into the barn which we had locked up and placed furniture in front of. But as the windows in the barn were without glass, there was a terrible draught. We had sealed the doors all round with celotape, and this had come loose and was vibrating in the wind! It was a long time before Bill let me forget my ghost!

This was not the only occasion when I felt afraid. The village was surrounded by fields of strawberries and hops – hence the oast house. And from time immemorial, the hops had been picked by Londoners who made their annual pilgrimage to the villages of Kent to enjoy the country air and help with the hop picking. Just up the lane from us was a row of hop pickers huts – primitive, with no sanitation, other than chemical closets, and only a tap for water.

Over the years the real Londoners seem to have fallen by the wayside – and their place was taken by gypsies. Moving in in September and being preoccupied with all the problems of babies, nappies, and trying to get the house in some semblance of order, we were not really aware of our neighbours up the lane, and our house looked so derelict I do not think anyone really knew we were in occupation. But our second September at the Oast brought us up sharp about our seasonal neighbours. First of all, a number of caravans arrived and rumbled past The Oast followed by several old and battered cars and equally battered lorries. Then a number of horses arrived – and a couple were tethered immediately outside our land.

At this time our land was still unfenced and we felt very exposed. The footpath leading up to the hopper huts passed within thirty yards of our back door and it was easy for strangers to walk up to the back of the house across the fields.

Within a few days of the arrival of the hop pickers, we found ourselves besieged. There were frequent knocks at the door with requests for a jug of water, or a drop of milk. One or two knocked and asked us to read letters for them or help them to fill in forms. Though we were among those who advocated a fair deal for caravan dwellers, we were uneasily aware that every request was accompanied by an inquisitive look through the door into the house. And our unease was increased when we found, on several occasions, the visitors peering through windows at the back of the house

One day about ten o'clock in the evening came a knock on the door. It was a man with a can. Could we give him some petrol. His wife was about to have a baby and he needed to take her to hospital. We could not see how we could get the petrol out of our car into his can – so Bill offered instead to drive the woman to hospital and said he would bring his car up the lane to the hopper hut. The man looked uneasy – and said he would go back and discuss it. Bill got himself ready and sat on tenterhooks waiting for the man to return and collect him. Nothing happened and well after midnight, we decided to go to bed. No call came during the night – and when next morning we saw one of the visitors walking past the house, we stopped them and asked what had happened about the baby. The man looked blank. 'What baby?' he asked. We looked at each other, and felt more uneasy than ever.

During the day, there were talks in the shop of fights outside the pub and there was an atmosphere of unease in the village. A few days later, we were sitting up late when we heard the sound of fire engines. Our lounge, in one of the roundels, has two large windows – one of which looks towards the village and the other across to a barn and the footpath. Responding to the sound of fire engines in the way I suspect most people do, we rushed to the window overlooking the village to see where the fire was. But there were no flashing lights and we felt very puzzled. We were even more mystified as we heard more and more fire engines arriving and yet could not see them. For some reason it did not occur to us to look out of the window which overlooked the barn, but eventually, curiosity overcame us and we put on our coats to go out and investigate.

Opening the front door the mystery was solved. Immediately across from the house, the barn was ablaze and there, almost in our front garden, were the fire engines – together with what seemed like half the inhabitants of the village in an assortment of overcoats, night caps, and dressing gowns reminiscent of a Victorian melodrama.

It transpired that the gypsies, angry at the farmer's refusal to increase their wages, had decided to take reprisals. They had set fire to the barn and had then gone up and besieged his farmhouse at the top of the hill, threatening him with guns if he tried to come out and deal with the fire. The farmer had been forced to enlist the help of our neighbour to deal with the fire brigade when they arrived.

It was a night to remember. Police arrived to deal with the siege, the firemen dealt with the fire, and the on-looking villagers got in the way till they finally decided it was time for bed. During the night there was a mass exodus of the gypsies, their dogs, caravans and horses.

Next morning, all that remained was a horse that was left tethered at the roadside for a couple of days before it mysteriously disappeared.

That, to our great relief, was the last of the gypseys. The next year, the farmer employed Asians who were bussed in and out from the Medway towns.

But that was not the end of the scares. One evening, it must have been some years later, we were sitting round the fire as a family reading *Wind in the Willows*, with Bill as Badger, Justin as Toad, Alex as Ratty and me as Mole, when there was a knock at the door. I felt uneasy and went to open it myself. As I opened it, a man, bleeding profusely, incoherent, unkempt and filthy and seemingly very drunk, fell through the doorway into the house!

Recovering from the shock of this sudden irruption into our house, we sat the man in a chair, mopped up the blood, wrapped him in a blanket as he was shivering from cold, shock and inadequate clothing – and tried to find out what had happened. More than a little incoherent, we eventually extracted the fact that he was working for the local farmer and was living up the lane in the hopper huts. He had been returning from the pub in the dark when he had slipped and fallen against the barbed wire fence along the lane. We phoned the farmer who said the best thing would be to get in touch with the police as he didn't want to get involved!

We gave the man hot coffee to try and sober him up while we waited for the police to arrive. Meanwhile, we hurried the children to bed – all hopes of continuing to read *The Wind in the Willows* at an end.

The local policeman arrived fairly quickly and it was then that our 'visitor' produced a card from the local hospital which stated that he had just been in hospital suffering from concussion and that if he showed any further signs of concussion he should be returned to hospital immediately.

The problem now arose – was he drunk or was he concussed? We looked at the man's pupils and we all decided that they were not as they should be. So we wrapped him in one of Bill's old jumpers and the local bobby carted him off to hospital. We cleared up the mess and were about to depart to bed when the farmer arrived on our doorstep with a box of apples – thanking us for dealing with the man. He said he had had endless problems with him since his arrival and had not wanted to get involved again.

He was to be disappointed. The hospital decided that the man was not concussed but drunk! As the farm was the man's only address, the poor farmer was woken in the early hours by the hospital demanding that he come and fetch him, and bring him back to the hopper huts where he was staying.

That, for us, was the beginning of several weeks involvement with Andy as his name turned out to be. At about 2.30pm the next day (pub closing time) Andy turned up on our doorstep with a packet of cigars for Bill and a box of chocolates for me – thanking us for our kindness the previous night and bringing back the jumper we had wrapped him in before he set off for hospital. We said he could keep the jumper (not a generous gesture on our part as it had moth holes in it and Bill didn't fancy wearing it again!) and thanked him warmly for the gifts.

That evening Andy asked if we could let him have a potato and carrot for his dinner. From that point on, for the next two weeks he was a frequent caller – 'borrowing' saucepans, milk, butter, and so forth. He was a gentle and amiable man who had no fixed abode but spent his life as an itinerant farm labourer, getting work as and where it was available. He travelled to Italy for the peach harvest, to Greece for the olives, to Norfolk for the peas, and to Kent for the strawberries and potatoes. His only vice seemed to be the drink – but even in his cups he was not raucous or belligerent but merely unsteady on his feet – hence the concussion.

But from the time onwards, we were always a little uneasy at unexpected knocks on the door after eight o'clock on a winter's evening!

The dining room and hall before conversion. We lived upstairs for the first months!

CHAPTER 11
The Playgroup Venture, January 1967

It was the beginning of November before our circle of acquaintances began to expand and I met Clare and her family. She appeared on my doorstep one afternoon with her son, Ewen, a toddler almost the same age as Justin. We quickly struck up a close friendship and spent a lot of time either together or looking after each other's children. Looking back, I feel really fortunate in that I met first with Barbara, my doctor friend, in Chislehurst, and then with Clare in Ulcombe – both of whom have remained close friends ever since.

Clare was apologetic about not coming to see us before, but said she had been unaware until then that anyone was in residence – not surprising considering the condition of The Oast at the time.

Justin was almost three, but I have always taken life stage by stage and had not really given much thought to the next stage of Justin's development, having been too pre-occupied with the new baby and the difficulties of our camping-out life at The Oast. But, not long before I met Clare, it had begun to dawn on me that we ought to be thinking about some sort of pre-school education for him.

I soon discovered that there was no nursery school in the village, and that the nearest one, four miles distant, was inaccessible by public transport.

Clare

Maidstone, ten miles away, had a number of playgroups and nursery schools, but they were equally inaccessible as the morning bus reached Maidstone far too late to make attendance possible, Moreover, we should have had to hang around for several hours after the nursery school sessions were over for a bus back to the village.

I was beginning to feel very anxious about this when the Health Visitor sowed the seed which led to getting a play group going at The Oast. She suggested that I should start a playgroup in the village myself.

Now, at this stage, I knew nothing about playgroups or pre-school education.

But I have never been daunted by lack of knowledge, being aware, perhaps from my academic training, that knowledge is always available if you know where to look for it. So, taken by this possible solution to the problem, I set about finding out as much about playgroups as possible.

What I did not realise was that this was to be the start of that voyage of discovery which occupied the next twenty-five years of my life. I had always been considered a good organiser although, up to this point, I had never been involved in any major innovative schemes. As a child I had organised my friends (bossed them around according to my sister) and my mother reminded me at this time that at the age of ten my first venture had been to start the 'Happy Club' for the children in the street. Later, I was to be the organiser of the 'Cricket Club' which operated on a nearby bomb site for many years until eventually the powers that be decided to replace the houses demolished by a V1 during the War.

I always felt the term 'bossy' was rather hard – but one has to accept that families have different perceptions of each other! But secretly, I think they were rather proud of my organising abilities, and they were not altogether surprised when later I embarked on a 'career' of public speaking. For when I was five years of age, such a career had been predicted. One Sunday morning my father had taken me for a walk in the park and I was chattering away to him in my usual fashion when an elderly and very stately gentleman, a total stranger, who had been walking behind us, accosted my father and raised his hat, saying, 'Sir, may I tell you that one day, your daughter will be a fine public speaker.' Raising his hat again he walked away, leaving my father totally bemused. The story was repeated to me a number of times during my childhood with a degree of both amusement and disbelief because I was at that time very shy and retiring with people outside the family, despite being bossy with family and friends.

My research into playgroups revealed that because of the inadequacy of state nursery provision, the playgroup movement was just beginning to gain public awareness. Bel Mooney had written a letter to *The Times* which had led to the self help playgroup movement. The Pre School Playgroups Association, familiarly known as PPA, had just been formed, and all over the country groups of young mothers and fathers were getting together to set up playgroups in village halls, church halls or homes.

PPA advocated the establishment of community playgroups which involved parents in the organisation and business side of the playgroup as well as in the playgroup itself. In the few years playgroups had been running PPA had discovered that the benefits were as much to the mothers (and fathers) as to their children. By participating in the organisation of a business, which was what playgroups had to be if they were to be financially viable, many mothers discovered hidden talents and developed resources within themselves which they were unaware they possessed. And by helping to run the playgroup sessions they learnt about the importance of play for the intellectual, physical and social development of their children.

PPA believed that the playgroup movement was responsible for a far more contented and self confident group of mothers who enjoyed happier relationships with their toddlers as they discovered the variety of basic and simple toys and materials which were both inexpensive but absorbing to the child.

PPA sent me specimen constitutions and gave detailed guidelines on how to form a committee; the local government and DHSS regulations one had to comply with; how to get free milk; what equipment was needed; and how to organise playgroup sessions. A whole series of cheap and simple but very practical booklets were available which were invaluable to those like myself who were quite new to the world of pre-school education.

Armed with all this information, my meeting with Clare at this time was fortuitous. She was a quick convert to the idea of starting our own playgroup. But we quickly realised, after doing a head count of under- fives, that there were too few children in the village of the right age to make one viable. Discussing this with our Health Visitor she pointed me to a possible solution. Her area of work included Kingswood, a nearby modern housing estate which was even more poorly served than Ulcombe for it had only one shop (Ulcombe had two), one pub (Ulcombe had three), no church, no school, and a dilapidated village hall. She suggested that we consider combining forces with the young mothers there who, like me, wanted pre-school education for their children.

She put me in touch with Eve who had come to the same conclusion as we had about numbers and viability. Kingswood and Ulcombe, though less than two miles apart, are separated by a very steep hill which defeats even the most intrepid cyclists. None of us had cars, and with toddlers and babies in tow, walking from one village to another was a prospect none of us viewed with any great delight. All our early discussions, therefore, took place via lengthy telephone conversations.

We set out on a fact finding exercise in each village, and quickly realised there was already a link between the two villages through the primary school which served both villages via a school bus. Enquiries revealed that there were sufficient toddlers in the two villages to make a viable number for a playgroup. Each village had a hall but Ulcombe's was a little more spacious and, built as recently as 1911, slightly less antiquated than the one at Kingswood!

These facts ascertained, we decided the time had come to meet. It is curious what false impressions one can get about people by just listening to their voices! I am always amazed when I see for the first time in the flesh someone I have got to know well over the telephone or through listening to them on the radio. I shall always remember my surprise when I first saw Brian Redhead, a man I had come to like and admire enormously from listening to his morning news broadcasts, so completely different from the picture of him I had conjured up. And so it was when Eve and I first set eyes on each other.

I discovered a woman with dark hair, positive features and of above average height, but had imagined her as petite, with delicate features and fluffy blonde hair. She in turn, hearing my deep voice over the phone, expected to find a big horsy woman, whereas I am 5 foot 3 inches high, have a thin face with lightly waved hair and know nothing about horses! Our surprise was so great that we could neither refrain from bursting out laughing and confessing to the images we had each built up of the other.

At that first playgroup meeting there were about eight young mothers and we concentrated first of all on the transport problem, knowing that unless we could find means of getting the children from one village to another the playgroup would not be viable. The Kingswood contingent reported that they had found two mothers with cars, and a possible third, who were interested, and calculated that each car could bring down three toddlers. We had been unable to identify any mothers in Ulcombe with cars, but had mustered a similar number of potential recruits in Ulcombe and we felt there was the possibility of increasing numbers once we were established. We therefore realised that if Ulcombe could be the venue, we had a sufficient number of children to make a playgroup viable.

I had been very taken with the philosophy of PPA and outlined it to the little group assembled. They agreed that the PPA model would be a worthy one to adopt. So we formed our committee – I taking on the role of Chairman, Clare the Secretary, and a friend of Eve's as the Treasurer.

We realised we would not be able to get very far until we had some money behind us – so decided that our first priority would be to organise some money making ventures to raise enough money to buy the basic equipment needed. We felt certain we could get most of the materials we needed without cost, but knew that a sand and water tray and a mini climbing frame and slide were essential items which we should have to purchase. Clare was on the school's Parent Teacher Association Committee and knew that stacked away in the store room were some old school chairs and tables which she was confident the headmaster would let her have! And we had a committee resourceful enough to beg, borrow or steal whatever else was needed to get the Playgroup under way.

We arranged to have a jumble sale and a Cheese and Wine party, feeling confident that these two events would raise enough to purchase the sand and water tray and climbing frame. Our confidence was justified. The two events raised more than we had hoped. The Headmaster duly disgorged the tables and chairs, and other equipment miraculously appeared, while Alex's erstwhile baby bath on a stand provided an excellent dry sand tray.

Money and basic equipment in hand, the next stage was the booking of the parish hall. This seemed a mere formality as it was empty each morning and we already knew how much was charged for an evening's hire. We felt confident that, as it was a parish hall, the Rector would be happy to see a children's group there, and would almost certainly give us reduced rents. How sadly optimistic we were! When Clare and I went to see the Rector, we were rebuffed. He told us that there was a heating problem; that the hall was wired for off-peak electricity which was not available until the evening; and that he was not prepared to consider any alterations or additions to the current electrical arrangements. After a second meeting, he did offer to let us install an alternative system of heating – if we could find one – but added the rider that if we did so, such an installation would belong to the Church!

The Rector had the reputation of being an eccentric character, but I was surprised by his lack of sympathy and understanding for our plans. I had assumed – remembering the old saying, 'Give me a child before the age of seven and I will show you the man' – that a parish priest would have been only too glad to welcome under its roof a venture serving small children. I was a non-believer at the time and his attitude did nothing to give me any confidence in the Church or its message. Even now, looking back, I am amazed at what a wonderful opportunity for outreach was missed.

Clare and I went away disheartened but such was our determination to succeed that it was not long before ideas began to germinate. We investigated the possibility of installing a small oil-filled boiler, and found that a small boiler plus chimney flue and guard would cost £150. It was an enormous sum and we knew it would take a good few months to raise. It was now January and the possibility of getting anything done for the winter was out of the question. September seemed to be the earliest date at which we could hope to be ready.

It was at this point that I started looking at our own property – the empty second oast behind the lounge, and the unconverted black kiln. Two possibilities suggested themselves: one was to have the Playgroup in the second oast and run a community based playgroup as we had planned; the other was to get a mortgage to convert the third oast, and run the Playgroup as a business, charging rent which would be used to finance the mortgage.

Our oasts were somewhat different from the majority of oasts in Kent. At one time there had been three kilns with conventional tiled cones. But, as we learnt from a ninety-five year old inhabitant of the village, there had been a fire at the Oast in 1887 and the three kilns had been burnt down. As it was a hop growing area the kilns had to be rebuilt, and were replaced with brick cones.

Obviously they were less vulnerable to fire – but they were also much more difficult to convert into houses once their original use was at an end. When the first two oasts were converted just after the War, the brick cones were knocked down and then rebuilt to half the original height with tiled roofs giving an appearance of stunted growth.

When we purchased The Oast, the third kiln was in its original state with a brick cone, but the top of the cone was open to the skies as the rotating top had been removed. We could not afford to replace the rotating top, but had planned just to cap the top in order to make it waterproof.

Later, when we had abandoned the idea of getting another mortgage to convert the third oast, we found a local farmer who agreed to cap The Oast for us for £25 – a heavy price at the time. We waited with great excitement for the job to be done – but

The unconverted oast

it was terrifying watching the man at work. He fixed hugely extended ladders to the oast by tying ropes around the kiln, and then proceeded to climb the ladder without a safety harness or any form of security and calmly installed a round wooden cover over the hole at the top of the cone. Justin stood watching fascinated, but I couldn't bear to watch and went indoors, only to peep out every few minutes to make sure the man was still in one piece.

We were delighted at the thought of having a nice dry storage area for Bill to use as a workroom while he worked on the house. But we were sadly disappointed. For, despite the protective top, the water continued to pour in through the cracks in the brickwork. What we had not realised was that the bitumen coating to the cone acted as waterproofing. It had to be applied annually for, as soon as the sun got to it, the bitumen started melting, leaving cracks which let in the water.

Our efforts at waterproofing being in vain, and the rain continuing to pour in, we could not help but regret the expenditure of £25 which at that stage represented a considerable proportion of our remaining capital. But there was compensation in the fact that the account for the job did not arrive – and by the end of three years, we came to the conclusion that the farmer had forgotten all about it. Then, three years and two months after the work had been done, an envelope dropped through our letter box with a bill in it, and we realised the farmer was dilatory rather than forgetful. One advantage, of course, was that by then inflation was beginning its upward spiral, and the bill was not quite as bad as it would have been had it been rendered on time.

The oast having a brick kiln limited us in other ways. Whereas with a tiled kiln it would have been easy to put in a floor and insert windows, with a brick kiln there were major problems. In the first place, the bricks on the kiln represented a huge weight. Secondly, we were reliably informed that it was not safe to knock holes into the brick cone because it would have caused the whole cone to become unsafe. So, if we were to convert The Oast, we would have to do as our predecessor had done and demolish the cone and rebuild it.

To go back to the Playgroup. The idea of converting the third oast for a playgroup was very attractive and I got estimates from local builders. For £1,500, one local builder said he could demolish the cone, replace it with a tiled roof, put in a floor, and knock out windows. This would provide two additional round rooms – one up and one down. We would have to put in windows, plaster the walls and finish off the work. It seemed an enormous amount at the time – representing more than a quarter of the purchase price of The Oast – and we knew that it could be a risky business to rely on the Playgroup as a guarantee of income.

So the idea was abandoned. But later, looking at the still unconverted oast and knowing that with prices in the 1980s it would have cost at least £30,000 to convert, we bitterly regretted we were unable to do it at the time. Later, when we sold The Oast, the current owners converted the roundel at a cost nearing £100,000!

The music room where the Playgroup was first held

Finance was not the only reason why we did not go down that particular road. The first, of course, was time. We should have had to wait many months to start the Playgroup while the conversion was completed. The second was that Bill did not really fancy the idea of having a nursery permanently in our home. The third reason was, for me, the most important. Though I liked young children, it was not my idea of bliss to make a career of looking after them. In fact, the idea of supervising a dozen or more toddlers each day filled me with horror.

So we decided on the second option and went back to the Playgroup Committee and offered it the temporary use of our back oast. There were two conditions. One was that the committee would help us clean and decorate the room. The second was that they would help us with the finance for new floor coverings – the present floor being too dangerous to use.

The proposition was accepted with alacrity. The committee felt that if we were to get the Playgroup going at The Oast it would give us time to raise the money for the boiler and good play equipment in time to move into the parish hall in the autumn.

A few days later a working party, which included some of the husbands, arrived at The Oast with scrubbing brushes, scrapers, and paint brushes, and set to work making the far oast habitable. After three sessions our derelict room was converted into a bright and attractive playroom with freshly laundered curtains from a junk shop at the windows and equipment set out ready for the children's occupation.

From the proceeds of the jumble sale and cheese and wine party we were able to buy a water tray, and a mini climbing frame as well as sand to fill the baby bath on a stand which Alex had now grown out of. Clare obtained the small tables and chairs she had noticed at the school, one of the mothers made aprons for all the children while another made special plastic aprons for water play. Books for the book corner, paper and paint, easels, building bricks and an assortment of equipment, not, perhaps, up to professional nursery school standards but adequate to start with, appeared from nowhere and we were all set to go.

We had applied for the necessary consent to hold a playgroup from the Social Services department and from the Borough Council. The Oast was inspected for fire hazard, the toilets and kitchens for proper standards of cleanliness, and the space outside for adequate room for parking. We organised free milk for the children and a loan of books from the Library Service.

One of our mothers was a primary school teacher and she very generously agreed to Supervise the Playgroup for the first month or two while we were getting on our feet. We organised a rota of mothers as helpers, another rota for transport, and we were ready for our first session in January 1967.

One of the consequences of having the Playgroup in the far oast was that our living room became a thoroughfare. The children had to pass through it to get to the toilet, and the helpers had to pass through to get to the kitchen for water. I had not bargained for the number of times small children needed to go to the toilet – and it was some time before I realised that much of it was due to curiosity and the desire to explore. For the first few weeks there was a constant stream of children and helpers to and from the toilet, and I soon accepted that I would get no peace whatsoever if I remained in the living room during the morning. This was disappointing as I had hoped to get on with some of my archive work while Alex had her morning nap.

Moreover, I was so unfamiliar with pre-school education that I little realised the impact that would be made by sand and water. That first day, when twelve under fives toddled through our living room was an eye opener. The devastation at the end of the morning had to be seen to be believed. Sand has a habit of creeping everywhere, and water play, though wonderfully educational, has to be very carefully organised and supervised if it is not to get out of hand. We were all novices at the game; the situation was new, and the children were excited. As I surveyed the chaos at the end of the morning I wondered whether I would be able to tolerate the situation for long!

But everyone was keen, people were sensitive to the fact that the Playgroup was in a home, and it did not take long for mistakes to be ironed out and for the Playgroup to settle down into a routine.

The primary school teacher did a wonderful job as Supervisor and we should all have loved to keep her permanently. Unfortunately, at that stage it was an unpaid job and we knew she was wanted back at her school in the autumn. We felt we had to make the most of her time with us, and were all eager to learn as much from her as we could.

Some people are a natural with young children and know instinctively how to work with them. Others, and I think I was one of them, needed to observe and learn from others. And there were some who really had no rapport at all with the pre-school child and could not wait unit until their own children were beyond that stage. But we were so convinced by PPA's philosophy that we were determined that a condition of entry to the Playgroup was that the mother should take her turn on the helper's rota. We did, however, make one exception to our rule.

One of the things that saddened us about the Playgroup, both then and later when it became well established in the Village Hall, was that we were unable to persuade the old villagers to send their children. We were an entirely self supporting group as were the majority of playgroups at the time, and had to charge a fee each day – I think it was 2s 6d a morning.

This was, of course, more than many of the poorer families could afford though it was considerably less than the fees charged by 'proper' nursery schools. As we were all struggling financially, there was no way we could afford to subsidise other children.

Although both Labour and Conservative parties subscribed to the necessity of extending pre-school education to all three to five year olds, no government seemed prepared to finance the setting up of state nursery classes or schools. Yet the general public was being made increasingly aware of the importance of pre-school education. Social scientists such as Halsey were publishing research findings which indicated the importance of the early years in later educational progress or failure. Research also indicated that it was social classes 4 and 5 which were still lagging behind in educational achievement despite the apparent equal opportunities provided by the 1944 Education Act. The Newsoms in their *Four Years Old in an Urban Community*, pointed to the very great variations in child rearing in the early years between the different social classes, and this seemed to point even more strongly to the fact that social classes 4 and 5 would benefit particularly from pre-school education.

These discrepancies were widely recognised in America, and *Operation Headstart* was introduced to try and give children from less advantaged homes special pre-school education.

The Playgroup movement was the British response to the recognition of the importance of the early years. But wonderful as the playgroup movement was, in that thousands of children had the benefits of pre- school education which the state consistently failed to provide, playgroups were always more oriented towards the middle class than the working class child because of cost. Though it would have been less expensive for government to invest money in supporting self -help playgroups, the money was never forthcoming in sufficient quantities to overcome this orientation. Later, under the Urban Aid Scheme, there were some urban areas where government input enabled playgroups to be subsidised for the less advantaged. But this was only the tip of the iceberg as far as need was concerned, and for hundreds of thousands of children, their first experience of organised educational play was still at the age of five when they entered primary school.

Twenty-seven years on, the debate still went on. In 1994, a report was published by the Royal Society of Arts and leading educationists and child care experts said once again that pre-school education should be available for all three to five year olds. To finance this, the Report suggests that the school starting age should be raised to six – a suggestion that received an immediate and emphatic thumbs down from the then Education Secretary, John Patten. The report also recommended education for parenting – something I was to find myself involved in a few years later with my pre-school playgroup courses and my secondary school teaching.

In 1967, pre-school education was available to a very limited number of three to five year olds, and in Ulcombe, the only real village child who came along to our playgroup was the son of the village coalman – and that was only with difficulty. His mother went to work each morning at 8 o'clock and the only way she could let her son come to the Playgroup was for one of us to look after him each morning from 8am to 9am. So, four days a week André was left with me at 8am and I had to entertain him until the Playgroup started at 9am. It should not have been a problem, but unfortunately André had not long before had a baby sister who had a lot of serious medical problems. His mother had to spend a lot of time with the baby and caused André unhappiness which he took out on Alex by prodding and poking her and muttering 'nasty baby'. Whereas I had previously been able to leave her playing happily in her playpen with Justin in the lounge while I cleared away the breakfast things and tidied the house, once André joined us each morning, I no longer felt it was safe to leave the children alone.

So, though the Playgroup provided a little time to myself during those mornings when I was not on rota duty, I felt the Playgroup was responsible for the loss of an hour of my time each morning, and another hour tidying up after the Playgroup children had departed. But it was something I did not regret, as I saw the pleasure the children got from playing together, and the way our little group of mothers blossomed over the months.

There were various crises during the early period – almost inevitable when you have a group of toddlers together. There was the child who fell off the edge of a chair and had to be rushed to hospital to be stitched up. There was the child who vomited into the water tray – not a pleasant experience. And there was the horrendous occasion when the entire drainage system seized up.

We were still on cesspool drainage. Our architect friend, when he had surveyed The Oast, had discovered that our drainage system was fairly complicated. Our pipes and those of our two neighbours some distance away followed a circuitous route to a cesspool in a field half way down the village, taking in, en route, the double privy which he had been so ecstatic about. He had observed, at the time of his discovery, that the pipes narrowed at that point – a factor that was material to the unblocking of the system.

This was the time when Alex was still in nappies and I had the habit of washing the less salubrious nappies in the lavatory pan. One day I inadvertently flushed a whole nappy down the toilet. I was annoyed as nappies were expensive – but thought no more about it.

On this particular morning, the mother on duty as a helper reported to me that she was unable to flush the toilet properly. During the course of the morning, the situation became worse, and by mid-day both toilets were on the point of overflowing. I was panic struck – even more so when my neighbour knocked on the door to say that both she and our other neighbour were also in trouble.

We called for help – and one of the local farm labourers who specialised in drain rodding came to the rescue. As ours was the only baby in the three houses, I was unable to decline responsibility for the very mangled and soiled nappy which, after hours of pushing and puffing, was finally extracted from the system and presented to me. I cannot now remember whether we were landed with the whole cost of the clearance, but I do remember receiving a very firm lecture from my husband on the necessity of retaining firm hold of nappies when washing them in the toilet. When I responded by inviting him to take over the nappy job in the future, as he was obviously more competent than I, he declined the offer!

As the time approached for us to move into the parish hall, we had to give a very careful look at our finances. We had run the Playgroup with twelve children at The Oast, but we needed twenty a day in the hall if we were to pay our way. For once we moved into the hall, there was rent to pay – with no hope of concessionary rates from the Church.

The problem was where we were to find our twenty children. There were a number of children in the village who were under three, and their mothers would have been very happy to send them to the Playgroup. But we were convinced by the arguments advanced by PPA that two year olds were not ready for playgroup nor able to cope happily with separation from their mothers and the hurly burly of a group of children. So, though we longed to say yes from the financial point of view, we stuck to our principles, and searched around for three and four year olds from elsewhere.

Ulcombe Parish Hall

Maggie helping Alex in the adventure playground

Fortunately, advertisements placed in parish magazines in neighbouring villages soon produced the requisite number of children. The arrival of one of these children was to have ongoing consequences for our family, for, some years later, his mother Sheila took on the job as my cleaner and has become a close and very valued friend of the family, virtually running the house for us and keeping us all on the straight and narrow while we were at The Oast. Since I have been a widow, she has continued a great support and friend.

Moving into the parish hall, we decided to pay a Supervisor. Our teacher had gone back to full time teaching and needed replacing. Our observation of the children's reaction to our teacher made us realise how important it was for them to have continuity. But none of us were prepared or able to give up five mornings a week without remuneration. So we had agreed we must pay someone to do the job.

We put advertisements in the local paper and a fortnight later found ourselves interviewing three candidates. It really gave the committee a great sense of importance in participating in the selection procedure – but we did not find it easy to choose between the three candidates: one had been a nurse, had experience of small children, and her own children were off hand; one had a lovely personality but no experience; and the third had been a nanny and had a nice personality, but her children, though at school, were still very young.

We felt we had to reject the person we felt most at ease with, and this left us with a choice between the nurse and the nanny. The 'selection committee' was divided two and two. It was a useful lesson for us and made us realise that when a vote is required, we should make sure that there is an uneven number of people voting!

The nanny was in nearly every respect the better candidate. She had experience with under fives, and was well versed in the needs of the pre-school child having read widely and worked with them for several years. But her own children had only just started school, and we knew that children of that age are vulnerable to a whole variety of minor illnesses. Some of the committee were frightened she might be very unreliable, particularly as she lived in a remote area and had no one lined up to take care of her children if they were ill when she was working. The nurse was clearly very competent and confident. She had not actually worked with under-fives, though had frequently encountered them through her husband's job. But we had doubts, which were confirmed later after we had appointed her, and realised she did not find it easy to work with volunteers.

Slide with Justin third from the back (photo now in Museum of Kent Life)

But she did help us to put the Playgroup in the parish hall on a good footing and we were grateful for her contribution, even though she didn't stay with us for long.

Our numbers sufficient, our equipment ready, the new Supervisor appointed, and the oil boiler installed with the help of the bank, we were ready to move into the parish hall. If I am honest, it was with a sigh of relief that I said good-bye to the Playgroup, and had the house to myself in the mornings.

The burden now fell unexpectedly on Clare who lived opposite the hall. Come the cold weather, we lit the oil boiler to heat the hall, only to find that the hall didn't warm up till the boiler had been alight for three hours – just as the children were departing. If it was to be effective, the boiler needed to be lit at 6 am. Without really thinking too carefully about it, Clare volunteered as she was an early riser. And for that winter, she went across to the hall each morning and struggled to light a boiler that proved to be extremely temperamental and had to be watched over for a long time before one could be sure it was really alight. Our second winter we persuaded one of the farm labourers, for a small fee, to light the boiler on his way to work.

Our first supervisor was replaced by a young woman with experience of nursery education. She was excellent and we were very sorry to lose her. But then, one of our local mothers, Maggie, came forward and supervised the Playgroup for several years. Her children, a daughter and a son, were the same age as mine, and we formed a close bond. When I took on a part-time teaching job at a local secondary school, she looked after our daughter, Alex, after the Playgroup session. It was a happy arrangement though it didn't last long as the teacher I was replacing returned to work sooner than expected.

At some point we managed to get a grant for an adventure playground. It was one of the best in Kent, and was very popular with the children. Unfortunately, the farmer who owned the land, was spraying his apple trees, and felt it made it hazardous for the children to be out of doors – so he withdrew the land, and we had to demolish the play equipment. However, it was moved on to the local primary school where it was used for many years.

The playgroup continued to flourish, and then operated in the 'new' village hall until 2014. It was, of course, more formally structured, and the fees of the children aged four and above were paid by the state. But not everything changes, for when I visited some forty years later, I was amused to find in the dressing up box a red, fur trimmed coat, that my mother had made for Alex when she was three!

CHAPTER 12
The Baby Sitting Club, 1968 onwards

The formation of a baby sitting club was a natural development. Most of the Playgroup parents were hard up, and finding that bit extra to pay for a baby sitter was not easy. A baby sitting club seemed the obvious answer. We recruited most of the Playgroup mothers and fathers as well as a number of others with school age children, and distributed a list containing all the members' names, addresses and telephone numbers, plus the ages and names of their children. The local postmaster printed tokens on card for us on his hand made press, and each member received tokens to the value of 20 hours.

The rules were simple. If you went out a lot, you had to do a lot of baby-sitting. Tokens were the currency and you had to pay tokens to the value of the number of hours sat. You were paid double time after midnight on a weekday, and on Saturdays and Sundays. You were at liberty to make as many cups of tea or coffee as you liked during the evening – and if you had no car, the husband or wife was expected to take you home when they got back.

The Club worked well. The only difficulty that arose was when an event was taking place in the village which most members of the Club wanted to attend. Even that was not too much of a problem as some of our members came from the next village. But it was a question of first come, first served and there were always a few unlucky ones who had to find a paid sitter.

It was interesting baby-sitting in different houses around the village. There was television to watch, a nice assortment of nibbles to eat during the evening, and the knowledge that one had the evening to oneself. I enjoyed studying other people's decor and browsing through different bookcases which were often very revealing of people's sometimes very unexpected interests. Rarely was the evening interrupted by the children waking – they were all so familiar with the club members they felt quite relaxed about their parents going out, and often looked forward to having a baby sitter for the evening.

Although most of the sitting was done by the women, it was not unusual for one of the husbands to take on the task, especially if their own children were unwell. They proved to be as popular as their wives.

One thing most of the houses had in common in the village was dripping taps! Ulcombe's water is extremely hard – and whenever one went into a house, there was the familiar sound of the drip drip of a tap whose washers had worn out. Bill owned a tool called a reamer which circulated round the village with alarming frequency – but the problem seemed beyond solution, and over the years, in common with most households in the village, we had to renew every tap in The Oast at least once – a costly experience.

There were the occasional bizarre situations. I remember sitting in one house when the back door suddenly opened and a man walked in. My heart started beating rapidly and I looked frantically round the room to see if there was a defensive weapon within reach. As my eyes alighted with relief on a poker sitting in the hearth, the man, without saying a word, sat down in the armchair opposite me and switched on the television. He rapidly became absorbed in the programme, while I edged my chair as close as I could to the poker. Time passed, the beating of my heart became less deafening and I managed to muster up courage to ask him what he was doing there. He replied, with surprise, that he lived there. 'Didn't Mary tell you?' he asked, and when I replied, 'No', he shrugged his shoulders and turned back to the television.

It was with a great feeling of relief that I heard the front door open, and Mary and her husband returned from their evening out. They assured me my visitor was a legitimate member of the household, but I admit to having felt more than a little angry that Mary hadn't bothered to warn me that a man might be returning to the house during the evening. From that point on, whenever I was baby sitting, the minute mine hosts left for their evening out, I rushed to the back door to make sure it was locked. I certainly had no intention of being frightened in that way again.

From time to time, sitting with slightly older children who did not go to bed till after one had been there for several hours, one discovered some very bizarre situations and relationships in what seemed from the outside to be conventional households. I often wondered what the parents would have thought had they realised how much their children inadvertently revealed while they were out enjoying themselves!

One evening, sitting in a very small house, the girl revealed they had a lodger. 'Where on earth,' I innocently asked, 'do they all sleep?' 'Well', replied the girl with perfect equanimity, 'sometimes Mummy and Daddy sleep upstairs and Jake sleeps on the sofa, sometimes Mummy and Jake sleep upstairs and Daddy sleeps on the sofa, and sometimes Daddy and Jake sleep upstairs and Mummy sleeps on the sofa.' What could I say other than a bemused nod of the head.

I think the most disconcerting evening was when the lights went out. The house was isolated on the very outskirts of the village and there was no other house in sight. I had no torch, and the only heating was an electric fire. The sudden darkness woke one of the children who, when questioned, informed me that the electricity was on a meter. As I had no money with me and the child did not know where her mother kept the coins for the meter, I spent the next two hours cold and in the pitch dark. Television, reading, writing, was all out of the question, and it was not even possible to make a hot drink as all the village cooking was done by electricity. I spent the two hours in total misery – apart from a telephone call to my husband who was tied to sitting with our own children. It made me realise how inadequate were my own inner resources, and it also led me into contemplating how awful it must be for those in solitary confinement. Little did one know then of the horrors later to be suffered by the western hostages – Terry Waite, John Macarthy and Brian Keenan

CHAPTER 13
The Oast Garden, 1967–1999

That first winter, trying to cope with the difficulties of the house compounded by the presence of a playgroup in the far oast, prevented us from giving much attention to the problems awaiting us outside on our one acre plot.

The weather was cold and dreary, and even had there been a suitable garden available, it is unlikely Justin would have wanted to spend much time outside on his own. But, as the better weather approached, the problem began to loom large.

In the first place, we had an area immediately outside our back door where the water collected into a sizeable pool several inches deep. In converting the barn, we had had to dig the floor out below the level of the land – and this included an area outside the kitchen and dining room. Because of the levels, there was no way the water could escape naturally. Justin was still too young and vulnerable to risk letting him play outside alone near water that was sufficiently deep for him to drown in. So one of the things we had to give our early attention to was to devise a means of draining away the water.

We soon realised that soakaways were the only answer, and before the summer had arrived, we had been forced to dig three of these – no mean task in heavy clay soil much complicated by vast quantities of rubble.

The land around The Oast had been used as a dumping ground for many years. The weeds were rampant – many, especially the nettles, as tall as I was, and it was sometime before we realised what lay beneath them.

As we hacked our way through the undergrowth we discovered old ovens, farm machinery in great quantities, long heavy metal rods which turned out to have been part of wartime aircraft landing strips, old water tanks, chain harrows which snaked underground for yards and yards, and were very difficult to dig out, and a dozen or more huge telegraph poles. To add to our difficulties, there was a vast quantity of rubble and rag stone which had been dug out from the village street and dumped on our land when main drainage was put into the village the year of our arrival.

This, of course, we were unaware of – being still on cess pit drainage ourselves. But it was, in fact, that first summer that the problem of our drains came to a head. We were, in this, as in so many matters, naive and never thought to question the lack of arrangements for having the cesspool emptied. In fact, until that disastrous day when we reaped the repercussions of my loss of Alex's nappy down the lavatory, we hadn't registered the whereabouts of the cesspool.

But in the early summer, the toilets filled up again in all three houses and when the man came to rod the drains, he informed us that the cesspool was full to overflowing. Until our arrival, a process of seepage had kept the level of the cesspool sufficiently low to avoid the necessity of having it emptied – an all too common happening in the countryside. But when we moved in with two young children and a washing machine which was used daily, the cesspool was no longer able to cope with the daily quantity of water flowing in.

We had to make a decision either to have a new cesspool or connect up to the newly installed main drainage. The cost of the former was cheaper but in the long run it was obvious that main drainage was the more useful, and so we had to dip into what were almost the last of our reserves of capital.

This had implications for the garden for it meant we couldn'y afford to pay for any assistance with clearing the land. It was heavy and backbreaking work – and looking back, it is clear that was this the time when the foundations were laid for later back trouble.

Our progress was very slow because the children were too young to be left alone. Work on the outside could only be done when we were both at home – or when some kind friend or neighbour had the children for an afternoon.

I remember one particular occasion when I desperately wanted to tackle a corner of the garden where the nettles had grown taller than I was. My neighbour kindly offered to sit with the children while I tackled the job. It being a hot day, I embarked on the battle wearing shorts and a sleeveless top. I felt rather like Prince Charming storming the castle of the sleeping princess which was surrounded by thorns and nettles. I used a scythe and gradually hacked my way into the centre of the nettles which covered an area the size of a small suburban garden. At one point, looking back towards The Oast, I found I was totally enclosed in a vast undergrowth of nettles, completely shut off from the outside world. It was an eerie feeling.

What did not register when I returned triumphant to the house, with all the nettles lying at my feet, was that I had been badly stung. My neighbour was horrified to see the state I was in. My face, arms and legs were bright red with nettle stings, and by nine o'clock that evening, I was in agony. No sleep came that night, and it was some days before the pain eased.

I have, ever since regarded nettles as major enemies. The feeling is obviously reciprocated, because I can never pass a nettle without it leaping out and stinging me, however careful I am to avoid it! I confess that, as a result, I am totally vicious in my approach to stinging nettles, even gloating over them when I consign them to the fire. Though it makes me feel guilty when I compare it to my attitude to the other plants of creation, with which I have a happy relationship, there is nothing I can do about it. The memory of the pain I suffered that night will always remain with me.

There are two other plants which I detest – though for rather different reasons. One is cooch grass which has caused me hours of heavy and backbreaking work, and the other is columbine with which I have had long and bloody battles over the years, and with which, even now, forty years on, the honours are even and the battle still joined.

Quite early on, as we started to clear away the weeds and rubble, we discovered that a large area which had looked like overgrown soil was in fact an area of concrete

Sandpit at the Oast

which had once been a bullock yard. When the bullocks were taken away, the farmer had left behind the straw and slush on which the bullocks were kept, and over this had grown a vast quantity of greenery. It had formed into a huge mat which we had to cut into blocks before we could remove it. It was rather like lifting omelettes from a pan – though considerably heavier!

It was a valuable discovery, for once we had cleared this area, swept it clean and washed it down, we were able to make a sandpit for the children and a small area for them to ride their bikes and play on. It was still too dangerous to allow them to roam freely, but at least it meant they could enjoy being outside when I had the time to sit with them.

We slowly and bit by bit humped all the rubble and metal into a corner of the garden and then turned our attention to levelling the land ready to put it down to grass.

After fruitless enquiries over a period of many weeks, we persuaded a local farmer to come along and harrow the land for us, hoping this would enable us to sow grass seeds ready for the following year. But, as with everything we attempted, there were snags. The harrowing exposed a mass of large stones and rocks, and there was no hope of making a lawn until they had all been removed. So Bill spent most of his summer holiday slowly raking the stones across the area that was to be a lawn – an area that was nearly an acre in extent. It was a boring and backbreaking job – and Bill did his best to eradicate from his memory the summer holiday he spent clearing the stones away.

The land round the Oast was fan shaped and we decided the best way to cope with the garden was to put it all down to grass and then slowly design it as we wanted.

Gardening had never appealed to either of us very much. and in fact, there was a time when, as owners of a flat set in landscaped gardens for which we paid a maintenance charge, we felt rather contemptuous of the hours my sister and her husband spent on their garden – something of which I have been frequently reminded over the years as I became infected myself by the gardening bug.

I believed I had inherited my father's dislike of gardening. He used to cut the grass but hated it so much that he did it as though he was in a race and completely exhausted himself in the process. My mother used to get furious with him, and feared he would have apoplexy as he came into the house red faced, sweating, angry and breathless, but she continued to insist he did the grass as it was 'the man of the house's job'. She would never, however, let him near the flower beds or vegetable garden as he could not be trusted. I remember one summer when she tried to grow strawberries – and became increasingly frustrated when on five separate occasions she discovered her precious strawberry plants lying on top of the bonfire. After the sixth rescue attempt, she gave up the struggle.

For some reason, there were two exceptions to his detestation of gardening. One was edging the grass. He was a tidy man and the sight of neat edges gave him immense satisfaction. And standing over a bonfire gave him a sort of atavistic pleasure – except when he couldn't get it going when he became enraged and swore he would concrete over the whole garden.

He was also enraged by weeds in the lawn and would rush out with his little knife and cut them out – often leaving the lawn covered with little holes from which he had removed the weeds. It is not surprising, perhaps, that in his seventies, he developed a love of bowls and took great pleasure in the perfect grass of his local bowling green.

I had, as I said, thought I had inherited my father's dislike of gardening rather than my mother's green fingers. But as our garden at the Oast slowly took shape, I found myself spending more and more time gardening and taking a delight in what was happening. I think it was the creative aspect as much as anything that attracted me. To see the gradual evolution of something that was beautiful and tranquil gave me immense pleasure – though it was many years before we began to see the fruits of our labours.

For in those first years, the disposing of all the detritus left on the land by the previous owners presented a major headache. There was such a vast quantity we did not know who to turn to for help. We sensed there was value in some of it and if only we could find the right outlet we could make some money. But we were so overwhelmed by the size of the problem, and the lack of financial resources to call in help, that we were delighted when we found some local gypsies willing to cart away all the metal which for that first year formed a great heap by the side of the Oast, making our place look like a tip rather than a domestic garden.

The metal gone, we still had vast quantities of rubble and ragstone to contend with. I fancied a large rockery and in my ignorance about gardening imagined that we could safely lose much of the rubble as the base for a large rockery.

I sat down and drew a plan for the rockery. It was very complicated with little footpaths snaking through beautiful shaped clumps of rock. It promised well and as I barrowed vast quantities of rubble into the rockery area and piled it into the shapes I had marked out, I had high hopes of a very beautiful area.

The view from our bedroom

On top of the rubble I threw earth and then placed rocks on top and begged, borrowed and stole rockery plants. For a while, it looked good. But I really did not know what I was doing, and it was not long before my enemy, cooch grass, began to poke through the rubble, not only destroying the look of the rockery, but also, because of the huge quantity of rubble below, proving extremely difficult to get rid of. Moreover. I had placed the rocks so unscientifically that they held in neither the earth nor the water so many of the plants soon died.

Over the years I was forced gradually to remove all the underlying rubble in order to defeat the cooch, and it was about twelve years before I had a rockery I was really happy with. It was another example of my innate impatience which makes me try to get things done quickly – an impatience which in the end leads to having to do many things twice over.

But we did have a number of first time successes. Many of the rocks were, as we became more adept, used to very good effect with raised beds and walls round the patio outside the music room and the front door.

The area in the front of the house was tarmacked. I think most people would have used it as a driveway and parking area for cars. But we had a very particular reason for not having cars near the house. My cousin, whose first child was exactly the same age as both Justin and my sister's eldest child, was killed in a horrific accident. My cousin got into his Landrover which was parked immediately outside his house and started to drive off to work. His son, aged two, rushed out after his father and was too small to be seen, and my cousin ran him over. The tragedy was so firmly printed on our minds that we were determined to keep all cars well away from the house.

The rockery

I think, even had this tragedy not occurred, we would not have wanted cars immediately outside the house. We preferred looking out on flower beds and grass rather than an assortment of parked cars.

I was therefore determined to get rid of some of the huge tarmac area in the front – and set to work with a pick axe, hacking my way through four feet of rubble. This was work that, though back breaking, was something I could tackle, leaving Bill to do the more skilled work inside the house.

Digging through tarmac was very heavy work, and at night, after I had been digging for some hours, my hands used to swell and become numb with pins and needles. Being short of money, we had very few suitable tools. Our new wheelbarrow soon succumbed to the burden of carrying heavy loads of rubble, and the wheel became buckled and distorted. One day, wheeling the barrow across uneven land, the wheel, by then square, got embedded in a hole. I heaved it out and felt my back go. For months after, I had constant backache, and used to go out into the outhouse that had once been milking sheds, and hang from the beams in an effort to 'unlock' my back and ease the pain.

To add to our problems were the monsters in the garden. Bill's summer spent clearing the stones, was only stage one on the route to making a garden. We then had to rake the earth smooth ready to sew grass, and dig out flower beds, and holes in which to plant trees and shrubs.

Small rocks protruding from an area where we planned to plant a tree or make a flower bed often proved to be the tip of a huge boulder, lurking below ground like an iceberg whose visible area represented less than a fifth of its bulk. These monsters took hours, sometimes days, to dig out. First we had to dig away the soil all round, and then by a process of leverage which involved two if not more people, we gradually prized the monster out of its hole. As time progressed, we had more and more of these huge boulders which, to start with, we placed at the side of the children's play area. Two years on, as the boulders accumulated and we realised they would spoil the garden, we had the task of moving them to another heap out of sight of the house. Here again, a little forward planning might have saved us a lot of heavy lifting.

In a garden as virgin as ours, there was always the possibility that we might uncover something interesting and rare. Bill was ever optimistic and hopeful of digging up buried treasure or some objet d'art which would restore our fortunes. Whenever he found something not immediately recognisable, he would put it on his treasure pile. Most of the objects later turned out to be farm implements, and over the years he had to put up with a lot of teasing about his romantic ideas.

But on his treasure pile were a large number of fossils, some of which were very interesting – and one of them, a smooth egg shaped fossil, triggered off the idea for a science fiction story which he wrote later to amuse the children.

For me the most fascinating find was a small piece from a statue – the shoulder and part of the upper arm of a woman, draped with loose clothing. It was clearly very old and of considerable quality, but it was a mystery to us how it came to be in the garden. We looked at old maps, but nowhere in the vicinity were there references to any old houses that had been demolished.

But in the Church on the hill is a large scar on the side pillar of the chancel and from early records, it is clear there was once a statue of the Virgin Mary attached to the wall. Though the fragment is small, no more than a foot high and nine inches round, I cannot help but think it is part of the missing statue.

And then one's imagination begins to work and wonder who tore down the statue. Was it during the Reformation or later, during Cromwellian times? Was it taken down by locals, or were the villagers forced to stand by and watch while zealous 'reformers' came from outside and tore down their much loved statue? Or perhaps, the locals, knowing what would happen, removed the statue themselves and buried it – not being able in their lifetime to restore it. And then perhaps there were calamities and deaths and the knowledge of the whereabouts of the statue was lost. And so there it lay safely below ground until our harrow unearthed part of it. Perhaps somewhere under our garden the rest of the statue lies hidden?

Of such small incidents are stories made, and perhaps one day I may use this fragments of statuary as a starting point for a novel. Who knows? Meanwhile, it sits safely in the corner of our patio.

But to return to the garden! Once the rubbish, rubble and stones were cleared away, we were at last able to start planting and this is when I really began to enjoy gardening. We had to plant carefully, for though the distant view was superb the nearer view was marred by some very unsightly and derelict farm buildings and hopper huts. We had to plan carefully in order to screen these unsightly buildings and yet keep the view free. One hut I particularly detested because it was clearly visible from the house. As it was both derelict and unused, I allowed my criminal tendencies full rein and tried to persuade various friends to come along by night and burn it down! Perhaps it was as well that no one was prepared to accept my ten pound bribe! A few years on, the farmer decided to let one of his labourers knock down the hut and take away the wood, and I was then able to move in and clear away the concrete base and rubble so that the area could be ploughed with the rest of the field.

Knowing very little about gardening, we made many mistakes with our planting in those early years. Because screening was important we took the advice of neighbours and planted a number of cupressus lawsoniana in strategic places and within a few years found it necessary to cut down a number of them as they grew to be too tall and oppressive. When confronted by a completely bare and naked garden, one is tempted to try and fill it as quickly as possible, and it is almost inevitable that the tiny trees and shrubs are planted far too close together. After five years I found myself thinning out and moving dozens of the shrubs I had so carefully planted. At one stage, when we had a builder friend here helping us convert the upper oast, he accused me of being a murderer. The accusation was not without justice as the garden seemed to be full of dying shrubs and trees. It was, therefore, with some satisfaction two years later that I was able to point out to him that, despite the traumatic move, all had survived.

One tree I was particularly pleased to have moved was a weeping willow. I have always loved their graceful shape, perhaps because they reminded me of my aunt's garden in which I had spent so many happy hours as a child. Quite early on we planted one opposite the front door where I thought it would look lovely. But reading about the devastation caused to foundations by willow roots which travel vast distances in search of water, we decided to move it well away from the house into the back garden.

There it thrived luxuriantly, but soon became shapeless, and I considered cutting it down. But before I had finally decided to do the foul deed, Justin and I visited my old friend in France. In the courtyard of their summer home was a beautiful willow beneath which the family had placed tables and chairs. I was intrigued as to how it had grown into this attractive umbrella shape, and learnt that my friends had quite ruthlessly shaved away all the inner branches so that it fell gracefully in an arc.

That decided me. The day after our return from France, I took a saw and pruning cutters and proceeded to hack and slash out all the central branches until I had achieved the same shape. For many years, , the tree sheltered tables and chairs, as in France, and provided a lovely shady sitting out area for hot summer days. When we sold The Oast in 1999, we cut down the tree in order both to enlarge The Oast garden, and to prevent debris from the tree falling into our swimming pool (of which, more later).

Often, as I sat on our patio on a summer's evening, looking across at the view which had first attracted our attention, watching the bats flying round the trees, and drinking in the tranquillity and beauty of our garden, I often wondered how someone else would have landscaped it. With its fan shape, endless variations were possible, and I am sure someone else would have achieved a completely different but equally attractive design.

But in a way the garden was not designed but evolved. In the early days we had vast expanses of grass across which the children careered on their bicycles, played cricket, camped out in their tents, and generally ran free round and round the house. I had flower beds round the edges and as my life outside the house grew busier, found I had less time to tend them and so grassed some over and filled others with shrubs which needed less attention.

The large expanse of grass proved a problem – taking nearly three hours to cut. So, I began to break the garden up into small areas making it possible to cut one lawn one day and another the next, without spoiling the effect. I did get some opposition from the cricketers – now in their teens – but as they were reluctant to help cut the grass I didn't feel the degree of guilt which they felt I should!

The utilitarian rather than design motivation in fact created an illusion of space, and there were interesting vistas as one moved through small openings from one area into another.

Later still, when my aunt died and left me a small legacy, we put in an outdoor swimming pool, landscaped in such a way that we were able to create various levels which added to the interest and beauty of the garden.

The pool from our bedroom window

CHAPTER 14
Pre School Playgroup Association and Adult Education, 1970 – 1973

If I had to describe myself, I think I would call myself a dilettante because over the years I have been involved in so many different ventures – a sort of Jack of all trades and master of none! But that is not really an accurate description. Perhaps the word 'enabler' would be a more appropriate word.

It is the creative aspect of a task that I find challenging and I tend to get bored with doing the same thing year in and year out. Once something that I have helped to create is on firm foundations and flourishing, I feel the need to move on and do something new.

So it was with the Playgroup. Once it was functioning well I was more than happy to move on to new pastures, and I became involved with the Kent Pre-school Playgroup Association as its Publicity Officer (1970) and then as its Chairman. My name had been brought to the attention of Kent PPA through the articles I had written about the playgroup movement for the local press.

The work as Publicity Officer was interesting, and in its turn brought me into contact with the national organisation which was doing a wonderful job in training and disseminating information across the country as well as putting pressure on government to fund and set up playgroups in Urban Aid areas.

It was apparent that those involved in the pre-school playgroup movement needed help, and adult education centres throughout the country responded to the demand for training by putting on pre-school education courses.

My first involvement with adult education came when I was asked at the last minute to stand in for someone who had gone sick. With great trepidation I travelled to Gravesend to deliver my first lecture. I cannot remember what it was about, but I do remember feeling very nervous as I stood up in front of a roomful of adults to talk about playgroups – being fairly convinced that they knew far more about them than I did.

But I came away feeling that lecturing was something I could enjoy doing, and when I was asked to set up playgroup courses at the Gillingham Adult Education Centre, I accepted with enthusiasm.

Playgroup courses in the main were introductory, and took place in the evenings when the husbands were free to look after the children. There were sessions on organisation and structure, on child development, and on various aspects of play.

I was given a free hand at Gillingham, and decided to organise two quite different courses. One was a conventional evening course as in other centres, and the other an all-day course.

It had occurred to me that if we could set up an all-day course, it could embrace some practical training which would be of great value. I also suspected there were mothers who would welcome a whole day out and who would be able to make judicious arrangements for their children to be looked after for the day by relatives and friends.

While I was, and still am, a passionate advocate of the importance of a mother being at home with her children in the early years, I felt that brief separations, carefully arranged, were of value to both mothers and children. I remembered how much I had valued my one day a week to myself when my son was small, and my neighbour and I exchanged children for a day a week each – she to work as a GP and me as an archivist. It was a great boon to both of us. Barbara and I enjoyed our day's freedom, while the two toddlers played together happily from a very early age. I have vivid memories of the two, aged about eleven months, crawling after each other all round our flat – Justin with his over-arm crawl and Ian humping along like a centipede. It was an amusing sight! The two children remained firm friends for years – even after our paths diverged and we moved down to Ulcombe.

So, I thought it would be helpful to offer an all day course – giving the students the opportunity of doing practical work in other playgroups where they could gain experience and observe how other playgroups operated. This involved me in visiting all the playgroups in the area to arrange the students' placements. The arrangement was very similar in concept to the teaching practice arranged by training colleges. I was also fortunate in securing the co-operation of a number of infant schools which were happy to have playgroup students in for a morning.

The adult education budget was then more generous, and it not only allowed me to supervise and monitor the visits as part of the course, it also enabled me to be present at every afternoon session with the addition of a visiting lecturer where necessary.

I felt quite competent to tutor many of the sessions myself with the help of some excellent PPA films. So I tutored the sessions on organisation and structure, on philosophy, on painting and nature play, on the book corner and manipulative play, and on sand and water and clay. Where I felt the need for additional support was in child development, music, speech therapy, and emotional problems.

One of the joys of these playgroup courses was to get the students involved in the messy activities that they would later be introducing the children to. I brought in huge lumps of clay which we all played with – happily thumping it into the right consistency, throwing it onto the floor to get rid of air (and our own aggression), and moulding it into fantastic shapes. We had huge bags of flour which we mixed in large bowls into just the right doughy consistency for a child to play with – to which we added bright and beautiful colours. We played with water and tried to enter into a child's wonder at the way it behaved. We had trays full of dry sand which would not stay in shape but which we discovered acted very like water, and we then added water to the sand and discovered we could mould it into shapes rather like clay.

Our painting sessions were hilarious. We had easels and paper and large brushes for the more conventional painting – but we also experimented with finger and foot painting, with potato printing and a whole variety of shapes. I collected a series of paintings by pre-school children and demonstrated the way one could trace a child's development – the circle which represented 'mummy', which became more complex and had eyes and mouth added as the child developed, and later still had arms and legs sticking out from the circle. Then, at around the age of four and a half, but sometimes quite a bit earlier, 'mummy' had a separate head and body. I brought in pictures in angry reds, or miserable blacks and greys; pictures which revealed problems; heads with huge ears where the child was worried by deafness; and pictures where the shapes were painted over and blanked right out revealing hidden miseries the child could not share.

The students were amazed at what paintings could reveal. Some were even more amazed at their own feeling of liberation as they were encouraged to play freely with the paint and to get as dirty and messy as they liked. Some expressed their reluctance to let their own children make a mess – and had not realised that the toddler who spilt his orange juice into his food tray and moved the liquid around into patterns was really involved in a learning process as well as developing manipulative skills.

They discovered, too, that clearing up the mess could be made fun rather than an irritating chore. And they began to realise that so much that seemed humdrum or 'naughty' was in fact part of the learning process.

There were some excellent films available to help the courses along. One memorable one, *I have an Egg* was about a group of blind Polish children. The students were able to experience, through watching these children, the tactile value of an egg in all its ramifications – smooth and hard, brittle and jagged, raw and slimy, hard boiled. We smelt with the children the smell of an egg, both raw and cooked. And we shared with them their puzzlement as they held the fertilised eggs to their ears and heard a rattling sound inside, and then their joy as they fingered gently the emerging chick. I think there was seldom a dry eye in the room at the end of that particular film as these blind children, with a look of absolute rapture on their faces, gently cupped in their hands the tiny chicks.

We learnt too about the problems of separation in the early years as we watched some of the Tavistock studies of children separated from their mothers by hospitalisation or the birth of siblings. These films always caused me anguish as I remembered my forcible separation from Justin (described above) when he was thirteen months old and had gastro-enteritis – so serious he became dehydrated and was rushed into hospital. And as I too caught the infection, I was sent away from the hospital and didn't see him for two weeks.

With this background, it is easy to understand why I found the Tavistock films on separation of mother and child in the early years so disturbing. But it did give me the opportunity to talk to the mothers on the course from personal experience, and make them think very carefully before deliberately leaving their children for long periods with others.

The playgroup courses continued and so increased in popularity that I found myself doing the equivalent of three days lecturing – spread over daytime and evening.

I spent some five years in this work, becoming as well, the Voluntary Area Organiser for Gillingham – a role that was both a communications and an advisory role. I finally gave up the work when, under the Urban Aid Scheme, a grant was made to appoint a paid Playgroups Adviser for the area. It was a job which I, and many of my friends, had expected I would get. But it went to a young and inexperienced lady. At the time I felt very disappointed. But, in fact, financially the rejection served me well, because instead of earning £1,500 a year as a Playgroups Adviser, I soon secured a job earning around £7,5000 as a teacher!

Once again, I was being pushed on in my voyage of discovery, although at the time, not being a Christian, I had no understanding of the purpose God had in store for me.

CHAPTER 15
Community Activities, 1966 – 2016

Over the years my life has taken a series of unplanned but interconnected turnings. Bill was of the opinion that I always opened my mouth too quickly and got involved in ventures before I had really thought about them. His favourite saying was, "Think and engage brain before opening mouth". I admit to not always engaging brain first, and sometimes to "rushing in where angels fear to tread". But I have no regrets. I can never resist a challenge, and each new venture presented exciting and irresistible possibilities.

Because of this weakness for ventures new I have found myself over the years involved in a series of voluntary community activities which eventually led me into becoming the official Appeal Organiser for a local hospice charity.

The first of these ventures was the formation of the local playgroup which I have already described. This had many spin offs. Involvement with the Playgroup was a significant factor in making village life so very enjoyable. A number of our playgroup colleagues became close friends – and remain so to this day. With judicious exchange of children we all managed to get time to ourselves during the week, and life was full of contrasts – one day a house full of noisy toddlers, the next, a peaceful house all to oneself.

The arrangement was of great benefit to the children who became very relaxed about being left in the care of other adults. Additionally they had the pleasure of the company of other children. We were mutually supportive in times of trouble or distress – taking in each other's children for days at a time when illness, hospitalisation or the demands of elderly relatives became imperative.

Our children, now in their fifties are still reaping the benefit of those early years. Though the majority of them have been away from home for long periods to universities and colleges around the country, many of them have gravitated back to the area to live. As a result they have a wide circle of friends to which are added those friends they have met during their studies who, after sampling it, have often decided that life in the area is good and have settled in and around the village.

KENT MESSENGER CORRESPONDENT

My next venture, unplanned, was to write for the local newspaper. How ill equipped many of us are for solitude! I have always found it difficult to sit doing nothing except when I am immersed in a book or a television programme. Other than my prayer time first thing in the morning, which is really an active rather than a passive encounter, I am incapable of sitting and just contemplating.

On those rare occasions when I have nothing to do, I always find myself reaching for pen and paper, or a book, or the telephone, and I know that solitary confinement for me without books, paper and pencil would be a real torture.

Paper is one of my passions in life. I love the feel of it and the sight of a pristine page waiting to be filled with writing gives me a thrill. I collect paper – all shapes and sizes – and have done so since childhood. I often think with pity of the Brontes who had access to so little paper when they were children that they were forced to write on tiny scraps of paper, every inch of which they filled with writing.

I think too of a dear old friend, the Earl of Harrowby, whom I met when I was training to be an archivist. He was one of this world's wonderful eccentrics. Though not exactly impoverished, he would use and re-use envelopes, sticking labels on top of labels on top of labels. His letters were always closely written in a near illegible hand and then crossed. Having filled the page both vertically and horizontally, he would then proceed to write in the margin. His letters were a joy to receive because one knew one had days of deciphering ahead, and the feeling of achievement when one had finally decoded the last hieroglyphic was enormous.

It was pen and paper that led me to my next venture. The playgroup committee used to organise a number of interesting outings for the children, and pleasant social occasions such as story telling by our local children's writer, birthday visits by our oldest inhabitant, pets days, etc. Though we tried to get the local newspaper to cover these activities, we never found any mention in the local press nor indeed any references to the growing playgroup movement. One day in 1969, irritated by a particularly blatant omission, I sat down and wrote a sharp letter to the Editor of the *Kent Messenger* complaining of his newspaper's lack of interest in an important section of the community. Almost by return I had a phone call inviting me to become a Village Correspondent. It seemed an interesting possibility – especially as the opportunity to promote the playgroup movement was coupled with the possibility of earning all of two shillings and sixpence for each story printed.

So I agreed, and set to and made contact with all the village organisations I could find. I visited the local school and met up with the headmaster. I attended parish council meetings; I contacted the Rector of the Church, the Chairman of the Conservative Association (the only political club in the village), the organiser of the weekly Whist Drives, the President of the W.I., the secretary of the Horticultural Society, and the Captains of the Cricket and Football Clubs.

In the ensuing weeks, the Ulcombe column in the local paper suddenly became long and at the end of the month I was delighted to receive a small cheque from the paper.

My news items had to be with the Editor by the Tuesday morning and this presented quite a problem as many of the more interesting events took place on a Friday or Saturday evening. To write them up and get them to the paper in time without a car was difficult as there was no guarantee, even in those days, that a letter posted on Monday morning would arrive the next day. How different today with emails!

Fortunately a solution was at hand. The husband of one of our playgroup members worked in the advertising department of the local paper, and he very kindly agreed to take my copy in each week.

I must have been regarded as a difficult lady because I always picked up the telephone and complained if my reports were cut short or not printed. As Ulcombe was at the end of the alphabet, and village news was always the lowest priority, I often, to begin, with found the Ulcombe news left out. But after repeated complaints, I suspect the editors found it easier to cut other village's news items than those from the 'awkward lady' in Ulcombe.

But it did not stop them from offering me more villages to cover and I soon found myself the village correspondent of five local villages. In the first weeks, I worked hard to make personal contacts with everyone – attending public meetings and making myself generally known. The local organisations were so delighted to have their news reported that I had little difficulty in persuading them to either telephone me with their news or pop the details through my letter box.

Very soon, I had trained most of the organisations to send me their news, and all I had to do was write it up. It was a very satisfactory arrangement and my monthly cheque amounted to around £40 – a very useful addition to our meagre income because The Oast was still eating up all our limited surplus funds.

The real excitement came when one or two articles I wrote were published with my *By line* – an excitement I understand is shared by all new journalists. Some of my articles were published in the Evening News which covered a wider area, and I like to think that these articles extended people's knowledge of the pre-school playgroup movement.

Although items printed in the village columns only netted two shillings and sixpence, a much greater amount was paid for items published in the body of the paper – so I was at pains to make the stories as eye catching and interesting as possible in order to attract the editor's eye. I would phone up and try to get photographers out to specially interesting events, and did interviews with various characters in the five villages when opportunity presented. As the years went by I filled more and more scrapbooks with my newspaper cuttings.

When I took up teaching full time I found the Sunday evening chore of writing up my reports too tiring to handle and gave up the job. Sadly, the Ulcombe column from being the longest village column in the paper dwindled over the years to almost nothing. My first successors had not developed the art of making a news story out of nothing – what I would call creative reporting! To be successful one has to have a nose for news – keeping one's ears to the ground, and looking at everything as a potential story. On the whole, people love to see their names in print and there is always plenty to report in even the sleepiest village.

NEW VILLAGE HALL

The playgroup was indirectly responsible for my next venture which was the building of a new village hall. The old village hall was far from ideal for the Playgroup. There were problems with a temperamental boiler, inadequate water supplies in the gentlemen's toilet, and no water at all in the ladies because the trustees of the hall had become tired of dealing with pipes which burst every time the temperature dropped to freezing point, and cut the water off altogether. Unpleasing smells emanated from the kitchen where the mould grew on china as soon as one's back was turned, and the storage space for the Playgroup equipment was so inadequate that the Playgroup supervisor had a daily battle trying to fit all the equipment into the tiny space available.

The hall had been built in 1911 by Albert Chapman, a local builder and undertaker, who was then in his nineties. In his very interesting *Memoirs*, he recalled the details of building the hall, and wrote that he put in some windows eaten up by woodworm, which he had taken out of a derelict building. The windows were still there when our village hall venture began, and in fact are still there now that the hall is part of the Museum of Kent Life! It's amazing what a good lick of paint can do!

The late sixties was a period when many villages were building new halls with assistance of grants from the National Playing Fields Association. In an irritated moment I decided to try and get a new village hall under way – and invited to our house representatives of all the village organisations – Playgroup, W.I., Library, Cricket Club, Whist Club and the Church – as well as one or two people who had muttered over the years about the inadequacies of the old hall. Everyone turned up – apart from a representative from the Church – the significance of which I did not realise until later.

There was immediate enthusiasm for the idea of a new village hall, and we decided to get information together about costs and grants and then hold a public meeting in the old hall. We learnt that grants of around 50% were likely to be forthcoming from the National Playing Fields Association, and that a new hall was likely to cost us in the region of £18,000. (Of course, by the time we got to building the hall, the cost had risen to £34,000.)

The meeting, which I chaired, was well attended and there was a very positive response to the idea of a new hall coupled with anxiety about whether a small village like ours could raise the eighteen thousand pounds needed. Unexpected opposition, however, came from the Rector's spokesman who not only asserted that a new hall was unnecessary but also stated that the Church would not be interested in joining forces to provide one.

Remembering the Rector's attitude towards the Playgroup, we should not have been surprised – but it was a disappointment as one of the possibilities we had talked about at our first meeting was to join forces with the Church to upgrade the existing Parish hall.

With such fervent opposition, it was clear we would have to explore our other two ideas. One was to obtain permission from the Parish Council to build on a corner of the village playing fields. The other was to purchase a run down oast that was on the market for £6,000, and convert it into a village centre. The second idea was quickly discarded as being too costly and too difficult. I was sad about this – and even more so, in later years, when I discovered two other villages had actually implemented such a scheme. But, in this as in everything else which involves group decisions, one has to go along with the majority view.

A committee was formed and we set out on the long, slow, task of raising the necessary funds. We very early decided that our main fund raising venture would be a weekly lottery. We roped in an army of 'sub collectors' who undertook to collect the weekly sum of one shilling for a lottery ticket. We had another group called 'main collectors' who, once a month, collected in the monies from the sub collectors. We had a monthly prize of £5 and a quarterly prize of £40 – the draw taking place in the local hostelry, and the winner's name being published in the parish magazine. As the value of the pound went down, so we put up the weekly tally – and, as far as I remember, the lottery brought in about £750 a year.

We ran a number of fund raising events – dances, bazaars, and coffee mornings – which did much to enhance the community life of the village. Our most exciting event was an Auction when we secured the services of a professional auctioneer. We wrote to everyone in the village and all the friends we could think of and invited them to let us sell their unwanted goods for the modest commission of 30% which would go towards the new village hall.

We had an immediate and encouraging response. The chance of selling unwanted possessions at a ready made auction presented an attractive opportunity to people who had not been able to summon up the energy to go to professional auctioneers.

We asked people to send in the details of what they wanted to put in the auction so that we could prepare a catalogue. The response was excellent and we soon became aware that we would have a number of quite valuable antiques in the sale. Realising the importance of good publicity I worked hard to get good press and radio coverage, and also wrote personally to all the antique dealers in the area suggesting it might be worth their while coming along.

These efforts happily produced the desired response, and on the day of the auction the village was a hive of activity. Cars, vans and lorries, delivering a vast assortment of items ranging from broken down lawn mowers to precious antiques, thronged the village throughout the day. The deliveries were only just completed when the public began arriving – among whom was a large number of antique dealers.

Traffic in the village came almost to a standstill as more and more cars arrived and tried to park in the narrow village street. Fortunately it was a fine summer's evening and those who had to park further afield arrived in good humour. The interest in the exhibits was very great and there seemed to be something there for everyone – I doubt whether any villager left the auction without bidding for something – whether it was an ancient garden fork, a sherry glass, a chair, or an electrical item, which they hoped to restore to working order. The antique dealers were very happy with their visit and asked to be informed of similar events in the future.

Sales amounted to well over £3,000 and the hall committee netted something like £850 – representing 30% of the total. It seems a small amount in today's currency, but at the time it was a considerable sum and we were all delighted with our endeavour.

Another very successful venture was an Antique Valuation Day done for us by Philips. Again, the venture attracted huge support, and we spent the day providing refreshments for the many people who came to have their items valued.

Rather different, but again very successful was a concert given by some talented locals at Ulcombe Place – a lovely house adjacent to the Church. It was an elegant evening which included a supper – and the ladies all wore long dresses – the fashion at the time – and the men black ties.

It took us seven years to raise sufficient money to start building. There were ups and downs on the committee – a chairman who was less than energetic, and a treasurer who worked extremely hard but had a quarrelsome temperament. But as we neared our goal we secured the services, *gratis*, of a local architect and he and I toured round Kent inspecting some of the more recently built village halls.

We were determined to have a hall that was maintenance free. We knew we would never be able to raise the money to build a hall that would compare with some of the more elegant and spacious halls we visited. This was something some of our newer residents did not comprehend when they looked critically at our utilitarian interior walls which were not exactly beautiful but which never needed painting. Over the years, the main expense in the hall was the repairs necessitated by vandalism – and the building of an extension for extra storage.

A few years ago, an energetic new village hall committee painted all the walls cream. The hall looked lovely – but the acoustics were ruined. A later committee had to install specially constructed baffle boards. Today the hall is acoustically sound.

The great day came on 20th November 1977 when the hall was finally finished. All the villagers rallied round to provide items for the hall, and our treasurer, who had worked extremely hard over the years, did some of the interior work himself.

His father donated a cooker and various facilities for the kitchen. We asked every villager to donate a plate, a cup and a saucer – and until recently, nearly forty years on, whenever one used the hall, one was confronted with old familiar china which took many of us back to our childhoods.

The hall is well used – with a playgroup and toddler club throughout the week, a badminton club on Fridays, a young children's tennis club on a Saturday, and many sundry bookings for local societies, private parties, weddings and social gatherings. At one time it also had a doctor's surgery, a weekly bingo session, and a second badminton evening.

Recent legislation requiring entertainment licences for public buildings used for public entertainment has caused problems for the village. Without a licence, the hall could no longer be used for dances and concerts unless they were strictly private. Yet, to obtain a licence, the hall had to be up graded with new wiring, new kitchen equipment, and outside paths – a costly operation. The legislation is, of course, designed to protect. But it causes major headaches to small communities like ours which have few amenities and even fewer resources. Pressure was then on to revitalise the hall committee and set it on a new fund raising path. This was one situation I didn't want to get involved in – especially as I was currently campaigning for tennis courts for the village! In fact, when I look back over the years, I realise that much of my time in Ulcombe has been spent in trying to extract money from people!

ULCOMBE HORSE SHOW

We got involved in the local Horse Show soon after our arrival in Ulcombe. I recall being asked very early on whether we would like to become Vice Presidents of the Ulcombe Horse Show. Enquiries revealed that it involved donating about ten pounds to the Horse Show Committee and receiving a programme. There seemed no other benefits, but as the proceeds of the Horse Show were to go towards restoring our local mediaeval church we agreed.

The Show was an affiliated Show lasting two days – Saturday and Sunday. We didn't know much about horses, but went along to the Show out of interest. It was a large show with a number of rings and a huge marquee which was marked 'Members Tent'. From the smells and sounds that emanated from the marquee, the 'members' were clearly having a good time – but us lowly Vice Presidents were not invited.

As our daughter was mad on horses, we continued to patronise the Show and for two years I was roped in to help with the Gymkhana – taking the money – while, Bill was persuaded to be a Steward. I shall never forget his disgust when he learnt he had to wear a bowler hat to carry out his duties!

Although the Show continued for a number of years, nothing was done in the way of restoration of the Church – and people began to mutter about what had happened to the money. After a year or two, many of us ceased to be Vice Presidents – and then the Show came to an abrupt end.

A few years later, we had a new Rector who decided to try and resurrect it. He persuaded the owner of the local shop, a keen horsewoman, to take on the task. She organised the Show on a Wednesday afternoon – the choice of a weekday being dictated by the fact that she ran the local shop and Wednesday was early closing. The Show was successful and in that first year raised £450. We were away on holiday so missed it, but everyone reported it as a pleasant occasion, and when, the following year, we were asked to help – me with the Gymkhana and Bill as a steward – we happily agreed.

Looking after the money at the gymkhana was a simple task which I was happy to help with. But it was a bad move. For the next year, in 1982 the show organiser decided enough was enough, and the Rector asked me to take it over.

Now this was, in fact, a crazy request for I knew nothing about horses. As a child I had longed to go riding, but the cost was way beyond my parent's means, and it was not until I went to university that I had my first ride ever. My college room-mate was a keen rider. She had been at Cheltenham Ladies College where she rode regularly. When she came to Bedford College she started riding in Richmond Park, and when she discovered I had never ridden, persuaded me to go with her.

I had no riding gear, and Cynthia felt that slacks were inappropriate for riding in Richmond Park, so she gave me a pair of her old jodhpurs. It was a generous gift – but as she was over 5 foot 10 inches tall and I was only 5 foot 3 inches, they were not exactly comfortable or elegant! But nothing daunted we set off. Sitting on a horse for the first time, I rode inexpertly and uneasily – although I did manage to stay on. But after a week or two, I decided I really was a fish out of water, riding with a group of young people who had sat happily in the saddle since childhood. Moreover, it was expensive, and it was not really a pastime I could afford. So I diverted my sporting activities to rowing, and joined the College Boat Club on the River Thames.

Holiday in Wales

I did not realise what a strenuous sport rowing was until I found myself in a boat with eight others. Rowing is, without doubt, the most strenuous of all sporting activities. Once in a boat, the rowers become as one person, and there is no way one can ease up without rocking the boat. I recall many occasions crying in rhythm with the oars sliding through the water, 'I wish I could die, I wish I could die,' knowing that if for one second I ceased rowing the whole boat would topple over. But for some bizarre reason I stuck to the sport and ended up as Captain of the College Boat Club – rowing two miles on the same stretch of river as the Oxford and Cambridge Boat Race. I shudder when I look back on College Boat Club photos and see the brawny muscles that one inevitably developed with the sport!

To go back to horses. From my college days on, I only rode three times. The first occasion was in 1959 when Bill and I had a holiday in Wales with our great friend, the Indian historian, Dr Bishwenath Pandey, and his girl friend, Jackie. On the last day of the holiday Bish decided we should go for a day's trekking in the hills. Now, while Bish had done a lot of riding in India and was perfectly at ease on a horse, Bill had never ridden, and Jackie was about as inexpert as I was.

We explained this to the owner of the riding school and he assigned us appropriate horses. Bish's horse was frisky and he was soon riding ahead, quite at ease. Jackie and I rode very tentatively, but Bill was the star of the occasion, sitting on his horse as though he were reclining in a comfortable armchair. His horse, Ginger, was elderly, idle and very broad. He ambled along very slowly – and when prodded and pushed by the leader of the expedition, trotted reluctantly for a few moments before settling down to a stately walk. Soon, Bill was way behind the rest of us and the real riders in the group had to keep trotting back to try and galvanise Ginger into action. How we ever managed to get to our destination at the end of the day remains a mystery.

But to take on a whole day's trekking when we were all so unaccustomed to riding was a crazy thing to do, even for Bish who had not been in the saddle for five years. That evening, flushed with the success of the day, we didn't really notice the damage we had done to our muscles. But the following morning, when we boarded the ancient train which was to take us across Wales and back to London, and sat on the hard wooden seats, we didn't know what to do with our aching limbs. It was as much as we could do to sit down – and never were we so glad to see home and bed when, after seven hours of agonisingly painful travelling, we finally reached our destination.

After that holiday I didn't sit on a horse again until 1976 when we took the family to the Lake District. Alex was by then riding regularly. On this Lakeland holiday the children and I booked an afternoon's ride while Bill went fishing. Two years later, when in Scotland, Alex and I decided to treat ourselves to an afternoon's hack. We arrived at the village where the riding school was situated and were directed to a large Victorian house. To our amazement, the tackle, feed and numerous dogs and cats were housed in what had once been a gracious drawing room. The garden had been turned into a ménage, and it was clear we were in the presence of a fanatic. We were disconcerted but not altogether surprised when the lady who owned the riding school decided we should spend an hour in her menage before we went out on the moors. She was very fierce, and bullied and shouted at us as though she was grooming us for a competition. She was very critical of the way Alex sat on her horse and said she had been badly taught. As for me, she shouted instructions at me with increasing ferocity and I felt thoroughly demoralised and vowed I would never sit on a horse again. But to my surprise, at the end of the ordeal, she assured me that, if I were to have lessons, I would be a good rider. Her last instruction to me as we were leaving was to book in for lessons directly I got home!

But I never did, and from then until the time I was asked to take on the Ulcombe Horse Show I had not been near a horse except to drive Alex to and from the stables. Alex was, by now, a regular rider in as much as she had one hour's riding a week. She spent each Saturday morning at the stables, getting there before eight in the morning to help muck out the stables, saddle the horses, and take the younger riders out on a lead rein. She then had her hour's ride – which she had to pay for out of her increased pocket money allowance.

My first response to the request that I take over the Ulcombe Horse Show was, therefore, ribald laughter. I had never saddled or groomed a horse, nor could I name any of the tackle, and I certainly knew nothing about the niceties of a horse show. But, after much persuasion by the new Rector, I reluctantly agreed provided I could find someone to help with what I called 'the horsey' side of the Show – organising the schedule, finding the judges, organising the jumps and setting them up.

I was told of a lady called Penny who, it was thought, might help me. I telephoned her – only to discover that news of my impending request had already reached her through the village grapevine and she was ready and prepared with a number of good reasons why she should say no. But she did agree to come round for a cup of coffee and discuss it. As occasionally happens in life, we struck up an instant friendship which, as far as the Horse Show was concerned, was fortuitous because she agreed to help me. Had we not had this immediate rapport, I am sure Penny would never have agreed to get involved, and the Ulcombe Horse Show would, for the second time, have come to an untimely end.

But Penny's agreement to help meant that the die was cast. It was a rash decision for it involved hours of work for both of us from January onwards, and for the whole of the school summer holiday we were involved in preparation for the Show which was fixed for the August Bank Holiday.

I had analysed the previous show carefully and realised what a lot of work and what a large number of people were involved in producing even a small half day show. It seemed to me that, were the Show to be enlarged, there need be very little extra input but there could be a considerable amount of extra revenue.

With any large scale event, the first time round always involves a lot of work on the organiser's part. I like to work with committees and share out the work – in

Judging the Fancy Dress Competition

contrast to my predecessor who had organised the Show with her daughter and two friends, and preferred going it alone. So, having studied the excellent game plan provided by my predecessor, I decided that we would need, in addition to Penny as the Show Secretary, a treasurer, a caterer, someone to co-ordinate the transport, and various odd bods who could be given special tasks. I assigned myself the title Show Organiser and that first year took on the job of sponsorship secretary, publicity officer, organiser of the Fayre, general letter writer and site co-ordinator, as well as undertaking to produce the Show Schedule. In later years, I found other people to take on each of these roles, but for the first two years I was responsible for all these tasks, and it proved very onerous indeed.

I regard myself as a developer rather than an innovator for I am not an original thinker. But given an idea I seem to be able to enlarge and develop it. So it was with the Ulcombe Horse Show. My predecessor had laid down an excellent basic framework from which we never deviated. But by widening the scope of the show, we were over the years able to increase its profits from £450 to £2,500 the first year, and from then on by several hundred pounds each year so that by the time seven years later I resigned as Show Organiser we were netting £3,500.

I suspect most people have little idea of what is involved in organising a major horse show. When I had assembled a committee, we started meeting regularly from November onwards to prepare for the Show in August. We decided that first year to keep it midweek and see how it went. It appeared that, during the month of August, there were dozens of shows on at weekends which would conflict with ours. Over the years, our mid week show has proved so popular that, although at each annual review, the suggestion came up that we should try a weekend, we always decided eventually to stick to a mid week show. But I was not happy with the August Bank Holiday weekend. I was by then teaching in a down-town secondary modern school in Chatham. That first year, the Show hung over my head like an incubus throughout the whole of the precious summer holidays, and I was determined that if I were to continue organising the Show, we would get it over and done with as soon as the schools broke up.

This particular decision did not suit two members of the committee – a couple we had recruited from the previous shows. They argued loudly for the August bank holiday, and when they were outvoted, promptly resigned. I am not altogether sure this was the main reason. There are some people who do not like working in a group, and I suspect they were people who preferred working alone.

The committee always met in our house. Somehow, we never thought of moving elsewhere. I produced coffee and biscuits – and it was only after I resigned, and the Horse Show was taken over by the horsy fraternity, that the meetings were enlivened with a glass of wine. We had a very happy group, and the meetings were short and businesslike. Over the years we had a change of treasurer, and a change of sponsorship secretary. Penny moved and we lost her services but managed to secure the help of Frank who was very experienced in the horse show world. When I resigned after seven years, he took over as Show Organiser.

From the first meeting, I stated as our main objective the need to raise a substantial sum for the Church Restoration Fund. Not being interested in horse shows as such, the Restoration Fund was my real reason for involvement and I had no intention of losing sight of this objective.

It was clear that the first priority was to increase the number of sponsors. My predecessor had approached only those she knew personally. I decided to write to everyone in the village – pointing out that the money from the Show would go towards restoring the village's heritage – our beautiful mediaeval church. Obtaining a copy of the Electoral Roll, I wrote a letter soon after Christmas to everyone in the village – inviting them to become Sponsors at £10 and promising to include their names in the Show Schedule. It was this promise that was to cause problems.

The initial response was excellent. Many people promised to sponsor the show, and a number sent cheques straight away. But by the end of March, less than half the people I expected to sponsor had replied. The time approached when I needed to get on with the production of the Schedule – but it was something that could not be completed without the names of the sponsors. So started a lengthy process of telephoning all the people who seemed likely to sponsor if pressed. The exercise was worthwhile. By the time the Schedule had to be typed, about a third of all households in the village had agreed to Sponsor the horse show and we collected in £1,200 – sufficient to cover all the expenses of the Show and guarantee a good profit on the day.

The next priority was publicity. We needed to get the show as widely advertised as possible, not only to attract entries but also to attract spectators. One of the few horse events I had ever been aware of was the Charing Races, and this was because of a huge notice board near the roundabout on the main A20 at Charing. I decided to approach a firm of estate agents and see if they would help, and was absolutely delighted when they agreed to sign-write and erect six boards for us, provided we could find suitable sites. Looking at the map, we decided on six strategic sites on the approach roads to Maidstone, and then set about locating the owners of the land. The exercise proved successful, thanks largely to a local farmer who was a member of the Horse Show Committee. In late June, I was delighted to see on six main roads huge boards advertising the Ulcombe Horse Show and Fair with the name of the estate agent discreetly written at the bottom of the board.

These boards plus a couple of articles about the Horse Show and the restoration needs of the Church, which I managed to get into the local press, resulted in a number of new enquiries from riders wishing to participate. Penny had, some months before, placed advertisements in all the appropriate riding magazines – some of which published schedules of all the major shows during the year.

Penny had a busy time planning the schedule, finding judges for all the events, stewards to help in the rings throughout the day, and scouts to help re-erect the jumps after they'd been knocked down. Rosettes, judges and stewards badges had to be sorted out, and cups assembled for the main events.

We were fortunate in having some beautiful cups from the earlier Ulcombe Shows which were stored in the Church safe. That first year, all they needed was a good clean. But in subsequent years, it was always a hassle trying to persuade the winners to return the cups before the show. It involved repeated letters and phone calls – and even trips to distant parts to collect the cups.

Producing the Schedule was a major task. It had to be typed first and then either printed, duplicated or photocopied. We needed it to send to all enquirers – and we also needed a large number of copies to distribute to all the horse shows in the county that took place before ours. But the cost of printing a schedule would have reduced our profits, and as our priority was to raise money, we looked round for ways of getting it done for nothing. That first year, we were fortunate in getting the Schedule photocopied by of one our parishioners who had his own business. The committee then collated it. In the following two years, one of our committee members had a husband in a senior position in a large firm and he produced it for us, also for nothing.

When he left the firm, we were at a loss. But remembering our friendly estate agent who produced the roadside boards for us each year, I thought we might manage to involve another Estate Agent with the schedules. I selected one at random, walked into the office and asked for the manager – and half an hour later came out with a promise to run off the schedule for nothing in return for a full-page advert. I don't think he quite realised what he had agreed to. Photocopying and collating 2,500 twenty-two page schedules is quite an undertaking – and I learnt later that some of his staff had to work overtime in order to get it done for us! The next year, I had to offer to do the collating before he would agree to photocopy it again. It was a task that took the committee two whole evenings. Finally, as funds became more robust, we decided to go to the expense of paying something towards the cost of production. We knew that the manager of the first estate agents, whose help we had enlisted for the roadside boards, had been a little hurt that we had involved a second estate agency in our enterprise. So our Treasurer took him out to an expensive lunch, and he agreed to process the whole schedule for us at a greatly reduced charge.

We realised that a horse show is not everyone's cup of tea, so decided to include a Fair to attract the non-horsy fraternity. I insisted on calling it a Fayre – much to the disgust of local purists – as I felt it had a more attractive look to it! The Fayre involved the village as a whole. Everyone was asked to contribute to a tombola and a cake stall. Various people were asked to organise stalls. The Bell ringers decided to bring along one of the Church bells and invite people to guess the weight, the Playgroup set up a play corner, the school had a stall, and considerable interest was generated throughout the village.

When organising a horse show and fayre there are all sorts of things one has to think of. We had to find about five caravans for the show – two for the judges to sit in on the two main rings, one for the secretary, one for the judges to eat their lunch in, and one for the judges' caterers. Many major shows hire a marquee but we were determined to make as much profit as possible and decided to avoid the expense of hiring.

We did have to hire toilets – but negotiated a good discount from a local firm. We had to lay on an ambulance from St John's Ambulance – later transferring our allegiance to the Red Cross. We also had to hire a tannoy system. This could have been a major expense, but I found someone who agreed, as we were a charity and running a mid week show, to reduce his fee considerably. He and his tannoy became an integral part of the show and he looked forward to his annual visit to Ulcombe.

So too did a firm to whom we gave the catering contract. I managed to negotiate some very good terms in return for which the firm provided food, a bouncy castle, a disco bounce, and roundabouts. The first year we ran our own bar – and made a loss. We then handed over the bar contract as well – and after one year when, inadvertently we booked in two ice cream vans to their mutual irritation, we handed over the ice cream contract as well. Over the years, it proved a happy partnership. The firm accepted our steadily increasing fee for the contract and at the same time was always honest in sending us an additional sum after the show which represented a percentage of their total profit. This contract was the subject of annual debate with new members of the committee who enthusiastically suggested we did our own bar and catering. But the old hands, aware of the amount of work involved, remained content to leave some of these more peripheral activities to outside firms, knowing that the difference in the profit margin was minimal, while the increase in stress was significantly large.

As the show approached Penny was overwhelmed with entries which had to be processed. It was clear that our publicity was paying off, as more and more entries poured through the letter box each day, while her phone never stopped ringing with last minute enquiries. It was something I could not really help her with.

I was busy organising the layout of the show ground and helping with the painting of road and show signboards. To attract the locals to the show we duplicated small handbills and paid local newsagents to deliver to all the houses in neighbouring villages while we got the local scouts to deliver in our own village.

The weekend before the show we spent erecting the rings. This involved hammering in stakes all round the arenas and roping them off. Over the years Penny and her husband, Bill and I, and the local farmer found ourselves doing the bulk of this work. Some years it was easier than others. If it had been wet beforehand, it was comparatively easy to drive in the stakes, but in a dry summer it was extremely difficult. We also put up home-made toilets to supplement the hired ones.

The night before the show, road signs had to be erected. As the approach roads to the show ground were narrow country lanes, we had to organise a one-way route to avoid road jams with the horseboxes.

The jumps were one of our major headaches. We hired these from a local farmer who was also a show enthusiast. The problem was their transport and erection. The hire fee was comparatively low – but in return we had to collect the jumps from a village eight miles away, load them onto a large lorry, then drive back and unload them. But that was not the end of the exercise. They then had to be positioned in the appropriate rings.

Unloading the heavy jumps with Bill and Stanley Tassell

Now, jumps are heavy and cumbersome. Their 'feet' have to be attached and screwed on so that can stand upright, and the heavy poles have to be laid across at the correct height and angle. Over the years, as we got older and less fit, this particular job became the most burdensome aspect of the whole show. What was even worse was that at the end of the show, when we had been on the show ground from seven o'clock in the morning and were already exhausted, we had to dismantle the jumps and take them on to the next show. After several years of this nightmare exercise, we decided to enlist help and managed to persuade the army to help us.

I shall never forget the excitement of the morning of my first show in August 1985 as we waited to see the result of our months of preparation. I set out from our house soon after seven to get down to the show ground early and, as I drove out of our lane into the village street, was amazed to see horse box after horse box rolling through the village like some mass migration. It reminded me of the War in 1944 when we were evacuated to the village near Reading when for three whole days army trucks, tanks and jeeps rolled through the village in a continuous stream making their way to the ports ready for their landing in France.

We were amazed and delighted to see so many horseboxes. But those of us who were new to the horse world were also amazed at the arrogance of many of the competitors. The people we had persuaded to marshal the horseboxes had a very difficult time persuading the horsebox owners to park where they were told – and suffered quite a lot of abuse. There were others who came in several cars who argued forcibly against paying an entrance fee. Since all the horseboxes came in free, it seemed not unreasonable to charge for a second car. But, though owning expensive horses and elaborate horseboxes, some did all they could to avoid paying the £1 entrance fee which was to go to charity. It is something that never ceased to amaze me.

But that first show was a great occasion. Everything went according to plan and at the end of the day we were able to announce a profit of £2,200 – more than four times the amount raised the previous year. We were all delighted and felt encouraged to do it again the following year. This time, there was no doubt as to how the profits were to be used.

The committee continued to work hard over the years, and one of the main stays of the committee was our Treasurer, Norman, a retired solicitor with a marvellous sense of humour. The Treasurer's caravan on the day of the Show was always a good place to visit – he had a plentiful supply of gin which was generously dispensed to all comers. He had a good understanding of what people liked – and was well aware that one of the main things a committee wants to know as soon as possible after an event is how much has been raised. Now, if one is the sort of person wedded to precision, that is not easy to do. But if one is flexible and prepared to hazard a guess, then it is perfectly possible to estimate the financial outcome of a show on the day. Such was one of our Treasurer's major contributions. At the end of each Horse Show, when all the clearing up had been completed, we would assemble at The Oast for a Chinese take away (ordered in advance), and after we had eaten, our Treasurer would stand up and announce the figure we had achieved. We would all return home at the end of the evening exhausted, but replete, and well satisfied with the result of our efforts.

Another key member of the committee was our local farmer, Stanley – our Transport Manager. That title gives no indication of his contribution to the Show which included the ordering and transporting of all the equipment, providing manpower, looking after the insurance for the Show, and answering every call for help from members of the committee. He was, in fact, one of the mainstays of the village – Chairman of the Parish Council, Chairman of the School Governors, Trustee of the old Parish Hall, and a Churchwarden!

The Ulcombe Horse Show and Fayre was by then well established as a major Kent show. It is one people looked forward to coming to, as it was such a happy and friendly event. Each year, the profits increased slightly – even in the two years when we had torrential rain. The first wet year, we had a thunder storm and hail – and the ground became so wet that the horse boxes were stuck in the mud, and the local farmers had to get out their tractors and tow the boxes out. The next time we had a wet show, the heavens opened while the fancy dress competition was being judged, and I stood in the ring with the Mayor, getting increasingly wet despite a large umbrella. The poor competitors, sitting on their horses waiting for the judges' verdict, looked cold and bedraggled as the rain soaked into their beautiful and lovingly made costumes.

But even on wet days the show made a profit because of the money received in advance from sponsorship, trade stalls, and entry fees, which were non-returnable. As we avoided expenses like hiring marquees, printing schedules, or feeding all and sundry, we continued to make a profit where other shows made a loss.

The Ulcombe Horse Show, with a new and enthusiastic committee, continued to be as profitable and enjoyable as ever – and I was able to sit on the sidelines and enjoy it from my privileged position of Show President (firmly resolved not to take on the task of volunteer toilet attendant which had been my lot since resigning as Show Organiser!).

The money raised from these shows was used to help pay for a new roof and a new window in the Church, and some money was set aside for a new heating system. Vast sums of money continued to be needed for the restoration of the Church but, sadly, the new committee decided to split the proceeds between the Church and the village school.

PARISH MAGAZINE

As I got increasingly involved with my work with the hospice, I fondly thought that would be the end of my village activities. But it was not to be. During a two-year interregnum which followed the departure of the Rector, the Parish Magazine ceased to exist. Many people bemoaned its loss, but no one did anything about it.

One evening, in 1991, at a joint Parochial Church Council Meeting with our sister church, one of the Readers, listening to moans about our lack of a magazine, suggested that PCC members might take it in turns, month by month, to produce one. Forgetting Bill's dictum to 'engage brain before opening mouth' I volunteered to do the first one. Our daughter had by then set up her graphic design enterprise in our house, and with access to word processing and a photocopier, it seemed not too arduous a task, particularly as I was already producing a monthly news sheet for the hospice, and had produced a school magazine over several years.

So, with enthusiasm and not much difficulty, Alex and I produced a magazine in the October. It was well received and people seemed delighted to have a parish magazine again after such a long silence. But where was the next volunteer? Two years on, my daughter and I were still producing a monthly edition, and Bill asked would I ever learn! But the Newsletter, in the same format, is now being produced by my fourth successor and continues to grow and be popular.

LUNCH CLUB

When I retired from the Hospice (about which more later) a local publican asked me whether I would consider organising a luncheon club at his pub, The Shant. This seemed a good idea, and a way of keeping up with old friends. So I said yes – and invited people from all the different areas of contact I had made over the years – the school where I'd taught for eleven years, the Hospice Appeal which I'd worked with for seven years, the local church where I'd worshipped since 1981, and the Church in the neighbouring village of Harrietsham whose fund raising I'd organised.

Most of those invited accepted the invitation, and to begin with we had over a hundred members. The number has dwindled over the years, and we now have a membership of just over forty. As with *The Friendship Club* later, I organised it on a monthly basis with a Membership Fee (rather more than the £1 for *The Friendship Club*) and a monthly raffle which provided money for cards, flowers for sick members and money to charity at Christmas. Initially we called it *The Shant Luncheon Club* but when the Shant burnt down (in suspicious circumstances) we had to find alternative accommodation. We tried out a variety of places until we settled on The Dog and Bear, a pub in the neighbouring village of Lenham.

This led us to the thorny question of a name. A lot of members wanted to call it *Molly's Luncheon Club*, but I hated the idea. Eventually a name came to me. We had moved round and about on a number of occasions so why not call ourselves *The*

90th birthday of Doris and Edie

Roundabout Club. The name has stuck. We are now in our twenty-fifth year, and new members are still joining us.

Occasionally, we have our lunches at Chilston Park – a more elegant venue but a little more expensive.

FRIENDSHIP CLUB

The next community venture was *The Friendship Club*. During an interregnum at the Church, I realised there was a real vacuum in the village and that nothing was being done for its elderly residents. So I called together a group of ladies – some churchgoers and some not – and suggested we set up a sort of Darby and Joan Club. The idea was well received and we decided to hold a monthly meeting in the Village Hall on the last Thursday in the month. We decided not to put an age limit on it – and consequently, our membership ranges in age from fifty to ninety – a good mix. We planned a typically varied programme – with speakers, bingo and beetle drives, Christmas parties, New Year lunches and outings. To cover the costs of the club, we had an annual membership fee of £2 and a compulsory £1 Raffle each month to which members contributed prizes. Tea, which proved the highlight of our meetings, was provided on a rota basis by members.

The club is now in its eighteenth year. Our earliest members are still with us – though now well into their seventies and eighties, which has implications for the sort of outings we can do. Membership continues to grow and we are known as 'the friendliest club' in the area.

HISTORY OF ULCOMBE

At the time of the Millennium we learnt that a number of villages were producing local histories. Some of the villages were giving a free copy of their history to every resident. This was a challenge. How nice it would be if we could do the same thing and produce a history of Ulcombe. So, in 2001 I invited twelve local people to my house and put the proposition to them: each of them to research and write one of the chapters.

I chose the people carefully: Don, the local postmaster who had lived in the village all his life; Bridget, the parish clerk; Geoff, the chairman of the parish council who enjoyed the local hostelries; Philip, an expert in agriculture; Jane who lived in the converted police house; John, a KCC Education Inspector, who was interested in old houses; Simon, an engineer who knew all about the workings of the village utilities; Joyce, a governor of the local primary school; Maria, a gypsy who lived on the permanent gypsy site; David, a local historian who kept us all supplied with books and information about sources; and me. Later we recruited Neil, an archaeologist from the neighbouring village, and Cliff, a former Mayor of Maidstone, later wheelchair bound, who took on recent housing developments in the village.

I had already written a number of chapters – on the Church, the Playgroup, the Village Hall, and the Horse Show, and undertook to research the two World Wars, Ulcombe's social life and personalities, as well as the local flora and fauna which no one else wanted to do. Rosemary, daughter of the local farmer, undertook to do some oral history with the older residents of the village.

To my delight, everyone said yes. It was agreed that Philip (the local agricultural expert who had good contacts in the publishing world) and I would co-edit the history. We were to call it *Ulcombe's Story: a millennium history of our village*

We knew we had available quite a large collection of old photographs of the village as a friend, David, and I had organised a local photographic exhibition some years before, and David had made copies of them all. John, who had undertaken the chapter on old houses, was also very competent with the computer and scanned in all the old photographs and the new ones which we were all taking.

My daughter, Alex, with her own graphic design business, took on the layout and design of the book, while Bill undertook the laborious task of proof reading.

We all started work on what was to take three years to complete. For it was not only the research that had to be done on the history of the village, there was also the thorny question of how we were to finance it if we wanted to give a free copy to every householder. We realised that, if we were to apply for grants, we would have to form ourselves into a local History Society. So we drew up a constitution with aims and objectives and formed ourselves into *The Ulcombe History Society*. We managed to obtain grants from The Awards for All Lottery Fund, the Kent Archaeological Society, the Allen Groves Local History Fund, Maidstone Borough Council, and Ulcombe Parish Council. We persuaded a hundred and fifty local and former residents of the village to donate a minimum of £20 in return for being listed in the history as Donors and Subscribers.

Some former and current residents were particularly generous, including members of the St Leger family whose connections with Ulcombe's church go back to the time of William the Conqueror.

We decided we needed even more funds if we were to achieve our aim. So Philip, brother to the local historian, David, undertook to find some local advertisers to swell the funds.

Over the next three years we met regularly at The Oast. We were a very harmonious group and had many very happy evenings – imbibing wine and coffee and getting to know each other better. But, in the middle of that period I was diagnosed with breast cancer and had a lumpectomy followed by chemotherapy and radiotherapy. For me, researching, writing and editing the history was a wonderful therapy, because it was something I could take up and put down according to how well I felt.

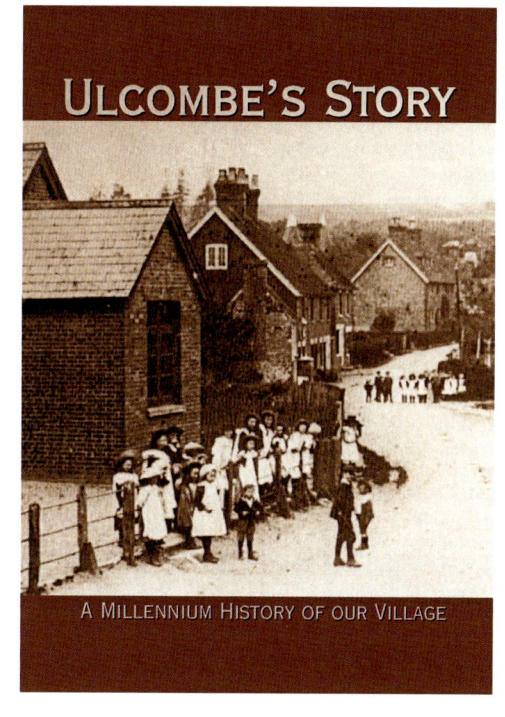

At last, the manuscript went off to the publisher who was a friend of Philip, and who gave us a very good quote. The proofs arrived which needed a lot of checking, and then came the exciting day when 750 volumes of the history arrived at our house. It was all very traumatic for me as Bill was very ill at home – dying of mesothelioma, an asbestos related disease which he had contracted at the age of seventeen when he was waiting for call-up and working in an asbestos factory.

We organised a formal launch in the Village Hall – a special occasion to which everyone was invited to come along and pick up their copies of *Ulcombe's Story*. It should have been for me a very happy occasion but I knew Bill had only a week or so to live. But he insisted I went to the Launch as he knew how much the history had meant to me. A very kind couple from the village, Sally and Steve, knowing how very ill Bill was, took a video of the formal part of the Launch and rushed it up to Bill the same evening so that he could feel part of the event. Bill died a week later.

TALKS AND MUSLIM LADIES

Among all my other involvements, I still continue giving talks on *The East India Company*, *The Watermen of the River Thames* and *Converting an Oast House*, while my most recent venture is teaching a group of Muslim ladies to speak English. Will I ever learn!

CHAPTER 16
Sharing a Car, 1973 – 1975

Village life is for me idyllic and I would never willingly live anywhere other than in the country, unless perhaps in a cathedral close. A return to the suburban environment in which I spent my first twenty years was the subject of a recurring nightmare – and I often woke sobbing because in my dream I was forced to leave The Oast and go back to the small suburban house in the road I lived in as a child. I can't explain the reason for these nightmares. My childhood was a happy one and I remember just after the War, when my parents contemplated moving to a different house, begging them to stay where we were because I didn't want to move.

But in my nightmare, the pain of leaving The Oast was intense and I found myself sobbing with deep gasping breaths. As the dream progressed and I gradually accepted the change and the new life in the suburb, all memory of our life in the country was erased as though it had never been, and the pain was intensified. I awoke with a searing sense of loss which stayed with me for the rest of the day.

So strong is my dread of living in a town that I have made my children promise that if I am left alone and become senile and they have to put me in a home, they will choose one with a room overlooking trees and fields or gardens rather than bricks and mortar.

But despite the joys of country living, there are many problems – the main one being transport. The rural bus service is almost non-existent and unless you own a car, life is very restricted. I was fortunate in our early years at The Oast in that my husband had a colleague living in the next village. From time to time they would share transport so that their wives could have a car for the day. This worked well for some years – especially when I was teaching at the Adult Education Centre – but then Bill's colleague moved abroad. It coincided with my being offered some regular part-time teaching in the town where Bill worked. Without a second car we knew it would not be possible to accept it. Bill's hours were erratic and would only occasionally coincide with my part-time teaching. But the expense of a second car was beyond our means.

I have always believed that if you work hard enough at a problem, a solution will ultimately present itself – and sure enough, after thinking about it for weeks and casting my eye round the village, the answer came to me. I would have to find someone to share a car with.

Living opposite was a young woman with children of similar age. She was a radiographer and worked in Chatham part time – as I hoped to. I knew she had for some time been having horrendously complicated journeys to work, and Bill had sometimes been able to help her out with a lift.

I went to see her and suggested that we shared a car. Her first reaction, as I had anticipated, was 'no'. It would be far too complicated. But when I outlined the scheme I had worked out, she began to see the possibilities, and after a few day's reflection, agreed.

The plan was to buy the car together and share the cost of the road tax and motor insurance. That was the simple part. The complicated part was to work out how to sort out the petrol and repair bills and any damage that might occur.

The petrol problem was easy to solve though a little complicated to execute. First, we had to work out how many miles to the gallon the car would do. We then agreed that we would purchase all our petrol from the garage at the top of the hill where Bill already had an account and ask the garage owner, a good friend of ours, to open a separate account for Carol and me. In this way, we would have a record of exactly how much petrol we used each month.

In order to know how much mileage we had done, we would keep a notebook in the car in which we would record the mileage after every journey. At the end of the month we would divide the petrol account in direct ratio to the amount of mileage we had each done. Not being mathematicians, we realised the sum involved would be fairly complicated, but we both had confidence in our sons' calculators.

It seemed fair to share our repair bills on the same basis of mileage. agreeing that whoever had used the car most would have been responsible for the most wear and tear. As it happened our use of the car was almost parallel so there was very little difference in our respective share of the repair bills.

The thorny problem, which was potentially the one on which the whole scheme could have foundered, was what to do if either of us had an accident. We had decided we should take out full comprehensive insurance but realised that if either of us had an accident, we would lose our *no claims benefit*. We agreed that it would not be fair to have to pay the extra insurance if we had not been responsible for the accident and decided that whoever was responsible for an accident, would have to make up whatever increased costs were incurred.

We then turned our attention to how we were to share the car. We were fortunate in that both our part time jobs were in Chatham and within a couple of miles of each other. With a little juggling, we decided we could travel together at least once a week, and share one of the morning journeys on two of the other days, making alternative arrangements for the journey home. This would enable us both to have the car for virtually two days a week. We agreed that if there were any special problems, we would do our best to make the car available on other occasions.

Having sorted out potential problems in advance, we wrote our decisions down as formally as possible and both signed a copy. It is something I would recommend to anyone. Carol and I shared a car for nearly three years and never had a wry word or argument despite the fact over the years we both had accidents and various traumas with the car.

Our first purchase was an A.40. It was cheap and fairly decrepit but it gave us good service for a year until the door by the driver's seat fell off and could not be put back. We managed to get a replacement from a breaker's yard, and for the next six months drove round with a blue car and one yellow door. It didn't matter. What was important was that we were mobile.

Difficulties then began with the gears. We found it almost impossible to get into second gear, and if you wanted to reverse the car, you had to take your hands off the driving wheel, place both hands on the gear lever, and force it into reverse. We decided the time had come to part with the car. We advertised it in the local paper and though several people came out to see it there were no takers until, one evening, a very well heeled looking gentleman came out and said he would buy it for his wife. We were a little worried as he had not bothered to drive our car before making the offer – and we were very aware of the car's deficiencies. But he waived aside our anxieties and told us he only wanted it for his wife, and the more problems there were the better. He told us his wife had already failed her test twenty times; he was only going to let her drive it round the fields as she wasn't safe to go on the roads; and the worse the car was the sooner she would give up the idea of driving altogether!

We couldn't help wondering what sort of tuition his wife had received – and what sort of relationship the couple had – or would have when she saw the sort of car he had bought her. But we pocketed the £100 with relief and set about looking for a replacement.

We were fortunate with our next car. My brother-in-law was about to purchase a new car and let us have his Hillman – very superior to our first car and in excellent condition. It did us very good service until a year later. Carol and I were travelling together to work and driving peacefully along the busy A20 when we were horrified to see a car hurtling towards us, out of control, from the other side of the central reservation. It hit the invalid car in front of us, tipping it upside down, ricocheted round and hit us hard on the side. The car behind us was too close and bumped into our back while an overtaking car hit us on the side. Our car was a write-off – but fortunately neither of us was hurt apart from shock and a few bruises.

The sadness was that, though the car would have given us good service for many years to come, it had no sale value, and though we managed to get compensation through the RAC for inconvenience and loss of earnings, we did not have enough insurance money to replace the car.

Fortunately the accident coincided with a period of change for both of us. Carol was about to move to a new job and I had decided to go into full time teaching as the children were now in their teens, and I felt it was not so necessary to be at home when they returned from school. Full time work meant a higher salary and the possibility of getting a loan for a car of my own.

But sharing a car is something I would strongly recommend to any young impecunious housewife who feels house bound and cut off from the outside world because of lack of transport. By anticipating problems and deciding what to do about them if they occurred, we avoided all conflict and difficulties and had a very happy relationship throughout. We are still good friends today.

CHAPTER 17
The French Connection, 1952 to the present

My French connection goes back to pre-university days when I spent six weeks in a Colonie de Vacance in the French Alps. My father worked for Shell and saw an invitation for an English student to work in the Shell Français Colonie de Vacance for the summer holidays. I received his suggestion that I might enjoy it with great enthusiasm, and one late afternoon in July set off for the Shell guesthouse in Paris where I was to meet up with my fellow monitrices and the children we were to be looking after in Chambery for a month.

My French was very limited. I'd managed to obtain a credit in my matriculation exam and had studied it for the first year in the sixth form – but had had to abandon it in the interest of getting an A' level credit in Latin which was then essential for entry to university for an arts degree

I always felt my comparatively meagre competence in French was due to the poor start caused by the tumult of war. At the age of ten I'd entered the local 'County School'. Though most pupils entered at the age of eleven the school had, for some reason, a small intake of girls at the age of ten following a fairly stiff entrance examination. As I have written before I passed the exam (despite a severe attack of 'acidosis') and became a member of this elite Lower Third class.

Evacuation took me away for the next year, and it was not until late in the summer term of the 'third' year (eleven-twelve year olds) that I returned to the school.

Special arrangements were made for those entering the school for the first time after wartime evacuation, and I was placed in a French class for beginners. Though delighted at the time, I subsequently realised that it was my misfortune to do so well that I was quickly promoted to the second division. Having missed all the basics, I struggled from then on. Had my parents been around I might have worked at home to catch up. But what with the travelling, missing the family, and not finding it easy to re-establish friendships made in the Lower Third (one could write a book about the cruelty of children to each other) I was not in a frame of mind to sit down and work at filling the gaps.

That, for many years, was my excuse for my comparative lack of fluency at French. But I think a lot more has to do with having an ear for languages, which some people seem to be born with. I've always felt that an ear for languages is connected with music and keying into the different rhythm of words in different languages. I had no opportunity to visit France as my parents, though not impoverished, were never able to afford to pay for me to go on any of the French school trips. So I never heard the language spoken other than by English teachers and, very occasionally, by the French mademoiselle whom we met about four times a term.

Thus, when at the age of eighteen I made my first trip to France my spoken French was very rudimentary indeed – and my comprehension of what was being said almost nil. This did not make it easy when, at the Shell guest house, I met up with the group of people I was to live with for the next six weeks – about a hundred children ranging in age from six to sixteen, a dozen French monitrices, and six 'etrangeres', myself included, from Holland, Denmark. Germany, Austria and the United States.

That first day I was not aware of the presence of the American to whom, had I known, I would have clung with relief.

Having eaten a delicious meal we boarded the train in Paris at around eleven o'clock in the evening and settled ourselves as comfortably as we could for a night's sleep. I had heard during the evening the word 'greve' mentioned on a number of occasions, but exhausted and battered by the noise of the children, I hadn't bothered to get out my dictionary and find out what it meant.

The train set off. After half an hour of excited chatter, the children fell into an exhausted sleep – and I too dozed off – only to be awakened with a start when the train, following a long loud hoot, came to a sudden stop. It was midnight. I kept expecting the train to start moving again – but nothing happened, and I dozed fitfully through the night and awoke to the sight of agitated monitrices conferring seriously together in the corridor. It was then that I became aware of our predicament. The entire French railway had gone on strike for twenty-four hours, and we were stranded in the wilds with a hundred hungry children, no sanitation, and no chance of continuing the journey till midnight, if then.

By mid morning bladders were full and stomachs felt empty. But no relief or sustenance was on hand until just after midday when we were all disgorged from the train, and walked two miles along the track to a primitive farmhouse. There we were able to relieve our bladders and enjoy a very simple meal of dry bread and cheese and some very watered wine, so pale in colour the proportion of wine to water was almost negligible.

This was my first introduction to French plumbing – two holes in the ground in a broken down outhouse, no toilet paper and no running water. I wondered what the next six weeks held in store for me!

We passed the afternoon in a field, and the monitrices managed to encourage the dispirited, dirty, and tired children into playing some simple games, and at about six o'clock we walked back to the train where we waited hopefully for the signal that the strike was at an end. Sure enough, on the stroke of midnight, the train set off – and we arrived at Chambery early the next morning where brilliant sunshine and beautiful mountains greeted us – a most welcome sight after the rigours of the journey.

The Colonie de Vacance was in the foothills of the mountains at a little place called La Feclaz – and there I spent six idyllic weeks walking the countryside, visiting castles and abbeys, improving my French, and getting to know a little about the French way of life.

Monitrices from Denmark, Holland, the USA, Germany and me

I shared a room with two French girls – Nicole and Bernadette. The monitrices had a day off each week and one day the three of us, together with the American, Katie, set off to visit Geneva. We were all students and all hard up, so decided to hitch hike. The outward journey was uneventful. We managed to get lifts together and spent a most enjoyable day in Geneva where, to my absolute amazement, I met a school friend at the United Nations Building. The return journey was another matter altogether. Cars and lorries seemed less willing to give lifts in the evening, and we were beginning to panic as seven o'clock approached and we were still ten miles away from the telepherique which we had to go on to get back up the mountain to La Feclaz.

Deciding we might have more chance if we split into two groups, Nicole and Katie went ahead and managed to get a lorry to stop and pick them up. But Bernadette and I were less successful and still tramping along disconsolately at eight o'clock. We were on the point of looking for a barn to bed down in for the night when a well dressed man in his early forties, driving a Bentley, took pity on us and stopped. He asked us where we wanted to go. We had no idea. The telepherique had closed. We knew we would have to find somewhere to sleep – but we had no money to pay for a night's lodging. Bernadette explained our dilemma to the motorist who said he was the proprietor of a hotel and offered us a bed for the night. Looking back, it was the sort of situation which would have made our mothers turn in their graves – but we were naive and blissfully ignorant of the dangers of such a situation

We accepted his offer and found ourselves, half an hour later, ensconced in what must have been the equivalent of a five star hotel. We were shown to a beautifully appointed room – more luxurious than anything I had ever seen. And there we bedded down for the night in our underwear. Food was not offered to us and our empty stomachs woke us early – and we were soon hastening on our way to the telepherique and to what we knew would be an angry reception by the Directrice.

At the end of the six weeks at La Feclaz my room mate, Nicole, invited

Nicole and me in Paris

me to stay with her family in Paris for a few days – and so began a close friendship and my French connection which continues to the present day.

Nicole's parents were warm and friendly and made me very welcome. There I was introduced to the delights of French family cooking – and was much intrigued to see Nicole's father and Nicole getting up to prepare different dishes during the course of the meal.

Nicole paid a return visit to England, and from then on we corresponded regularly and exchanged interesting presents at Christmas. But the opportunity to return to France did not occur until Bill and I had been married some twenty years and we felt our son – aged twelve – needed a trip to France to improve his French.

Though passionate advocates of the state system of education we were not sufficiently indifferent to our son's welfare to accept happily the thought that he might spend all his schooldays in a high school. The Thameside system of education was in operation in our area. Children at the age of eleven all went to the local high school where most stayed till the age of sixteen. The academic pupils were creamed off at thirteen and went to the Upper Schools (in essence the old grammar schools) and those who were left behind, especially those on the borderline, suffered a loss of self esteem which often damaged them for years to come.

A rigorous system of assessment took place – based mainly on achievement in four subjects – English, Maths, French and Science. Our son had no problem with maths and science at which he excelled. His English was poor (at that stage he was not a willing reader and his primary school teacher always related with amusement that it took him four terms to get through his reading book *Custers Gold)* but as Bill and I were both English teachers we felt we could deal with his inadequacies in English. But French was a different matter and I decided to accept Nicole's repeated invitations to visit France and accompany Justin over for an exchange visit with Nicole's son, Thierry, who was the same age.

Twenty years is a long gap – but there was instant recognition and immense joy when Nicole and I met up at the Gare du Nord in Paris and chattered happily in Franglais all the way to Guanville where Nicole's parents-in-law had a holiday home.

I had not realised when Nicole invited us that we would be arriving on the wedding day of the youngest member of the family, Katherine. We arrived in the evening and the formal wedding had already taken place But there at Guanville, at eight o'clock in the evening, some thirty-five members of the family were present.

As soon as we arrived and introductions were over, we all sat down to eat at a table that snaked through the dining room into the large farmhouse kitchen. The talk wafted round us, and from time to time members of the family tried to engage us in conversation. They soon gave up the attempt at verbal communication, but made us feel included in the happy family gathering by their warm and friendly smiles – and we felt quite content.

When the bride and groom and many of the family departed the next day, those remaining turned their attention to making our visit as happy and interesting as possible.

The place was a perfect holiday setting. Monsieur Masson, Nicole's father-in-law, had brought the farm at Guanville many years before. It had a beautiful courtyard with a huge willow tree, sculpted out to form an umbrella for white garden tables and chairs. Around the courtyard were some eight outbuildings – the number coinciding with Monsieur Masson's eight children. To each he gave an outhouse for them to convert in whatever way they wished as holiday chalets – and in this way he found it possible to assemble his whole family which by then numbered nearly forty members as most of his children had produced numerous offspring.

On one side of the complex was a dense wood within which were the remains of a huge castle. It was not possible to get near it because it was fenced off with barbed wire, but walking round the perimeter of the wood, one could see tantalising glimpses between the trees of huge round towers, battlements, and crumbling walls. There was a brooding air of mystery about the place and I longed to get nearer and explore it. I felt that, had it been in England, it would have been made into a tourist attraction, but M. Masson told me that the place was dangerous. There had been extensive tunnelling beneath the buildings, and no one was allowed near it. No one had any idea to whom the castle had belonged, or what was its history as all records had been destroyed during the French Revolution. I had the feeling that we were living beside the castle of the sleeping princess, hidden from all eyes by the machinations of a wicked fairy queen!

Nicole's mother-in-law was charming and she and I very quickly established a good rapport. She spoke no English but was extremely patient with me and helped in the development of that confidence which is so essential if one is to make any progress in a language. We used to sit in the courtyard happily playing scrabble together. Sadly, she died a year or two after my visit so I did not meet her again.

M. Masson was a tall, stately and aristocratic gentleman who had had a very successful business in South America. Returning to France he had contacts at a very senior level with the French government. He spoke the most beautiful but complex French which was not easy to understand – particularly when he tried to engage me in conversation about the state of politics and affairs in Britain. But we got on well and when I returned to England we started an annual correspondence which continued right up to his death in 1991 at the age of eight-nine.

We met up with him on a number of occasions after that and stayed in his flat in Montmartre – just a hundred yards from the Sacre Coeur. Nicole told us he had always had a great rapport with students who visited him in great numbers whenever they came to Paris.

For the person trying to understand a foreign language, it is the speed and quality of the spoken word that makes the difference between understanding and incomprehension. Nicole's husband, Bernard, spoke beautifully – enunciating each word carefully with a nice cadence. I understood nearly everything he said. But their daughter, Florence, aged fifteen, spoke so rapidly that I understood not one word. Nicole and I conversed in franglais – and still do – as being the quickest and easiest way to communicate. Even now, though rather more proficient at French that I was then, it still depends very much on who I am speaking to as to how much I understand.

Our visit to France was a great success and Justin seemed happy. I had no qualms about leaving him when, after a week, I returned to England to Bill and Alex who had been coping alone at The Oast.

Two weeks later, Justin returned to England with Thierry. Thus began a series of exchange visits which eventually seemed to involve the whole village. When Alex's turn came to go to France, Nicole arranged for an exchange with her niece Isabelle. When Nicole's daughter Florence eventually decided she would like to come to England, I found the daughter of a village friend for her to stay with. Then Isabelle's friend wanted to come to England – and then her cousin – and, before we knew where we were, there were French exchanges going on all over the village.

I think back with a certain degree of amazement that, when Justin was twelve, we sent him to France on his own, having arranged for Nicole to meet him off the train in Paris. We put him on an overnight boat at Dover and didn't feel unduly worried. It's certainly not something one would be happy doing today. He returned with Thierry – and I must admit we were worried when we couldn't see them coming off the boat. But, at last they emerged, telling us they had got a job helping the waiters to clear the tables. They were, understandably pleased with themselves!

Over the years our contacts with Nicole's husband's family have extended more and more. We have stayed with various members of the family in Paris, Guanville, and in Annecy where the family have a lovely holiday home – while a number of the youngsters have been over to stay with us. Nicole and I write regularly two or three times a year – she in French and I in English – and we are both grateful that our correspondence has enabled our two families over the years to enjoy such a happy friendship.

CHAPTER 18

The Swimming Pool and the Guest House Venture, 1982 – 1985

As the years passed, although The Oast gradually became more habitable, our financial situation failed to improve – largely of course because we continued to pour money into renovating a house that had a voracious appetite.

We were, perhaps, not as wise as we might have been when I received a small legacy from my aunt. She was my godmother, and after her husband's death spent a lot of time with us, as well as every Christmas, until the time she had to go into a nursing home with advanced senile dementia.

I loved swimming, and had always longed for a swimming pool. The garden was large enough to accommodate one – but of course the idea of having a pool of our own seemed a luxury beyond our wildest dreams. We had, however, examined the pools of several of our acquaintances and realised it was possible to buy a liner pool and do it ourselves.

Though I had very tentatively talked with Bill about having a pool, the idea met with very little response, and it receded into the back of my mind. But two things galvanised me into action. One was that Bill, quite uncharacteristically, talked about getting a greenhouse. What prompted this desire I have no idea for anyone less interested in gardening it would be hard to find. However, not averse to a greenhouse, I went along with the idea until I saw where he proposed to put it. I realised it would block the possible entry for all time of a digger to excavate a pool. And knowing Bill, I knew he would produce it as an insuperable argument against having a pool.

Unfortunately for Bill, my legacy arrived at the same time. One Easter Saturday morning, working in the garden in unseasonably blazing hot sunshine, the longing for water and our own pool became stronger than ever, and on the spur of the moment I downed tools and whispered to Alex that I wanted to investigate something of interest to all the family, and asked her to come with me.

We crept away secretly and drove off to the next village where John, an acquaintance of ours, had a swimming pool firm. He was at home.

I put to him a simple question. How much would a do-it-yourself swimming pool kit cost? His reply – £3,500 – fell well within my legacy of £5,000 so I asked for more details. "Why don't I come round and look at your garden now?" said John, realising he had got the fish on the hook already.

Alex and I looked at one another and decided that it would be a very good idea – though we both felt a little trepidation at Bill's likely response. We set off for home, John following in his Landrover.

Bill hadn't noticed our absence, although we had been gone more than an hour, and was still working on the gutters at the back of the house. We decided to show John the area where we thought the pool might go before alerting Bill to our presence.

John walked round the garden, got out his tape measure, and was marking out the possible area for the pool when Bill realised there was a stranger in the garden. He walked over and greeted John courteously, but looked totally bewildered when John started asking him questions about what shape pool he wanted, blissfully unaware that Bill had no knowledge of our mission.

Bill's reaction can be guessed – but, being the gentleman he was, he remained courteous and agreed to think about the idea. John dined out for years afterwards on the story of Molly commissioning a pool for Bill to install, when Bill knew nothing about it!

John explained that with a do-it-yourself pool, his firm would send in a digger to excavate the pool. We would then have to fix the plastic sides, install the filter system, and lay the concrete base. Then his firm would return with a special suction machine and install the liner. We would then fill the pool with water and – hey presto – we would have a swimming pool. It all sounded very simple and, it being our Silver Wedding year and Bill having just taken early retirement, he reluctantly agreed that we should have a pool.

Three weeks later, the pool kit arrived – all neatly boxed up – followed by a digger. We had borrowed a video camera to record the event. That was another story! Unlike the modern camcorder, the video camera necessitated the use of two wheelbarrows and a very long extension lead to get the equipment from one place to another.

The family, especially Bill, proved extremely uncooperative over this venture – refusing after the first two hours of filming to help me move the wheelbarrows, let alone pose for me. I felt they were totally unreasonable – and the language on the film that finally emerged was not exactly ladylike!

However, we did manage to record the entry of the digger, and the first scoops of earth that marked the beginning of the devastation of that part of our lovely garden. Within two days, it looked like a First World War battlefield as mounds of thick sticky yellow clay emerged from the bowels of the earth.

As always with our ventures, problems emerged. The first was the discovery of an enormous block of concrete at a crucial corner of the pool. It was one of the bases of the huge barn that had once stood there and been demolished by the farmer just before The Oast was put on the market. The digger managed after a time to winkle the concrete base out – but in trying to raise it to the surface, it slipped out of the claw of the digger and rolled to the bottom, damaging en route the beautiful smooth sides that the digger operator had been so proud of. This accident necessitated the hiring of an additional machine to lift the concrete out – and of course, caused extra expense – something we were well used to.

These events took place in early May – and Bill set about concreting in the intense heat of the 1982 summer. He was constantly diverted to help Alex with revision for her O' level exams, and Justin with his A' levels – and as I was heavily pre-occupied with finishing my MA thesis, he had to cope with the cooking as well. He really deserved a halo for the way he coped during this period, but I fear he received nothing but irritability from me. For I was bored to tears with writing my

The swimming pool now

The day I received my MA

thesis on Management in Education, and longing to get out and start straightening the garden – and was extremely irritable and frustrated.

However, the great day came in August 1982 when we started filling the pool. It must have been a period of intense irritation for our neighbours for, during three whole days and nights, there was the continuous sound of a running motor which, as the pool gradually filled with water, extracted all the air between the liner and the concrete so as to ensure that the plastic liner lay smooth and flat against the sides.

I couldn't wait for the pool to be filled – and as the square at the bottom of the pool (eight feet deep) filled up, I slid down the slope and dabbled my feet in the water. It was a great moment.

The pool gave the family endless pleasure – but Bill endless work – and he never ceased to bemoan the fact that making the pool was the direct cause of all his aches and pains, and of a vast quantity of additional work. But he admitted to its pleasures and enjoyed a regular swim during the warmer summer months.

I had promised Bill that if we had a pool in the garden I would not want to go away on holiday for a long time. The garden was by now well established and a source of great pleasure. We had open views in two directions across the Weald of Kent – and though we were in the middle of the village there were no houses in sight from the garden, nor indeed from most of the windows of the house.

It was an idyllic place for a holiday but what, of course, I had not taken into consideration, on making my rash promise, was that it is not easy to holiday at home. Somehow, people know you are there. The telephone continues to intrude, the post arrives daily with all its news good and bad, and callers continue to knock at the door. Moreover the house needs cleaning, food has to be prepared and cleared away afterwards, and relaxing in the garden one is made very aware of weeds and growing grass. So, though The Oast was an idyllic setting for a holiday, it did not really provide us with the sort of holiday we needed.

However, the seeds of an idea was sown. We were even more impoverished than before and always on the look out for additional sources of income. Why didn't we take in holiday guests?

The idea was attractive. We were used to entertaining endless numbers of visitors. We had two spare bedrooms, three toilets and two separate sitting rooms. We were ideally placed for foreign visitors – less than an hour from Dover and an hour and a quarter to London. The area abounded in stately homes and castles – and was just the sort of place to attract foreign visitors.

So, that winter in 1983, we started planning. The first thing was to turn our son out of one of the two bedrooms he occupied. One room was once the playroom and the other his bedroom but over the previous two years the two had become indistinguishable – overrun with a vast and incoherent mass of clothes, chairs, books, papers galore – and war game impedimenta. As an enthusiastic war gamer, he had gathered round him friends from the locality who seemed to spend most of their waking free hours.

Main guest room

in our house. The playroom was large and in the centre was a table tennis table – something we had bought as a family Christmas present some years before in the fond hope of playing table tennis. But Justin and his friends thought otherwise. They fell on it with enthusiasm as a marvellous base for Napoleonic warfare. Covered with a dark green sheet which he had stolen from my linen cupboard, the table was set out with an elaborate reconstruction of the area round Waterloo – with houses, farm buildings, woods, roads, streams and trees – and a vast army of tiny metal soldiers, horses and guns – all beautifully painted.

These little silver figures were purchased unpainted – and littered the tables, cupboards, bookcases and window shelves round the room – awaiting adornment. A former kitchen table was appropriated as a painting table – and it was quite usual to see a group of large six foot lads sitting round the table totally absorbed in painting, with fine detail, these miniature figures. They were true works of art and a great tribute to the lads' patience and skill. In fact the whole panorama was a real work of art. But somehow the lads' aesthetic appreciation did not extend beyond the battlefield – and the chaos and confusion of the rest of the room and in Justin's bedroom next door was beyond description.

Sheila, my cleaner, made valiant attempts to hoover the carpet – but would frequently give up in despair and leave imperative notes on Justin's bed demanding that he removed the rubbish from the floor so that she could clean his room. Dust seemed not to bother him. It was only when I brought in the heavy brigade and threatened cessation of meals that he responded reluctantly and made a half-hearted attempt at clearing up.

The thought of potential revenue from Justin's bedroom galvanised me into action. We turfed Justin out of his bedroom, lock, stock and barrel – moving his bed and his overflowing chest of drawers to join the chaos in the playroom. We then completely redecorated and refurnished his bedroom apart from the carpet which we now discovered to be really quite presentable. We had scarcely seen it for the last two years. When the work was finished we realised we had forgotten that the room was nearly as attractive as our main guest room in one of the roundels. We had always managed to keep that in pristine order – and this, I suspect, was one of the reasons why so many friends came to stay with us.

Our next task was to invest in several sets of non-iron sheets, some good quality towels, and a complete new set of china – our wedding china now being very much depleted.

We devised our own brochure – an A4 card folded into three with pictures of the Oast on the front and photos of our garden and some of the interesting stately homes in the area in the middle. A detailed map on the back gave careful instructions as to how to find us – an essential requirement we thought, remembering the trouble our visitors had had trying to locate us in our early years at the Oast.

We registered with the Tourist Board, the South East Tourist Board and the Maidstone Tourist Board, and put adverts in Farmhouse Guides and the Kent

Holiday Guide. It was quite a costly exercise and we spent what was in fact a quarter of our net profit in our first year.

What turned out later to be our best source for visitors was the car park attendant at the local and very poplar castle – Leeds Castle. We had seen him chatting to visitors on several of our visits to the castle and I approached him to find out if he was ever asked by visitors about accommodation in the area. He replied in the affirmative, saying he was frequently asked by foreign tourists to direct them to somewhere nice to stay.

It did not take long for us to make a mutually beneficial agreement with him – and we loaded him up with a pile of our yellow brochures and the promise of a commission for every visitor he sent us. He proved a regular source of visitors. We always knew that he had sent them when, at about 5.30 in the evening, visitors would walk down our garden path to the front door clutching one of our yellow brochures in their hand. 'The man at the castle said he knew just the place for us to stay and gave us this brochure. Do you have a room for the night?'

A few days later I would drive down to the castle car park, a five pound note folded carefully in my hand. The car park attendant would see me coming, wander over casually for a chat and I would discreetly pass over the note through the window. It was a very happy arrangement which lasted until we gave up the guest house venture five years later.

We planned to start our venture in the early spring but had most of our preparations in hand by the late autumn. But we were far from prepared for visitors when Charlotte and Ben turned up on our doorstep in the middle of October. Our friends at the local garage at the top of the hill knew of our plans and rather jumped the gun when two charming elderly Americans stopped for petrol mid-morning and asked about accommodation in the area. They sent them down to us. The lounge looked chaotic as I had, the day before, removed all our loose covers from our lounge suite and washed them. As it was raining they were still damp and I had draped them over the banisters to dry. They had shed bits of cotton throughout the house which could not have looked more unkempt had we tried.

However we invited the Americans to join us for coffee and explained that we were really not planning to receive guests until the spring. Charlotte begged us to show her our guest room. She took one look and fell in love with it, and announced that this was exactly the sort of place they had been looking for. They would stay – despite the chaos! She was a determined business woman – had headed the buying department of one of America's leading fashion stores – and said she was quite sure we would have the whole house in order by the time they returned that evening! She was charming and far tougher than I, and I had no choice but to agree to them staying.

We took their cases up to the guest room and Ben and Charlotte departed for the day while I frantically set about ironing the loose covers and restoring the house to normality. We worked like beavers (Bill was on a mid term holiday) and by the time Charlotte and Ben returned the house looked immaculate.

We sent them off for dinner to one of our local pubs which did excellent meals, and when they returned we sat late into the night talking. They had spent many years in Japan and had some fascinating tales to tell. During the course of conversation we learnt that Ben was to celebrate his eightieth birthday the next day and, finding them very congenial company, I offered to cook dinner for them.

They were delighted with the suggestion and the next morning, after breakfast, Charlotte took me aside to discuss the arrangements. I said that, as it was a special birthday, they should be our guests. But Charlotte then proceeded to subject me to one of her business lectures which were to be a feature of her stay with us – something I was very much to appreciate as she gave me some invaluable advice.

"You can't go giving away extras like dinners without charging," said Charlotte. "You'll never make any profit!' I insisted that an eightieth birthday was something very special and thought I had won the argument when she agreed, and said she would provide the wine. But little did I know Charlotte! For that evening, when they returned from their day's sight seeing, she brought along a whole crate of very expensive wines as their contribution to the celebrations.

We loved their visit and they promised to return the following year. But Ben became ill and they were unable to make the trip. But we continued corresponding for many years afterwards – and Charlotte's letters were always full of interest. They wanted us to visit them, but we couldn't afford the trip. They were near neighbours of President Reagan and the letters were full of interesting anecdotes. When the letters eventually ceased coming, we feared that old age had finally overtaken them, and felt sad that we had not seen them again.

We had no more visitors until the early spring when we were once again taken unawares – thanks again to our friends at the garage who took a keen interest in our affairs. Early one evening they sent us a Danish couple. Quite excited we welcomed them, asked them to sign our brand new Visitors' Book and showed them to their room. We invited them, as our first official visitors, to join us for a drink on the terrace before they went out for dinner.

We were in the middle of cooking a barbecue and helping Alex with some revision for exams. The Danish couple were a charming professional couple and we had an interesting conversation with them before they went off to have dinner. Time went by. We had our barbecue, Bill and Alex were quietly working together when I suddenly remembered that there were no flowers in the guest room. I got some scissors, cut some flowers, arranged them in a vase, and took them up to the bedroom. We had put no locks on the door and I walked straight in, thinking our guests were still out having dinner. Imagine my consternation when I discovered that, not only had they returned from the pub and entered quietly through the front door without letting us know they had returned, but they had also gone straight to bed!

In great confusion, I dumped the flowers on the nearest available surface, muttered something under my breath and fled! That was lesson number one. Put locks on the bedroom doors, and never ever enter a room without knocking first. But it did not put off our Danish visitors. For that was in Spring 1984 and in July 1987 they made a return visit and wrote in the Visitor's Book , " We **had** to come back"

Our first two sets of visitors had come from overseas, were charming, middle aged and professional. They were characteristic of the visitors we were to receive over the next few years and what was to make the venture so enjoyable. But we did make one mistake in the first year and that was to accept Minnehaha.

That was not her real name, but she so resembled one's picture of a red Indian princess that we nicknamed her Minnehaha. Alas, she did not live up to her in character. The letter from Canada asked us to accommodate an eighteen year old for a complete week with full board. We were told she was interested in horse riding, swimming, and in music, and wanted to be with young people. She seemed to possess all the qualities needed to fit in easily with our children and their friends, and so we agreed to take her.

We met her at the airport and drove her home. She was very silent in the car but this we put down to shyness. As it was late in the evening, she said she didn't want a meal but went straight to bed. Next morning we waited and waited for her to get up – and she eventually emerged at noon. Bill's face was a study when, asked what she would like for breakfast, she said, "Bananas, a fried egg and treacle."

She proved to be a loner who didn't want to join in with anything at all. The children and their friends were a happy and friendly crowd, and did their best to make her welcome – but she rebuffed all their approaches. She moaned about the cold, about the food, about going out. She skulked in her bedroom for hours on end, and was a thorough pain. We took her to several places of interest but she was bored by them. We organised riding for her, and she never said thank you. It was a moment of great relief when we put her on the plane at the end of eight days and we vowed we would never take in youngsters on their own again.

Among our early visitors was a family who have, over the years, become very good friends. We had had a a church fund raising event in our house on the Saturday night – and were busily organising an impromptu luncheon party to eat up the leftovers when the phone went. It was an English family, on holiday in England from Germany. They had seen our Oast advertised in the Maidstone Tourist office and were keen to stay in Ulcombe because Graham was into family history, and one of his Victorian ancestors had lived in the village.

They arrived in time for morning coffee – and when I said I was just off to church, they decided to come too. So I then invited them to join the gathering for lunch – in return for a small donation to the Church. This was the beginning of a long association. Every time they came to England to visit their family in the north they stopped off with us overnight. Later, when the children went to boarding school in England, they stayed here for the exeat weekends. We always looked forward to their visits and watched their two delightful children grow into interesting teenagers.

Sadly, their marriage broke up, but Graham not only continues to come and see me on his visits to England, he also takes a great interest in the village and its church, and contributes to The Friends of Ulcomeb Church which we set up in June 2013.

An interesting time was the visit of a French family with two small children who came at the same time as a Frenchwoman of thirty. For some reason, I had agreed to do dinner as well as bed and breakfast. It proved far more onerous than I had expected and, again, was something we did not repeat. The first two nights I despaired. The children were aged eighteen months and three and a half, and Marie, the mother, insisted the children ate dinner with the rest of us. I organised dinner promptly at seven, feeling it was far too late for tiny tots of that age to be eating. And, of course, the inevitable happened. The children were tired and grizzled through the meal – and when Marie put them to bed, they were over tired and unable to sleep.

Graham Homewood

I put up with this for two days, and then decided something drastic had to be done. It was not fair on Brigitte nor on my family, who, I felt, were entitled to a peaceful evening. But I realised diplomacy was needed. So, after breakfast, I took Marie aside and said, in my broken French, that I thought it would be nice for her, and she would enjoy her holiday more, if she and her husband had the evenings free of their children. I suggested that she brought them back a little earlier, and I would give them their tea at five o'clock. She and Alain could play with them for a while, then give them a bath and read them a story in bed while I cooked the dinner.

This, of course, was the normal routine that we had followed very happily with both our children. To Marie, it seemed quite alien and it took a lot of persuading before she agreed to try it. Needless to say, the change in routine worked like a charm. The children gained their parents' full attention before going to bed, and then, not overtired, were able to fall asleep immediately.

Marie was astonished and delighted – and followed the routine for the rest of the stay. When she left she declared that she would continue to do the same when she got home – that their evenings up to then had been purgatory. It was nice to think that she and Alain had not only had a nice holiday but had also gained a useful new experience.

It was the next week that we had one of our most amusing incidents. We had a young French woman, Brigitte, staying with us when Graham and family turned up unexpectedly. Fed up with cooking, I suggested they might all like to join us for a Chinese takeaway. All agreed that it was a good idea and soon after breakfast I ordered the meal. The Chinese restaurant asked me to come in and pay a deposit as it was for so many – but I assured him that I would not let him down and persuaded him to agree to forgo his deposit on this occasion as I didn't want to make the trek to pay him.

Come the evening, the table beautifully laid for ten, Bill and Graham set out for Lenham to collect the meal while the rest of us sat in our lounge drinking sherry. It was all very relaxed and we expected the men to be back within twenty minutes. But an hour went by – and then another half hour and no sign of the men folk. Then the phone rang. It was Bill, furious. "Where, in heaven's name, is this Chinese meal we're supposed to collect? We've been to Lenham and its not there. We've been to Headcorn and they know nothing about it."

A moment of horror – I checked the card and realised I had ordered from a Maidstone take-away – nine miles in the other direction – and from a place Bill did not know. His sense of direction was so poor I knew there was no chance of explaining how to get there over the phone. I said he had better come home and I would persuade Brigitte to take me to Maidstone.

Explanations hurriedly offered, I persuaded Brigitte to drive. She was none too happy on English roads in the daylight – and was appalled at the thought of night driving – but valiantly agreed. Her reluctance increased when we found that, in the last hour, a hail storm had blown up. However, we set off – driving in the middle of the road – and eventually reached the take-away where a very irate Chinese gentleman awaited us and said he would never again take an advance telephone order without a deposit.

When we returned with the meal, everyone fell on it ravenously – but not before I had been made to crawl with abject apologies. "But why," said I, "did it take such a long time for you to discover you were in the wrong place?"

The explanation was bizarre. Bill and Graham had gone to Lenham and when they asked for Mrs Poulter's order, they were told it would not be long. They sat down and waited, quite content, chatting and watching the beautiful coloured fish in the take-away's large aquarium. But time went by and people came and went, and there was no sign of the food. They eventually woke up to the fact that a long time had passed and went up to the counter and asked what had happened to their order. The manager told them that it had already been collected. Further enquiry elicited the fact that an order had been collected, almost unbelievably, by a Mr Porter!

Bill had then assumed that I must have ordered from another Chinese take-away five miles in the other direction, so he and Graham had raced to Headcorn, only to find the food had not been ordered from there either. It was then that Bill phoned me in understandable anger.

With the prolonged pre-dinner drinking session and the whole nature of the evening, it was a riotous meal. The final climax came when I brought in from the oven a most beautiful cherry gateau which sat elegantly on a silver foil dish. As I placed it on the table, the foil dish collapsed and the gateaux landed upside down on the tablecloth. We were by then too far gone to worry about niceties – and all scooped up our portions direct from the cloth. It tasted good.

Perhaps our most unusual visitors were three Japanese students. We had a phone call from a Japanese official who asked if he could come and see us. He worked for Mitsubishi and said that one of the Directors wanted his son and daughter and their friend to stay with a family in England. He had seen our brochure and thought we would be a suitable place.

We were then subjected to a detailed interrogation, and the house and garden were inspected with great care. A week or two later, we had a visit from another official – and then received a letter to say we had been approved! We were told that the students would be brought here by the firm's chauffeur and that the chauffeur would arrive each morning to take them around Kent. Our role was to give them breakfast and dinner, and to entertain them in the evenings.

Come the day of their arrival, they were brought over by the two officials who treated the students very deferentially. We settled them into their three rooms (Bill and I had, once again, to sleep on the music room floor as the Japanese officials had insisted that each girl should have her own room – and we really only had two guest rooms). The Japanese boy was extremely good looking and so was the friend. But the boy's sister was far from prepossessing to look at, though she proved to have a delightful sense of humour and was the most friendly of the three

We sat down to dinner. Throughout their stay I prepared typical English meals as this was what I had been asked to do. But before I could bring in the food, the girls brought in presents – one for each of us, very carefully chosen to suit our age and sex. I rather suspect we should have given them presents in exchange but no one told us this was the custom.

At the end of the meal, the girls leapt up and cleared the table. When I protested, they said that their father had insisted they do this so that they would behave as the English do.

We got to know a fair amount about them through the daughter. It transpired that the father was hoping to make an arranged marriage between his son and the friend who was with them. Although she was a very beautiful girl, we didn't feel that the son was any too keen.

He was the least friendly of the three and we never got close to him. He was apparently a very good tennis player and we had been asked to organise both tennis and riding for the students while they were with us. One day we were allowed to take them off for a walk and a pub lunch at one of our local pubs – something they seemed to enjoy.

They left with great protestations of thanks and promises to write – but we never heard from them again.

One of the pleasures of our guest house venture was getting to know so many interesting and pleasant people. The majority were from overseas – Swiss, Dutch, Danish, Swedish, French, German, Canadians, Americans, New Zealanders, Australians, Indians and South Americans. We never had any Italians, South Africans, nor in fact from the continent of Africa. It seemed that our type of accommodation appealed to the professional middle classes who wanted something more personal than a formal hotel. The English couples who visited were from a similar background.

An Australian dentist was one of our more loquacious guests. He had a Swedish wife and had spent five months in Sweden with her family. He spoke not a word of Swedish and they spoke not a word of English. He arrived here on his own – and talked non stop until the early hours when Bill, almost dead with fatigue, insisted we all went to bed. The tirade continued at breakfast the next morning. He was like a geyser that had suddenly been uncorked – and we waved him good-bye with a great sense of relief, though we did feel very sorry for him.

A Swiss family – he a chef, she English and a secretary, and their daughter a student, made many visits. They came for a night and stayed ten days – returning many times over the years. She was especially interested in my hospice involvement as she had recently lost her mother in very sad circumstances, and had obviously never had a chance to talk about it with anyone.

Another family with hospice interests came from America. He was a Senator and a Rotarian and was involved in hospice work in America. His daughter was an air-hostess – a beautiful girl with honey coloured hair and the most delightful personality. Arriving one evening when, dressed in evening dress, I was off to an official dinner escorted by 'another man', they felt so sorry for Bill that they took him out to dinner with them, and gave him a far more enjoyable evening than I had at my very formal dinner. But the senator needed some convincing that my behaviour was not somehow improper! We made some informal links between his Rotary club and that of one of my hospice colleagues, which provided some interest to both sides.

One family we were specially fond of came from America. He was a solicitor, she an English teacher and they had three delightful teenage children. We spent many happy hours in the garden discussing education, Jane Austen, and children. We still write regularly and hope one day they will come to England again.

Judy, like so many Americans, was passionate about antiques and brought a small grandmother clock to take back. Trying to work out the best way to transport this somewhat unusual shaped object took up hours of our time – and we anticipated difficulties at the airport. But the grandmother clock travelled back in style because Judy managed to secure a whole airline seat for it – much to the curiosity of their fellow travellers.

A very attractive Frenchman turned up one Saturday afternoon while Bill was fishing. He turned out to be a racing driver and had arrived in a Porsche. I made him a cup of tea and joined him on the terrace. In the course of an hour I heard all about his life – his wife who had left him, his daughter who had lived with a man and had a son by him – and then was killed in a car crash, his other son who wanted to be a racing driver but was currently a ski instructor. He was then working as a pilot in Saudi Arabia but was having a difficult time with his boss. He also turned out to be deeply religious.

He stayed several days and we got to know him well. His visit coincided with the breakdown of my car. So he drove me to school in style each morning in his Porsche – much to the envy of the pupils who were filled with admiration not only for the car but for my dishy companion!

His son and a friend some time later came to stay with us for several weeks. They were making plans for the coming motor racing scene. They became good friends with my son and his group, and joined them on their trips to the pub and out and about – and for a time was like one of the family.

Michael and his friends descended on us unexpectedly the morning of the Open Air Concert at Leeds Castle. They booked two rooms and set off for the castle soon after – asking for a key to get in as they would be very late. They were clearly very well heeled and well bred. They had a great time at the concert and stayed on next day to swim and laze in the garden. I was more than a little shocked to see the two girls sitting there topless – it was something quite outside my experience at the time. We called them our Sloane Rangers.

This was the first of many visits by Michael . He was an interesting character, an Australian – very good looking and very arrogant – but I liked him (perhaps because he once told me, when I was in a bathing suit, that I had beautiful legs!). He came each time with a different girl – each one glamorous and very well bred – and we used to have fun speculating what his next girl friend would be like. But then he started bringing Emma. She too was glamorous and titled but was warm and friendly and we hoped he would settle down with her. But it was not to be. At the next Open Air concert he came on his own – and this was a very different Michael. The stuffing had been knocked out of him. After all the years of being the one to drop his girl friends with casual abandon, Emma had given him the push – and he was devastated. We did not see Michael again.

One especially amusing occasion was when both we and our guests were wedding bound. Our wedding was in Sussex, theirs in our village. The guests were friends of people living in the village whom we scarcely knew. They had booked our two rooms for the weekend. There was a slight problem in that we had to leave for our wedding before they were expected to arrive, but we arranged with a friend to let them in and give them a key to get back to the house if they needed to. We were very trusting in those days – but our trust was never abused.

We got back from our wedding at about nine in the evening, passing the Village Hall on the way home where the reception was still in full swing. When we reached the Oast it was shrouded in darkness, and the first thing we did was to put on all the lights and draw the curtains.

I thought it would be welcoming if I drew the curtains in the guest bedrooms so went upstairs, opened the guest room door, put on the lights, walked to the other side of the room, drew the curtains, turned to return to the door – and saw to my horror a bald head sticking out from under the bedcovers. It was the father of the family – sound asleep and snoring loudly! I don't think I have ever got out of a room faster in my life.

I did not dare to go into the other guest room, and it was long after midnight when the rest of the family returned. I dreaded meeting the family at breakfast next morning but I need not have worried. The husband had clearly been oblivious of my intrusion, and his wife confided in me later that her husband had drunk too much at the wedding and had had to be brought home and put to bed early. But she had been determined not to let it spoil her enjoyment and had gone back to the wedding. She hadn't realised that someone other than herself had drawn the curtain in their bedroom – and I certainly wasn't going to confess! But, remembering the incident in our very early days I really should have known better than to walk into a guest bedroom late in the evening!

We were very trusting of our guests and, if we wanted to go out, would give them keys to get in and out of the house, would show them how the television worked and where they could make coffee.

I remember one occasion when we had three couples in the house. They had no connection with each other but met up over afternoon tea. My sister and her husband had just moved to a new house in Sussex and we were making our first visit there. Before setting out, we left the three couples sitting happily chatting in our lounge.

We got to Horam where my sister had moved and suddenly realised we'd forgotten to bring their new address or telephone number with us. We stopped at the local telephone box and asked Directory Enquiries for help. The move was too recent for their new number to be recorded. We called at the local pub and asked if they knew of anyone who had just moved into the area. The publican was friendly but couldn't help. He gave the impression that he thought we were a little mad as Horam had quite a large population.

What to do? I knew where I had left my address book and decided the only solution was to phone home. So I rang our number, hoping against hope the guests would have the courage to pick up the phone. Eventually, after I had let the phone ring for many minutes, one of them answered the phone. 'This,' I said, 'is your hostess.

We don't know where we are going. Could you help us. I left my address book behind and I think it is on the dressing table in our bedroom. If you find it, perhaps you could look up my sister's address?'

With much hilarity, I gather, the address book was found and we were told where we were going. The incident so amused all three couples that they went out to dinner together – and by breakfast-time next morning had become the best of friends. I suspect it was a tale they dined out on when they got home!

Partly because of my archive training, and partly because we hoped that some of our visitors would make return visits, we kept a notebook in which we recorded such information as we had gleaned about them. We knew that people can feel hurt if they think you have forgotten them, so we recorded as much as we could remember – their jobs, their children, their interests. It stood us in good stead over the years.

It is amazing the information our guests imparted. Our first entry recorded the visit of the Danish couple whom we noted as middle aged, he an EEC economics adviser and his wife a doctor with two children. The next note recorded that our visitors had two adopted children, the husband was in Europe with the U.S. army and had a Mormon brother who was a missionary in England – and the family was distressed because he had deserted the Presbyterian church in which he had been brought up.

We had quite a few Mormon visitors, and could easily identify them because they always refused the cup of tea I offered them on arrival. This was something that the Tourist Board had recommended we should do as it was an easy way of getting to know what sort of people you had under your roof. It was good advice.

An early entry recorded that the wife had studied English at Lancaster University and the husband was a historian. I took them up our church tower, and cooked dinner for them – and they made a donation of £10 to the Church! One lady I recorded as being a doctor with high blood pressure – left a number of her possessions behind!

One couple I noted as being farmers from Norfolk. They were keen on riding and had a son who was a musician and in publishing. They must have enjoyed their visit because they recommended us to Elizabeth Gundry for entry into her book, *Off the Beaten Track,* a well known guide to guest houses that were a little different. We later had a visit from Elizabeth Gundry who wanted to include us in her next edition – but we had by then decided to give up.

Looking back, many of our visitors seem to have been doctors, nurses, lawyers and university lecturers. Two nurses from America who stayed with us, one of whom was a Lay Reader, told us their church had helped to pay for the restoration of Canterbury Cathedral's west window. Several of our visitors were involved in work with cancer and hospices and were interested to hear of my involvement with a hospice project. They liked to talk to our youngsters and hear about higher education in this country.

Our guests told us about their children, their illnesses, their marriages and divorces, their work, their leisure activities, their churches and their problems. For me, newly a Christian, it was good to find how many had a deep religious faith, and to be able to share with them my belief – something I was unable to do with Bill who remained militantly agnostic. Some joined me in worship at our local church.

Quite a few Americans and Canadians stayed at The Oast because they had been posted to the area during the War and wanted to revisit old haunts. Some of their war time stories were enthralling – such as the story told by the American airman who was posted to a local airfield that was being prepared for the invasion. The men were told to place all the jerry cans full of aviation fuel in the hedges round the field for safety. Unfortunately a tracer bullet hit one of the cans, and within minutes the airfield was surrounded by a ring of fire!

A number of our guests made return visits over several years and were disappointed when we stopped taking in guests. We had done our best to make them feel like personal guests rather than paying guests. We always had sherry in the lounge before they went out for dinner. And inevitably they would want to know all about the house, look at our photographs and hear all about our work, our family and our local interests. Many joined us in local activities if they happened to be here when something was going on.

We prepared a book with information and pictures about all the places of interest in the area, and had details of local pubs and restaurants, places to ride and play tennis, and travel details. Invariably, after breakfast, we would be nabbed by the guests to help plan their day. I was a little more adept than Bill at escaping and getting on with my chores (and by then, I was heavily involved with the Hospice Appeal).

It was, in fact, these morning sessions that eventually turned Bill off the project. He was far too gentlemanly to cut people off in full flow and never managed to develop a technique to extricate himself from the breakfast room. And as his desire to write burned ever stronger, so his interest in the guest-house venture diminished. He also began to feel the need to have his own house to himself, and didn't always feel like being sociable during the evenings.

The time came when we used to race to answer the telephone. If Bill got there first, he would tell callers that we were full – and I would be cross. If I got there first, I would accept the booking – and Bill would be cross! My increasing involvement with the Hospice Appeal meant that Bill was left to deal with the guests more and more often, and I no longer had a leg to stand on when it came to discussions about giving up. I agreed to close.

Our decision was made when we were really getting well known, and we could have been almost fully booked. We were receiving lots of visitors through recommendations from others. And we had also joined a group called **Distinctly Different** – people who all owned interesting but unusual houses such as mills, railways stations, barns, old churches, pig sty's, etc. We had a brochure which advertised our premises, and the leader of the group was marketing it very efficiently, getting mentions in national and local newspapers and holiday revues. And, of course, we all recommended **Distinctly Different** guest houses to our visitors, many of whom, especially the Americans, did the grand tour of England, covering as much of the country as possible in their week or two 's vacation.

This was something that always amazed me. I remember one difficult conversation with an American couple who planned in one day to visit Chartwell, Stonehenge, and Bath, and then return to us in time for dinner. They couldn't understand the impossibility of such a trip, and it took a long time to persuade them to adjust their plans.

Looking back through our Visitor's Book it is clear that The Oast had something to offer that people were looking for. Many wrote of the peace and tranquillity of the place. Others spoke of warm hospitality, and others again of the beauty of the house and gardens.

Many were the promises in our Visitor's Book, 'We'll be back', and many were the invitation to 'Come and see us.' We were given the accolade a number of times of 'The best B & B we have stayed in.' The last entry in the book reads, 'We toast your Oast. Thank you!'

It was a most interesting and enjoyable five years and a period I shall never regret.

CHAPTER 19
Back to School, 1973 – 1986

When I looked at the faded carpet in our sitting room, I smiled wryly. For it was this carpet that was really responsible for the next eleven years of my life.

Work at the Adult Education centre ended at the beginning of June. We needed a carpet and had no money to buy one. I knew another six weeks remained of the school summer term, and I also knew, this being the 1970s, that there was a great teacher shortage.

I wrote to the three Education Officers in my area to ask if there was any supply teaching available. The following day I had no less than five head teachers on the telephone, begging me to call on them the same day as they were desperate for help. It was good to feel so wanted! What a contrast to later when there are so many people out of work and even highly qualified scientists, doctors and computer experts are unable to find a job!.

I visited all five schools and, what would have been gratifying had I not known how desperate schools were, was the offer of a job by all five Heads. They all wanted me to start work the next day!

Although all the schools seemed pleasant enough, I had no difficulty in choosing. It was a somewhat quixotic choice – a down-town secondary modern school in rather run down buildings with pupils whom the Head described as 'difficult'. But I liked the Headmistress. She was elderly and tired looking, but she had a lovely smile and a warm personality.

I liked the way she spoke about her pupils. She obviously cared about them, and had a carefully worked out educational philosophy which I felt I could relate to.

She told me that many of the pupils came from difficult social backgrounds and had so many problems to cope with at home that they found it difficult to adjust to school life. She said the children needed to feel they were loved before they could respond and learn, but with the right teachers, many of them blossomed and were able to achieve success at school.

She told me she had a number of long serving staff, and that this was very important for the pupils. She also had several men on the staff. Again she regarded this as important as many of the pupils had no father or a succession of 'uncles', and found it difficult to relate to men. The men on the staff were mature and provided the pupils with standards by which to measure the men they would meet in later years.

What warmed me even more to the head was the interest she showed in my playgroup work. She said that playgroups were something the pupils at the school would have benefited greatly from had they had the opportunity of going to one. She suggested that if I were kind enough to come to the school, I could perhaps use some of my teaching techniques with the pupils in their General Studies lessons.

I felt challenged, and agreed to start the next day. I then went home and phoned the other four heads to decline their offers.

Although I had now visited five secondary schools as well as the schools my two children attended, I had never worked in one nor really taken in the environment. But as I walked into the school the next morning, all my senses were alert, and the first thing that assailed me was the smell. It took me back years to my own school days. It was an unforgettable smell, compounded of chalk dust, rotting plimsolls, chemicals from the labs, and young sweaty bodies. I remembered with a sense almost of panic the feeling of relief I had had twenty years before when I finally said good-bye to school at the age of eighteen and vowed I would never enter a school again.

But the smell apart, I had no sense of anxiety or lack of confidence. I had by now been teaching (or perhaps I should say lecturing) for five years with great success. My classes were always full and I had never lost a student. I was now involved in the teaching of English as well as pre-school education so I knew what I was about. And our own home was always full of school age children who never presented any problems. So, although I had no experience of secondary modern pupils, I had no sense of foreboding.

I was to take over the timetable of a teacher who had been rushed into hospital for a major operation. She taught a mixture of subjects – English, needlework and General Studies. I had warned the head that the sight of a needle was anathema to me – but she didn't seem to take it in, and assured me all would be well.

As a supply teacher I had no responsibility for a form, so that first morning, once the daily staff meeting was over, I had half an hour to myself while the pupils were registered and went to Assembly. It seemed good to be paid to sit idly in a staff room – but there was little I could do as I had not been given a timetable, and had no idea what or who I was to be teaching.

I heard the first tramp of feet as the pupils marched down to the assembly hall – and twenty minutes later another loud tramp as they all returned to their classrooms. A school day is governed by mass exoduses every half hour or forty minutes, depending on the length of the lesson periods. The change over from one lesson to another is rather like a mass migration with the whole school on the move. Unlike primary schools where pupils stay put, in a secondary school the pupils have to move from one special area to another – it being easier to move pupils than books and equipment. Such moves inevitably take up valuable time and, in a school where discipline is lax, it provides the opportunity for all sorts of misdemeanours.

Good management of this regular migration is one of the keys to good discipline as I was soon to discover. In fact, discipline is the key to successful teaching in a secondary school – but I will come to that later.

I recall my first day as being comparatively uneventful. Pupils usually give a new teacher a few day's grace while they assess their potential – and as I was relaxed and had no particular desire to succeed they did not, during those six weeks at the end of the academic year, discover any weaknesses which they could probe and play on. For me, it was merely a means of earning some money to buy a carpet, and the girls sensed my lack of anxiety coupled with a confidence spilling over from my previous activities, and gave me an easy time.

But some things stay in the mind. I remember noting with pleasure that all the pupils stood up when the Deputy Head and I walked into my first class. I thought it was the norm – and was somewhat disconcerted later to discover that it didn't always happen. In fact it was a courtesy that had to be demanded by the teacher; not all the staff felt it was important, and some did not have the confidence to impose such a demand.

I remember also being slightly baffled in an English lesson with a third year form by their apparent lack of comprehension of what I was talking about. Later, when I returned to the school on a regular basis and had to start getting to grips with what teaching in a down-town secondary modern school was all about, I realised that my vocabulary and the girls' vocabulary were miles apart. I had to learn, quite consciously, to simplify what I said – not only in the vocabulary I used but also in the construction of my sentences.

I learnt a lot from the Deputy Head who had been at the school for years and who was an excellent teacher. We did some team teaching together and, looking back, I realise we did a sort of *Two Ronnie's* double act (or perhaps it was more like speaking in a foreign language and having an interpreter alongside). I would tell the pupils something and then the Deputy Head would explain what I had said in what seemed to me very childlike language. It was a good learning experience for me, and by the time I left the school eleven year's later, I think I had mastered the pupils' language. But I also hope that I had been the means of enlarging theirs.

Another thing that struck me in those first weeks was the inquisitiveness of the girls. They wanted to know whether I was married, had children, and where I came from. This instantly expressed curiosity was something I had already experienced when I was working in the India Office Library. The Indian students there had no hesitation about asking a great variety of questions about one's private life – and many even went as far as to ask how much one was earning. Yet this openness was coupled with a deep inner reserve, and a suspicion and lack of trust – a contradiction which was vividly exposed and analysed in a study done by Maurice Cowley of a village group in India.

One of my early lessons was needlework. The Needlework Department was housed in two adjacent rooms with interlocking doors. The class of thirty was divided into two halves – one half to each needlework teacher. I had warned the Headmistress that needlework was not my forte, and had reiterated this to the needlework teacher who was now in charge. But she assured me all would be well as the needlework taught was of an extremely simple nature. And she added that if I did have any problems I need only pop into her room and ask for help.

It must have been in the first few minutes that I realised my fears were justified. A pupil came up to me with an extremely complicated looking garment and asked me how to do a particular seam. I have not, perhaps, expressed fully my deep antipathy to needlework. The sight of needle and cotton plunges me into a deep gloom which turns very quickly to rage as I struggle to thread a needle or try and sew without dripping blood from my finger and completely wrecking my skin for weeks to come. My family soon learnt to avoid asking me to do anything in the sewing line. Bill darned his own socks from our first year of marriage and would secretly try and repair trouser zips and splitting seams rather than risk the storm that inevitably ensued when I was faced with sewing. Alex asked for an electric sewing machine on her seventeenth birthday and this helped to ease the tension. In the early days of our marriage Bill had purchased a sewing machine for the princely sum of £4. But it was as idiosyncratic as I was, and never worked properly even though it sported the name of *Singer*.

I have often wondered why I hated sewing so much. Both my grandmother and my mother were excellent needle-women, and on the maternal side we are supposed to be descendants of the Flemish weavers. One of my earliest memories is of my grandmother arriving for a visit and settling down happily with a sewing box and a vast pile of socks to darn. My mother enjoyed making clothes, doing drawn thread work and a whole variety of esoteric ventures with needle and cotton. But somehow the sewing gene slipped me by. My encounters with needle and cotton were invariably a disaster. The cotton got knotted the minute I started sewing, and no sooner had I sorted out the knots than the cotton broke off and I was forced to start all over again. And, to make matters worse, I always pricked my index finger so badly it was painful for days after.

I recall the unutterable boredom of needlework lessons in the first year at the Grammar School when for two whole terms we made knicker linings to go inside the appalling navy bloomers we were forced to wear. I gave up needlework at the very earliest opportunity.

Perhaps my aversion is due to the fact that, being left handed I am, as my grandmother used to say when she saw me knitting, "kack handed". It would really be more accurate to say I am ambidextrous. I write and throw a ball with my left hand, hold a tennis racquet in my right, play cricket with my right, and use a knife and fork the conventional way round.

You can perhaps, therefore, understand when I say that the sight of an unfinished garment and a pupil standing before me asking for help sent me into a cold sweat. I had no idea what to do and, mumbling some excuse, slipped into the next room to ask discreetly for advice. To my dismay I found a long queue waiting to see the teacher. Brought up to respect that most British of traditions, the 'queue', I felt the only thing I could do was to join the back of it! I felt a little ignominious standing, garment in hand, among the pupils but it seemed my only option and I confess to a mild feeling of success when I returned to my own classroom and was able to help the patiently waiting pupil.

I staggered on in this fashion till the end of term, and as my need for assistance was repeated time after time, I got quite used to standing in the queue chatting pleasantly to the waiting girls who were very amiable and friendly, and soon accepted my presence as being perfectly normal.

Fortunately, my own pupils were happy with the arrangement. It meant there was no pressure on them to work and they could continue to chatter (their favourite pastime) and avoid all pretence of work while I was out of the room. They were wise enough to keep their voices down so that no prowling Head or Deputy would pop in to investigate the noise – and this happy arrangement continued till the end of term when I said good bye thankfully to teaching needlework, and vowed I would never ever venture into that arena again.

One class I had later in the week was entitled Child Care. It was with a group of fourth year girls who, I was warned, were very difficult. As the Head had told me to use some of my playgroup techniques with them I decided to do a session on children and paint, and took in my collection of the paintings of under fives and explained what they meant. The girls were fascinated. A week later, I decided to do with them the sort of session we had had on the playgroup course where they experimented with various paints and techniques and tried to experience the joys of a child playing with paint. Once again they soon became totally absorbed – as had the adults on my playgroup courses.

Not really understanding the calibre of this particular class, I was unaware that I had scored a real success. But apparently, the Head of Child care was so delighted with the pupils' response that she reported back enthusiastically to the Head.

It was this as much as anything, I suspect, that led the Head to call me in a week before the end of term and ask me to stay on the following year. The offer came at an opportune moment. I had been on the point of giving up my playgroup courses and moving over entirely to English. I was already committed to a whole day's teaching at the Adult Centre – and also to an afternoon a week looking after my aged aunt who was suffering from senile dementia, and for whom I was responsible.

I told the Head I was prepared to teach for three and a half days a week but my existing commitments prevented me from offering any more time. As I felt I was very well qualified and had a wide experience of life in other areas and was now of quite mature years, I felt justified in asking for a scale post. Although it was almost unheard of for a part-time teacher to be given one, the Head agreed to try and persuade the authorities. She succeeded and I was appointed to a Scale 3 part time-post with special responsibility for "humanities".

She also asked me to be a form teacher. I liked the idea. It gave a pastoral dimension to the work which I knew I would enjoy. But it did present a problem. I felt that if I was to be a form teacher I should be there every morning at least –

otherwise continuity would be lost – and I was already aware that continuity and security were very important in a down-town school which had an Urban Aid allowance as a school of special difficulty. We arranged that, on the day I was at the Adult centre, I would come in to school, register my class, and accompany it to assembly before going on. I also stayed on till after registration on the Friday afternoon before I set off for my stint with my aged aunt. It was worth doing, for it enabled me to develop a close rapport with the girls in my form and do pastoral work with them which I felt was as valuable as any of the academic knowledge I was able to impart.

So, come September I was all set to enter the real world of secondary teaching. It was not until this point that I was really aware of culture shock. The previous half term had been but a taster in very easy conditions. The next term was an eye opener.

But that is another story.

CHAPTER 20
Culture Shock

The first shock came early in the term when a pupil (aged fifteen) walked into my classroom one Monday morning with a black eye and what looked like a broken nose. Expressing sympathy, I asked how it had happened. She replied, quite nonchalantly, that she had been in a fight with another girl. I had never before encountered physical fighting between women. I knew they were capable of vicious verbal fights – but the thought they would resort to physical violence was another matter altogether.

"It was a fair fight, miss," my pupil assured me. "We had seconds out". And this statement was corroborated by several of her friends who were standing round listening.

Reared as I had been in a comfortable suburban environment, with a good grammar school education followed by four years at university and seven years in an academic library of world renown, I had very little idea of this other world where academic success counted for little, and survival was the name of the game. I am ashamed, when I look back, to think how cocooned I was from the harsh reality of the life of so many in our country. I feel I was really only half educated and cannot help being angry with a system which was so selective and exclusive. Much of it was my fault. I was perhaps too introspective and didn't have that curiosity about the world outside which would have drawn me to find out how others lived. But I think the system itself was as much at fault, and still is, in the upper echelons of academia.

One of the differences I noticed early on was the lack of trust. Whereas in the grammar school we were all assigned a cloakroom with our own special peg on which we hung up our coats each day, and where we left our PE bags with all our PE clothes and equipment, such facilities were totally lacking in the secondary modern school. The pupils dragged everything round with them throughout the day – coats, bags, shoes, notebooks. No one dared to leave a coat unattended because it was likely to get stolen.

The result was that every lesson began with a battle to get coats removed. The success or failure in this exercise was an indication to the pupils of whether the teacher was 'weak' or 'strict.' I soon got to know those pupils one would have to battle with. They would walk into the classroom with a challenging swagger and sit near the back of the room, hugging their coats tightly to their chest. I learnt very quickly that the class would be uncontrollable if, having asked a pupil to remove her coat and been refused, I tried to start the lesson with the jacket still on. So I would delay the battle, ignore the troublemaker, and start the lesson. This would take the wind from the troublemaker's sails because her main aim was almost inevitably to draw attention to herself. With the rest of the class settled, one could have a quiet and semi-private conversation with the pupil who would usually remove her coat without any further fuss and settle down to work.

Another thing that hit me early was the general disregard for education, which manifested itself in such simple things as coming to school without a pen. I was amazed at the number of girls who would announce, the minute you asked them to write anything, that they didn't have a pen. My own schooldays memories are of carefully kept pencil cases, with a full complement of pens, pencils, rubbers, crayons, rulers, set squares and compasses. But for many of our pupils, such possessions were non-existent. To survive, the teacher had to keep a stock of pens, pencils, rulers and rubbers – and at the beginning of each lesson, lose time in the distribution of these basic implements of education.

As an inexperienced teacher, unaware of such problems, I didn't always remember to count the pens out at the beginning of the lesson. As a result, when I collected the pens in at the end (if I remembered to do so), I was frequently short-changed, and was always having to replenish the stock from my own pocket.

I was also horrified to discover the lack of basic text books. Again, I recalled my own secondary school days when, at the beginning of the academic year, we were all issued with at least one text book for each subject. We had to cover the books in brown paper and put our names and form number on them. The books were all numbered and the teacher meticulously entered the numbers in her record book. Each pupil had her own desk in her form room where books were stored when not in use. These desks were inviolable. Any interference with another pupil's desk met with the most dire consequences.

What a far cry from this secondary modern school. Pupils were never issued with their own text books. There were not enough to go round to start with, but no one ever seemed to see the need for it. When it came to homework, pupils were usually given duplicated work sheets to work from, and as a consequence never had the opportunity to browse through nicely printed books. On the rare occasions books were issued, full sets were never available and one had to make elaborate arrangements for the sharing of books, and the provision of enough time to make the sharing possible.

Teachers in secondary modern schools have far more logistical problems to battle with than the outside world realises, and I always feel angry when I hear teachers being criticised as lazy or ill prepared.

The culture shock manifested itself as much as anything in the appearance of the girls. I had been used to a rigidly uniformed school where neatness was all-important, and any deviation was immediately jumped on. Hair had to be above the shoulder or tied back, and socks were de rigeur.

The appearance of the girls at this particular stage in the school's life was especially depressing. The school had a policy of uniform for the first four years (not strictly enforced) while the fifth year were allowed to choose their uniform colour. In my first year at the school, the fifth year had chosen brown and black and the girls walked round in a variety of drab outfits, which did nothing to enhance their appearance. At the end of every lesson, they donned their coats before moving on to the next class, and they all, invariably, had brown or black coats to match their uniform, so whenever one encountered a group of fifth years on the move, one seemed to be confronted by a heavy and threatening wall of people.

The girls had a physical maturity which I did not remember from my own school days. The long and lank hair which most of the girls sported seemed to reflect both their apathy, and their depressed attitude to school and life in general. They had no pride in their appearance and they dragged themselves round the school on tall platform shoes as though they were carrying all the cares of the world on their shoulders. In fact, I was to discover that, for many of them, this was not so far from the truth.

There were those girls in the fifth year who were happy and well adjusted, but I seemed to encounter many more who detested and resented school and could not wait to leave. It was just after the raising of the school leaving age to sixteen, and they felt trapped in an environment they could see no point in belonging to.

They were resentful of authority and extremely difficult to handle. They were physically mature and were eager to embark on the next stage of their lives. It seemed to me that many had exhausted what academic potential they had, and now wanted to "work" in the real world. The school had comparatively little to offer them – and many of the staff had no idea how to handle them.

Their resentment took the form of rudeness: deliberate attempts to flout authority, sullen responses, and constant disruption of lessons. Their main topic of conversation was boys – and many of them were sexually mature.

The school had an excellent Child Care course which was probably the only course they really enjoyed. The Child Care teacher was a wonderfully warm, motherly and caring teacher, who acted as confidante and friend to the girls – and who spent much of her time helping sort out their personal problems – which were legion. I listened on the wireless the other day to the Education Minister saying that teachers should only concern themselves with teaching their subject – but I was made aware that for very many pupils, personal cares lay so heavy, they impeded in very large measure their capacity to receive the educational input on offer.

I also discovered very early on that you had to obtain the girls' trust and respect if you were to get anywhere with teaching them. All teachers have their own techniques which vary enormously. Some have a natural authority which the pupils recognise immediately – others have to work at it, and yet others never achieve it. But what they do recognise very quickly is those teachers who really care about them. And it is to these teachers that they give their trust.

As I got to know the pupils better and was able to understand some of their problems and discover their strengths and weaknesses, I was moved to write a poem about them:

Our Girls
You can tell our girls
Any place, any time
Breasts tightly swathed
Protruding. Ships' figureheads.
Clothes high fashion
Yet drab –
Colours black and brown
Faded and lifeless. Shoes – oh, those shoes!
Platforms four inches high
Weighted, heavy,
Symbols of the cares
That cling round them – ivy,
Poisoning a childhood
They have never really known.
Eyes dull, lacklustre
Mascara shrouded
Peering sullen at all around
Vested with authority.
Full of hate
Or fear
Or just a dull unknowing
Yet, sudden shaft of light appears
At sight of child, or dog
Or someone old.
Pity? Love? Compassion?
Yes, but more – or less
A moment's sense of power, of self esteem,
A recognition that here is one
Who will not spurn, diminish, scorn,
But seek or even welcome
Attention and a little help.
Response! The face transforms.
Eyes relax,
Lips break into a smile
Contours of body soften
Warmth released.
Our girls. Enigma. Challenge.
Is school a fitting place for such as these?

In those early days I found the girls intimidating – in their height, in their maturity, in their aggressive manner, and in their unkempt appearance. It was not until I embarked on a Social Studies course which involved the girls in writing a personal profile that I realised I had been labouring under a complete misconception.

As part of their personal profile they had to record their height and weight. Few of them had any idea how tall they were – a fact that surprised me when I thought of our own household and that of many of our friends where the height of the children was recorded solemnly on every birthday and marked prominently on a kitchen or hall wall. And there was always great excitement as the children discovered how much they had grown during the year.

I had tape measures and scales at the ready, and as the pupils removed their tall platform shoes, the room was suddenly transformed from a roomful of mature young women to a group of innocent looking schoolchildren. The girls who, until that moment, had towered over me now suddenly dwindled like Alice in Wonderland and revealed themselves the children they really were. It was a moment that did much to restore my confidence.

It also made me aware that I had been treating them in a far more adult way than they were able to respond to. In fact I soon discovered that teaching in a school like this is not an easy job. Unless people have experienced it, they can have no real idea of the difficulties involved. After taking early retirement I did supply teaching for a while in a variety of schools, and was made deeply aware of the vast difference between teaching in a grammar school and in a secondary modern or high school.

It has much to do with motivation and expectation – and a lot to do with parental background. It has also to do with sanctions. In the privileged situation of a grammar school there is always the unspoken knowledge that if you don't conform you will be asked to leave. But in a secondary modern school there is nowhere lower to go – and the pupils know it.

In a grammar school it is possible to set a class work, and know the pupils will get on with it (even if they have to be left alone for a time). In a secondary modern school the teacher has to stand over the pupils much of the time to keep them working – and there is very little hope of work continuing if the teacher has to leave the room.

In making such a statement one could be accused of being sweeping and dismissive – and it's certainly not fair to the many hard working and well motivated pupils one finds in such downtown secondary modern schools that I am talking about. But the problem lies with the disruptive pupils who are, sadly, to be found in almost every class.

These are the children who, through no fault of their own, cannot cope with school life. Their domestic experiences are such that they have been badly damaged emotionally, and respond by hating the world, school, authority, police, teachers, and the whole gamut of education. Coming from disrupted homes, lacking the discipline of firm caring family life, they come to school determined to disrupt and disturb all lessons with no consideration for the harm they are causing those around them. They cannot see the point of being at school, and they deeply resent the authority of the school, and teachers in particular.

The problems of the pupils in our school were legion. Looking through my diaries I noted at the beginning of one academic year that the Head told me 'You've got a nice easy class this year'. But I was soon to discover that this so called 'easy' class contained a number of pupils with very serious domestic problems.

There was Betty whose father was a sailor and who had no settled partner. She and her father had moved from port to port over the years and Betty was quite clearly familiar with all the attractions a port had to offer!

There was Abigail who came to school very distressed one day because she had found a note in her mother's coat pocket the night before addressed to her father saying she 'couldn't go on with it any more'. She said she was sorry about the effect it would have on the children and asked her husband to look after the children and make sure they worked hard at school because she didn't want them to 'turn out bad'.

Abigail's father had left home and Abigail didn't like to speak to her mother, but was scared about leaving her alone. She did not know what to do, but was understandably very frightened about the situation.

It was a tricky problem. The note was clearly a suicide note – but how far was it within our province to interfere? After questioning Abigail closely it appeared that her paternal grandmother lived close by, and had quite a lot to do with the family. Discussion with the Deputy Head then ensued and we decided to get in touch with the grandmother. She was aware of her daughter-in-law's depression, but was house bound and could do nothing. Eventually, with her agreement, we decided to get in touch with the Social Services department who sent someone round straight away.

Next morning, Abigail came to school looking really cheerful with a note from her mother thanking us for our help. It said 'A nice man from the Welfare came out to see me and is going to help sort out my problems.' It seemed that, on this occasion, we had made the right decision – but I was well aware that such interference doesn't always produce the right results, and I confess to having spent an anxious night wondering whether our intervention would be thrown back in our faces.

Another child in the class, Marcia, went absent for five or six days and returned to school in a dreadful state. It transpired that her brother's wife had died, leaving him with two young children to bring up. They had all come to live with Marcia and her mother. But her mother was very ill indeed – a diabetic with heart trouble – and had been taken to hospital. Marcia, aged fourteen, had been left looking after her two young nieces and the household. But this was not the end of the story. For Marcia revealed that she had been fostered, and there were hints that she would 'be sent back'. There was no way Marcia could concentrate on her school work until her domestic problems were sorted out.

Annie was another lass with problems. She was alternately wild and withdrawn, and one could not get through to her. She was extremely difficult to handle – and by the end of the year, one knew why. Her father was sexually abusing her, and her mother had eventually reported him to the authorities. When the court case came up, Annie had a very bad time because somehow, all the neighbours knew what was happening, and the story got round the school.

A more unusual case was that of Henrietta – a bright and cheerful girl in her final term at the school for whom I had great hopes academically. She worked hard, was always helpful and took on a number of responsibilities in the school. But she suddenly became very difficult and totally out of control. She stopped working in class and became disruptive. One day, in a lunch hour, she daubed the classroom with lipstick and obscene comments. She tore up paper, wrote all over text books, and provoked fights with her classmates. We spent a lot of time trying to find out what was causing this sudden change of behaviour, but were quite unable to get near her to help her. She closed up like a clam and responded rudely and even violently to our attempts to help. We summoned her parents to the school but only her mother turned up, and she expressed herself totally bewildered by her daughter' behaviour.

It took a very long time to find out what was really wrong – and this only came about because Henrietta got involved with the production of the school play, and in the less formal atmosphere of after school rehearsals, she told the drama teacher, a man who worked only part time, that her mother had got involved in a lesbian relationship. She had left home, taking Henrietta with her, and moved in with her woman friend. The only way Henrietta was able to express the horror she felt was in this outrageous and wild behaviour. But though we discovered the reason for her behaviour, we didn't have the expertise to help her and, as she was on the point of leaving school, we had very grave anxieties about her future. I felt she was likely to end up on the streets, pregnant or drug abusing – but there was little we could do to help.

Then there was Samantha. Her father had left her mother with a family of six to bring up – four boys and two girls. Two of the boys were in prison, and Samantha's sister had an illegitimate baby. Samantha was a big girl – very good at sport and at drama. She was not averse to using her fists and was a real bully in the playground. She had a reading age of eight and was averse to learning. She always managed to arrive late to a lesson – and would invariably make a dramatic entrance by throwing open the door and standing glaring in the doorway at the class. She would then shout across the room at her friends. At first, I would get angry with her and try to modify her behaviour, but I soon realised that any attempt at trying to impose a normal standard of behaviour would provoke rudeness and a long drawn out battle with the inevitable disruption of the lesson. So I developed the tactic of welcoming her with a warm smile and saying, 'Hello Samantha. Nice to see you. We were just talking about …. I wonder if you have any ideas about it?'

Samantha would immediately glow, and speaking loudly, would make a number of comments on whatever topic we were discussing. She was, in fact, good at discussion and could often see the essence of a problem we were discussing. Having satisfied her need to be noticed, she would settle down as a comparatively normal member of class.

There were, of course, occasions when this ploy was not successful and I always felt we were sitting on the edge of a volcano. It was usually when things were particularly difficult for her at home. It emerged during our discussions that she did most of the cooking and ironing at home, as well as all the housework, because her mother was out at work. Her big brothers frequently wet the bed – and she often had to vacate her own bed if her brothers' beds were very wet. Is it any wonder she was unable to cope normally with school life?

Maladjusted children like Samantha, handled gently and skilfully, will often settle down and work, whereas if one takes an authoritarian stance, the chances are that the teacher will get a mouthful of abuse and constant interruptions of the lesson. But the gentle approach takes time and is often misinterpreted by the class as 'softness'. This then exposes the teacher to the danger of unruly behaviour by the rest of the class.

Were a teacher able to take a class into her confidence and say, 'Look I am treating Jane in this way because she is very unhappy and finds it difficult to behave properly. But you don't need to behave badly and so you cannot expect the same leniency', the chances are that the pupils would respond. But not many teachers have the confidence to do that, and there is always the danger that such a statement would be reported back to the problem child's family, with the inevitable consequences.

For many, the only response these disruptive children have received through school life is punishment, and they are driven further and further into feelings of resentment and hate.

The only way through is love – but that is something intangible and is slow to take effect. It was something which the Head recognised and tried to inculcate among the staff with, in many cases, considerable success. But love works slowly, and meanwhile lessons have to continue and disruptive pupils have somehow to be contained so that the rest of the class can continue learning.

The teacher who is aware of the problem, and who has the necessary emotional confidence and stability to work on this basis, has the unenviable task of trying to balance the needs of the one or two disruptive pupils and the needs of the class as a whole. What the disruptive pupil needs is time – ideally the undivided time and attention of the teacher. But when much time is given to one particular pupil, the rest of the class suffers.

Whatever the long-term solution, the immediate and urgent problem for the teacher is to deal with the disruption. Unless it is nipped in the bud, the lesson deteriorates. But there are no easy solutions. One method is to tell the pupil to wait outside the door, settle the rest of the class, and then go outside and try and sort out the transgressor. This is not easy. You dare not leave the class for more than a few minutes – and those few minutes are not sufficient for the counselling that is really needed if progress is to be made.

The Head's successor would not allow the teachers to make a pupil stand outside the classroom. She insisted they be sent straight to the Year Head who would most likely be teaching. And here another set of problems arose. For in going to the Year Head a confrontation situation is set up straight away – and the pupil who, perhaps, could have been sensitively dealt with by the teacher, now feels a resentment towards that teacher because she has involved her in a disciplinary situation.

For the inexperienced or less confident teacher, his or her so-called inability to cope has now been exposed to a senior teacher on whom references and recommendations for promotion depend. Many are reluctant to tread that path – and retain the difficult pupil in the classroom, forced thereby to spend the rest of the lesson alternating between trying to teach the class and trying to deal with a pupil who, feeling she has won, causes increasing mayhem.

Schools with this sort of problem have tried all sorts of solutions. Some have very small special classes for disruptive pupils with specially trained teachers assigned permanently to them. These classes are expensive in manpower and with the cuts that so often take place, difficult to staff.

Some schools have disciplinary 'sin bins' where pupils endure a very hard discipline for a few weeks. Often, when they are sent back to their class they are more resentful than ever. In our area there was a special unit for disruptive pupils which did very good work with them. But the demand was so great that it was very difficult indeed to get a pupil transferred – and they were often sent back before anything had been achieved.

The only real 'sanction' the school had was to suspend a pupil for three days. This was seen by many as derisory – an extra holiday whose only merit was to give the teachers a breathing space. A far more formal procedure is needed with parents having to enter into some sort of agreement to guarantee good behaviour before their child returns to school

For what it really came down to was not school inadequacy. My blood boils when I hear politicians deriding inadequate teachers when they have so little idea of what really goes on in many classrooms. It is impossible to teach effectively with a disruptive in the classroom – and that is a problem that the government then (and now) has given no serious thought to.

There was also the problem of the school truant, rounded up by the school welfare officer and sent forcibly back to school. One cannot criticise the law which makes provision for getting all children of school age into school – but it does place a burden on the teachers faced by a reluctant pupil who then disrupts the lessons of those around them. Thought should be given to making special provision for children who truant, but when I was teaching no assistance with this sort of problem was forthcoming.

Looking through the diaries of my early period of teaching, I found the following entry:

"English lesson. Had just started to get the girls writing about something that happened yesterday in order to explain to them what we mean by Reported Speech when Tracy bursts in (late as usual) saying breathlessly (as usual) 'Sorry I'm late' and walks straight to the back of the class and starts talking to Jane. Once again, a battle with Tracy – as humorous as possible otherwise one is likely to get a mouthful and waste the class's time in a confrontation. I get her settled in the front away from Jane. Her home life is appalling and Tracy can be extremely difficult. Best way to deal with her is to swallow hard, accept some of her loudness and treat her gently and humorously. She can then be very sweet as she was today.

But it was not my day! Half way through the lesson, Lorraine and Sissie decided they had done enough work and downed tools – not an unusual occurrence. I had to devote most of my attention to them in order to keep the class under control. Sissie has only just been sent back to school by the Courts after being found by the Welfare Officer serving in a shop. Lorraine's father, a gypsy, has just come out of prison. Her three sisters have all been through the school and she's definitely the best of the bunch. Her father has a violent reputation in the area and I suspect Lorraine is feeling the effects of having him home again. It can't be easy at home – her brothers have also been in prison. I like Lorraine. She has a number of redeeming characteristics – she is kind hearted and has a sense of humour, and is intelligent enough to understand both what she is doing and what is being said to her. But her response to criticism and discipline is immediate and violent.

I've found that gentle teasing and chivvying seem to be the best way to deal with her and I can usually persuade her to keep quiet – but no way can I persuade her to work if she feels she has done enough. I established a rapport with Lorraine when she learnt that Alex (my daughter) was passionate about horses – and I brought in some of Alex's horsey books for her to read which she appreciated – as she did the day I allowed her to bring her pet ferret to school and give a talk about it. She was docile for several weeks afterwards. But today it took all my patience and concentration to prevent her causing chaos, and once again I was faced with the dilemma of keeping control by concentrating on the 'baddies' at the expense of those who wished to work.'

"Baddies" and "goodies" were terms used by the Head. They somehow get down to the level of the pupil's thinking, and the childlike phrase lessens the sense of guilt and wickedness that a more formal phrase might have had. They were certainly words the pupils related to. And the pupils related to the Head. They loved her and she loved them. It was good for them – but not always quite so easy for the staff for, as I discovered, the Head tended to take the side of the pupils in any confrontation.

It was partly because of this that the staff started a *Baddies' Book* in which the serious misdemeanours of the pupils were recorded. One of its purposes was to have available 'evidence' of a pupil's misdeeds if they came up before the Suspension

Panel. The second was to give the Year Heads an overall picture of some of our more difficult girls; and the third, as mentioned above, was to provide proof to the Head that a member of staff was not the only person who had difficulties with a particular girl. The implication in any confrontation with a pupil was that the teacher had in some way been inadequate. The Head listened sympathetically to the pupil's accusations that the lesson was boring, that the teacher hadn't got down to the pupil's level, had not understood the problems of the pupil, had inadequate control, had singled out the wrong troublemaker, had insufficient tolerance, and so forth.

I have never been able to decide whether the Head had a deliberate policy in this direction, and was determined to throw back on each teacher the responsibility for the conduct of his or her own classroom; whether she felt this was a good way of getting to know what went on in the school; or whether she was unaware of the undermining effect her sympathetic ear to the pupils had on the teacher's authority. Many teachers felt she was afraid to be unpopular with the girls to whom she liked to appear as a loving mother figure.

Whatever the motive behind her approach, it had a singularly unhappy effect on some of the staff – many of whom refused to invoke her help in difficult situations in case they were accused of being inadequate. Because of this, they put up with troublemakers much longer than they should have, and difficult situations became cumulative and gradually the level of discipline in the school (and the threshold of tolerance) became lower and lower. It saddened me that many members of staff did not have the confidence to be open with the Head about their problems, because she was, in the main, a very wise and caring woman.

However the introduction of the 'Baddies' Book' promised to help solve this particular problem in that any member of staff having trouble with a particular girl, could quote the book for support of their story. The book produced much amusement in the staffroom. Incidents were recorded almost as soon as they happened and were therefore full of emotion – usually anger. In retrospect, the entries seem unreal – but they are reproduced exactly as written at the time of the incidents:

"Tracey. Passing cigarettes round during the lesson. When asked for them, refused to give them to me.

Susan H. Very rude – interfering when I was talking to another girl.

Told me I could only tell her to be quiet if I was taking the lesson.

Jane and Karen arrived ten minutes late and came into the room fighting each other.

Kim barged into the room while 3R was waiting to be dismissed. Shouted across room and was very rude and unpleasant. When threatened with being taken to see the Head, said 'You'll have to catch me first.'

Sissie said 'You are a cow, miss'.

Margaret threw a ruler at Ann and almost hit her and made her cry. When corrected she swore – using an awful mouthful.

When told to go to Assembly became most difficult and told me to 'shut my mouth'.

Gale banged the arm of another girl (which was already sprained). When spoken to severely by me told me I couldn't tell her what to do – only her mother had that right. When told to wait, pushed on past me and went up to dinner.

When told not to use the milk door because there was an exam going on, her reply was 'Oh, fucking hell'. Solution – decapitation?

Anita. Putting on make up. Doing hair and applying lacquer instead of doing history.

On Thursday Julie would not stop talking and was a disruptive influence on the girls round her. I thought moving her would be the answer. After telling her to move three times, she reluctantly moved and as she passed me called me a 'Stupid Woman'. I sent her to the Head to whom she told a completely different story and she was soon back in class without an apology. I felt like sending her out again but did not like to make a fuss.

I have had these girls for three lessons so far today and their behaviour has been beyond description. I am speechless with disgust.

Very unco-operative. No pens or pencils. Goading Margaret G.

Telling foul tales in a loud voice. Vanessa tried very hard not to work. Fight brewing between her and Annie – planning to meet behind the gym.

They were playing a word game and began to needle each other over their respective scores. Then they began name-calling, challenges were issued and they began to fight. I separated them with the help of Jane. By this time a certain amount of hair had been pulled out and the shirt Jane was wearing was ripped.

Sissie. Noisy and abusive through the lesson. She ended by emptying the waste bin over Jeanette. When asked to pick it up shouted 'You miserable four eyed cow.' However, she had to do as asked and grudgingly apologised because the door was locked.

Disgusting behaviour. Throwing sugar and wet towels around cookery room, shouting and screaming and uncontrollable behaviour. Would not stop.

Arrived fifteen minutes late for maths and stood at door of mobile yelling like fishwives at the boys across the road.

Nicola arrived half way through the lesson armed with a lolly but no pens and pencils. Would not stop sucking the lolly. She tells me she has enough detentions to last till the end of term.

Wrote on another girl's face with a biro she had pinched from another girl.

Screamed out of the window at two boys at the bus stop – Jane was particularly crude and suggestive.

Yvonne. Unspeakable behaviour. They began by making paper darts with the paper they were supposed to be writing on. They quietened down for a few moments and then began playing tennis with screwed up paper. They screamed, shouted and sang. I sent for the Deputy Head but she was unavailable. Eventually they became bored and quietened down.

Ran across the room and caught her ankle in the heel of my shoe. She then screamed 'You kicked my toe you f…ing old cow."

Perhaps the most serious incident of all was when, after a major confrontation in a classroom, a girl was sent to the Year Head who interviewed her in a little room at the end of the corridor. The girl rushed screaming out of the room and locked the teacher in. The only way the teacher could get out was to climb through the window onto a ledge and call for help!

I found in my eleven years at the school that the only way through was to treat the pupils with unfailing courtesy, show that one cared for them, and demonstrate slowly but surely that there were boundaries beyond which you would not let them go. I tried to keep the boundaries as wide as possible, and my classes were often fairly noisy. But the work got done and the pupils and I developed a mutual respect.

It was not an easy road to follow. Such an approach takes time – and the early days with a new class were often hard going as the pupils slowly discovered that though I was gentle I was not 'soft'. But over the years the pupils' response was positive and I recall one letter from a pupil after she left which said 'I know I played you up a lot to begin with, but you were the only teacher who cared, and I am grateful to you.' She kept in touch for many years, as do others.

In the avoidance of confrontation with disturbed and disruptive children, one's antennae have to be finely tuned, and extreme sensitivity and skill is required to defuse a situation before it gets out of hand.

But teachers are vulnerable – and never more so than in the presence of colleagues. They are always looking over their shoulder, knowing their future careers and promotion are dependent on the references of the Head and their seniors.

Where a teacher might handle a situation in a particular way on his own, the presence of a colleague can often destroy a sensitively contrived link, and a minor incident becomes a major confrontation. Children who lack confidence, as do most disruptive pupils, often feel threatened at the presence of two teachers – hostile alien adults – and do not know how to cope with the situation. Often their reaction, occasioned by fear, becomes aggressive. And since the teacher before a witness is also experiencing a form of fear – 'What will my colleague think?' – the situation becomes fraught with difficulty before any verbal exchange takes place whatsoever. Only the supremely insensitive teacher can cope with such a situation in a really relaxed manner.

The whole question of discipline is a complex one and I feel it is not given enough attention in the training of teachers. For unless a teacher can control a class there is absolutely no way he can teach it – even though he may be in essence a very good teacher.

How often, for example are teachers forced to look at schools from a pupils point of view?

The pupil is, more often than not, happy in his primary school where he spends his time in one classroom with one teacher who gets to know him really well.

He then comes to a secondary school where he finds himself having to relate to a different teacher for a whole variety of different subjects. The only continuity is provided by his form tutor whom he will see briefly once or twice a day at registration time and who may or may not teach him.

During the day therefore, at forty minute (or thereabouts) intervals, he will meet up with some eight different teachers – some male, some female. Each has a very different style of teaching and each has very different ideas on discipline. What is tolerated by one is abhorred by another. The easy relationship encouraged by one teacher is regarded as rudeness and presumption by another. One teacher makes them stand up on entry; another makes them line up outside the classroom before entering. One encourages a little quiet discussion between the pupils about their work; another demands absolute silence. One does not notice (or does not bother with) minor infringements of uniform; another is down on them like a ton of hot bricks. One teacher encourages pupils to question and challenge them; another regards questioning as presumption or an attempt to delay getting down to work. For a child who is not secure in himself, these constant changes and different role models are difficult to adjust to. And for the child who is not very bright, these constant changes are totally confusing.

And for the teacher there is another aspect to this problem of different styles of teaching and discipline. What goes on in the previous lesson often affects the next one. The pupils who have been screwed down into total silence and obedience by a strict disciplinarian whom they fear, will often feel such a sense of release in the next lesson that the teacher will have a difficult time trying to calm them down and get them working again.

This was something I discovered from personal observation after I had been at the school for quite a time. I had occasion to observe on a number of occasions the pupils coming out of the class of a particularly strict disciplinarian – and then hearing the rumpus in their next class, which happened to be next door to my room, with a teacher who normally had no trouble with her classes. The strict disciplinarian was superior about the other teacher's difficulties – but I couldn't help but ask whether she benefited by receiving pupils from teachers who had held the pupils on an easier rein.

Discreet research, questioning and observation gave strength to my theory – and I wonder whether it has ever been researched seriously.

Although discipline is one of the major problems of teaching in a down-town school, another equally serious one is apathy and lack of motivation. I speak now of the 1970s and early 1980s, but the current situation is not so very different – and perhaps even more so with the high levels of unemployment that abound.

Half the pupils came from the centre of the town – an area of nineteenth century houses built cheek by jowl, with doors opening straight onto the pavement, and with tiny gardens at the back. The others came from a pre-war extremely dilapidated council estate. There were few open spaces around, and the town itself was dark and depressing. The school's playing field was the only sizeable open space in the area, and the local primary schools had to make do with small tarmac playgrounds – many of which abutted onto busy main roads.

I couldn't help contrasting the beautiful surroundings in which our own children were brought up – an acre of garden, panoramic views, and fields all around – with the dismal environment in which the pupils lived. Was it any wonder that so many of them rebelled and were disruptive – while others lapsed into apathy and gave up in despair.

Once a year, near the end of the summer term, I used to take my own class for a day's outing. The day started with a visit to one of our local stately homes, and I would then bring them back to The Oast where we had a barbecue. I gave them the run of the house and garden, including the swimming pool – and we put up the badminton net and the croquet posts in the garden, and the table tennis in the house. My husband always joined in and helped look after them – and I tried to make it as much of a family day as possible.

The girls were, of course, amazed at the size of the house and garden and I was always very careful to show them our 'before and after' photographs, and tell them how little it had cost us and how we had done most of the work on the house ourselves. I did not want them to get the impression that we were very wealthy and had life easy, but I did want them to see what hard work and enterprise could lead to if one was determined enough.

These outings were always a delight to me because the girls were so happy. They were always extremely careful with our property, and insisted on washing up and leaving the place immaculate. Some of my colleagues used to say I was mad – especially bringing home some really difficult troublemakers, and some who were known to be light fingered. But I never lost anything and there was never any damage. The girls appreciated the trust that was placed in them by coming into 'miss's home' and they responded accordingly.

On the coach going back, the girls would often persuade me to bring my daughter along – and they would take her over and make a great fuss of her. I must confess that there were one or two occasions when I wondered whether their singing on the return journey was entirely suitable for the ears of our 'innocent' little daughter, but in later years she assured me that she heard nothing she had not heard before at school! So perhaps it was me who was a little naive.

I was constantly made aware of the contrast between our own children, with their secure and loving family, and so many of the children at the school (probably as many as a third of the pupils) who came from one parent or broken families. Many had to cope with stepmothers or fathers or 'uncles' who changed with alarming rapidity. Many had fathers or brothers in prison or borstal – and in any Social Studies lesson when Crime and Punishment was discussed, more than half the class invariably admitted to having close associations with someone who had seriously transgressed the law.

Many children came from large families – often seven or eight children – and were crowded into small council houses. At a time when the national average number of children per family was 2.4, the school average worked out at 4.5.

In those early days at the school I was frequently brought up short by differences in attitude and outlook. The children were aware of our different backgrounds and were not afraid of talking about it. I recall one occasion when we were reading 'Great Expectations' and had come to the part where the convict, Magwitch, returns to England to seek out Pip who is living as a young gentleman in London. We read of Pip's horror at discovering that his benefactor was not the refined, if dotty, Miss Haversham, but a low working class convict. It seemed a good moment to pause and talk about the great social divides of the nineteenth century. But, before I knew where we were, we were into a heated discussion about 'Them' (the snobs) and 'Us' (the common people). I asked them to define what they meant by 'snob' and suggested a better classification might be between nice people and nasty people (the good and the bad) because both sorts were to be found in all walks of life. But no! The girls were very aware of class divisions and felt there were very deep divisions between people. They felt a detestation for 'snobs' who, they said, were horrid and without any virtues. Their definition of a snob was a little hazy. They were people who looked down on them, spoke posh and 'never have any fun and never laugh'.

They hastily excluded me from being a snob by saying, 'You're posh, you speak nice. But you're not a snob cos you don't look down on us.'

One girl actually said, 'Well, you see miss, if someone falls down in the street, a snob will stop and pick him up. But we common people would just stand and laugh at them'. This was a definition which horrified me at the time and still does – but as I write this I have before me a copy of the local paper whose front page story is about a policeman who was attacked and knocked down in the street, and when his girl friend asked for help, the people stood round and jeered. It is a depressing commentary on our times. But it also highlights some of the class differences which the girls were aware of but could not define.

Whereas we were brought up to trust and respect the police and would have no hesitation in calling on them for help, many of the girls and their families detested the police and would do anything to avoid contact and prevent them from doing their duty. It was a reflection of the criminal record of many of their families, but it was very sad.

Later in our Social Studies lessons, I tried to break down this barrier by inviting in the local Community Policeman who was sensitive and had a great understanding of the area. He did much to break down the prejudices of the girls he taught, and became a familiar and welcome figure in the school. Unhappily, his particular style of working did not go down too well with his new superior at the local police station, and he was moved on – and, disillusioned, soon left the force altogether.

But, to go back to class distinctions, I think what really got to the girls and angered them was when they were treated as inferior beings and were 'looked down on'. I had a lot of interesting discussions following the showing of the BBC films 'Seven Up', 'Seven plus Seven' and 'Twenty-One' which followed a group of children from different backgrounds through the years and tried to discover the effect of environment on educational progress.

The girls hated the thought of private education – especially boarding schools, and had absolutely no illusion about the sort of reception they would get if their parents suddenly came into money and they were sent to a 'snob' school.

Speaking 'posh' was one of the big distinctions, and in fact was a problem that exercised a number of our pupils who lived on the edge of the catchment area in owner-occupied houses. Some had only just missed getting a place at the grammar school. A number spoke with fairly polished accents but in school, in order to survive, adopted the local accent – knowing full well they would have a bad time of it if they used their 'posh' home accents. It was always intriguing to meet them on Open Days with their parents and hear the transformation.

I found the girls extremely warm and friendly and was happy to relate to them in a far more personal way than my teachers had to me. I felt it was important. They knew about my children and what they did, about my husband and my senile aunt. One day I came into school a little late and apologised explaining that my daughter was ill. They were concerned and wanted to know who was looking after her. I explained that my cleaning lady was with her. This loosed a torrent of questions and comments which went something like this:

'You have a cleaning lady miss?'
'You mean someone goes into your house when you're not there?'
'Why yes, I do.'
'Ow does she get into the house?' asked Patsy – always the practical one.
'Well'. I replied, 'I give her a key'.
'Cor, I wouldn't trust no one with a key to my house', said Patsy (not perhaps, surprisingly, as her family was notoriously light fingered.)
'Oo, I wouldn't like no one going into my house poking her nose into all my things.'
'Coo miss, you aint 'alf a snob'
'How much do you pay her, miss?'
'About eight pounds a week. She works for seven hours so it's just over a pound an hour.' (This was 1975).
'But that's an awful lot of money. Why don't you do your own work like my mum? She don't have no one to help her.'
'Well,' I explained, 'When you're a teacher, you have an awful lot of marking and preparation to do when you get home. And there's the cooking and the shopping – and I like to spend time with my children and help them with their homework. If I had to do all the cleaning as well, I wouldn't have any time to relax. So I think it's better to have a little less money and a little more time.'

I watched the girl's reaction to this. Some could see the sense in my statement and nodded agreement, and when I explained that my cleaning lady was able to choose the time when she came to suit her own timetable, Karen said thoughtfully, 'You know, miss, it's not a bad job for someone, is it?'

But some of the girls were not convinced of the morality of letting someone else do your housework. Anita announced that she thought it was 'downright lazy not doing your own work', while Susy, when she discovered my cleaning lady also hung out my washing and did the ironing, indicated that I had sunk to the depths in her estimation.

One of the things I really enjoyed was having my own class. The Head was innovative and when I first arrived there was Family Grouping. My pastoral group comprised pupils of all ages, ranging from eleven to sixteen. There was a lot of merit in this – giving the older pupils a chance to care for the younger ones and being able to feel looked up to and valued. But there were disadvantages when there were 'baddies' in the group as the young ones were easily led astray.

In my second year at the school the Head reverted to the more conventional arrangement and I found myself then and in the following years with either fourth or fifth year girls (fifteen to sixteen) with whom I was most at ease.

In having a class one took on pastoral responsibilities – and in a school like ours, these were considerable. In fact, in such schools, there is a conflict between being a teacher and being a social worker. A teacher is appointed to teach – but when pupils are facing insuperable domestic problems they are unable to learn. The teacher then either has to give up or develop some of the social work skills. It's a question of survival.

For many of the children the secure person in their lives was granny – and as the extended family was commonplace, granny usually lived nearby and did a lot of the caring. At Open Days one could identify those parents who had major domestic problems to cope with. They were downtrodden in appearance and looked years older than their years. Many had neglected their teeth – and it was difficult to believe we lived in a welfare state. Much of it was due to ignorance caused by low intellect – and this was one of the reasons for the high birth rate. But poverty was very great.

But it was not necessarily ignorance of contraception that led to fourth and fifth year pregnancies. The pupils had the most excellent lessons on contraception by our dedicated Child Care teacher. But some of our girls had had such an especially difficult childhood that they sought pregnancy, albeit unconsciously, in order to possess something of their own to love. And so the cycle of deprivation continued.

Girls who became pregnant would proudly bring their babies into school with no sense of shame or wrong doing. And the Child Care teacher spent many a Sunday at christenings and even some Saturdays at shot gun weddings – trying to support these girls who had so little support from home.

How, I ask, can one really tackle 'standards' in those schools where such major social problems exist. Surely these need to be tackled and incorporated into the thinking if any real progress is to be made?

Molly with staff of Christchurch School, third from left in the front row, wearing tartan

CHAPTER 21
Curriculum Innovations

My first four years at the school were, in fact, very enjoyable – largely I think, because the Head not only encouraged me to experiment in my English and Social Studies teaching, but also in certain other areas of the curriculum. This was something which pandered to my enjoyment of innovative challenges.

Some of the experiments were bizarre and a far cry from a conventional academic curriculum. I am sure they would be would be regarded with horror by some of our recent Education Secretaries who have pontificated loudly about the need for 'standards' and have been deeply critical of the teaching profession.

But when one regularly had an intake where nearly a third of the pupils had a reading age of less than ten, and took into account the very deprived social background of many of the children, one understood why the Head felt it needful, and indeed worthwhile, to try curriculum innovations which might capture the pupils' interest and help break through their problems and their lethargy, and inculcate a desire to learn.

One has only to recall the story of Kes about a boy from a similarly deprived background, whose refusal to learn and conform is overcome only when he finds a baby kestrel. His urgent need to learn how to care for the kestrel propels him into the local library where he discovers the relevance and the joy of being able to read. Of course, that particular story has a tragic ending when the boy's new found joy is shattered when his corrupt but equally deprived step-brother murders his kestrel.

Looking back, one of the more bizarre curriculum experiments was the Free Activities period. I say bizarre but that is to belittle what I think had a sound educational basis. The pupils lived in an area where 'there's nothing to do, miss.' I don't think it was any different from other urban areas. The problem here, as elsewhere, was that the children did not have the understanding or imagination to involve themselves in the activities on offer.

It was a period when there was an awareness that changes were taking place in society and that people were going to find themselves with far more leisure time than ever before. Unemployment hadn't raised its ugly head in quite the way it has now, but there were numbers of people on a short working week, and numbers more who were unemployed.

The Head said, 'Children are growing up into a world where they will have an increasing amount of leisure time and many of the children in our school do little with their leisure time other than watch television. It is our responsibility, as part of the education of these children, to help them make better use of it.'

The Head therefore proposed to try and encourage their creativity by giving them one hour a week when they could choose to do whatever they wanted within the confines of a classroom. I, with four others, was one of the teachers she asked to be involved in the experiment.

Many of our colleagues were deeply suspicious of this 'new subject'. The very name, 'Free Activities' suggested a woolly option which would open the door to indiscipline and mayhem. Those who saw life in terms of black and white were deeply suspicious of the statements she used to justify the experiment: 'Children need an opportunity to make choices in order to develop their personalities'; 'Freedom not licence is what we should aim at'; and, 'The child who cannot play cannot learn'

The budget was small – but I was allowed to gather together books (fictional and instructional), painting and craft materials, a number of board games and a record player.

At the start of the experiment, the pupils were given the choice of using either the materials on offer by the school or those they had brought in themselves. When we started I soon found that the girls seemed unable to concentrate on one activity for any length of time, and would jump from one thing to another with great rapidity. There was a restless atmosphere in the room and I decided something drastic needed to be done if the experiment was to succeed.

I felt they somehow needed to be pinned down in one place, while at the same time having the freedom to choose what they would do in that place. I hit on the idea of a train journey.

I explained carefully to the class that they had to imagine they were going on a very long train ride. I told them they had to bring with them the activities they would like to be involved in for the duration of the journey.

The idea touched a chord and the next week when they arrived in the classroom they set to with great enthusiasm to arranging the classroom like a train with various compartments. They then all took their seats and started sorting out their goods and chattels for the journey.

It was not long before a discussion ensued as to whether or not there was a lavatory on the train. (After careful observation over a longish period, I had come to the conclusion that, in our school at least, there seemed to be a correlation between low intelligence and weak bladders. I know such a statement is open to the accusation of naivety, and that people would say it was the lure of escape from the classroom to the toilet that was the reason for the frequent requests to go to the toilet! But I think it was more complex than that. In those with lower intelligence, there is an absence of planning and of understanding the consequences of an action. This, I suspect, is one of the reasons for the high incidence of pregnancies among the unmarried, and for the large size of families in the area. It was not that contraceptives were not available – rather that they did not plan ahead. Similarly, where people are more physical than cerebral, the discomforts of a full bladder seem more likely to be dominant.

So, after thinking about it for a moment, I told the children that the toilets on the train were not working properly – and then added that the restaurant car was out of action because the staff were on strike. The girls accepted the statement meekly and settled down to their activities. It was a far more peaceful lesson and at the end the girls all declared that 'that was a good lesson, miss' and 'Could we do it again next week?'.

I readily agreed!

Come the next week, the girls rushed into the class to arrange the desks, and then stood solemnly at the front of the class without sitting down. I was puzzled and asked them what was the matter. 'Oh miss! We're waiting for the train to arrive.' Such an obvious explanation had quite eluded me! A few moments later, there was a realistic hoot as the train arrived at the platform and all the girls piled into their respective compartments.

No sooner had the train 'left the platform' than the children dived into their bags and brought out an assortment of knitting, books, games and newspapers. They had really thought about what do on the journey and I realised, not for the first time, how important it is to stimulate the imagination of children if one is to get a really good response.

But I watched open mouthed as I observed one girl bringing out a paper bag and unwrapping a pile of sandwiches. I was even more dumb struck as she proceeded solemnly to eat the sandwiches. When I recovered sufficiently to ask what she thought she was doing, she replied happily, 'Oh, we always eat sandwiches on a train journey,' and continued to munch happily.

Her friend brought out a bar of chocolate and said, 'You see, miss, there was a notice at the end of the platform that said the restaurant was closed because of a strike so we thought we'd better be on the safe side and bring our own food.'

What could I say? I was, as the saying goes, 'hoist with my own petard'!

As might be imagined the Free Activities lessons were regarded with considerable suspicion by the more conventional members of staff, and as it had not been resourced very generously, and two of the staff involved in the first experiment moved to other schools at the end of the year, it was dropped from the timetable the following year.

But it did, in fact, stimulate a lot of discussion in the staffroom. The school was in an Educational Priority Area and, as I said before, had a higher proportion than most secondary modern schools of children with a low reading age. There were a large number of children with reading ages of around eight and nine and very significant learning problems. A lot of effort was put into the remedial department, but the school had very few qualified remedial teachers, and many of the children of very low ability were in 'normal' classes and had to be dealt with by conventional subject teachers who had little or no training in special education.

One of the problems that was apparent to all was that the girls did little or no reading for pleasure at home. When talking to them, one became aware that few had had the joy of being read to as children. The nightly bedtime story was not part of their experience – and to them books were a chore – a part of dreary school life.

So, after the end of the Free Activities experiment, we embarked on another curriculum innovation. The last half hour of each morning was devoted to a Reading period. Each class was provided with a box of books, carefully chosen (as we hoped) to suit the girls' tastes and abilities. A lot of careful preparation went into the selection of the reading boxes and we started the experiment with enthusiasm and high hopes.

In some classes it went well – with the teacher from time to time reading out to the class snippets of books she had enjoyed and encouraging the girls to do likewise. They were allowed to bring their own books from home – but comics (perhaps unwisely) were not allowed. For many of the girls, the reading period was an oasis in the day which they much enjoyed. For others, it was a torture.

The experiment was particularly difficult with fourth and fifth year girls, many of whom were settled into the non reading habit, and resented having to sit still and read for a half-hour. Many teachers of senior classes dreaded the Reading Period, knowing they would have endless trouble with the disruptives in the class. This experiment survived for two years before, by popular consent, it was jettisoned.

Longer term benefits, we felt, were more likely to arise from Library lessons during the first two years. We were fortunate in having a dedicated teacher in charge of the Library who had an intuitive understanding of the sort of environment likely to appeal to the girls. The Library was light and airy, with fitted carpets and armchairs, lots of plants and interesting wall displays. She had Library Monitors from both Junior and Senior parts of the school who were given considerable responsibility in the running of the library. And, above all, she had a dedicated woman who was the Library Assistant and manned the library throughout the day.

Having spent half a term learning how to use the Library and discovering its contents, the girls were then given a Library project to do. Each chose her own subject, and it was obvious they enjoyed doing their projects and put a lot of effort into them.

At first, I felt these project were valueless. The girls copied out information verbatim, often using at most two books as source material. There was no critical analysis at all and very little individual input. I started to think about project work in general and looked round at the different subject departments in the school. It was clear that there was a great emphasis on project work for CSE – particularly for the Mode 3 examinations.

I was, to begin with, fairly critical of this project work and eschewed it altogether in my own subjects, but I came to realise that I was cutting out an area of experience which the girls enjoyed and from which they could benefit if the work were structured carefully. So I started doing project work in English – using it as a vehicle for learning about the make up of well prepared textbooks so that the mechanics of the project became as important as the text. I insisted on a beautifully prepared title page, introduction, list of contents, list of illustrations, text, bibliography, appendices and index. I encouraged them to incorporate first hand information and ideas, and I never allowed them to copy anything direct (except the occasional quotation) but always insisted they paraphrased information in their own words. When I extended project work into Social Studies, I encouraged interviews and questionnaires which added to the interest of the work.

But to go back to the Library. I realised, when I had been at the school for a time, that the Library was one of the most popular areas of the school. It was always full during the lunch break and for many was a quiet refuge from the noisy and at times frightening playground where it was quite obvious that bullying and intimidation took place, although it was not always easy to identify.

An experiment of a rather different nature was the Water Project which we embarked on in the midst of another curriculum innovation where we rotated girls among a small group of teachers on an Environmental Studies course. As we were in the midst of a period of severe drought such as we have several times since been threatened with in the south east, we decided in the summer term to do a Water Project. We had a happy and successful term studying water from a variety of angles – starting by listing all the ways water could be saved in the home.

Not having given a great deal of thought to it, I encouraged the girls to do some measuring of water at home. The girls' response was varied. One conscientious pupil actually persuaded her mother to measure how much water she used during her weekly Monday wash! She must have been a saintly and long suffering woman! But another girl came into school with the comment, 'My dad says you must be bonkers, miss', and I could not but agree with him.

We did some fairly elaborate work, with the help of the Geography Department, on the water cycle, and we enlisted the help of the Science Department to measure rainfall – but, as we had virtually no rain the whole of the term, this was not exactly a success.

We then moved on to water transport and studied rivers and locks – and were able to hire from the County Education Film Library some very interesting films on canals and the major rivers of the world.

We made a visit to the local Waterworks where the water was extracted from deep underground reservoirs. Some of the explanations were over the heads of the girls – but outings were always enjoyable – an escape from school – wherever they went.

As the end of term approached, the little group of teachers involved in Environmental Studies was feeling very satisfied with the success of the course, and decided to set a small end of term exam to see how much the girls had, in fact, absorbed.

We prepared the exam paper very carefully – setting it out as attractively as possible in keeping with our stated aim of making the girls more environmentally aware. We felt we had produced a model exam paper and looked forward eagerly to reading the answers.

Our eager anticipation was justified – but not in quite the way we expected. The answers produced hilarity in the staff room for some weeks to come. I reproduce some below:

The first question,' List four ways in which you can save water' elicited the answers: 'Put a brick down the lavatory; use less water; people try to save water by using less; and, put wood up when it rains to stop water coming fru.'

The second question,' What is the average consumption of water per day in the average household?' left us with a choice – 3 pints or 600 gallons!

Asked to describe the water cycle, one child did a beautiful drawing of a bicycle attached in a mysterious way to a stream, while another replied: 'The water cycle is a whirlwind stream which rushes round and round very fast.'

It was difficult to unravel the thought process behind the answer 'We get most of our water from sawsers' to the question 'Where does most of our water come from in the area?'

Following a brilliant exposition of the working of a canal lock by one of my colleagues, with a clear diagram which all the girls had copied into their notebooks, we asked them to describe how a lock worked.

On one answer paper, we found an elaborate drawing of a key and keyhole. Another child wrote: 'A lock works if you put a key to a shed.' And another said, 'A lock works by putting a catch on it.'

Perhaps the best answer was from a child who said, 'A lock works by getting out of a boat, then you open a gate and a man dives into the lock, and the water in the lock gets higher by the water going in and then they open a gate.' We couldn't help but wonder what happened to the man!

At the end of the exam paper we put in a couple of questions about volcanoes and earthquakes which we had studied just two weeks before. I was informed by one pupil that 'Japan was completely destroyed by an earthquake', and that among the world's best known volcanoes were Big Ben, China, Mount Everest and Mount India.

Such results brought sharply to the fore, as so often happened in this school with pupils of low ability, the question, what was one doing in this teaching game and what, if anything, were we achieving. The answer, as always, was very elusive.

I have already touched on the excellent Child Care course in the school which was probably the most popular on the syllabus. Maggie, the Child Care teacher, was a jolly, well upholstered lady in her late fifties. She radiated warmth and motherliness and I felt instinctively when I first met her that she was the sort of person a girl would turn to if she were in trouble. My instincts were correct. Maggie had a wide-ranging knowledge of the girls and their problems, and a rapport with them which many of us envied. Her laugh was infectious and she had a fund of stories – many of them earthy and not fit for polite company – about the girls who had passed through her hands during the twenty years she had been at the school. She had lived in the neighbourhood all her life and many of her current pupils were the offspring of pupils she had taught years before.

Weddings of former pupils were a regular feature of her weekend activities, and on many a Monday she would regale us with detailed and lively accounts of the wedding she had attended over the weekend – with gloomy predictions about the outcome of the union. As she often knew the backgrounds of both bride and groom, her knowledge of the respective families went back over several generations. We knew her pessimistic prophesies had a good chance of being fulfilled.

Maggie's aim in life was to try and break the cycle of deprivation by making the girls aware of the importance of good mothering in the early years – a mothering which included not only good physical care but also the introduction of good early play materials and books. I felt deeply in tune with her thinking, and did all I could to reinforce her work through my Social Studies course which I introduced in my second year in the school when I started working full time.

Saddened by the problems of unmarried mothers in the area, her first priority was sex education – giving the girls explicit information about contraception (including the handling of a variety of contraceptive devices) and showing them films about reproduction and childbirth. There were some excellent films available through the Education Library which were an invaluable part of the course.

Looking back over the years, I remember my feeling of anger when, just before Aids became so prominent, there was a Government initiative to make parents rather than schools responsible for sex education. We all felt threatened for a while and worried that we would be hauled up for our sex education courses. For this was an area of work which we felt was very important. We knew many parents were unable or reluctant to teach their children adequately about sex.

One of the moral problems involved in sex education was how far explicit information would encourage pupils into early sexual experiment. It was easy to talk about the mechanics of sex – not so easy to discuss relationships and even more difficult to try and uphold a moral code in which one knew a number of one's colleagues, and many of the pupil's families, did not believe. This was the seventies when casual sexual relationships were considered both normal and emotionally healthy – when the barriers about the explicit portrayal of sex in films and television were falling down rapidly despite the efforts of people like Mary Whitehouse, and when many of one's colleagues were enjoying open relationships which many of the pupils were fully aware of.

Maggie's approach to this problem was indirect. She spoke warmly and frequently of her own husband and children and their happy family situation, and involved her husband and children in a number of school activities. She radiated such warmth and contentment that the pupils had the opportunity of observing at first hand the values of a conventional and strictly moral family situation.

She organised a Community Service programme for the fifth year girls who went out once a week to a variety of playgroups, nursery schools and primary schools, and helped with the toddlers. Each pupil had to do a project – a study of a pre-school child.

The course included child birth, health, nutrition, clothing and hygiene, and play. It was a Mode 3 course which inevitably involved a considerable amount of internal work and moderation for the teacher.

This was, of course, before the introduction of GCSE with its emphasis on course work. As someone who had been brought up on conventional end of year formal examinations, I was very interested to see how the Mode 3 examination worked and spent quite a time trying to evaluate it.

I came to the conclusion that it was an excellent way of measuring a pupil's understanding of a subject and the degree of his interest and effort. Where, of course, it was not so effective was in measuring the amount of solid learning and memorising that the pupil had done. The Mode 3 examination certainly provided the opportunity for a pupil to explore a subject in his own particular way and to bring to it his own particular slant and interests. But for many, of course, the input was minimal and the system was open to abuse by the less conscientious teacher.

CHAPTER 22
English and Social Studies

Given the area the school served and the problems that so many of our pupils had to contend with, the type of curriculum offered to the pupils had a very significant bearing on the way they coped with their lives once they left school. Literacy and numeracy were, of course, the first priority – although the low level of literacy among the pupils, which horrified me, suggested at first glance that this had not been given the priority it should have been at primary school. As I got to know the pupils better I realised that, although some of it was attributable to the very low IQs of many of the pupils, it also had much to do with low levels of motivation and self esteem which was caused by poor and inadequate parenting rather than poor teaching.

I had great sympathy with the Head who was prepared to experiment with curriculum innovations which she thought might help the pupils cope with life better.

But it was clear to me that basic literacy was the priority and I was very happy to be involved in the teaching of English. As I got to know the staff better, I realised that very few in the school taught their specialist subject: although I was a History graduate, I was responsible for Humanities and also taught English.

I felt deeply committed to my English teaching and over the years achieved a measure of success that made it seem well worth while. But I had to work very hard at it. A number of observations led me to develop my own particular strategies to encourage the pupils. I observed quite early on that, whereas if you read a pupil's work it was illiterate, if you let them read it out loud to the class, it was totally comprehensible. There was a serious gap between the thought process and the mechanics of writing it down. Lack of specialist training made it difficult for me to know how to cope with this problem, but I discovered that if a pupil received praise for her verbal offering she was more likely to work hard at improving the written work.

Dyslexia was not widely accepted as a problem at that time in state schools, but looking back, I am sure a number of pupils who struggled in the lower streams were in fact dyslexic.

I have already mentioned the problem of language and the need to simplify the way I talked to pupils but I was determined that their vocabulary should be enlarged and we spent a lot of time playing a variety of word games.

But perhaps my major contribution to the girls' educational development was discussion work. This was something I enjoyed doing and was good at. My aim was to free the girls' from inhibition and shyness and get them to express verbally their ideas and anxieties. Although discussions were often heated, the girls began to listen to each other and respond analytically rather than negatively or aggressively to each other's point of view. Of course it took time and patience but most pupils eventually succumbed to the relaxed environment, and joined happily in our discussion work.

What I found particularly valuable in this kind of work was that those girls who were poor in written work were often able to express themselves quite coherently in their oral work. By making the girls aware that their contribution to discussions was valued, they developed that self esteem which is so vital to educational progress.

Discussion work, of course, enabled one to raise issues about life in the outside world, which the girls were soon to face. In trying to get them to think about these issues and how they might affect them personally, I felt I was contributing to their social development.

The development of a pupil's imagination was another very important area which I tried to stimulate by talking about colour, playing music, showing them pictures, thinking about people in different contexts. I remember one beautiful spring day when I asked them to sit back and listen to some music. I gave them all paper to write on when they felt ready, and suggested they should write about whatever came into their heads. I then played a record of Beethoven's *Pastoral Symphony*. The music flowed round these pupils whose normal musical fare was pop, and the atmosphere of peace and stillness (and perhaps surprise) was quite amazing. Some of the written work that ensued was of a very high quality and quite beautiful – and it was an experiment I repeated from time to time – moving on the next occasion to Sibelius's *Tone Poem*, and on another to Holsts' *Planets* – each of which evoked very different responses.

Colour is something that is to me of immense significance in life. I respond to surroundings very much according to the decor and colour – and I know my initial response to people is governed in part by the colour of the clothes they are wearing. It was because of this that I got the girls to think about colour in their descriptive writing – whether of people or place.

I was also, of course, very much aware of colour and decor in the school itself. Like so many schools, it had not been decorated for years and was drab and dingy in the extreme. A number of staff, in desperation, started decorating their own classrooms and I decided to do the same. My form sold hot chocolate drinks at morning break and ran raffles and competitions to raise the money for the paint. Having read round the subject a little and knowing my own preferences, I chose a light turquoise for the walls – feeling it would be restful and have a calming effect on the girls. I remembered how we had been told on one of our visits to the new Magistrates' Court that green had been chosen specifically for the carpets and furniture to defuse feelings of anger in the courtroom.

The girls stayed on after school to decorate their form room, and my son came along and painted the ceiling for us. The room was transformed by being cleaned and decorated, though we were still left with the old dark maroon curtains. Fortunately, they toned in with the turquoise, and the whole room had a restful feel.

That we had chosen well was soon corroborated by the girls who expressed their pleasure in the change – and over the next year or two, many came up to me and said my room was their favourite in the school.

But I digress. In the attempt to stimulate imaginative thinking and writing I would seize on any ploy I could think of. The girls were always rude about my handbag because there were so many occasions when I couldn't find my classroom keys. 'Oh miss,' they would cry, shaking their heads sadly over my inefficiency. This 'miss' I found most endearing – especially as I was just about to enter my fifties. It somehow made me feel young again!

One day, after a frantic search for my keys, I emptied the contents of my handbag onto my desk. As more and more articles came out of the bag, the girl's astonishment increased, and less than complimentary comments flew round the classroom. I decided I needed to defend myself and started telling them that, having been a Queen's Guide with the motto 'Be Prepared' instilled firmly into my psyche, I always carried round with me items I might need. As I pulled out a large bunch of safety pins, I reminded them how grateful they often were when I was able to give them a safety pin to hold up a skirt, or pin up shorts that had lost a button. Many had made use of my needle and cotton – and as far the large bundle of pens, pencils and rubbers, few could deny that they had found them useful on the many occasions when they had come to school ill equipped.

As they looked at my diary, they were reminded of the enjoyment they had had in keeping a diary over a period of a month. The London Underground Map and my address book were less easy for them to understand until I told them about my trips to London twice a week to do my Master's Degree. This provided an opportunity to discuss jobs, qualifications, salaries, and promotion, and helped them to realise that education did not stop when people left school.

Make up, purse, credit cards, elastoplast, tweezers, notebook and handkerchiefs were accepted as being part of the normal contents of a handbag – a penknife and fruit knife less so!

But what really provoked discussion were the small New Testament, the little wooden cross, and the enormous key I unearthed from the bottom of the bag. I explained to them that it was the key to our mediaeval church which I unlocked on my way to school each day. This prompted a long and very interesting discussion about Christianity with which very few had any contact apart from what they had learnt at school.

This unexpected diversion led me to the 'handbag exercise'. I had done a lot of work with character descriptions, getting the girls to write about themselves, and then jumbling the descriptions up and reading them out to the class so that they could try to guess who it was. Later, they had written a description of someone else in the class, and again had to guess who. Occasionally the descriptions were a little spiteful which led to discussions about love and tolerance. I then collected together character descriptions from different novels to demonstrate the many different ways there were of describing people – some detailed and lengthy, some pithy but very much to the point.

My spontaneous handbag emptying prompted me to create four imaginary characters whose handbags were found at a police station. I asked the girls to try and work out what sort of people owned the different handbags, and then write a story that would bring all the characters together. It was an exercise that covered several weeks and which we all enjoyed.

Another ploy was to write the first or last paragraph of a story and let the girls write the rest. In all these different exercises, the real key to enlisting the pupil's enthusiasm was to get the girls to read their work to the class. It made sense. It made them realise that written work was for a purpose – and that purpose was the sharing of ideas and communicating through writing. They began to accept that writing was not a sterile exercise done for teacher's benefit, but was something they could share with others.

Like all English teachers, I felt it was important that the pupils should have knowledge of their rich literary heritage. But much of it was in language too difficult for them to understand. A moral dilemma for me was the use of what I called 'expurgated' versions of the classics. These were, in fact, classics rewritten in simplified language, which in reality only included the story line. Some of the girls loved them and would quickly lose interest if one tried to introduce them to the real version. But for some of the girls I felt we were not giving them a service if we did not encourage them to read the 'real thing'.

I recall an occasion when we had been reading an expurgated version of *Wuthering Heights*. We read round the class the chapter in which Catherine discovers that her cousin Linton is living nearby at Wuthering Heights. In the expurgated version by Kennet, the events leading up to it and the incident itself are described in a few pages. Catherine's importuning of Ellen to take her across the moors, and the skilful manipulation of Catherine by Heathcliffe was nowhere hinted at – while the evil undertones of Healthcliffe's character and the feebleness of Linton are completely lost.

Exasperated, I told the girls how much they were missing by reading this easy version and told them I would read to them what Emily Bronte had really written.

While I was reading there was not a murmur or movement from the girls – and there was an audible sigh of appreciation at the end. When I then suggested we returned to the easier book, the girls with one voice protested. I went down to the English stock cupboard and found right at the back a half set of the 'real' version of *Wuthering Heights* and from then on we read from the original.

I felt this was a most instructive incident – a comment on our failure to extend pupils fully and a sad commentary on the way the school's meagre resources were being used.

But with Shakespeare, we did manage to make progress. We started with the simplified version, listened to records of such plays as 'Romeo and Juliet' and 'The Merchant of Venice', acted out some of the easier scenes, and even managed to hire films for the girls to see full-blown Shakespeare productions. I also took parties of senior girls to London from time to time, and I remember they especially loved a very black and gory production of Macbeth.

Two contrasting English teaching successes stay in my memory. One year I had the lowest fifth year stream for English. I was determined that at least some of them should get a CSE pass. We worked hard throughout the year although many of them were still nearly illiterate. Though it was a difficult class, there were some sufficiently well motivated to want to do the CSE exam and produce the requisite amount of work. One especially pathetic girl, so timid she would seldom speak in class, was determined to do the exam. Her work just about merited Grade 5 marks and, come exam time, she had done all the necessary course work and we were able to enter her.

She passed with a Grade 5 and came back proudly in the Autumn term to receive her certificate. She was accompanied by both her parents and several of her sisters and brothers – all dressed in their Sunday best. They were over the moon with excitement for it was the first time anyone in the family had ever passed an exam! Their pride and joy in this very minor achievement – but such a major one for them – made me wonder what we do to children with our academic examination system of passes and failures which marks out so many people as failures for life. What right have we to so judge people and set them apart at so young an age?

But who am I to say that when I recall how proud I was of that other success I remember so vividly?

I disliked the 11 plus system which directed children into grammar and secondary modern schools on the basis of rather narrow criteria, and where the percentage of children going to grammar schools depended very much on the area you lived in, and the wealth of the local education authority. Had the schools been equal in terms of educational opportunity and resources, there could be justification for such a system, but my observation of different types of school was that there were vast inequalities between schools, and that those who went to secondary modern schools had a very poor deal.

Having said that, I realised that there was a small group of children in secondary modern schools who sometimes derived benefit from the system. These were the borderline children who only just missed getting into the grammar school. In the secondary modern school, they were the star pupils whom the staff loved to teach because they were able to achieve what most of their pupils did not have the ability to. Because they were often well motivated, they were a joy to teach, and gave the teachers welcome relief from the more difficult pupils they had to contend with most of the time. Where secondary modern schools were streamed, these pupils got special attention – and instead of being at the bottom of the heap, as they would have been in a grammar school, they were at the top, and given every encouragement to succeed.

My form

Such was a class I was fortunate enough to teach English to over a period of four years – something that did not often happen. It was a class I established a particularly close rapport with, and in the Fourth Year found a number of them in both my form group and in my Social Studies group. It was a situation that could, of course, have been detrimental for their progress had there been any personality clashes, but such, happily, was not the case.

Having a class over so many years, I didn't have to waste time at the beginning of the new academic year initiating them into my system of work, and they were able to settle down quickly, knowing exactly what I expected of them. They developed really good work habits and I was able to stretch them to the limit. At the beginning of the fourth year, I felt they had enough ability and were sufficiently well motivated to be entered as an experiment for O' level English at the end of the fourth year. In previous years we had occasionally entered a few girls for O' levels in the fifth year but without a great deal of success.

As the school could only pay for CSEs, I had to enlist the support of their parents and get them to pay for the exam. I was absolutely honest with them and told them it was a very long shot – but they all, to my delight, agreed to support the experiment and pay the entrance fees.

The girls were excited by the challenge, became highly motivated and worked very hard throughout the year. To our mutual delight, no less than seventeen out of the thirty girls in the class achieved B or C passes – and one got an A pass. The following year, most of the seventeen gained an O' level English Literature pass as well – three of them with A grades – and a number of those who had failed to get their language pass in the fourth year achieved it in the fifth. It was a real feather in their caps – and did much for their morale and their job prospects when they left school. This is something they could never have achieved in the grammar school as they would probably have been in the bottom stream and would certainly not have been entered for O' level in their fourth year.

I think over the years I enjoyed my English teaching as much if not more than Social Studies which was my main responsibility. But I was certainly landed with a very heavy marking load as both subjects called for large quantities of lengthy written work. What people do not always realise is that marking English essays by less than literate pupils takes up an awful lot of time. For not only is one looking at content, one is also having to spend a disproportionate amount of time on correcting grammar and spelling mistakes. I did not make it any easier for myself by demanding large quantities of work from the pupils – but it was worth it to see how well some of the low ability children in particular improved and became interested.

One of the things that we all found most difficult with English (and Social Studies) teaching was grading essays and examination papers. As I write there is a lot of discussion going on in the press and the radio about the GCSE examination results this year which are better than in previous years. The Inspectors' report suggests that the grading may have been over-generous.

The marking of English papers is especially difficult as one's response to creative writing is often very subjective. I remember one occasion when we had a fairly detailed marking schedule for an end of term examination – and we all marked the same five papers. The discrepancy in the marks we awarded was frightening – ranging from 42% to 74 %. All were careful and conscientious teachers and in the discussions that followed it was quite clear that each teacher had valid reasons for the way she or

O' level success a year early

he had marked the papers. It took a lot of discussion before we could agree a mark – and these were inevitably compromise marks rather than based on objective criteria.

Arising out of my English teaching but a voluntary lunch time activity, was the production of the school newspaper. I gathered together a group of girls from all years and started producing a termly paper. I had hoped to get the girls involved in the whole process of production – and from time to time found fifth year girls who were sufficiently competent to type the stencils. But it was a difficult and uphill task.

I must also admit to a certain sense of disillusionment with my colleagues who did comparatively little to assist in finding interesting material for the paper. But each term we managed to produce something which the girls enjoyed reading and found readable – and I believe it added to their awareness that there was a purpose in writing. I also managed to involve some of the more artistic girls in simple graphics.

The duplicating was a more hazardous procedure. Gestetners and I always seemed to enter into warfare. I invariably found myself covered in ink within minutes of approaching the machine. It frequently jammed and tore – and I was very unpopular with the school secretary to whom I turned frequently for help. However, often at the eleventh hour, the school newspaper was ready for collation. This is when the girls came into their own. I would borrow three staplers, place the numbered sheets in order round the periphery of the room and enlist the help of some twenty girls who would spend a couple of happy hours, starting work in the lunch hour, putting the paper together. The next day it would be sold for a few pence per copy.

When our Head announced that she would be retiring at the end of term after some twenty years in the school, I decided it would be nice to organise something rather special. I got in touch with a local printer and persuaded him to print a school newspaper for us in the same format as a 'real' paper. He agreed to do it at cost, and I then approached the Deputy Head for funds to cover the cost.

We collected together old school photos and anecdotes from former pupils and members of staff and, on the last but one day of term, with all the school assembled in the hall and the Head sitting on the platform, four girls dressed as newspaper boys, with a loud bell in their hand, walked into the hall shouting, 'Read all about it' and distributed the newspapers to the assembled pupils. One pupil went up to the head and formally presented her with an inscribed copy. It was a great moment and one which I think the Head appreciated.

My main area of responsibility, the Social Studies Course, was studied by all the pupils in the fourth and fifth years. The Head gave me a free hand to plan the curriculum, and I spent a lot of time reading, visiting other schools and looking at their social studies courses, and in the summer holiday spent a week at Norwich University on a Humanities Curriculum Project Course.

I decided it was important for the girls to have the objective of an examination pass at the end of the second year, but opted for a Mode 3 syllabus which I could write myself. I decided to pin the course on five areas of study – the Family, Education,

Housing, Work and Leisure, and Community. I had no difficulty in persuading the Head that it should be a team teaching situation, and I had on my team the Deputy Head, an English-cum-PE teacher, a Science Teacher and a Religious Studies teacher – giving us five teachers to cover four classes – thus enabling us to have smaller groups which we knew would be valuable for discussion work.

There was already material in the school, which had been purchased by a previous teacher but never used. But we needed a lot more, and I was determined the pupils would have access to decent textbooks. Again, the Head was supportive and I had a generous allocation of money to purchase books, a projector and screen, and files and stationery in generous measure.

I also managed to get a grant from one of the inspectors to cover the cost of hiring films and financing the occasional educational trip, for we all believed quite passionately that if a trip was part of the syllabus, it should not depend on the ability to pay as to whether or not a pupil could go.

I was timetabled for one whole afternoon a week for each of the Fourth and Fifth years, and was allotted the large hall for when we wanted to meet as a whole year group. Looking back, I suspect that, as a newcomer, I was none too popular with my colleagues. It must have been difficult for them to accept the very generous resources I was given for this new subject, and I don't think I was as sensitive about it as I should have been!

I designed the course quite specifically to help the pupils understand the world in which they lived. The first term we studied The Family and started with the pupil herself – recording, as I have mentioned before, personal details and statistics.

We then turned to compiling a family tree. This was a tricky area. Most of the girls were intrigued with the idea of setting out the names of all their relations. But a very high proportion of them had complicated families with both step and half brothers and sisters – sometimes on both sides of the family. It was an opportunity to talk openly about the problems that arise from living in mixed family set-ups, and I think many valued the chance to share their problems in a sympathetic environment. But it needed very sensitive handling.

I encouraged the girls to bring in photographs of themselves in order to stamp their own identity on their files. Next we turned to family size which introduced us to sociological statistics. We soon discovered that the average size of family in the school was quite a bit higher than the national average, but I am afraid I fudged the issue of differentiating between real and half or step-brothers and sisters. That was far too complicated for us all.

We explored other family patterns – looking at the Kibbutz in Israel and families throughout the world. The film *Four Families*, which described the baby rearing patterns of families in India, France, Canada and Japan, revealed to them very different approaches to child rearing. We began to get used to sociological terminology and discussed heredity and environment, monogamy and polygamy. We looked at family relationships and the need for care in choosing a marriage partner.

I showed them a most delightful Swedish film on childbirth called *Barnet the Child* where the mother remained radiant throughout the birth and was attended and helped by her husband. We discussed sexual relationships and looked at contraception – in this way reinforcing what Maggie was doing in Child Care.

Halfway through the term I suggested the girls started to look round for a young child on whom they could do a child study. The idea met with enthusiasm as most seemed to have contact with under-fives. For those who did not, I made arrangements for them to study one of the children in the school crèche. This is something which the Head had set up for the teachers' children, and which Maggie used for her Child Care studies.

The girls seemed to enjoy the term's work and I preened myself on success. But how is success measured? At the end of the term I set a little test – and felt more than a little deflated by the exam answers – some of which were very amusing but hardly accurate:

QUESTION: What is the alternative to the family in Israel?
ANSWER: A Caboose

QUESTION: Explain the difference between heredity and environment
ANSWER: Heredity is when you inherit some illness from your family, and environment is outside when the weather changes from rain to sun.

QUESTION: Why was there a hiccup in the post-war birth rate?
Answer: Because there were no men about to have intercourse with the women, and if they were born, most died.

ALTERNATIVELY
Because many soldiers went out to work and the women and children were left in underground caves for protection.

QUESTION: Why has the death rate declined?
ANSWER: Because more elderly people die quicker and more babies are dying of ill health.

QUESTION: There are different forms of marriage throughout the world
What is the name for
(a) One man one woman
(b) One man – several wives
(c) One woman – several husbands

ANSWER: (a) Marriage
(b) Greedy
(c) Greedy

QUESTION: What do we mean by Rites of Passage?

ANSWER:	A passage in a book
QUESTION:	What is the Infant Mortality rate?
ANSWER:	Children without a mother or father
QUESTION:	What is the name given to children born out of wedlock
ANSWER:	Surigiout
QUESTION:	Why has the birth rate declined?
ANSWER:	Because not many people are being born.

But one had to keep on trying! The next term we embarked on the topic of Education. The underlying theme was meant to be that education starts the day one is born and continues throughout life.

It was at this stage of the course that I used again some of the material I had used during my playgroup days. What the girls most enjoyed was the session on painting. I brought in my collection of paintings and drawings by under fives and explained what some of them indicated. I also brought in some of the playgroup films on sand and water, clay and dough, and imaginative play.

A film I loved to show was *I have an Egg*, one of the most beautiful films I have ever seen about a group of young blind Polish children who were having a lesson about an egg. It is a tender demonstration of the way blind children bring into play all their other senses to compensate for their lack of sight. I have described it before as I used it regularly on my playgroup courses. The girls' response to the film was similar to that of the adults I used to show it to, and there was seldom a dry eye in the classroom when I showed this film.

We spent a lot of time looking at schooling in all its ramifications – selection, 11 plus, comprehensive education, Thameside, and private schools. We discussed the merits of streaming, setting and mixed ability. We talked about examinations and qualifications; about university and further education, and education for life. We discussed equality of opportunity and touched on the cycle of deprivation. We looked at pre-school education – playgroups, nursery schools and nurseries – and mothers going out to work. One hoped that some of this would rub off when they became parents themselves. We knew that for some of them, this would be all too soon.

A series of films they found absolutely fascinating and which prompted endless discussion were the films, *Seven Up*, *Seven plus Seven*, and *Twenty-One*. These were a series of television documentaries which filmed over a period of years a group of children from different social backgrounds. The theme of the study was, 'Give me a child at the age of seven and I will show you the man'.

The films were fascinating. The girls all identified with the cheeky boy from the East End of London who wanted to become a jockey but ended up as a taxi driver.

They found the three lads from exclusive boarding schools, two of whom ended up at Oxbridge and the bar, as from an alien culture. But they felt very sorry for the girl, daughter of a headmistress, who was brought up by a nanny and then went to Benenden. When they saw her at twenty-one and learnt that her parents were divorced and that she had clearly been involved in the drug scene, they felt no envy for her expensive way of life – but great pity for her lack of love and security. This was something the girls valued most highly – especially those who lacked security in their own lives.

In the film *Twenty-One* the children were brought together. The class barriers were very apparent – though some of the more securely based did seem to be able to relate to each other. But the films demonstrated in a way that was chillingly convincing that different educational patterns produce very different people, with totally different social and material expectations from life.

Inevitably during this term there was a lot of discussion about teachers and their role, and I realised that the girls had very decided views about what teachers should and should not do, and how they should behave.

Several years into the programme, with one of the brighter classes, I decided to ask them to write freely about what they thought schools and teachers should be like. It was after the arrival of the new Head and the introduction of fairly rigid streaming and different timetables for the able and less able. I give below some of their answers:

'I think that all pupils, irrespective of whether they are clever or not, should be allowed and encouraged to learn the same subjects. In no way should the less able be allowed to feel inferior or not as good as the brighter pupils as this will discourage them totally from the inclination to work.'

'The teachers should spend just as much time, and sometimes more, with the less able pupils than with the able. I do not think the teachers should give up at any time because the pupil finds the subject difficult. It should encourage the teacher to find new and more interesting teaching methods, and different approaches to different classes. For example, a teacher who talks all through the lesson will inevitably lose any interest the class might have had in the subject, whereas if she tries to include the pupils more in the lessons they will be much more interested and willing to learn new things.'

'I feel that a system which allows bright pupils to learn more than the not so bright pupils is not good. By stating that pupils cannot do a subject, you are rejecting them and making them feel inferior. This should never be done as it will make them never want to work and to feel that the teacher is not interested in them.'

'I think that any pupil, whatever her intelligence, should be able to learn any subject she wishes to, and the teachers should be willing and able to take on the challenge of teaching the pupil a subject she knows they will find difficult.'

'I do not agree with mixed ability classes because in such a class there may be some very bright pupils who are being held back because of the work being done for the less able. They will be learning what they already know. This is a terrible situation because I think that bright pupils should be pushed to their fullest ability and not held back at all.'

'I think that all pupils should be taught the same thing even if they find it difficult or boring. For everyone is equal, except that clever people just know how to use his or her brains more usefully. The teacher should never give up. It may be difficult but the teacher should slow down and explain the subject more fully if the pupils do not understand it.'

'I think streaming is a good idea ONLY if the classes are unaware of their status. In no way should the less bright pupils feel failures. They should be happily encouraged and praised all the while as this will boost them into working harder and trying to achieve higher goals.'

'Irrespective of whether a child is clever or not, they should all have the same chance in life.'

'Even if you stream a group there will still be clever and not so clever in each stream.'

'In infant and primary schools some teachers teach the whole class the same subject and pull all the clever ones down to the same level as the not so clever. This is unfair and an awful waste of brainpower. I think a system should be adopted where everyone can learn things at their own rate.'

'Sometimes the weaker pupils do not bother because they believe they cannot improve, but if it is shown they can achieve the same sort of results as the pupils that are clever, they will to a certain extent reach a higher standard.'

'The clever pupil will soon get bored if he has to keep waiting for the not so clever pupil to catch up.'

'If a person is particularly thick a range of practical subjects should be offered so that his or her school life is not a waste of time. An effort should be made on the teaching side to try and arrange it so that everyone has the subjects on their timetable which are of both practical use and interest. No one should be forced into a subject as this causes a defiant attitude on the pupil's side and often they will behave badly and refuse to work.'

Many of the girls had a real understanding of how pupils are motivated. I felt that their comments, above and below, justified the enormous amount of time I spent on discussion during our Social Studies lessons:

'I think making the group take part in discussion and let their opinions out is a way in which a pupil becomes interested. If you make them feel they are really good (when they are not really) it gives them the feeling that they are worthwhile and can do well if they try. The teacher should support the weaker ones so that they can try and not feel left out. A sense of belonging is necessary.'

'The teachers seem to think and try to get over to us that older people are important and that we should be polite to them. This annoys me as I think we should be allowed to say what we feel because we have as many ideas as our elders and should be able to voice them.' (This from a fairly bright but very difficult lass.)

'If a pupil or a class find a subject boring I believe it is up to the teacher to do something about it and not just give up. The teacher should try to find a method of teaching which stimulates the class, gets them asking questions and playing an active part in the lesson... Perhaps more communication between pupils and teachers is the answer, with both parties putting forth their views on how to go about learning.'

'I think it is very important to teach pupils subjects that are needed to help them get a job. Some pupils, may for example, find maths boring or difficult, but the teacher should not give up the attempt to teach them because maths is an important subject. The teacher should make the lessons more interesting and maybe they could spend more time in explaining certain things if they find it hard.'

The girls quite clearly had very high expectations of their teachers:

'It is not always the teacher's fault that pupils lose interest. Sometimes the pupils have decided they do not wish to learn anything and will not co-operate or join in the lesson. They become just plain stubborn and in the end unable to sit down and concentrate on doing any work. If this happens I still feel the teacher should not give up. She should discipline the pupil and try to show them in a friendly way that they must work. If this approach does not work, then she should be harsh and angry and insist that they will work.'

(This comment was particularly interesting as it came from a very disruptive girl whom I had for English and Social Studies over a period of two years. When I first started teaching her, she was quite impossible, but after many battles and much 'friendly encouragement' she ended up a most helpful and hard working girl – although never shy about expressing very positive ideas during discussion and form time.)

'I think it is a teacher's job to make the work interesting. If the pupil is bored it is only because of the teacher's inability in teaching to get the child's attention. Different approaches should be taken to the subject every time and they will respond. If they know they are going to do the same sort of work they will get bored.'

And the girls' perceptions of what teachers value and why they did certain things was interesting:

'The staff values the good examination results of the bright girls so that the reputation of the school does not drop. Most of the staff have different expressions which convey this message.'

'Responsibility is connected with the streaming system.'

'Uniform is important for the appearance of the school and shows smartness, and is a form of discipline by the teachers.'

'I think the main things our teachers are worried about is the reputation of the school. They want the public to have a good impression of our school.'

'Because we are in streams according to brightness, this shows that our school feels the top streams should be taught the most and the teachers should spend most of their time with them. I do not agree with this.'

'Teachers show us we should not be late as this creates a bad impression.'

'Teachers show us the things we should value in life. They expect us to be truthful and some teachers feel that a nice person is much more important than what we can learn.'

'When girls in the school are made prefects the parents think this is because their daughters have achieved a good standard. I do not feel it is. I think that the teachers just choose who they like for prefects.'

And in answer to, 'What are the qualities that make a good teacher?' one of the girls summarised them as follows:

A teacher should be friendly and listen to what the children have to say.
A teacher must have a sense of humour.
A teacher should be interesting.
A teacher must be able to control the class – but not too strict.
A teacher should dress nicely and look smart.
A teacher should be understanding about children's problems.
A teacher should not shout at children.
A teacher should learn us something!'

These were the comments of some of our more able girls. Sadly I only have one comment from the girls in a lower ability stream which was passed on to me by a colleague. She said, 'Teachers didn't ought to teach us out of books. They ought to teach us out of what they've got in their heads like Mrs Smith and Miss Peters (cooking and needlework teachers respectively). They are good teachers because they don't never use books but teach us what they know.' What can one say to this?

At another time, in some desperation with an extremely difficult and disruptive low ability fifth year class, I tried to get them thinking about why they should be at school. I asked them to imagine that they all had to apply for a place in school, and could only come if they were accepted. It was a novel thought for them, and they set to work with interest. Sadly I did not keep their letters – but the theme that came through time and again was that they wanted to come to school in order to be able to get a good job when they left.

One of the words that appear so often in these comments and was in daily use in the school was the word 'boring'. I banned it from use in my classes and insisted they found a different way of saying it.

I found it interesting that whenever we discussed the merits of single sex or mixed schools most of the girls expressed a strong preference for single sex schools – this despite the fact that the seats near the windows which overlooked the adjacent boys' school were always the most popular!

Another thing I found interesting was that there were no strong feelings of resentment among the brighter girls who had only just missed getting into grammar school. They thought, rightly I think, that they had more attention in our school than they would have done had they been selected. But they did regard their grammar school peers as 'posh' and 'snobby' and expressed no wish to be like them.

In the ensuing terms we looked at Housing, Work and Leisure and the Community.

I chose Housing because I wanted the girls to have some understanding of how one went about getting a council house, saving money for a deposit to buy a house, and the problems and responsibilities of renting. I also tried to help them understand the complexities of the rating system.

We looked at buildings old and new and visited the new town at New Ash Green. We also looked at some of our interesting old houses in Kent, visiting Stoneacre and Knole Park. And we looked at films of housing in other parts of the world.

We showed the girls the documentary film *Cathy Come Home* about a couple who got married at a very early age, partly because the girl was unhappy at home. It traced their deteriorating situation as they quickly produced a large family, over-extended themselves financially, and got into such severe financial difficulties that the husband walked out on the family and Cathy finally had to let her children go into care. It gave the girls much food for thought.

Then we moved on to a look at local government, local services and the welfare state. Though we worked hard at it, and it had great relevance to their future lives, it was not easy to capture the same interest as for our other topics.

Work and Leisure we tied in very closely with the Work Experience Programme which we operated in the first term of the fifth year. All the girls had to do a fairly detailed Work Experience Report as part of their studies.

We took a very careful look at leisure activities. One of the girls' biggest complaints about living in the area was that 'there's nothing to do in this town, Miss.' Their comments were far from justified and we tried to stretch their imaginations and horizons about what was available – I am not sure with total success.

The Community session was the most interesting as we looked at all the problems of society – drugs, crime and punishment, deviancy. We called in our Community Policeman to give talks to the girls. We showed the film *Gale is Dead* about drugs and *Edna the Inebriate Woman* about a drop out from society.

We looked at the law and visited our local magistrates court. These were trips that the girls found fascinating. But they were not without problems. The court ushers were not always as careful as they should have been about the cases we sat in on. One very difficult occasion was when we were in court, and one of their neighbours was up on a charge of incest. Fortunately the case was sent up to a higher court. But I had to take the girls aside afterwards and impress on them the need to keep what they heard to themselves. Fortunately I think the girls trusted and respected what I had to say, and there were no repercussions.

I was however, very angry indeed when we found ourselves sitting in on a most unsavoury domestic case of assault and rape within a marriage. Although rape in marriage was not then accepted as a crime, all the extremely sordid details of what was clearly marital rape came out in court. I was very worried indeed about how their parents would react if they knew. But when I expressed to them my anxiety the girls indicated that I was very old fashioned and naive to imagine that they would be shocked or surprised by what they had heard. 'We know all about these things,' they assured me and told me not to worry!

It was during this term that I introduced a fun 'role playing' exercise which I had devised to try and demonstrate to them how the interaction of personalities and factors have a great bearing on decision making, and how in such situations people have to compromise to reach a decision.

I managed to get access to the adjacent classroom to mine so that I could have two separate groups doing the exercise at the same time – flitting from one room to the next to see how the girls were getting on.

I asked them to imagine they were the Board of Directors of a cosmetics firm which needed to employ a new senior executive to set up a new factory and lead a big expansion drive into the chain stores. I told them that four people had applied for the job and had been interviewed. I handed them the details about the applicants, each of whom had qualifications and experiences which made them very evenly balanced. I located the new and old factories in areas which had significance for the travelling arrangements of the candidates. And I indicated that each of the applicants had links with one or more members of the selection board.

I then assigned roles to each pupil telling them who they were – and then gave each pupil, in confidence, more details about the character they were to role play. In order to make the decision making more difficult I gave each character a reason why they favoured one or other of the candidates and opposed on principle the preferred candidates of other members of the Board. Knowing that their imaginations would be captured if a little romance was included, I threw in the potential for a little sexual jealousy.

I set out the desks in a large oblong as in a boardroom, sat the girls down with their assigned roles, and left them to it.

THE ROLE PLAYING EXERCISE
The Task
The Blossomtime factory at Canterbury requires a Senior Executive to share in the running of the factory and to be eventually responsible for opening a new factory at Sittingbourne.

The factory manufactures cosmetics; it is already selling its products to a number of shops but has not yet broken into the big chain stores. A big expansion drive is planned for the future. The new Senior Executive will be responsible for this as well, and therefore needs to be someone who has flair and enthusiasm and is a good salesman.

Four people have applied for the job. They have all been interviewed and your job is to decide to which of the four applicants to give the job.

THE APPLICANTS
Peter Anderson: Aged 40. Has worked in cosmetics since leaving school at 16 and has been working in the rival firm Yardlane. He has just been made redundant. He is married with three children. He has a lively personality, a good sense of humour, and has a lot of drive and energy. He is well liked by the factory workers. He has worked his way up the ladder. His father was a works foreman. He lives in Maidstone.

Alastair McViney: Aged 39. He is the nephew of the Managing Director. He is a graduate. After leaving university he worked in Blossomtime for ten years. He then moved to Fairtones, a rival firm, to get experience and inside knowledge of a rival firm. He is divorced with no children. He is very efficient but rather arrogant and considered snobbish by the workers in the factory. He lives in Canterbury.

Mary Barton: Aged 38. She is a graduate. She is married with two children aged 12 and 14. She is very attractive and has an excellent dress sense. She has worked in cosmetics since leaving university – first of all in a factory and then in Boots and one of the other big chain stores as a cosmetic buyer, so she knows both sides of the business and has many contacts. She has never had contact with the workers on the factory floor. She lives in Sittingbourne.

Stephen Finch: Aged 27. A graduate. He is engaged to the Chairman's daughter. He is a very handsome man with an attractive personality. He has worked in three cosmetics factories and for a brief time ran his own cosmetics business. He has also taken a special course in market research and has studied particularly carefully the promotion of new products. He has had no contact with the workers. He lives in London.

THE BOARD
Chairman: Mr Craig. His daughter is engaged to Stephen Finch. He is very eager to give Stephen the job because he thinks he is a whizz kid and will do very well with the new factory.

Managing Director: John McViney. He wants his nephew, Alastair McViney, to have the job. He has no children of his own and hopes Alastair will inherit his shares and his position in the factory.

Secretary to the Chairman: Miss Macey. She is 55 and has been with Mr Craig for years. She respects him and thinks he knows best so supports his choice.

Assistant to Managing Director: Alan Evans. He is very jealous because he wanted the job for himself. He dislikes Alastair McViney and does not want him to get the job. He also dislikes women.

SENIOR EXECUTIVES:
Mrs Mary Edwards. She wants Alastair McViney to get the job. She used to work with him and thinks he is very good.

Eric Lyall. He supports the Chairman, Mr Craig, because he is hoping for promotion from him.

Paul Stephens. He supports the Managing Director but also has a secret liking for Mary Barton. So he is in a cleft stick.

Stuart McGregor. He has worked with Mary Barton and thinks she is very efficient and would do the job well. He is engaged to Alison Mark.

Alison Mark. She is engaged to Paul Stephens – but is afraid that he likes Mary Barton too much.

Michael Young. He used to be at school with Peter Anderson and dislikes him intensely.

George Harris. He is working hard to try and take over the Managing Director's job.

Nigel Saunders. He is only interested in the efficiency of the factory.

Mark Newhouse. He also worked his way up the ladder from the factory floor so is in favour of Peter Anderson. He also thinks that if Peter is appointed he will have a better chance of promotion in the future.

Antonia Fraser. She is beautiful and well connected and very snobbish. She does not think a non-graduate should have the job. She has a secret liking for Alastair MvViney. She is a very jealous lady.

Frances Potts. She is secretly working for the rival firm Yardlane and is not interested in the Blossomtime factory's success.

It was a fascinating exercise, and one which the girls took very seriously. It was wonderful how they entered into their roles and argued in accordance with the prejudices and preferences I had attached to their characters. Because the applicants were so evenly balanced, and because each member of the Board had motives for appointing or rejecting certain of the candidates, it was an exercise which necessitated the girls working out a strategy to resolve their differences of opinion.

This was an exercise I gave the pupils over many years and I think it was evidence that I had created a real balance between the candidates and the Board in that the groups all came up with different choices. And the strategies they adopted to resolve their problems were very different and always interesting.

Often the exercise would start with loud and aggressive argument but invariably it settled down into sensible discussion about the candidates and the way to resolve the difficulties. I gave no instructions as to how the decision-making session was to be conducted, other than that the chosen candidate must receive all but two of the votes. Some used a written voting system. Some eliminated one or two of the candidates early on, others later. Some reached a decision solely through persuasion.

A week or two after the exercise, I usually showed them the wonderful Henry Fonda film *Twelve Angry Men* about the jury in a murder trial of a young coloured man. The jury was impatient to get away from the jury room and hastily voted 11 to 1 that the man was Guilty. Henry Fonda cast a lone vote of Not Guilty – not because he was certain the man was innocent but because he felt the jury should not send a man to his death without exploring his innocence or guilt with great care.

The whole film is shot in the jury room where the jurors, hot and sticky from the sultry weather outside, impatient to get away, and full of prejudices and hang ups, gradually work through to a verdict of Not Guilty. It is a film I have seen a dozen times and could still see again without getting bored – so subtle and clever are the interactions of the jurors and the revelations of their prejudices and problems.

Seeing the film so soon after their own role playing exercise the girls found it reinforced what they had discovered about the interaction of people in a decision making exercise.

Social Studies was one of the most popular lessons on the timetable, and I believe that the girls derived a lot of benefit from it – not only in the information we gave them, and the sort of analytical work that we set, but also in the many opportunities we provided for discussion and debate in a very free and open atmosphere where the girls' ideas were analysed and discussed in a non judgmental way by their peers.

The course was valued by the first Head, but ideologically it did not accord with the views of the second Head who, over a period of years, changed the subject from being a core subject to a choice between Child Care and Social Studies, and finally was reduced to an examination Sociology course for the brighter girls.

There was little I could do. Philosophically the Head and I were poles apart. I found it difficult to accept the educational approach of a head who concentrated on the three Rs at the expense of the arts and education for life. I was deeply unhappy at a Head who was prepared to use the cane. I was unhappy that a Head should have been appointed who had two children under the age of three when we were trying to get across the importance of good parenting. I disliked the way a united and happy staff was divided on the issue of teacher unions, and the way in which promotion seemed to depend on one's political persuasion.

For me the final disillusionment came when I was asked to move lock stock and barrel out of my classroom which I had, over the years, built up as a resource centre, into a tiny mobile where it was not even safe to store the department's film projector and overhead projector. I felt the time had come to depart

An opportunity presented itself when the local Education Authority announced that the school would have to lose one teacher. Anger ensued when the staff learnt that the redundancy was to take place in six week's time. And outrage was felt when the Head announced that she would get rid of one of her non-specialist staff. She put up on the notice board a 'hit' list which included members of the English department, the person in charge of the school Library, and two remedial teachers. All were members of the National Union of Teachers, which the Head detested. This Machiavellian use of the situation caused uproar in the staffroom and many of the staff were determined to fight the redundancy tooth and nail. Hating to see such blatant injustice done, I accepted the responsibility for writing the letters to the local Education Authority, the County Education Officer, the Governors, and the local M.P.s. Urgent meetings were called, local and county education officers came out to meet the staff, and within a couple of weeks, the demand to make a teacher redundant was withdrawn. The staff had won the battle for justice.

But the incident had sickened me, and during the summer holiday, I went to see the local education officer and said I would be prepared to accept early retirement provided I got ten years enhancement and could choose the time of my departure. He was so delighted that he agreed to my terms, and at half term in the autumn term, I left the school – my only real regret was saying goodbye to the pupils whom I had come to love over the years. For, though I had a number of friends among the staff, I had no regrets at leaving a staffroom where the staff were disillusioned and divided.

I left the education system in 1987. Looking back, I am saddened by the many teachers one meets who would do anything to get early retirement. They are overwhelmed and exhausted because of the mountains of paper work thrown at them by various government innovations. I am incensed by constant criticism of incompetent teachers and poor schools; of league tables which take little account of the levels of children's intelligence and the appalling domestic situations they have to contend with. Equally, I am horrified by the abuse many teachers suffer from out of control children – many of whom are so street-wise they manipulate for their own ends the controls put on society by traumas such as child abuse and violence. I am angered that the education of our children is often debated by cabinets, many of whose members opt out of state education altogether, and presume to tell the rest of society that they have a choice. But equally, one has to acknowledge that there are poor schools (often because they are inadequately resourced) and poor teachers (often because they find it difficult to control disruptive pupils).

Despite my own grammar school education and the four years I spent at university, I was early convinced that something should be done about the inequalities in educational opportunity, and was a firm supporter of comprehensive schooling. I still believe that comprehensive schools, well organised, have an enormous amount to offer. No child needs to feel superior or inferior because of selection or rejection. Adequately resourced and staffed, schools should be able to organise the curriculum in such a way that bright children are put on the 'fast track' while slow learners are provided with specialist help. The key to success is not to separate the children in all subjects but to bring them together with their peers in subjects like art, games, physical education and music, and in their tutor groups. This, of course demands good organisational skills – and many comprehensive schools have achieved this blend and produced excellent results, managing to develop an 'ethos' which values all achievement, whether academic or practical.

I was never able to experience comprehensive education at first hand because the area in which Bill and I lived had a bastardised selection system – known as Thameside. All the children in the area (apart of course those who opted for private education) went to their local (high) school at the age of eleven. Then, at the age of thirteen, the academic ones were creamed off to the Upper School. These were, in all but name, the old grammar and technical schools.

The system fell between two stools. The two years between eleven and thirteen were felt by the Upper Schools to be wasted because there were significant differences in the quality of education offered by the seven feeder High Schools. So, nearly a year was spent by the Upper Schools in getting all the pupils up to the same standard – particularly in Maths, Science and English. Meanwhile, those left behind in the high schools felt themselves to be failures.

But I must confess that Bill and I were greatly relieved when both our son and daughter proved to be of academic bent, and were transferred at the age of thirteen to the grammar schools – and were thus set on the road to a later university education. Despite my absolute belief in the need for equality of opportunity, I confess that we would have been deeply distressed if our children had been 'left behind' at the High School. This was because we knew from personal observation what poor schools they were, with a high incidence of disruption and poor academic results. Moreover, we had observed that the local children, who failed to get transferred, left school with low self-esteem.

Some years later, Kent, instead of taking the fully comprehensive route, reverted to the Eleven Plus.

I can only count myself fortunate that, with an enlightened Education Act in 1944 and the early post war reforms, I was one of the lucky ones who went to university with fees paid and a grant according to one's financial circumstance, secure in the knowledge that we would get a good job at the end of it; that we would be able, if we wished, to embark on a career that was secure and progressive, and that at a later period of our lives we would be able to retire with a pension. Such security no longer exists.

Today, I am distressed by the plight of thousands of young people who have gone through the rigours of higher education and study, only to find themselves loaded with a huge debt which constrains their future.

It is ironic to think that the varied and somewhat erratic career I have followed from choice, ending up with a very tiny pension, is one that this generation of young people will have to follow of necessity. I would change very little in my life – even though I have envied at times the financial security and status of those who have followed a more conventional career. But I have been blessed with a secure and happy family life – and that is what one must hope and pray will underpin the lives of those who are now embarking on a desperately uncertain labour market.

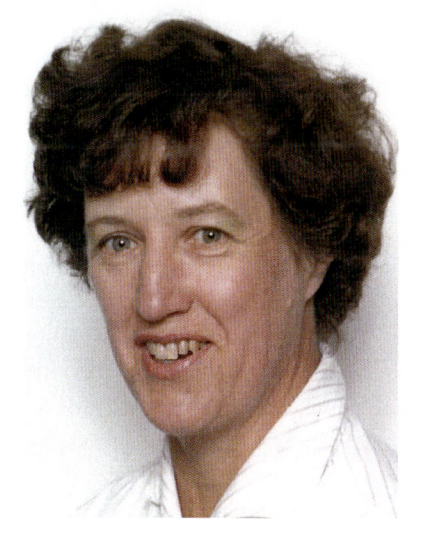

CHAPTER 23
Reflections on my Teaching Experience

When I look over the notes I kept during the eleven years I spent in the school there seem to be a number of things worth commenting on – albeit in a rather haphazard fashion.

I came across the diary I had kept of a typical day and was amazed at the enormous variety of interactions one had during the eight hours one was in school, the constant moving from room to room at the sound of a bell, and the dozens of different minor activities with which one was involved. In the course of one day, I could attend a staff meeting, mark a class register twice with appropriate symbols to denote lateness, sickness, attendance at the doctors or dentists, the bringing of a note etc., collect money for an outing, escort pupils to assembly, take eight lesson registers, check out books, teach, show a film, mark a set of exercise books, hand out and collect in sets of books four or five times over, do a break duty, listen to pupils' problems (several times over during the day), attend a departmental meeting, order books and equipment, help sort out a dispute or confrontation, discipline a pupil, have a discussion with a colleague, phone a parent, get the girls to tidy the classroom, have an inquest into why a girl has missed a colleague's lesson, help a girl find a missing article, write a note of explanation to another teacher, enter marks in a register – and go home wondering why one was tired!

It was, of course, not only the changing interactions that caused fatigue but also the constant problem of discipline. Our Deputy Head, who was one of the most efficient and pleasant teachers I have ever come across, wrote out some notes for students on teaching practice. They were of such a practical and helpful nature for the type of pupils we had in school that, by popular request, a copy was distributed to all the staff. They read as follows:

AIDS TO TEACHERS IN THE CLASSROOM

1. Be in the classroom first if possible. Insist that the girls come in quietly and if you are not satisfied make them do it again.
2. Try and look as if you are pleased to see them. Have plenty of work prepared, making sure there is something even the least able can cope with at first. Work written on the board is a good starter.
3. Have an adequate supply of spare paper, pens, pencils etc. **Count** everything borrowed.

4. Allow some work to start on arrival. Don't let children get bored waiting around.
5. When they are all busy, look round and check for coat wearers, chewers etc. Sometimes it's a good idea to speak to offenders quietly – often more effective than a shouting confrontation.
6. Do not tolerate unnecessary noise. They **know** when they are being too noisy and **expect** us to stop it.
7. Be '**angry**' at any kind of rudeness. Tell them they are being rude and that you do not like it, and will not tolerate it. Talk about it – don't suffer it hoping it will go away. It won't! It will get worse!

   At the same time, don't sulk! Be approachable as soon as the storm has passed. Answer even the more annoyingly stupid questions with consideration, not ridicule. The lines of communication must be kept open.
8. **Never** try to talk above a noise.
9. Insist on proper clearing up. Allow plenty of time for this. They are not very co-operative after the bell has gone. Check numbers of all text books and equipment. Make a **BIG FUSS** if anything is missing.
10. Check floor for bits. Get someone to go round with a basket. Make desk writers clean it off – or at least try to. Clean the board when finished with.
11. **NEVER** let them go before you say so. The bell is a signal for the **teacher.** Make it clear that no one is going anywhere until you are satisfied that all tasks have been completed.
12. Put chairs back tidily. If desks have been moved put them back as they were. Dismiss the class reminding them about quietness in the corridors etc. They will carry away the right impression for the next time. **Remember** they will be back! A little extra effort at first can make life a lot easier later.

These practical suggestions were of considerable help, and the more successful teachers were those who took time over these minutiae of classroom management. But, as will be recognised, they took up time and when one remembers that in most schools lessons last for forty minutes, one will realise how limited is the amount of pure teaching time in any one lesson. One could argue, as indeed I would, that getting pupils to adhere to these practical modes of behaviour is a form of education in itself. But, in those schools where disruption is rife, these matters take up a disproportionate amount of time at the expense of pure academic learning.

While I was teaching, the James Report came out with its suggestion of teacher tutors in school. The Report's recommendations have never really been implemented, and yet new and inexperienced teachers could learn so much from people like our Deputy Head. Sadly, in my school, although the Deputy Head did as much as she could to help those struggling in the classroom, she had no official time assigned to tutoring – and I often felt what a waste of her talents that was – and what an opportunity missed.

I am sure there must be hundreds of teachers in schools throughout the country who would make wonderful teacher tutors given the time and opportunity.

One of the things I found most difficult to get excited about was infringement of rules about school uniform. That is not to say I did not believe in uniform. I did for a number of reasons. School uniform is a great leveller in that no pupil can flaunt expensive clothes at the expense of the poorer members of the class. It is good for morale and pride in their school, in that the girls can feel on a par with those from the grammar and technical schools who rigidly adhere to uniform. And it gives them a feeling of group identity. Moreover, it is, as my social studies pupils so astutely realised, an aid to discipline.

But that said, confrontations over infringement of uniform often caused unnecessary problems. I saw absolutely no point in manufacturing a confrontation over a pair of yellow socks when a normally difficult pupil comes into the classroom with a pleasant smile on her face and a willingness to work.

Nor, I must be honest, did I always notice aberrations of uniform. I was far more concerned with the expression on a girl's face, the way she walked, the angle at which she held her shoulders, than with what she wore on her feet. I was often amazed, walking into the staffroom at lunch time, to hear staff complaining loudly about the awful confrontation they had had over Clare's slippers and Mary's socks – when the same Clare and Mary had been very agreeable and had worked hard in my lesson earlier in the day. I sometimes felt guilty that I had not noticed the offending articles of clothing – but at the same time knew that the socks and shoes were unimportant in comparison to the girls' willingness to work.

It is this sort of situation and moral dilemma which causes stress. In the eyes of my colleagues, I was lax because I didn't always act upon infringements. In the eyes of my pupils I was a good teacher because I understood, and didn't cause an unnecessary fuss!

Sometimes, one had to intervene between pupils and colleagues. What the girls detested more than anything was nitpicking. They particularly disliked an R.E. teacher who was always needling them and holding inquests over trivial infringements of rules. She was like a terrier worrying at a rat, and would never let any breach of school rules pass. She always taught the younger age group because she couldn't handle the girls beyond the second year. But the girls she had taught during their first two years detested her – and none more so than Tracy of the fifth who was one of our brightest, but most notorious and difficult girls. She was in my form.

The girls had nicknamed this teacher Miss Pug Face because of her somewhat squashed up nose and little protubarent eyes which indicated a thyroid condition. Though she no longer taught Tracey, she had been her form teacher in the first year and had antagonised her from the start. Over the years she had waged a war of attrition against Tracey, looking for faults whenever they met. Though Tracey was one of the most difficult girls I have ever taught, there were ways through to her from time to time. It was clear from the outset that the one thing she would never tolerate was nit-picking over trifles. Enraged by constant confrontations, Tracey and her gang decided on guerrilla warfare. They waited for her round corners, and when they saw her coming would call out loudly, 'Here comes Miss Pug Face' and disappear quickly.

Now 'Miss Pug Face', not surprisingly, didn't tell any of her colleagues what was going on. No teacher likes to admit to defeat – especially such a personal one as this – so she attempted to deal with the situation on her own.

One lunchtime, Tracey, who was now in my form, broke yet another rule, and 'Miss Pugface' was determined to have blood. She followed Tracey and her gang to the classroom (fifth years were allowed into the classroom at lunch times) and tried to haul Tracey out of the room. Fortunately for her, I'd decided to return to the classroom early. I arrived to find Miss Pug face holding open the door of the room, her face white and her hands shaking with fear, as the whole class bayed at her like a pack of wolves, while Tracey, with hands clenched into a fist, was on the point of attacking her. It was an ugly moment and I had to exert every ounce of my authority, not only to quieten the girls, but to insist that Miss Pugface walked away and left the situation to me. Even at this most dangerous moment, she tried to insist that I dragged Tracey out of the room straight away, and I had to take her firmly by the arm and walk her back to the staffroom to prevent her being physically attacked. I then had to return to the classroom to sort it out.

Miss Pugface refused to accept that she was at least part of the cause of the trouble. Tracey, of course, was suspended, and I felt very sad because, apart from this incident, Tracey had mellowed and started working hard, and might have done well had this confrontation with 'Miss Pugface' not happened.

Over the years I observed with interest the teachers in our school – the single teachers, the newly married, the married with children and the men. It seemed to me that the married teachers with children had a number of advantages over their colleagues when it came to teaching the sort of pupils we had in the school. As mothers, they had a better understanding of how children react – and were often able to provide the sort of motherly figure so many of our girls needed. Some people, of course, would argue the contrary view – that teachers who were mothers tended to transfer their own experiences of children to every situation rather than look at it objectively.

But the married teacher with children also had a number of difficulties not faced by her colleagues. There was the perennial problem of what to do when their young were sick. And there was the problem of fatigue. Returning home at the end of a tiring day's teaching, wanting nothing better than to put her feet up for an hour and have a quiet cup of tea, the mother is faced instead by children who want to tell her all about their day – their achievements and their problems – and who need their tea and her full attention for the next three hours until bedtime at around seven thirty.

With teenage children the demands are different but no less tiring. I was amused to find the following account I had written of a typical evening:

'Arrived home just before the kids and made us all a cup of tea. Drove Alex to her music lesson. Came back and started to cook the dinner. Justin wandered in and asked me to help with his Latin homework. Have forgotten most of my Latin. Amazing to think I read three Latin mediaeval Latin Chronicles for my special subject at University! Trying to help him I burnt the onions – and had to start all over again. Got cross with Justin because he really wanted me to do his homework for him and I refused – irritably. Left him to get on with it while I rushed down to collect Alex. Got delayed by her teacher (a personal friend of mine) who wanted a chat.

Got home. The dinner overcooked. Alex upset because she had had a quarrel with one of her friends. Tried to get her to see how important it was for her to stand up for herself and sort out her own battles – but this upset her further. (Why is it I can help sort out the problems of the girls at school but get nowhere with Alex? Feel I must be a very insensitive mother. Perhaps I shouldn't be teaching at all!)

Bill arrived home. He'd had a bad day at college so wasn't very happy. We had dinner. Bill helped wash up then went, not very enthusiastically, to a Parish Council meeting. Alex wanted help with her history homework – 'You did do a degree in history, mother!' It's surprising how much one has forgotten. Spent time looking out some relevant books and Alex seemed satisfied and settled down in her room. Then Justin asked me to check his French homework – a cautious approach after our battle over the Latin. 'I have done it **on my own** but I would understand much better if you checked it with me. I never understand the teacher in class – I can't understand his accent!' What can I say to that?

It gets to the stage sometimes when we and our friends compare the marks we get for homework! 'I only got a C for my English yesterday – does the teacher really know what he's about?'!

Alex goes to bed, then comes down and asks for a note for the next day for the dentist. That reminds Justin that he needs £1.50 for a school trip and the consent form to be signed. He starts thinking about going to bed and suddenly remembers he needs his PE kit for the next day. Where is it? After a frantic search it emerges from the bottom of his school bag – damp and far too dirty to wear again without washing. I go resignedly to the kitchen, wash it by hand, spin it out and drape it over the radiators – and tell Justin irritably that if it's not dry by the morning he'll have to wear it wet – that will teach him!

By now, it's 9.45pm and I haven't even started marking the set of English books I had promised the girls I would give back to them in the morning. They were so enthusiastic when they wrote their pieces this afternoon that I agreed to follow it up tomorrow when I see them again.

Just settled down to mark when Bill gets back – wanting to talk about the inanities of parish council business. Make a cup of coffee and at 10.20pm actually start marking. Heigh ho – it will be well past midnight before I can even begin to think of bed.

This was a very typical sort of evening, repeated I am quite sure, in the homes of hundreds of teachers throughout the land. But after evenings like this, I could not help but feel a certain envy of my childless colleagues!

As I said earlier we had quite a proportion of men teachers in the school. Some were a great asset in the sense of providing the girls with excellent role models. These were the older men with families of their own, men who were caring but were also good disciplinarians. But with younger men there were a number of problems.

The most obvious, of course, was the problem of sex. It was difficult for the older more mature girls not to try and flirt with the young and attractive men on the staff. Fortunately many were professional enough not to respond – some may even have been unaware of the fluttering eyelids and suggestive smiles. But there were those who did respond and became far more friendly than was wise. It was not always easy to know what to do – especially with those men teachers who remained behind in their classrooms talking to pupils well after school hours, and those who accompanied pupils on school holidays and intruded into the girls' sleeping quarters. It caused disquiet among the older teachers who could see the dangers. But expressing anxieties about a colleague was like treading a minefield. It was sometimes construed as professional jealousy, and one had to be extremely careful about alerting the Head – especially when there were members of staff who were part of her social circle outside school.

Another quite different problem was that many of the pupils found it difficult to relate to these courteous, well spoken and gentle teachers who were so very different from the aggressive and sometimes abusive men they knew at home.

When there are young attractive men on the staff in a girls' school, they need very firm and clear guidelines with fairly careful surveillance by the senior staff. This did not always happen – and there were a number of potentially dangerous situations which only just avoided exploding into scandal.

I have touched in an earlier chapter on the conflicting roles of the teacher in a school of special difficulty – a conflict between teaching a subject and being a social worker. A friend of mine, a counsellor who has now returned to New Zealand, came along to an in-service course at the school and talked about 'some counselling skills and tasks of the teacher.'

She presented a document which included a list of the contrasting skills of the teacher/counsellor role:

Teacher	**Counsellor**
Disciplining	Nurturing
Keeping them in order	Caring for them
Aggressive teacher behaviour	Active listening
Punishment and reward	Suspending judgement while supporting client towards agreed goal
Imposing ideas and telling them	Listening, clarifying and supporting
A group, a class, a year	A single family or an individual

Secondary subject teaching	Primary individual teaching
Institution	Individual conforming or not
Social or emotional distance	Opportunity for closer and more trusting relationship
Conforming to a given norm	Tolerance, encouragement of individual differences
Control	Influence
Pupil worthy of respect	Client centred counselling

Ideally every teacher is a counsellor. In reality this is still difficult to achieve. Although we might like to think that everything we do in the classroom is aimed at developing the pupil's self confidence, his curiosity about life, and his consideration for other human beings in his environment, it is indeed not easy to teach an examination subject, remember every child's name **and** show by example **and** present a model lesson everytime

When one considers the conflicting and demanding nature of a teacher's role, it is a wonder that teachers ever succeed. And, of course, the public's perception of a teacher's role is often very limited. I remember with wry amusement the remark of one of our mothers at a school Open Evening. She was talking to our remedial specialist – a woman with teaching qualifications as well as a degree in psychology – about her daughter, Cheryl, who was behind with her reading. The remedial specialist told the mother that Cheryl was receiving special attention in school but suggested it might be helpful if her mother helped her with her reading at home. With a certain degree of irritation the mother said, 'I don't see what you are making all this fuss for. After all, Cheryl only wants to be a remedial teacher like you.'

Groups that particularly wanted their daughters to do well and enter the professions were our Indian families. About an eighth of our intake of pupils was Indian – some were Sikhs from the Punjab, some were Pakistanis, and many were from Uganda.

The families from Uganda in particular had seen better times. Many of the girls had had private schooling, servants in the house and a cultured social background. The impact on these gently nurtured Indian girls of the pupils from our downtown school, with their crude and rough ways, their ready resort to verbal and even physical abuse, must have come as a tremendous shock to them.

But, to my surprise, they seemed well integrated into the school community. Although many of them made friendships within their own race, as many more made friendships across the barriers of race – and this was good to see. In the years I was at the school I never heard any personal abuse or prejudice towards the Indian girls **in** the school.

But this, sadly, was not to say the girls were without racial prejudice. In any discussions about race, a fairly deep-rooted prejudice was evident – derived directly from their parents. They were particularly virulent about 'Pakis'. When

I gently tried to point out to them the contradictory nature of their views, they would say, 'But Anita, Surinda etc, is different'. They were careful to disassociate the individual they knew from the group they had been told about.

In two different years while I was at the school the Head Girl was an Indian. The school's Senior Prefects were elected jointly by the staff and the fourth year girls in the last half of the summer term. The Senior Prefects then chose their Head Girl. That an Indian should have been chosen on two separate occasions was a fair indication of the degree to which the Indian girls had been integrated.

A little exercise I did on one occasion was interesting. Pairing all the girls in one class, I asked them to interview and write a profile about each other. I paired the two Indian girls in the class with English girls. When I read the profiles later, there was no mention whatsoever that the girls were Indian. The nearest comment was that 'Punum has long dark hair and brown eyes. When she leaves school she wants to be a typist. She is a very nice girl and I hope she gets the job she wants.'

This, sadly, did not always happen. Though, as I said, many of the Indian parents had high ambitions for their children, often well beyond their abilities (medicine was a favourite ambition), there were some from the lower castes whose ambition was to bring the girls into the family business and be an extra pair of unpaid hands as soon as possible. Such was the case with Sushila – a bright girl who wanted to go on to college and train to be a teacher – an ambition she had the ability to fulfil. But her parents adamantly refused and insisted she worked in their local fish and chip shop. Over the years following, it was sad to see Sushila languishing behind the counter looking more and more down at heel and unhappy.

Others suffered in other ways. Their parents had come to England only in recent years, and though they were keen for their daughters to have an English education, they wanted them to retain their Indian customs. As many of the women made little or no attempt to learn to speak English, they were ignorant of English culture and retained their aloofness from all that was English. They seldom left their homes and their children had to help them with form filling, letter writing and contact with the outside world. It meant the girls got little help with their education and found themselves straddled between two cultures.

Being born in England and mixing freely with their peers in school they found it very difficult to conform to their parent's wishes in the home. They saw their friends going out in the evenings to clubs, cinemas, dances and to each other's houses. They heard them talking about their boyfriends and their plans for the future – and knew that they would never have the freedom to go out and choose their own partners as their parents would insist on an arranged marriage.

One felt deeply sorry for these girls. I remember vividly the plight of Anita. She knew that her parents would insist on an arranged marriage but had hoped that her parents would allow her to go to college first. Her hopes were dashed when the parents announced that they were bringing over a boy from India for her to marry in the autumn – a boy she had never set eyes on. Anita argued endlessly with her parents, even invoking the school's help. But the parents were adamant and, as if to ram home her subservience to the family, they insisted that now she was of marriageable age, she should take on all the household chores.

Anita started coming to school looking utterly exhausted. She was getting up at 5am to do the household work and prepare meals before coming to school. Determined not to give up her aspirations (I had pointed out the possibility of adult education once she was married and away from her parents) she tried to do her homework during the lunch break and in whatever free time she could snatch. She seemed to be heading for breakdown but there was little more we could do to help. In the September after leaving school, Anita was married off.

Sometimes an Indian girl in the fourth year would disappear for a year – only to return and tell us she had been to India to be betrothed. At this time we knew nothing about female genital mutliation.

We had several incidents where girls tried to run away from home to escape an arranged marriage. But they had nowhere to go. Their own community would not condone such defiance – and Social Services were reluctant to intervene in what was really a cultural matter. Within a short time, even the most determined were forced to accept the inevitable and return home.

One of the things that angered the more spirited girls was the freedom granted to their brothers who were allowed to go out with English girls and visit clubs, cinemas and even dances in the evenings. But it was only a short term freedom. These boys were allowed to 'sew their wild oats' before being brought to heel and married off within their own community

It is the offspring of these young people, the third generation Indians, who have the greater chance of being free to do as they choose, especially in those areas where they are in the minority. But as we have seen in other parts of the country the demand for ethnic education and freedom to practise their own customs grows stronger as time passes – so one would be very unwise to make any predictions whatsoever about the future.

However strongly one may feel about arranged marriages, there is little one can say in defence of the western idea of marriage when, in Britain, one in three marriages is currently ending in divorce!

When I had been at the school for three years, I started thinking gently about a move. I decided, rather ambitiously, to try my hand at applying for a deputy headship and was agreeably surprised to find myself on the shortlist. Thus encouraged, I continued to apply and was shortlisted about eight times – on three of which I found myself in the final two. But I never made it! I like to think it was because, despite the variety of my educational experience, I had only taught in the one secondary school. It may well, on the other hand, have been because I did not project myself well in an interview. Sadly, one never got any feedback, so had no way of knowing why the other candidate got the job. This was particularly frustrating when one felt, as objectively as it is possible to feel about oneself, that one was the better candidate!

Whatever the reason, it was a disappointing period and the false hopes engendered by being shortlisted so often prevented me from applying for lesser posts. That was clearly a mistake – but by the time I gave up hopes of attaining a deputy headship, I felt it was too late to apply for a humbler post. So I vegetated and got more and more involved with my life outside school.

Interview processes for these deputy head posts were costly in time, in money, and in nervous energy. They were usually drawn out over two days and involved often as many as ten interviewers and six candidates.

I wonder how many people realise the effort that goes into getting a deputy headship in a secondary school? First, there are the weeks spent scanning *The Times Educational Supplement* before a suitable job turns up. Then one has to write for details of the post – remembering always to enclose a stamped addressed envelope (necessary as post like these attracted well over a hundred applicants in the 1970s).

When the details arrived, a good evening's work lay ahead in filling in the application form. It asked for minute details about your educational qualifications and previous jobs, but it provided only tiny spaces in which to insert the information. Next, you had to write a resume of why you felt suitable for the post – and you tried to tailor your qualifications and strengths to what you perceived to be the needs of the post – a really tedious chore. Finally, you were asked to send a *Curriculum Vitae* (running in my case to eight pages because of the variety of my experience).

Then, just on case you were called for interview, you photocopied what you had said. Once the letter had been posted one forgot all about it, for acknowledgements were rarely made.

The first stirrings of hope begin some week's later when you are informed by the Head that references have been taken up. Sometimes a caring Head will find out more about the appointment by discreet enquiries over the telephone or at a meeting of head teachers.

Then one morning, a letter drops through the letterbox inviting you to interview. The unlucky applicants remain in ignorance until an appointment is finally made.

The interview day approaches. The adrenalin begins to course faster through one's veins. Wardrobes have to be inspected and serious decisions made as to whether new outfits are called for, and whether, being a woman, it would be a good idea to wear nail varnish and have one's hair specially set. These are not problems that the male candidate has to wrestle with. Most Heads of mixed schools are men and one has to decide what sort of impression to make – do you opt to be feminine and pretty, or do you try to look very businesslike and efficient? If you are too feminine, are you likely to be considered too weak to take on disciplinary responsibilities? If you project yourself as too efficient, will you upset male egos? Do you try and demonstrate that you have two sides to your character – or would that give the impression that you are inconsistent? These uncertainties put the woman at an immediate disadvantage beside the male candidates.

The day of the interview arrives. You've probably had very little sleep the night before – and you take longer than usual to get ready.

You set off. If you're wise, you will have tried out the journey beforehand to make sure you are not late on the day. Once you get to the school, you realise it is a replica of the other schools you have visited – either pre-war drear or post war glass house.

You are ushered into a room where you meet the other candidates – all equally nervous and tense, and all equally well groomed. The men probably have not had their hair set – but one can't be quite sure!

You sit making polite conversation while carefully weighing up the potential of the other candidates. The Head walks in and greets everyone warmly – then outlines the plan of battle. First, a group session with the Head, then lunch with various members of staff. After lunch half the group to be conducted round the school while the other half have individual sessions with the Head. Then a tea party with senior members of staff to wind up the day.

The second day – interviews all morning with the Head and the Chairman of Governors. Then lunch. Then the final all-important interview by the panel – Head, Chairman of Governors, Divisional Educational Office, Inspector, and two other Governors.

These are the notes I made after one of these interviews was over.

"After a cup of coffee to soothe the nerves, the Group Discussion began. We sit in a circle trying to look relaxed. Must strike the right note here. Is the Head looking for someone to take a lead in the discussion and really dominate it? Or would that frighten him and make him feel he would get too strong a deputy? Perhaps it's better to keep a low profile to begin with and let others make mistakes before coming in with pertinent and wise comments that demonstrate your ability. But perhaps the Head is not perceptive enough to pick up the wisdom of your remarks. Perhaps I ought to join in right from the beginning and take the lead. Should I appear as an enabler – giving others the opportunity to show their mettle? Could be good – but on the other hand that might enable others to shine at my expense. Depends so much on how much the head knows about group dynamics. Oh dear – it's too late for further reflection. We're in action.

Well, that session didn't go too badly. Am beginning to get an idea of the strength and weaknesses of the opposition. The blonde is a lightweight – no need to worry about her. And the tall one is too dogmatic – unlikely to be considered seriously. What about the fat dumpy looking one with no personality? Should think she has nothing to offer. But the one with the glasses and the pleasant manner seems a strong candidate – not very attractive to look at, but thoughtful and sensible comments – clearly on the ball. Then there's the inevitable inside candidate – but we don't meet her till tomorrow.

Off to lunch. Who am I partnered with? Yes, I see, the head of department in my own subject. Interesting. He takes me off to the canteen. Cafeteria service I see. Food – not too bad. Yes, as to be expected, we sit at table with a group of others – Director of Studies (must watch what I say in that direction) and Head of Maths as well as some younger ones. Are they going to be asked to comment on the candidates? Must try and charm them – not too formal yet not too flippant. Best thing is to bring them out – ask questions and make them feel good. Give a little of myself and my interests – but not too much.

Lunch over, the candidates assemble. A fair amount of chit-chat about the morning session The inevitable interview camaraderie beginning to build up. Ah, here come our escorts for the afternoon.

Tour round the school – conducted by the male Deputy Head. That's why all the candidates are women. Must make an impression here – he's sure to be consulted later. School really is rather nice – paint work fresh, no graffiti and very little litter about considering the lunch hour is only just over. Nice atmosphere of work in the school – very little noise emanating from the classrooms and some classroom doors left open. A good sign – no one with discipline problems would expose themselves by leaving their door open.

Staff room for tea. It's very full. Deputy laughingly says that everyone has come to tea with express purpose of seeing The Candidates! It's like being on show in the zoo!

Now it's my turn for interview with the head. What a pleasant man he is. Very relaxed discursive conversation. Could easily work with him. Leave feeling quite pleased with myself – though on reflection realise I have not picked up much about his philosophy of education.

Summons now to the tea party. We all troop off to the Home Economics area for a really splendid bun fight. Food very tempting – but realise just in time one is still on show! Mustn't waste time eating but must circulate. Say good-bye reluctantly to tempting food. Chat to Head of English – just getting into an animated discussion when the Head claps his hands and asks the candidates to withdraw in a few moments. We all walk out – feeling proper Charlies – and collapse in giggles in the cloakroom This, if nothing else, has cemented the group together. It wouldn't take much for us to withdraw collectively at this moment. Fancy discussing us in this blatant manner!

Drive home realising the ordeal has really only just begun – another whole night and day to get through!

Arrive at the school at 9 o'clock. Slept a little better last night – but woke very early. Wonder what order we'll be interviewed in. Alphabetical – forwards or backwards, random or in order of preference. Think the best place to be last but one – am sure they forget what the first one's like by the time they get to the end!

Head comes in – 'Good morning ladies.' He puts up interview list. I'm the last. Does that mean it's alphabetical? No, my name is near the middle. Could this be a good omen? Don't get excited – probably just a random order. Do some calculations

– and realise I've got about two and a half hours to sit around getting more and more nervous. What a waste of time! Why not tell us the day before so we can come in just before our interview.

The morning passes very slowly. Conversation somewhat stilted – no one wants to give away too much – but group camaraderie's very evident. Every candidate wished good luck as they go off – temptation resisted to discuss their potential as they leave the room.

Coffee very welcome first time round – but refused second time. Can't risk a full bladder just as one is called in for interview. Laughter as candidates return nervously giggling. Would love to ask what sort of questions they faced – but that wouldn't be cricket!

Funny how the clock is so loud – don't usually notice electric clocks. But perhaps it's not the clock – goodness, it's my own heart thumping.

Five minutes to go – a quick final dash to the loo. Now it's my turn.

Well, that was a very pleasant interview. The Head and Chairman of Governors very charming and friendly. What am I worrying about? I've got as good a chance as any. Now for lunch – in the Home Economics block this time. Let's hope it's good.

What a splendid lunch. Table beautifully laid, flowers, wine, and food that certainly didn't come from the canteen. Found myself placed next to the Head and on his other side the nice lady with glasses. Is this significant? Certainly no choice as to where to sit – all the places had name cards. Tried to watch the conversation carefully – not too much 'shop' over lunch. This is a social occasion and one doesn't want to be considered a bore. Woman with glasses very pleasant – but rather prissy. A spinster – that's probably the reason. Think she would be a good solid and reliable Deputy – but without much spark. Feel I've got more to offer. Hope they will think so too.

Lunch over, the Head tells us the candidates are to be narrowed down to two. All repair to our little room for coffee while we wait for the decision. This time, no attempt at conversation – the situation too nail biting. A heavy silence. Time drags interminably. A stranger enters the room. It's the internal candidate – we haven't seen her before. Wonder what she's like? She seems very confident. Perhaps it's all a fix and she's got the job in the bag already. Mustn't think like this. The head seems a man of integrity.

Wonder what sort of woman he'd like to work with. He's very presentable and obviously very confident. There's a danger he might prefer a single lady because she might look up to him more. What an agonising wait.

Door opens! All heads turn in unison – but it's only the Deputy to offer more coffee. We all say no. Now is not the time for coffee. Further long silence broken by nervous giggles. Door opens again. This time it's the Head. He says he would like the lady in glasses and ME to stay behind – glory be! The rest he thanks graciously and sends on their way.

The lady in glasses and I smile sheepishly at each other. Say we both felt hopeful when we found ourselves placed next to the Head at lunch. Wish each other luck –

while secretly wishing anything but! Lady with glasses to go first. Each interview to take about an hour.

She goes off. I sit in solitary state in the little room. It suddenly feels very empty and very bleak. No one comes nigh or by. I can't settle to anything though I have reading matter with me. Keep going over in my mind my attitude to all the items listed on the job description. Think I've got them off pat. Several trips to the toilet. Never has an hour dragged so slowly. Finally woman with glasses returns and it's my turn. Go in. Six members of panel. An introduction all round and then told to sit on the hard chair facing them. Do hate these hard chairs – you never know what to do with your knees. Try to look relaxed.

First question – 'Perhaps you'd like to tell us about yourself'.' I look blank and feel very surprised. That's exactly what he asked this morning. Surely he doesn't want me to go over it all again? It must be a test question to see if I am an interesting character. How can I make it different. Tell them about my family and community commitments. As I launch into an account of my domestic life, realise I have made a BIG mistake. They will think I have far too many commitments to give sufficient time to the school. What a blunder. But launched, I cannot pull back.

'Right. Now tell is something about your career.' Am feeling flustered – so burble on about all the different jobs I have done over the years and completely forget to emphasise the aspects of it which I think make me suitable for this job.

Move on to the question about mixed ability teaching. Am on firmer ground here – though during the two days I have been in the school I have been unable to find out the school's views on this thorny issue. Best be honest and expound my personal views. By the nods and smiles, guess I've hit the right note.

Exams – views on 16 plus and CSE Mode 1 versus Mode 3. Have very mixed feelings here, especially in view of changes going on in my own school under the new regime. Can see both sides of the argument – but have not yet formulated an opinion. Best way round this one is to put both points of view and then ask to sit on the fence for the moment. Don't think that pleases the Head – he looks a little grim. Really have no idea of his standpoint – he has resolutely concealed his own views throughout.

Remedial teaching? Are we talking about the same thing here? Suspect his remedial kids would be among our high flyers! Hold on – my school isn't as bad as all that – must watch how I go.

Do I get much help from the Head? Loaded question this. If I answer 'yes' they will think my ideas come from her. If I answer 'no' I may appear disloyal. Better plump for 'yes' – even though it's blatantly untrue. Smirk on Inspector's face. Obviously thinks I've culled my ideas from her. Drat!

Courses? Yes, I've attended several – Course 11-16 on Curriculum Planning – yes, very interesting. Have I read the follow-up document? Now which one is he referring to? There have been three documents since then and I always get them muddled up.

Better confess rather than make myself look silly. Mistake! It didn't go down well with the Inspector – obviously thinks me ill informed which is far from the truth. But the Chairman of Governors smiled sympathetically.

Realise I am flapping my hands around too much and sitting forward tensely rather than in a relaxed position. This really isn't going too well. What a contrast to this morning's interview. It was that first question that threw me.

'What would you do if a pupil came to you and said she was pregnant?' Answered this very well – at least, so I thought till I remembered I had forgotten to say I would discuss it with the Head. What a blunder! Now he'll think I'm the sort of person who will assume too much responsibility and by-pass him. Should have indicated that I knew all important matters had to be discussed with him first. And I did the same this morning. This just isn't good.

Manage to recover my balance and the last part of the interview goes smoothly. But I don't trust the woman Governor. She hasn't opened her mouth once during the interview – but I sense she doesn't like me.

Finally, 'Is there anything you would like to ask?' Know this is important so raise one or two matters in the job description and how they view the role of the Deputy.

Leave with very mixed feelings about the interview – know I haven't done myself justice.

Return to the little room. Lady with glasses sitting there very quietly. We sit chatting – outwardly calm but I can hear my heart beating. Now the interviews are over, we can let our guard down and talk about what we are doing. She is obviously a very experienced teacher – already holds the post of Senior Mistress. A spinster, as I thought, and a deeply committed Christian. She's never done anything other than teach. Clearly, a formidable rival.

An hour goes by. The tension builds up. Surely no one should have to go through this sort of thing – it's enough to cause a heart attack. Why can't we go home and let them inform us by post. This being kept waiting is sadistic.

The door opens. I have my fingers tightly crossed. The Head walks in. He turns to the lady with glasses and asks her to go in. I find myself shaking his hand. 'Thank you for coming. It was very close indeed.'

And that's it. Got to go home and break the news. Then back to my down-town school with all its problems and its dilapidated building. And the staff at school to face. Some will be sympathetic – some, I know, will secretly be pleased at my come-uppance. Jealousy is rife in the staffroom. What a disappointment – so near and yet so far. This job would have been a sinecure compared to my present one – nicer surroundings, better facilities, well motivated children and the sort of job I would really have enjoyed and got my teeth into.

Hey ho! Perhaps there will be another opportunity later. Perhaps I can persuade my husband to take us all out to dinner – I couldn't face cooking after all this."

The schools I was interviewed at seemed to be unaware of the problems faced by down-town schools like ours, and I am sure this contributed to my failure to secure a deputy headship. There was a certain lack of understanding of what I was talking about, and the means we used to combat our problems.

A school of special difficulty like ours demanded a united staff. Sadly, over the years, with a change of Head, and with increasing union activity, the staff that had once been warm and united, became divided into factions. We all see things differently. I was at the time a member of the National Union of Teachers which I joined without giving it much thought when I first started teaching, being the union to which most of the staff belonged.

With the arrival of the new Head, staff were encouraged to change to the National Association of Schoolmasters and Schoolmistresses because it renounced strike action – and the perception of many on the staff was that those who changed allegiance received favourable treatment by the Head. As union activity got more militant, the atmosphere in the staffroom deteriorated into a 'them and us' situation – exacerbated by the missives that came from County Hall. It was no longer a pleasant staff room to be part of.

It was during this period that one became more aware than ever of the power of the Head. In a report **Twelve Good Schools**, published some years before, the author whose name I now forget, demonstrated that good schools are very much the product of a good Head Teacher. This I believe to be the case. Over the years I was at the school, I had the opportunity to see in action two very different Heads. My sympathies were with the first whose philosophy accorded with mine. But the second had organisational abilities and made the school a more disciplined place to work in. They were both enablers – but the first enabled creativity while the second seemed to enable those whose views coincided with hers.

Over the years, I discovered that many teachers felt very dependant on the Head. For it was the Head who wrote the references on which a new job depended; she who could choose who was to receive the scale posts; she who would decide what subjects should be on the curriculum; how many periods they should be taught for; and in which rooms the teacher should be based.

One of the things I found most difficult to adjust to was the way that every new idea that came onto the education scene was immediately adopted and implemented. New educational jargon was in regular use, and there were constant changes in the curriculum. Before we had time to implement and evaluate a new development, it was thrown out and a new one was introduced. Although there had been many changes under the previous regime, the motivation for change was educational rather than political. Staff were constantly being sent on in-service courses – and one felt that the whole school was being run on the basis of a personal P.R. exercise. I could not deny that some of the ideas were good – but there were others which did more for the reputation of the Head than the benefit of the pupils

This, in common with many of my colleagues, I resented. But I found that, on the whole, the teachers lacked the courage to speak out about injustices, or to call for help when in difficulties because their image might be tarnished. When it came to strike action, many of us joined in against our personal inclination because we believed it was the only way to achieve a better deal for teachers and ultimately for the pupils. But it was only the strongest who remained in the NUT and the group as a whole suffered as a result.

It was not an easy period and it laid for me the seeds which led to my early retirement which I mentioned earlier. But I cannot conclude this little comment on the power of the Head without recounting a small incident which gave us all great amusement.

A new teacher came to the school who was very gullible. She had previously worked in a middle school and arrived soon after the new head. She was unaware of the calibre of our girls, and arriving in her classroom for registration one day, she found the girls in a state of high excitement. Having much on her mind, she did not take in the details of what the girls were saying to her, and signed, without reading it, the petition they thrust in front of her.

Returning to the staffroom for the afternoon break she heard her colleagues talking about the petition the girls had organised. Her face was a study when she realised that it was her form that had organised the Petition and that the Petition was a request to remove the new Head!

As I became increasingly disillusioned, I found it difficult to restrain myself from barbed comments and attacks on what was happening. To relieve my feelings I indulged in some humorous but cynical 'Black Papers' which I rather wickedly distributed among the staff. My Black Papers caricatured some of the cherished ideas that were being propounded from the top. Enough was enough. It was time to go!

CHAPTER 24
The Hospice Charity, 1985 – 1993

Over the years I seem to have stumbled into new areas of activity almost by chance. I was aware that, by contrast, many of my university friends followed a more conventional path which has led to greater success both financially and career-wise. At times, it has been difficult not to feel a little envious of the security they have enjoyed.

Two friends, whose children were the same ages as ours and with whom we spent a lot of time when the children were very young, were particularly well organised. They appeared to have mapped out their lives for years ahead – planning where they would live, what sort of career they would follow, which schools their children would go to, and the cars they would buy at different stages of their lives. Their holidays were planned well in advance, and weekend visits booked months ahead, while arrangements for return visits were always made before we parted. Doubts about the direction in which their lives were going seemed not to have entered their heads – nor did they seem bothered by fears that financial problems would impinge on their way of life.

We found this both amusing and intimidating. But we were too far down the erratic path of change and variety to try and emulate them. I seemed to hurl myself into one venture after another, and the family lurched from one financial crisis to the next – Bill never daring to leave the job he hated because of the voracious appetite of The Oast and the demands of my varied involvements. The only really fixed point in our lives was our oast house and our happy family. We felt we were doomed to be 'last minuters' – planning holidays a few days before, and jumping blindly into each new venture that presented itself. We knew we would never be rich and that we would never reach dizzy career heights. I had no doubt of my abilities (my erstwhile assistant at the India Office Library became the first woman head of MI5!) but I had no specific career ambitions, while Bill concentrated his hopes (but sadly not his time) on being a successful writer.

For me, the great thing was that life was never dull or uninteresting, and I know that, had I the chance to live my life over again, I would probably want to change it very little. That of course is, intrinsically, a very selfish statement. I could never have become involved in so many community activities without Bill's support – but in accepting that support without question, I was, in fact, restricting Bill's own opportunities. It was not till much later that I became aware of how much people's achievements in life are dependent on the support of those around them. I suspect that behind every successful person there is a strong silent partner – whether spouse, parent or friend – providing the stability, the support and the encouragement that enables them to go forward against all odds and achieve what they have set out to do. I know that without Bill, all the projects in which I have played a major part would never have come to fruition had Bill not given me endless support and encouragement.

Because my life seemed to lack any coherent strategy, it seemed just another random involvement without special significance when I first stumbled into a new area of community involvement – the Hospice Appeal. I hadn't long been a Christian, and as time went by I began to sense that there had, in fact, been a pattern to my life, and that there was a Guiding Hand directing it: that I had been led into all these different experiences in order to develop the skills needed for the particular task in which I found myself the leading player. I didn't articulate this idea for a long time – and when I did eventually talk to Bill about it, he, being a non-believer and a cynic to boot, laughed and said that that was one way of interpreting life which anyone could indulge in. We agreed to differ!

As with all my other ventures, involvement with the hospice was not planned. We spent a weekend with friends in Bristol – the wife was the daughter of a colleague at the India Office Library who had worked for me during vacations while she was at Oxford, and her husband was Reader in Economics at Bristol University. He had been on the point of accepting a professorship when he developed a brain tumour. The prognosis was bad, and he and his wife became involved with the Bristol Clinic in an attempt to stave off the progress of the disease.

While staying with them we learnt a lot about the philosophy of the Bristol Clinic, as well as seeing at first hand both the positive approach to cancer that the clinic engendered, and the less than attractive diet that patients were encouraged to follow.

Soon after our return I was introduced at a healing service at our local church to a lady who had advanced cancer and who, our Rector said, was thinking of going to the Bristol Clinic. She was keen to find out more about it before committing herself, so I put her in touch with our friends in Bristol, and she went down to visit them, and soon after spent a week in the Clinic. On her return, she and I became close friends, and she stayed with us on a number of occasions while her husband had some much needed breaks.

At about the same time, one of the sharper tongued members of our congregation commented that my community involvement always seemed to be with buildings rather than people. This touched a raw nerve and made me think a lot about what I was doing in my spare time.

A week or two later, I noticed a report in the local paper of a public meeting about a local hospice project which had been under way for just over a year. The meeting had apparently been stormy. The following week the paper carried a letter from the chairman of the project, answering some of the criticisms that had been made at the meeting and in the news report, and asking for help, especially with fund raising.

Life is full of coincidences or, as I have said I now believe, the guiding hand of God. The following week in June 1985 I was asked by a friend in the village to help with a Fair that she and her fellow flower arrangers were organising to raise money for the Hospice Appeal. Would I sell raffle tickets for her?

Now, selling raffle tickets is something I pride myself on being good at. There's always a sense of achievement in being able to relieve people of money for a good cause. I suspect the feeling is not dissimilar to that of the hunter who sets out to track down his prey. I usually set myself two targets: to nab everyone present, and to raise a certain sum of money based on an equation of the number of people at the gathering multiplied by one pound. I am not often disappointed in the result!

So, on this particular sunny afternoon, with a young French friend and a rather dotty relative in tow, I set off for the Fair. It was well organised and varied – held in a couple of barns and the surrounding yard. There was an exhibition of paintings by local artists on the upper floor, and an exhibition of beautiful flower arrangements below. The other barn contained refreshments- delicious home made cakes, tea and coffee – while dotted round the yard were stalls and a large cardboard wishing well into which people were throwing money.

The contacts of the past weeks – the Bristol Clinic, the comment in church, the newspaper report, and the Fair, all happening at about the same time, seemed to speak to me. I'd already been moderately successful with the fund raising I had done for the Playgroup, the Village Hall and the Church, and the thought nagged at me that here was a charity for people in great need, and that I ought to offer to help with fund raising. It was a niggle that I tried to suppress. My life was already very busy, and I was teaching full time. But the niggle wouldn't go away, and I felt I was somehow being pushed into making a new commitment.

The commitment was not so much to the idea of a hospice as to helping with something worthwhile. If you look round the charity world, it's interesting to discover who is involved in what, and the motivation for that involvement. There are so many hundreds of charities calling out for help – equally worthwhile and providing invaluable help for people in need. It would be difficult to try and evaluate the relative merits of these different charities. Is it, for example, more important to help young children in need at the beginning of their lives or to help the old and destitute who lack support? Is it more important to alleviate the effects of illness, or to concentrate on research to prevent such illnesses ever developing? One charity looks at the immediate – the other at the long term. Is it more important to provide food to prevent people starving in the here and now, or to provide help that will enable the more certain production of food in the future? These questions are impossible to answer. You cannot say to a man starving to death 'I am not going to give you any food because my money is going to an irrigation scheme which will help your children'. He may well reply that his children will not survive to see the irrigation scheme if they do not get food now. But if the irrigation scheme is not put into place now, the same story of lack or food and starvation may be repeated time and time again in the future.

So it is that most of us, without the knowledge to weigh up the pros and cons, don't attempt to answer these complex questions but become involved with a

Cynthia's family and friends with the artist Graham Clarke

particular charity either by chance or because of some personal link with the charity's cause. Many of the specialist medical charities, for example, arise directly out of the efforts of the relatives of sufferers of such medical conditions as diabetes, multiple sclerosis, motor neurone disease, Parkinsons, celiac disease, cystic fibrosis, rheumatoid arthritis – to name just a few. Other charities, concerned with the widespread incidence of diseases like cancer and heart disease, attract a wider support as people realise that they too, could find themselves among the victims. Some charities have an emotional appeal like the Blind Dogs and Lifeboats – an appeal that cannot be understood in intellectual terms when they are weighed against similar but less popular charities such as Mencap and the Deaf charities.

Hospice charities fall into the emotional category, and attract people from all walks of life. There are those who have experienced hospice care and want it for others; those who desperately needed hospice care but none was available, and so want to make sure others do not find themselves in the same predicament; those who feel that cancer, knowing no bounds and striking one in five of the population, may well claim them as a victim; and those who feel that dying is such a traumatic event for patients and families that specialist help and support is of vital importance.

But of course, with hospice charities as with all the others, people get involved for a whole variety of reasons, totally unconnected with the purpose of the charity itself. There are those who have a purely altruistic desire to do something worthwhile in the community; those who get involved because they are lonely; those who are bereaved and need to rebuild their lives; those who want their personal identity affirmed; those who are retired and having lost both their status and their purpose in life, need to be reaffirmed as valuable members of the community. There are those who are bored, those who want companionship, and those eager for new challenges.

Those involved in charity work need careful nurturing and support if their involvement is to continue and be of significance. This was something I was to learn later – but at the time I became involved in the Hospice Appeal, none of these thoughts entered my head.

At that first hospice Fair, all that concerned me was whether or not I should respond to the urge to offer my services. When I saw that the Chairman of the Hospice Appeal was present (his photograph had been in the local paper and, being very tall and dark, he was easily identifiable) I felt rather like a fish caught on a fly, being gently but inexorably drawn in. Wandering round selling my raffle tickets, I kept on passing the Chairman, and eventually, gave in and approached him to offer my services.

I laugh when I think back to his response. He didn't seem in the least enthusiastic about having a new volunteer. He asked me a bit about myself and whether I'd done any fund raising – but didn't seem any too impressed with what I had to tell him. The reason seemed obvious when he told me that he'd already managed to gather together a team of high-powered people, and that a retired business man was to take on fund raising. This somewhat deflating response was followed by the comment that he might be able to find something for me to do for the Appeal, and that if I would like to join the rest of the team at a social gathering the following week, he would see whether I could be fitted in!

I was more than a little amused at this response, and felt I had got myself 'screwed to the sticking point' for nothing. But I was curious, so decided to go along to the gathering and meet this high-powered team of people. The local town was an unknown quantity to me, and so were its citizens. Though it was only nine miles distant, I very rarely went there, and had no acquaintances let alone friends in the town. Our lives revolved round our rural community, and the town where I taught which was seventeen miles distant in the opposite direction.

Feeling a little nervous at the thought of walking into a roomful of total strangers (Bill had declined the invitation to accompany me), I dressed rather carefully for the gathering, and arrived to discover a room full of people, with a happy buzz of conversation.

In time honoured fashion, we were all asked to introduce ourselves and tell the assembled company about our backgrounds. As we went round the room, a faint memory stirred as we got to an elderly gentleman with glasses who said he was a retired businessman. Further round the room I was delighted to see someone I knew – Peter, the former editor of the *Kent Messenger* whom I had worked for when I was a local correspondent years before.

When the introductions were over, the elderly businessman spoke again, and as I looked at him the stirrings of memory became even stronger. I asked him if he had ever been known as Chalkie? He dismissed the suggestion somewhat brusquely saying that everyone with his surname carried that nickname. But memory was beginning to be certain. I named my father and asked if the name meant anything to him. At that, recognition came to him. He had served with my father in the War, and, when he was demobbed, had been a regular visitor to our house until he married and moved away. My sister and I had been very fond of him and used to call him 'uncle'.

Ron White

I don't quite know what triggered the memory. The young soldier had been slim with fair curly hair. The man in front of me was portly and his limited crop of hair was white. We had met up once just before my mother died eleven years before – but that had been such a sad and traumatic time that all memories of the encounter had been quite obliterated.

But now, memory flooded back for both of us. He jumped up from his chair and, to my embarrassment and the curiosity of everyone present, embraced me on the spot. I was overcome with amazement – and if anything, bemused even more when the chairman told me later that this was the retired businessman who was to head fund raising, and that he had already decided that the best way I could help was to be his assistant!

That evening was, apart from the introductions and a brief resume by the chairman, purely social and we all fell on the scrumptious food and drink set out in the corner of the room, and started chatting nineteen to the dozen. I naturally gravitated towards my erstwhile 'uncle' and the newspaper editor, Peter, and we had a wonderful evening, reminiscing about old times.

A week later, we had the first formal meeting of the new Management

Committee. The Chairman had picked his team well and had gathered together a group of people with varying skills and interests: Peter, who owned a local PR firm as well as being editor of the local 'freebie' newspaper; a local businessman with his own typesetting and printing business; a nurse who agreed to take on the role of Speaker Secretary; two Borough Councillors of different political persuasions; and two Funeral Directors; as well as a smattering of well dressed middle aged ladies with secretarial skills and time on their hands.

These new members were grafted on to the existing team which had been struggling to get the project off the ground for the last eighteen months. The key positions of Secretary, Treasurer and Newsletter Editor were held by the original members, while my 'uncle', Ron, was to be the Fund Raising Director, replacing a young married woman with children who had resigned because of the effect fund raising was having on her family life.

At that first formal meeting we learnt that the project had, to date, raised about £11,000; that the local health authority was hostile to the idea of an in-patient hospice, insisting that it was not part of its forward plan; and that there was a rival group that wanted to set up a hospice home care organisation which the health authority seemed ready to support. Being at that time unfamiliar with the charity world other than our own small scale village efforts, and being bowled over by the enthusiasm and conviction of the chairman, I was unaware of the implications of this information. In retrospect, it was clear that a charity with such an emotional appeal as a hospice should have brought in far more than £11,000 in the first eighteen months and that, without the support of the local health authority, there were bound to be problems.

But at that first meeting it was clear to us that the chairman had done a lot of research into hospice care, and had already produced a well researched paper on the need for a local one. We were all given a copy. It was a thoroughly professional piece of work with statistics about the number of deaths from cancer in the area, the number dying in hospital and at home, details of cost, population, and population growth forecasts, likely bed occupancy, and careful comparisons with other areas.

The chairman believed that the Health Authority's attitude was governed by financial rather than medical considerations, and convinced us all that an in-patient unit was badly needed. We left the meeting feeling that we were up against difficult and implacable enemies in both the Health Authority and the rival hospice group, and convinced that we should do all we could to persuade the local health authority to change its mind.

At the same time, I felt more than a little superfluous. During the course of the meeting, one of the funeral directors had outlined such a wonderful sounding scheme which, he assured us, would bring in £10,000 within a few months that, remembering my own more modest achievements (I had by then run two Horse Shows bringing in £2,200 and £2,600 after a considerable amount of work) I felt my contribution to this enterprise was going to be very limited indeed.

Shortly after this first meeting, Ron called the first Fund Raisers' Meeting at his house. He lived in a suburban area of town in a 1930s house, slightly more spacious but built in the same style, and with the same feel to it, as the house I had lived in until the age of eighteen. As a child, I had loved the house, and when, at the age of thirteen, my parents had contemplated moving, I was deeply distressed. The move didn't take place. But by the time I was at university, I disliked the house and the area and all that 'suburbia' and 'middle class values' represented. How snobbish we were as undergraduates! When my parents moved to the ground floor flat of a very large Victorian house with a beautiful garden round the house, my contact with 1930s suburbia came to an abrupt end.

My parents later moved to a spacious bungalow at Bexhill with a large garden, and our first married home, as I've said, was a flat in a Victorian house above a hairdresser's shop where the rooms were large and spacious and overlooked an orchard – mitigating the downside of the flat – a loo which we had to share with the staff of the hairdressers, a primitive bathroom with a geezer, and a basement which was flooded with water three quarters of the year and sprouted mushrooms! Later we moved to the modern flat in three acres of beautiful gardens, and then into The Oast and the open countryside. So, going to that first Fund Raisers' Meeting in a 1930s house in a suburban area of town was like going back in time.

It was at this first meeting that I really began to realise what we had taken on. The retiring fundraiser, who was present, gave us a list of names and addresses of about eighty people who, she said, were the Members of the Appeal. She also handed us some packets of sunflower seeds, and said she had been in touch with several schools about them. She didn't seem to have any other projects under way, and explained that the fund raising had been such a strain on her marriage that she had decided that her family had to come first, and she would be giving up any further involvement with the project.

This meant, of course, that we were virtually starting from scratch. The list of names was very basic, and hadn't been sorted into areas. The two others at the meeting both worked full time, as did I, and said they had only a limited amount of time to devote to the appeal. It was a daunting thought.

As with any new job, to begin with one has no idea where to start. There is a feeling of lassitude – almost of boredom – as one begins tentatively to get to grips with what is involved. I shall never forget my first few weeks at the India Office Library way back in 1956. It was a new post. No one had ever before looked after the European Manuscript Collection. Although, as I later discovered, it occupied half a mile of shelf life, it was but one section of a vast collection of oriental books and manuscripts in all the major languages of the Indian sub continent. I was the only one with archival knowledge on the staff (and, being my first archive post, that knowledge was fairly limited!) and for the first few weeks, I was bored and uncertain about what to do, and where to begin. But within a couple of months, my time was fully occupied, and the parameters of the job extended daily as I discovered the enormity of the task I had taken on – a large collection of manuscripts, some of which had come in during the nineteenth century, and were neglected and in need of repair, while vast new deposits of papers relating to the Viceroys and Secretaries of State for India waited to be taken out of chests and listed. The storage space was inadequate; there were dozens of small collections tucked away in cupboards because no one had known what to do with them; there was a vast collection of early nineteenth century photographs, unlisted and many still wrapped in brown paper, tucked into odd corners throughout the Library; there were no catalogues; there were thousands of manuscripts in need of repair and binding; and there were appalling fire risks which had somehow to be addressed, with the whole building (part of the old Commonwealth Relations Office) heated by open coal fires. Within a few months of my arrival I was overwhelmed by the thought that even if I had a hundred years to work on the material, I could only accomplish a small part of what needed to be done. I never again knew boredom in the seven happy years I spent there.

But to go back to the Hospice Appeal. In those early days we proceeded gently. I was still teaching full time, and Ron was in the early stages of widowhood. We were fortunate in that we found that not only did we have the link from the post war days, we also got on remarkably well, and complemented each other. He had a large circle of friends and acquaintances in the town and belonged to various men's clubs, while I had drive and organisational ability. It was a good combination and we soon moved into an easy working relationship where he made the contacts and I did the organising and paper work.

As with the India Office Library, I don't think at first we realised the size of the task we had taken on. We talked at that stage of raising £450,000 to build and equip the hospice. By the time it was actually built, we needed £1.3 million!

I felt the first priority was to do something about the Members – people who had indicated an interest in the appeal but whose support was not being utilised apart from the payment of an annual £2 subscription. So for the first few weeks I pored over a map of the local area and sorted the Members into local groups. It seemed to me that if we could get people to work together, they ought to be able to do some more effective fund raising rather than running the jumble sales which had, apparently, up to that time (apart from the Fair organised by my flower arranging friends) been the apogee of their achievements.

So I set about organising a network of support groups, following a similar pattern with each group I set up. I would look at the list of Members in an area, pick a name at random and telephone to ask whether they or any of their friends would host a gathering for the Appeal – ideally a cheese and wine party so as to attract the men as well as the ladies. The response was always positive. They either said 'yes' straight away or, if they lived in a small house, would refer me to someone with a larger house. At these gatherings – some of which were coffee mornings – there would be a bring-and-buy stall, a cake stall, and a raffle, but with the emphasis on the social aspect of the event. At some time during the evening (or morning) there would be a short talk about the Appeal, and what we were trying to achieve. I would suggest that the people present formed a local support group – but at that stage did not press them into any formal organisation – leaving it for a week or two before making contact again.

I soon discovered that unless one could identify a leader among a group of people, nothing would happen. My very first excursion turned out a bitter disappointment. There were about twenty people present and our Speaker Secretary gave an excellent talk. Lots of questions followed and there seemed to be lively enthusiasm for the hospice project. The gathering raised about £40 and I felt we were all set for ongoing support. But despite many visits and telephone conversations, I was unable to find anyone willing to take on responsibility for organising the group. As a result, support in that village dwindled to nothing, and it was not until some years later that I eventually managed to set up a group there.

Yet, on another occasion, a tiny gathering of people produced a leader who was so energetic that the group flourished and over the years produced regular and valuable support.

I soon felt very much at home with the Speaker Secretary and for the first few months we worked closely together – she giving the talks and I organising the groups into effective working committees. She knew far more about hospices than I did, and was a good speaker, so it was a happy arrangement. Then, on one occasion, she was taken ill and I had to take on the speaker's role at the last minute. She lent me her notes and I gave my first hospice talk. I was very nervous, but her notes were excellent and I got by. But using someone else's notes is difficult. We all express ourselves in a different way, and as I went through her talk I felt that there were things I might have said that she left out, and things I would have preferred to say in a different way and in a different sequence. I had much enjoyed giving the talk and, feeling more confident, decided that in the future, when I was trying to get a support group off the ground, I would give the talk myself, thus freeing the Speaker Secretary for other engagements.

I was by this time more familiar with hospices. I had joined the appeal in June 1985 and during that year my friend from the Church, who had gone to the Bristol Clinic, gradually deteriorated and it became obvious that her long fight with cancer was nearing its end. A few days after Christmas 1985 she was admitted to the hospice in Chatham where I was teaching, and spent the last four weeks of her life there.

The school where I taught was round the corner from the hospice, and I popped over most days at lunch time to see her. There I saw the work of a hospice at first hand – the loving care given by the nurses to my friend, the way her pain was at last controlled so that, though very weak, she was at peace and able to participate in the life of her little four bedded room. One lady was there for respite care for most of her time in the ward, another was in for symptom control, while the fourth bed was occupied by terminal patients, often for just the last day or two of their lives.

Their deaths could not have been easy for my friend to witness, but she seemed to take it all in her stride, and was accepting that her own death was inevitable. I remember on one occasion saying from memory, at her request, the twenty-third Psalm. Whether it was a Freudian slip or a quite genuine lapse of memory, I don't know, but I omitted the verse 'Yea though I walk through the valley of the shadow of death'. She gently chided me and made me repeat the Psalm with the verse in its rightful place.

She was keen that we should support the Hospice Appeal and, in the early period of my involvement with the project, had not only assisted with some of our fund raising activities, but had encouraged her husband and family, and her many friends, to help all they could. Even a few days before her death she was eager to know what was going on, and I remember with amazement how, just two days before she died, she wanted to know about a large raffle we were organising, and insisted I get her purse from her bag to buy some tickets! Her courage was amazing.

It was for me a very sad time. I had, years before, lost a university friend in her early thirties from cancer of the womb. Her husband was a busy GP and Bill and I spent some weeks living in their house and looking after her four children plus our own two while she was undergoing radiotherapy. But I had not been with her during the last weeks of her life, and so had not seen her final deterioration and death.

But this time I was at the hospice most days, and saw her slow decline, and I was with her the afternoon she died. It was deeply distressing seeing someone who was a contemporary, whose children had been at school with mine, and who had been such a vital and energetic person, dying at the age of forty-six.

But the hospice was wonderful, not only in the loving care it gave to my friend and her family, but also in the care that I, a mere friend, received. The nurses and matron were always at pains to see that I didn't leave the building in distress – and there were times when the matron took me into her office to have a good cry and a cup of tea before sending me on my way, or taking me back to the bedside to say a calm good-bye. And I felt that if the hospice could give such loving and generous care to a friend, how much greater was the care it would give to the family. It somehow made one feel that, despite their grief, the family was safe.

It also made me realise how little our family had been supported when our mother was dying. She was in hospital for the last three weeks of her life. She'd had cancer for several years, and had come through a series of operations with great courage and resilience, and somehow, we had put into the back of our minds the thought that we might lose her. But this time, we were more anxious. My mother, the day before she was taken into hospital, lying in bed, had turned to the wall and said she couldn't go on fighting any longer. But even the implications of that statement didn't really sink in.

On our frequent visits to the hospital – not easy as I was working full time and my parents lived about fifty miles away – we could see that she was deteriorating – but we could get no information or help from the nursing staff or doctors about the progress of her illness. Finally, I was so desperate that I chased the nurse in charge down a corridor and demanded to see a doctor. He was very irritable in his manner, and told us brusquely, and without preamble, that my mother would not survive, and then walked away, leaving us feeling devastated and utterly without support.

It must have been the next day that, sitting beside her bed, I felt so desolate that I wanted to cry. I went out into the corridor and leaned against a pillar and wept. A nurse came bustling down the corridor and said, not unkindly but without warmth, 'Come along now, Mrs Poulter. You've had enough. Go home', and she propelled me out of the hospital.

How different from the care I received in the hospice – and the care I have since seen extended to the families in our hospice. It was not that the nurses and doctors in the hospital were not caring people. It was just that they didn't see it as part of their role to care for, and support, the relatives of their patients. Their job was nursing the sick. Part of the reason for this was lack of time and resources. But part was due to the hospital's philosophy of care. Death is the enemy and everything possible must be done to prevent it. It's a philosophy that emphasises the physical aspect of care. Hospice philosophy, by contrast, emphasises the need to care for the whole person, and to embrace their emotional, material and spiritual needs as well as their physical. This care has to include the family of the patient because they are an intrinsic part of the patient's life, and the unit of care is, quite unashamedly, the patient and his or her family. This, of course, has implications for staffing, as the family can be quite large and complex and has very varying needs.

The control of pain and unpleasant symptoms are, of course, the first priority, and enormous strides in the development of pain control have been made in recent years, largely due to the work done in hospices. But it is implicit in hospice care that attention to a patient's emotional needs helps patients cope with their physical symptoms. Being able to express fears, anxieties, and anger, being able to be open with their families about the seriousness of their condition, all assist patients in coming to terms with their illness. Being more relaxed and at peace emotionally, a patient finds that the physical symptoms are more easily controlled. This philosophy is now slowly permeating hospitals. Doctors are receiving some training, albeit limited, in terminal care. And the importance of the emotional side of care, of a holistic approach, is being increasingly recognised. But there is a long way to go.

But for me, and for thousands like me, the experience of a loved one's death in the climate of care in which my mother died, leaves scars that will never totally heal. For, when our mother's cancer was first diagnosed, my father was told but not my mother. We were told by the doctor not to tell her. But she knew, and we knew, and she knew we knew – and a barrier entered into our relationship which had not been there before. We weren't able to talk about what was happening; we felt we had to try always to be encouraging about the outcome of the many operations she had to undergo, and we were never able to share her fear of dying and comfort her with the open expression of our love. It is something I shall always regret.

How much easier it was when our father was dying. By then, I had experienced hospice care and philosophy. My father was told, out of the blue, when having a cataract operation, that he had lung cancer and probably only had three months to live. We talked about it, we cried about it together, and then he and we lived life to the full. He was able to get about quite a lot, and was only bed ridden for a few days. The day before he died, the children went down to see him and said good-bye. He and I talked about immortality and the existence of God. He told me he wasn't at all sure whether God existed – but said, 'I will find out in a day or two, won't I?'

A few hours before his death, as my sister and I and our husbands sat by his bed, he said to us, 'Now, say good-bye – and bugger off and let me die in peace!' He wasn't a swearing man, but this phrase somehow expressed his courage, and I have always found it very comforting to remember.

Looking back, I realise that my mother's death in 1975 was the beginning of a long and sad encounter with death. We all have to face up to the death of elderly relatives – but it doesn't always come all at the same time. But for us, for a few years in the late 1970s and early 1980s, death was a constant accompaniment to our lives. Within five short months, Bill lost his eldest sister, her husband and his mother who lived with them. I lost a favourite aunt and uncle, and a not so favourite aunt. We also lost four friends within our own age group, followed not long after by the death of my father. It was perhaps this constant acquaintance with death and all its sorrows that drew me, albeit unconsciously, into my commitment to the Hospice Appeal.

So it was that all these experiences, and my direct contact with a hospice, gave me more confidence in talking about hospices and what they had to offer. As the years went by and our Speaker Secretary moved away and left the Appeal, I took on more and more speaking engagements.

While I was working on setting up a network of local support groups, Ron was working on the people he knew in the area and persuading them to raise money for the Hospice. It seemed important for our 'Group Leaders' and the growing band of fund raisers, to meet on a regular basis so that they could be kept up to date with what was going on. So we set up regular group meetings. These turned out to be vital to the success of the Appeal. A wonderful family feeling developed, and over the years close friendships were formed, and people in trouble were wonderfully supported.

I always organised and chaired the meetings. I don't quite know how that happened as Ron was officially the Fund Raising Chairman. I think it was because, to begin with, I knew everyone, and prepared the Agenda and all the papers for the meetings. But it was a happy arrangement. Ron and I always sat together at one end of a rectangular table. He said he was my 'minder' – there to keep me in order – and would be at pains to tease me light-heartedly, thus ensuring an atmosphere that was informal and humorous as well as businesslike.

From the outset, I felt that the secret of success was good communication, and was at pains to keep everyone apprised of what was going on. I very early suggested we should send out a monthly Information Sheet to our key supporters which would tell people how the money was coming in, where it was coming from, what help we needed, and what events were forthcoming. As time went on, we included with this Information Sheet posters, lottery books, and tickets to sell for events.

Gradually, during that first year, we developed a network of support and local groups across the area. Peter made sure that stories about the Appeal appeared on a fairly regular basis in the local press and in his own freebie newspaper – though he tried to avoid overkill. His philosophy was that the public needed to be able to identify with people- and so he began projecting Ron and me as the two main fundraisers of the Appeal. This of course was a sensible approach as far as the Appeal was concerned – the public preferring to identify with a person rather than an object – but over the years it was to have hurtful repercussions. For people are jealous, and some resented my regular appearances in the press.

A small group of people joined together to form a marketing team under the leadership of a man who owned a small printing and marketing business. It was at this point that one began to realise the significance of the bonds created by hospices. For the group contained not only one of the Appeal's very first supporters, but also the friends and family of my friend who had just died in a hospice. The group started looking at Christmas cards, appeal sashes, pens, rubbers, mugs and key rings – all stamped with the appeal's name and logo.

Bit by bit we extended our horizons and became involved in more and more fund raising initiatives, improving and refining our first efforts as the years went by. A Street Collection had been started before I became involved and was organised by Margaret, one of the Appeal's earliest supporters, who was representative of the many wonderful people who helped to fund raise over the years. She never wanted to serve at management level, but would give her help wherever it was wanted. Always cheerful, never critical or complaining, it is to such as these that the Hospice owes so much.

She, together with our Management Committee Councillor, became involved in the House to House Collection when we decided to do one in the town. A successful House to House Collection requires a lot of careful organisation and that first year we laid the foundations of what was to become one of our major fund raising endeavours.

Our local Councillor, who was also a funeral director, had a very good knowledge of the town and helped us identify people to take on the role of Main Collectors. The scheme was that they would each organise the collection in their own small areas by finding local collectors, sorting out who would cover which road or street, distributing the collecting boxes, and gathering them together afterwards. We gave our main collectors a list of all the Members living in their area, and though the calibre of our main collectors varied that first year, we were off to a good start, and collected about £5,000. As the years went by and our organisation became more efficient, we were able to recruit more and more collectors and we regularly collected over £16,000.

In this, as in many other endeavours, once I'd laid the foundations, I looked out for someone to take over responsibility. With the House to House Collection I was later very fortunate in finding a most efficient lady, Heather, who had recently retired from an office manager's job in London. We were given the whole of August to do our collection – not a popular month because so many people were away. But it allowed flexibility for our collectors, and they were able to choose their own time within the month to collect. Moreover, as we used collecting boxes rather than envelopes, collectors only had to make one visit. This was far more popular among our collectors, and it prevented the Appeal being discredited as happens when charities fail to pick up filled envelopes.

We were, in those early days, all amateurs, and, although I quickly found myself the main organiser of the fund raising, I was a volunteer like the rest, for I was still teaching full time. It was not till three years into the Appeal that I retired from teaching and started receiving a small honorarium of £5000 for my work.

Charity fund raising is now big business and there are more and more professional fundraisers with a corporate identity and the backing of the Institute of Charity Fund-raising Managers. Fundraisers for large national charities can command big salaries, and professional qualifications and training are now widely recognised. In a large organisation, fundraisers specialise in one or two areas – concentrating for example on charitable trusts, or corporate giving, legacy marketing or community fund raising. The larger charities usually have a separate marketing arm – and the proliferation of charity shops over the years has been quite remarkable.

But ours was a small local appeal. We had no big organisation behind us to provide back-up and capital. There was no expertise to call upon, and we had to make our own way. I found myself a 'jack of all trades', learning on the job and pushing out the boundaries in whatever direction I could, and wherever I was able to find support in terms of manpower. Even when I started receiving an honorarium, I still had to rely on volunteers for support, and it was not until the Hospice had been up and running for nearly a year that I was at last given some part-time paid secretarial help.

We all worked from home, scrounging whatever facilities we could from friends and relations. I was fortunate in that I had my own computer – a small Amstrad – on which I typed all the early reports, memoranda and minutes concerned with fund raising. A friend on the Management Committee allowed me to use his photocopier whenever I was in town, and another friend in the village made his firm's photocopier available for the Appeal when I was at home.

But we all felt the need for an office and for a shop, and spent a lot of time looking round for suitable premises. Eventually, Ron got in touch with the Health Authority and persuaded them to let us have a small room in an old hospital which was being run down in preparation for its closure and demolition a couple of years thence. The Chairman had, meanwhile, managed to persuade the National Westminster Bank to second for three days a week one of its managers, who was approaching retirement, while our Information Sheet produced cover for the other two days in the form of two volunteers. One of them, Elsie, was still with the Appeal beyond her eightieth birthday. The other, Olive, sadly, died just before the Hospice was built. Her death touched everyone deeply, and made us all aware what a close-knit family we had become.

There was no doubt in our minds that we were making good progress on the fund raising side, and gradually building up a really effective network of support. But there were problems and it was only bit by bit that we realised how serious they were.

On the one hand, there was the continued difficulty with the Health Authority. Although the Chairman and other members of the Management Committee had a number of meetings with Health Authority representatives, reports came back of difficult and contentious meetings with the Health Authority, which was still insistent that a home hospice set-up was the only way forward. Suspecting there might be someone who had a personal reason for opposing the hospice project, Ron and I suggested that it might be a good idea to ask the Health Authority to provide a neutral chairman to bring the two groups together and see if something could be sorted out. This suggestion was accepted and a new committee was set up. Ron and I delicately offered our services on such a committee as we felt we might perhaps have something to offer in the way of negotiating skills. Our offer was accepted – albeit a little reluctantly.

But this was not our only cause for unease. We had been aware for some time of an inexplicable hostility to the Appeal among the more influential members of the community – a hostility that even went so far as to advise us not to get too deeply involved. At first we thought some of this hostility was due to racial prejudice because our chairman was of Asian origin. We all felt racial prejudice was abhorrent and were determined that, if this really was the cause of the problem, we would fight the prejudice and struggle on.

But although the fact that our Chairman was Asian may have added to the difficulties, we were to discover that the problem lay in quite another direction. With hindsight, we should all have looked more closely at the structure and constitution of the Appeal before getting too deeply involved. But as it was a registered charity for a very good cause, had official printed stationery and literature, had supporters of good standing in the community, and was led by a man who had good knowledge of hospices and had done his homework well, there was no obvious reason why we should have questioned the structure.

But we couldn't get away from the fact that doubts existed. We were unable to enlist the support of any GPs, and I found that even the clergy were reluctant to help the Appeal. By this time I was in touch with the wider hospice movement, and I knew that hospice projects usually take off quickly because of their emotional appeal. We hoped that racial prejudice was not the problem, and puzzled over what other reasons might be causing this reluctance to 'come aboard'.

Six months into working for the Appeal I uncovered the underlying problem when I managed to persuade the secretary to let me see a copy of the trust deed on which the charity was based. There was no problem with the document itself.

It was all in order, legally drawn up and approved by the Charity Commissioners. But it contained no mention of a hospice, and it revealed that the charity only had two trustees, both of foreign origin, one of whom was the Chairman, and the other was living overseas.

The Trust Deed, dated 4 November 1983, stated that "the objects of the Trust are the relief of poverty, distress, sickness and homelessness and the advancement of education".

I feel the Charity Commissioners have much to answer for in registering, without detailed questioning, so many imprecisely worded charities. They are open to abuse and to misinterpretation. In this case, as I was to discover later, the charity had been set up by two idealistic young students who had had, I am sure, ideas of starting a mini Oxfam which would provide help for a great variety of needs. But it was not a suitable trust for a local hospice appeal – and it laid the trustees wide open to suspicions of abuse. People, who had seen the trust deed and knew the trustees were of foreign extraction, immediately suspected that the funds would be siphoned off and sent overseas. Their anxiety had been added to when one of the trustees left England and returned to his homeland.

Bill's reaction on seeing the trust deed was the same as mine, and following his advice, I alerted Ron and the members of the management committee to the wording of the trust. Had we had any idea at that stage of the problems that lay ahead I suspect a number of us would have opted out altogether!

The majority of the Management Committee (those who had joined with me in the June of that year) agreed with Bill and I that the trust deed was almost certainly the cause of our problems. However, in order to make sure we were not making a mountain out of a molehill, we got legal advice from a solicitor before approaching the Chairman with our anxieties. He confirmed that our anxieties were justified and suggested that the Chairman should be asked either to set up a new trust specifically for the hospice project, or write a subsidiary trust under the auspices of the existing trust. We also felt that it was important that some additional trustees should be appointed as the second Trustee was now out of the country, effectively leaving the Chairman as the sole trustee.

The setting up of a subsidiary trust, or a specific hospice trust, seemed to us a very simple answer to the problem. To our great surprise, the Chairman did not see the need for change – and thus began a protracted period of discussion and negotiation.

I first saw the trust deed in October 1985, and it was not until October 1987 that the matter was finally resolved. My file, eight inches thick, containing copies of all the letters, memoranda and minutes I wrote during the course of negotiations bear witness to the complexity and difficulties we encountered. For immediately we startsed delving into the legal arena, other problems and questions arise. We realised we had been going happily along raising money without any formal authority, a proper constitution or terms of reference. There were 'Members' of the Appeal but we had no idea of our accountability to them – in fact the whole set up was vague and without a formal structure, and we began to feel anxious about our own accountability.

In November we wrote to all the members of the Management Committee inviting them to a special meeting to discuss the situation. It became apparent that we were a divided committee. The nine of us who had joined the Hospice Appeal at the social gathering in the summer of 1983 and had been largely instrumental in getting the Appeal vigorously under way, came to the meeting. The original members declined.

Because of this impasse, it became obvious that the way forward was to set up a separate charity, but we were aware that that could be very damaging and could destroy our credibility with the public altogether.

On the 2nd of December 1986 I wrote to the Charity Commissioners outlining the problem and asking for their advice. I particularly wanted to know whether the funds raised (by now over £100,000) could be transferred if we decided to set up a separate charity. They took six months to reply! They affirmed the need for change.

I also wrote for advice to Paul Rossi of *Help the Hospices,* the umbrella organisation for hospices throughout the United Kingdom. Paul said we were right to raise our worries with the Charity Commissioners and that 'All the hospice trusts I know are specifically set up to build and run a hospice and a service for the terminally ill. In this way the aims and objectives of the trust are absolutely clear and open to inspection and scrutiny. Other hospice charities have also found it useful to appoint several trustees representing different walks of life in the area – e.g. doctors, clergy, etc. This demonstrates that the charity has wide support and it is a great bonus to fund raising.' He also suggested that the charitable company route might be a good one to explore.

The next six months were very difficult, and too complicated and distressing to describe. because repeated attempts to come to some agreement failed.

It was difficult to understand why the Chairman was so opposed to change. It was not a personality clash as some people later suspected, although there were strong characters involved, myself and the Chairman included. And it was certainly not racial prejudice as, later, some of his more dedicated followers tried to suggest, for as a group we all had many friends across the racial divide.

But there were religious and cultural differences which, I believe, made it difficult for the Chairman to understand and appreciate our conviction that change was imperative. And perhaps, had we really understood how devastating it is for a Muslim to lose face, and how serious were his religious convictions, the situation might possibly have been handled in a more sensitive way.

I suspect that the attitude of Muslim men to women was another factor in the dispute. As I have indicated, I began to have a more significant role in the organisation as our fund raising got under way and it could not have been easy for a Muslim to work with a woman on equal terms. There may even have been an element of jealousy as my name and that of Ron were given prominence in the local press. Additionally, as was natural, I am sure there was a fear that his 'baby' was being 'taken over'.

Whatever the reasons, by February 1987 we had still made no progress, so

Ron, Pat Saiz and I went up to London to discuss the situation with the Charity Commissioners. They expressed anxiety about setting up a separate charity because they felt it might abort the whole appeal. They wanted accommodation with the Chairman and asked him to come to London for discussion – a request he declined.

It was an incredibly difficult time because, as I said earlier, we seemed to be making progress with the Health Authority. They had produced, as we'd requested, a 'neutral chairman' in the person of a Member of the Health Authority, John Stacpoole. Ron and I had by then been attending these meetings, and our aim to pour oil on troubled waters and make an accommodation with the Hospice in the Home group seemed to be meeting with some success.

At the end of February 1987, while our Chairman was in India for a month, John Stacpoole, the Health Authority representative, came up with a very promising Draft Document about the hospice project which he wanted to put before the next meeting of the Health Authority – a meeting that was to take place before our Chairman returned from India. It contained an offer by the Health Authority to provide a site for the Hospice. This was progress indeed. But we were faced with a dilemma. There was no way we could contact our Chairman in India, and we felt we dare not delay agreement to the document. Ron and I decided to send a copy of the document to all the Management Committee members and ask for their reactions.

Approval was unanimous and we wrote to the Health Authority our acceptance of the document, and sent copies of both the document and our letter to the Chairman to await his return from India. Returning just one day before the Health Authority meeting was to take place, we learnt he had countermanded the Management Committee's decision, telephoning the Health Authority Chairman to refuse the offer of a site. As a result, the offer was not presented to the Health Authority Meeting, and once again, we felt frustrated and in despair.

I wrote to the Charity Commissioners to apprise them of the latest development who then replied that as the Chairman had refused to go and see them, they would now ask his solicitor to meet them instead. This he did – and shortly afterwards, resigned!

Meanwhile, though we all continued with our fund raising, we felt deeply frustrated by the way some of our fund raising activities were being blocked. Things came to a head in April 1987 when the Chairman told us that three new trustees had been appointed, and a new constitution introduced. We felt hopeful – until we learnt that the new trustees were all people who had not been involved with the fund raising during the last two years, and who lived well outside the area, while the new constitution did not seem to meet the needs of a hospice appeal.

We expressed our unhappiness at this development, and the result was that Ron and I received a letter from the Chairman saying that we were no longer to represent the Appeal at meetings with the Health Authority.

Then, a few days later, each member of the Gang of Nine received a letter, by recorded delivery, terminating our association with the Hospice Appeal. It would have been laughable had it not been tragic. Here was a group of intelligent people, highly motivated to raise the money to build a hospice, giving of their time voluntarily, dismissed out of hand because they and their Chairman could not agree about the best vehicle in which to carry forward the project.

We felt the time had come to let the Health Authority's representative know about the difficulties we were working under, and I wrote him a long letter outlining the problem. I also wrote again to the Charity Commissioners.

The protracted nature of the dispute, and the conviction of the correctness of our views, united us in a very strong bond. We knew that it was to our endeavours that there was now well over £100,000 in the Appeal's funds. We also knew that we had built up an excellent network of support among our grassroots members. We were not prepared to let it all go.

So followed an intensive period of meetings and writing of letters and memoranda, meetings with our solicitor, meetings of the Gang of Nine as dissident members of the Management Committee came to be known, long telephone discussions with the Charity Commissioners, letters to the chairman of the Health Authority's Hospice Committee, and last ditch attempts via third parties of reconciliation with the Chairman. The Chairman himself was similarly engaged in meetings and letter writing. We were all in turmoil. I found most of my spare time taken up with the dispute – at the expense both of our fund raising and of any family life at all. For on my shoulders fell all the burden of letter writing, phone calls, and the preparation of memoranda, minutes and agenda. My file of papers grew rapidly.

Up to this point we had kept all knowledge of the dispute from our loyal and hard working support groups whom Ron and I had been meeting regularly for the past twenty-one months – meetings which the Chairman had never attended although he had been given an open invitation. But despite our care to keep the problem under wraps, snippets of information had inevitably begun to leak out. Peter, for example, discovered that the Appeal's secretary had been spreading news round the town about the dissensions, and we had received some direct questions from one or two of our more astute supporters.

We had still refrained from going public as we believed it would damage the credibility of the Appeal. But by the time of our next Group Leader meeting on the 8th of June we felt we could no longer keep the situation quiet. The matter was raised under Any Other Business. I outlined to the Group Leaders the problems that had led up to the present impasse, and the possibility that we might be forced into setting up a separate charity. One of our members then read out a letter he had written to the Chairman asking for clarification of the situation and another letter he had written to the Charity Commissioners expressing anxiety.

Chairing the meeting, I felt it was wise to let the group leaders discuss the matter fully and express their views. I was aware that if it came to having to set up our own charity, it would only be possible if we had the support of the grass roots membership. The discussion was lively and sensible. Total support was expressed for the fund raising work that Ron and I had been doing, and for the actions of the Gang of Nine. But the Group Leaders felt that, before decisive action was taken, another attempt at accommodation with the Chairman should be undertaken. A formal proposal was therefore made that he should be asked to meet the Group Leaders and discuss the situation. A small sub committee was set up to plan the meeting and we agreed that neither Ron nor I should be present.

During the next few days I was encouraged by the many phone calls and letters I received expressing total support for all we were doing, and thanks for the way we had developed the Appeal. I was also heartened by the Charity Commissioners who told me that the Chairman had at last been up to see them but that they had had no more success than we had in trying to persuade him to alter the trust deed. They felt there was no hope of accommodation and said they would no longer stand in the way of our setting up a separate charity.

One further meeting on the 23rd of June between the Chairman, the new trustees and the Gang of Nine broke up in disarray. It was nearly the end of the road. But there was still the last ditch chance that the meeting with the Group Leaders would produce results.

There are some occasions in life that remain in the memory with a clarity and recall of detail that is quite amazing. The evening of the meeting between the Chairman and the Group Leaders was one such. The Group Leaders had arranged for the meeting to be held in the hall of a small primary school in a nearby village. We decided it would be best for none of the Gang of Nine to be present, and we found someone, Jo Russell, who we felt would be totally impartial, to chair the meeting.

But the Gang of Nine felt the outcome of the meeting was so important that we decided to spend the evening together and await reports from the Group Leaders after the meeting. We all wished we could be flies on the wall because, by now, tempers were very high, and we would all have liked to be present. Instead, we all gathered at The Oast. There was a tangible air of excitement as we and our spouses, waited for the Group Leaders to return. We laid on a light supper, and everyone brought a bottle of wine to ease the waiting time.

It was one of those warm balmy evenings and a many of the group brought swimming costumes. We swam, and sat on our terrace drinking wine, looking across at the view, and seemingly enjoying a relaxed social evening. But there was an undercurrent of excitement and expectation as the clock passed ten and then eleven, and we became more and more impatient and restless. It was not till well past eleven that we finally heard cars drawing up outside, and a dozen people walked into the garden, flushed and excited, to report the events of the meeting. It had been stormy. The Chairman outlined his understanding of the facts, insisting he had done his best to accommodate all the requests of the dissident Management Committee.

The Group Leaders quesioned the Chairman closely, and at the end of the meeting said they could not accept his interpretation of the situation. They passed two resolutions: one of no confidence in the Wishing Well Charity as it stood, and the other to suspend fund raising until the situation was sorted out. A last minute proposal was accepted that someone should try and arrange a three way meeting with the three Trustees, the dismissed Management Committee members, and the Group Leaders.

All this was relayed to us in bits and pieces, and it was not until the early hours that our little gathering at The Oast finally broke up. Later, we were given a shorthand report of all that had been said during the meeting.

This was the signal for us to start making earnest preparations for the setting up our own charity. Our solicitor and I had produced a draft document for a charitable company limited by guarantee, and we decided we would start recruiting trustees – 'Subscribers' as they were to be called. We drew up a list of potential names, targeting the better known members of the religious, medical, legal, educational and business fraternity, in order to give the new charity credibility in the community. We also felt we needed someone with a title among our subscribers. On my shoulders fell the responsibility for writing a number of very delicately worded letters eliciting support from those we did not know well. Members of the Gang of Nine also started making tentative approaches to their contacts.

To date, it was only the Management Committee and Group Leaders who had been consulted. We now felt we should go public to the body of our supporters, and I wrote to them inviting them to an informal meeting to 'discuss the way forward'.

The meeting was packed out. I was once again in the chair and, armed with material to use on the overhead projector, explained in detail our reasons for wanting change, and how we proposed to constitute the charity. Our supporters were intelligent people and plied us with questions, but we left the meeting with their total endorsement for what we were doing. Their only caveat – which we were totally in accord with – was that as the hospice project was the brainchild of the Chairman, every effort should be made to include him in the new structure.

It was suggested that a couple of weeks should be left for discussions with the Chairman and representatives, and that we should meet again before the summer holidays. To my personal dismay, the only date we could agree on was the 20th of July – the date of our 30th wedding anniversary. Bill had been planning a special weekend away. I was faced with one of those hideous dilemmas that are impossible to resolve without hurt. I decided that the hospice project was at such a crucial stage, and my role in the negotiations so key, that I should sacrifice our anniversary celebrations in order to chair the meeting. It took Bill a very long time to forgive me or the Hospice Appeal for this decision.

Three days later, life was made even more upsetting when our solicitor received a disturbing letter from the Charity Commissioners saying they were 'saddened by the turn of events and hoped that local good will would not be diluted.' They went on to say that 'the promoters of the new charity cannot rely on the possibility of getting control of the funds so far raised by the Charity.' It was a change from the view they had expressed earlier both in letters and in person, and was very disquieting. But our solicitor wrote to the Charity Commissioners that he had discussed the matter with our newspaper editor and 'had no hesitation in accepting their judgement both as to the need for setting up a new charity and its effect on public opinion'. This seemed to reassure them.

The next two weeks I was very busy preparing notes, copies of the proposed new constitution, and writing to all our regular supporters. Fortunately, it was near the end of term and the marking load at school had lessened, although the end of year school reports still remained to be written.

A last ditch meeting between myself, the Chairman and one of our supporters took place at the home of the Chairman. We took with us the draft of the proposed 'Charitable Company Limited by Guarantee', and explained how we saw it working. There would be up to fifty Subscribers representing all the groups involved. Members of the Gang of Nine would become Subscribers as would our solicitor. We hoped that the Chairman, his Trustees and his three original Management Committee members would also join us as Subscribers. We planned to recruit about twenty senior members of the community and told him about some of the people who had already agreed to join us. We said we hoped to fill the other places with representatives from our grass roots supporters. We told him we were happy to continue with the original name of the charity but would want to add the words 'Hospice Appeal'. Finally, we said we should very much like him to be our President.

It was a civilised meeting, but it was clear that, despite our suggeston that he should be the President of the new organisation, he felt anxiety about the security of the role. Various suggestions were made as to how the breach might be healed, and we left the meeting hopeful that a further meeting, to be held a week later with representatives of all the groups involved, would heal the rift.

Sadly, neither the Chairman nor his trustees turned up at the meeting. At the last minute, we received a message asking us to postpone it. It was far too late and complicated to contact people, some of whom were coming from a distance, and some of whom were away from home, and we felt unable to postpone it. This was the end of the road. We reported back to our supporters that the meeting had been aborted and recommended that we should go ahead with our plans, prepare a statement in readiness for the press, and ratify the decision to set up a new charity at the meeting on the 20th of July.

The next day the Chairman circulated a memorandum saying Ron and I had been responsible for the cancellation of the meeting, because we had refused to change the date,

Even despite the aborted meeting, we still hoped agreement might be reached. We all sat at the end of our telephones. The Chairman and his new trustees telephoned many of the Group Leaders to try and elicit their support – a support they refused to give, feeling that the problem had dragged on too long and was damaging to the Appeal. They were determined that a decision to set up a new charity at the meeting on the 20th of July should go ahead as planned.

But at the eleventh hour, the Chairman came up with a compromise offer. At one o'clock in the afternoon, Peter received a call from a P.R. firm asking for a meeting to discuss a statement from the Chairman. The meeting took place, and Peter then read the statement to me over the phone. It contained some new proposals which went some way towards meeting our demands and although Peter and I felt that we had now gone almost too far down the line with our arrangements for a new charity, we agreed that the proposals must be put to the meeting that night without prejudice.

Boughton Monchelsea school hall was once again packed with supporters and the excitement was tangible. Despite the spoiling of our anniversary celebrations, Bill had come along with me to support what he knew would be one of the most important meetings I had ever chaired. We were both touched when, before the meeting started, we were presented with a large bouquet of flowers, and Bill was thanked most sincerely for his support and for foregoing our anniversary plans.

The meeting opened with reports of the discussions, phone calls and written communications that we had all been involved with since the previous meeting of supporters. I also told the gathering about contacts with potential VIP supporters.

Peter then stood up and read out to the meeting the statement he had received from the Chairman. It was lengthy. It said that although there were differences of opinion we were all committed to the same cause. That if we set up a separate charity, the publicity could be damaging and would alienate support. The trustees were, therefore, willing: to accept six new trustees nominated by the membership; to consider the election of the Management Committee (although they had reservations about its practicality); and in due course, when the Hospice was ready to open, to set up a limited company to manage the Hospice. The statement also said that it would be happy to welcome back the nine dismissed members of the former Management Committee. The statement then went on to say:

'After all these points have been considered, we hope the meeting will at least defer any decision on forming a new organisation. Further dialogue must be preferable to a move which could even mean the demise of a project which is dear to our hearts. If, however, this is not the case, the present Trustees, rather than see the conflict continue to the detriment of the hospice project, offer to stand down and, after consultation with the Charity Commissioners and a ballot of all the members, they will pass on their legal responsibility to the nine former Management Committee members who have called this meeting. We will co-operate in this transfer in every way possible. We feel that the hospice project itself must come before any personal recognition and we make this offer in the hope of averting the damaging effects to the Hospice if the news of this conflict is made public.'

The offer was discussed, but in a half hearted way. It had come too late and after too many hurts. Moreover, everyone knew that we had now obtained the support of a number of influential people including one of the leading consultants in the town, and representatives from the General Practitioner Committee, as well as the Hospice in the

Home group. By stating that he would hand over the funds if we rejected his offer and set up a new charity, the Chairman had in effect signed the death warrant of his organisation.

The Chairman's proposals were rejected and a motion to set up a new appeal under a new name as a charitable company limited by guarantee. was proposed and passed unanimously. It was then agreed that the Chairman should be invited to become the Honorary President for, in the first instance, one year. Six representatives from among the grass roots supporters were to be elected that evening and the voting papers I had prepared in anticipation were passed round immediately.

Ron then wound up the meeting with an emotional speech in which he spoke of the immense amount of hard work and anxiety the situation had caused over a very long period, not only to the Gang of Nine but to their families. He said the strain on individual families, especially to ours, had been enormous. I was again touched when I received a personal tribute from the husband of my friend who had died in a hospice.

As it had all been so traumatic, I suggested we should cement the new arrangement with a social gathering – and invited them all to The Oast for a picnic and swim on a Sunday in August. Thus began what was to become an annual event.

We left the meeting with instructions from the Group Leaders to meet the Chairman and his trustees to sort out the change-over and to invite him to continue his involvement with the Hospice Appeal both on the Management Committee and as our President.

Up to this point we had managed to keep all mention of the dispute out of the press. But four days before our scheduled meeting with the Chairman and his trustees, a bombshell occurred. I received a phone call from the local paper asking about the 'rift in the charity'. Who spilt the beans we never found out. I told them that there had been a little difficulty, that there was to be a big meeting on the following Monday which would resolve it, and that we would give them a statement the day after the meeting. But the press felt they were on to a good story and were not to be put off. They said that if there was a rift, the public had a right to know **before** the meeting. I begged them to wait till they had an official statement the following week – that to publish anything now would be damaging to the Appeal. But they were not to be held off. They immediately contacted the Chairman who was less reticent and told them his version of events. An hour later the press came back to me and read to me the statement the Chairman had made. I realised I too would have to make a statement and said I would come back to them. I telephoned Peter and we concocted a statement which was as little damaging as possible. The next morning, photographs of the Chairman and I appeared on the front page of the local paper with the heading, 'Bid to heal hospice charity rift'.

The article was not as damaging as we had feared. It opened by saying:

"Trustees and fund-raisers of a hospice project meet on Monday to thrash out their differences. Both sides say that whatever happens at the meeting the plan for a hospice for the terminally ill will go ahead. They also say that the £150,000 already raised for the Hospice project is safe. One faction aims to create a new charity, the Maidstone Hospice Appeal, because it feels the present charity is 'too narrowly based'. The charity's founder and president said on the other hand that he and his fellow trustees hoped for a compromise." The article then went on to explain in more detail the different points of view.

It was a fair article. But, of course, it alerted the public to the problem, and our telephones were red hot over the weekend. But, in many ways, this public exposure proved to be more helpful than damaging.

Our meeting on the 17th of August was attended only by the Chairman. He said he represented all his trustees. We outlined to him all that had been discussed at the supporters' meeting and explained exactly what we had in mind for the new charity and the people we had already recruited. We urged him to remain with the new charity. But after very lengthy discussion, it became clear that he would not be able to accept the changes and had no intention of staying with us.

When he left we all felt sad at the parting of the ways. But we were hopeful that the transition would take place without acrimony and that he would honour his promise and in due course hand over the funds. It was not to be. On the 21st of August a huge statement, ringed in black, appeared in the local paper saying, 'An increasing rift has developed in the Hospice Appeal over the past year or so and all attempts to reach a compromise with Mrs Poulter and her group have failed. The charity will be handing over responsibility for the Hospice to this group in order to prevent further damage occurring if the conflict were to continue.' It was a long statement, outlining the Trustees views as to why they thought a new charity was unnecessary. It of course gave no hint that most of the trustees had only been brought in during the last few months, and had done nothing towards raising money for the Hospice.

Inevitably the local papers picked up on the announcement and wrote a prominent article headed "New Hospice Appeal launched after row". Once again, there were statements from the Chairman and myself. But that, fortunately, was the last of the press coverage about the dispute.

The way was now opened for formally setting up the Hospice Appeal. It was fortunate that I had some of the summer holiday ahead of me to get down to detailed planning. We all had conflicting emotions. There was a great sense of relief that the problem had been resolved, a feeling of deep sadness at the parting of the ways, and a feeling of excitement that after so long a period of uncertainty, we could really get down to building a hospice.

CHAPTER 25
Fund Raising for the Maidstone Hospice Appeal

As Ron had said at that crowded meeting of supporters on the 20th of July 1987, it had been a difficult and anxious eighteen months. For me, it had been especially demanding. I had taken early retirement in October 1986 at just about the time when I first saw the Trust Deed and was alerted to the nature of the problem. On retiring I had taken on a job with a company in London selling life assurance. Looking back, it was a crazy idea as I didn't have the temperament of a salesman. I had no hesitation in wringing money out of people for a good cause, but found the idea that I would get a good commission if I managed to sell someone a life assurance policy very inhibiting. However, I went into it in all good faith, had a week's residential training which I much enjoyed, and came out second in the end of week examinations. Then began the business of 'cold calling' which I detested.

I did manage to make several promising contacts – and at one point had hopes of landing a very good piece of business. Unfortunately (or perhaps fortunately) I was not given any backup from my bosses to help land the deal, and felt very disheartened when the man decided to go elsewhere. Even more disappointing was my failure to write a pension policy for a very wealthy friend of my son. He hesitated for many weeks before finally deciding against it.

The terms of appointment were payment by commission only. Some people managed to earn a very good living – but it needed a lot of time and application. Bill had by now retired from teaching and, as he had only been in teaching for a comparatively short time, his pension was very meagre indeed. If we were to stay at The Oast, I needed to bring in a reasonable amount every week. I was therefore doing three days a week supply teaching at a boys' high school in Maidstone – a job I found quite tough especially with one particular group of fifth year boys I had to try and get through the GCSE English examination. They had had five different teachers during the previous year and were, to begin with, totally out of control. This was partly due to the change of teachers, but also to the presence of a very bad troublemaker in the class. He was large, good looking and sexually very mature. He had terrorised the teachers and his fellow pupils almost from his entry to the school, but, as so often happens, the headmaster was intimidated by the boy's father, and fearful of the effects on his reputation if he admitted defeat. Moreover, the staff were fearful of admitting they couldn't cope, and so the boy remained in the school, frequently truanting but on his return, disrupting the whole class. I felt sorry for the boys in the class who had had to put up with his disruptive behaviour for five years. They were, by secondary modern school standards, quite bright, but with this boy in their class, they rarely had a lesson free from disruption.

As a supply teacher, I had nothing to lose, and I certainly didn't feel like putting up with the anti-social activities of this boy who was spoiling the chances of the rest of the class. So I documented in detail every incident over a period of two weeks and presented it formally to the Headmaster. He was forced to suspend the boy for the statutory three days, and many of the staff came up and thanked me for making a fuss. Of course, the boy was back in school again the following week, and for a while was fairly subdued. But the action was really too late. He should have been dealt with in his first year at the school. A year after leaving the school, he was had up in court for assaulting one of the teachers in the street!

Teaching three days a week meant that I had a limited time in which to sell life assurance. But this time was eroded even further by the growing demands of the Hospice Appeal. Had I achieved some early successes in the insurance business, I might just have got into the job and stayed. As it was, my career as a life assurance salesman didn't have a chance, and after six months I was (much to my secret relief) 'terminated'.

Looking back I am amazed at what I managed to fit in during those three years. During the period when I was involved in trying to unscramble the problems of the charity, I was teaching at least three day's a week – to start with in the boys school, and then in a girl's grammar school. Teaching fourth and fifth year English examination courses, I had a very heavy marking load, and to come home day after day and turn to the writing of innumerable letters and memoranda about the Hospice Appeal, after coping with lesson preparation and marking, was not easy. It was fortunate that there were half term holidays as well as school holidays when the pressure was lifted slightly.

But it was the emotional tension that was the most exhausting. We all knew that the change was vital, but we were terrified that in making the change we would lose all the money we had worked so hard to raise (by July 1987 it amounted to nearly £150,000). We felt an immense responsibility both to the project and to the public, and from time to time had to stop and analyse our actions and make sure we were acting wisely.

What did emerge most strongly from those anxious months was a wonderful feeling of family unity. Close friendships and loyalties were forged which continue to this day, and peoples still rush to support each other in times of crisis, illness and death. I really felt that the love and care we were hoping to achieve once our hospice was open was already in evidence. Because of this, we all felt immense sadness for our former Chairman. The hospice project had been his baby and it was being taken from him. We felt even sadder when he declined to take on the Presidency of the new charity.

But despite our regret, it didn't take long for us to be certain that we had made the right decision. More and more people came forward in support, and our funds began to grow at an encouraging rate.

It was fortunate that the split had occurred just as the long summer holidays were about to begin because this gave me time to get the new structure and membership sorted out. We met frequently to sort out the way forward, usually at The Oast. I went to see our potential Subscribers, and I also seized every opportunity to gain new supporters for the Hospice Appeal.

It was at this time that we recruited three people who were to make a major contribution to the appeal – our old friend, the neutral chairman of our meetings with the hospice at home group; a former High Sheriff; and the Chairman of the Finance Committee of the local Health Authority.

Lady Monckton

I hadn't met Lady Monckton, but wrote to her outlining what had happened and explaining our reasons for wanting her support. I was quite open with her and told her it was her title we were after! She invited me to go and see her. She was very friendly and agreed to give us the support of her name, but was equally frank and said she could give us neither time nor money as she was already heavily committed to other charities. This was fair comment and I accepted her name on those terms. But in fact, over the years she proved most generous not only in the money she raised for the Hospice through friends and trusts, but also in the amount of time and support she gave us. It was a most happy choice, and just before the Hospice opened we asked her to become our Patron.

John Stacpoole who had chaired the joint meetings between the Hospice at Home group and ourselves had been a good and impartial chairman and we felt he would be a valuable addition to the team if he could be persuaded to join us. I had kept him informed of all our negotiations and now wrote him a formal invitation while Ron made arrangements to take him to see a hospice as he had never visited one. He was completely won over by his visit, and agreed to join us.

The third person, Gavin Hearn, was a man who, unbeknown to me, was the Chairman of the Finance Committee of the Health Authority. I first met him when we used his house for a Cheese and Wine party to get a group going in his village. This had come about via a *Women's World Day of Prayer* service which I organised for many years in our church. Members of neighbouring churches always joined us, and after the service, I met Pam Bland from a village where we had no support group, and persuaded her to organise a Cheese and Wine Party as a preliminary to setting up a group in her village. She agreed, but as her own house was too small, looked round the houses in her village for a suitable venue for the gathering. Her eyes lighted on the old vicarage which was now a private residence, and approached the lady of the house for help. She very kindly suggested we both went to have coffee with her after the Sunday morning service to discuss what we had in mind.

The outcome of that meeting was a most enjoyable Cheese and Wine party some weeks later, attended by a large gathering from the village. We had the usual stalls and raffles, and half way through the evening I gave a short talk. Had I realised who the owner of the house was, I might have been a little more hesitant! But the talk seemed to be well received and a flourishing group was soon established in the village.

During the evening my host, Gavin Hearn, took me aside and asked a number of fairly searching questions. But it was not till later that we learnt of his association with the Health Authority and realised what a valuable addition he would be to the team.

His response to my invitation was to invite me to lunch to help sort out the organisational structure. We had already some fairly clear ideas about this – but his assistance in firming them up was invaluable.

It was obvious that one of the key decisions that had to be made was who was to be Chairman. Several people had indicated that they would like me to take on the job – and later, our two new and rather senior recruits said they would be happy to serve under me. But I felt that that was not necessarily the wisest course. There was a lot of work to be done in various directions. Fund raising was vital – but so was forward planning about the building of the Hospice itself – where, how, when and by whom. I also felt that if I took on the Chairmanship, it might look as though I had engineered the change in order to taken over the charity.

Another possible candidate was Ron, but we all felt his talents lay more on the fund raising side. It seemed obvious at the time (though there were some doubts later) that it would be valuable to have two members of the Health Authority associated with the Appeal in a senior capacity. So the outcome of all our discussions was to suggest to the Steering Committee that when we set up the new charity formally, we would invite our 'neutral' chairman to be Chairman, and the Chairman of the Health Authority Finance Committee to be our Vice Chairman. Ron would take on the title of Chairman of Fund Raising (we had by then learnt he was shortly to go into hospital for major surgery) and I would become the Appeal Organiser.

These recommendations were accepted by the Steering Committee and formally adopted in the October when the new Hospice Appeal was formally set up.

The 'VIP' members we managed to recruit came from wide ranging backgrounds which was just what we had hoped. Among our recruits were our solicitor friend who had advised us throughout the dispute; a senior consultant at the local hospital; a Methodist minister who had been associated with the Hospice at Home group and chaired the local group of free churches in the town; a lady who had been National President of the Professional and Business Women's Association; a former Mayor of the town; the senior partner of a local firm of accountants; the Headmaster of the local technical school who had just retired; the wife of the Chief Constable; two well known local artists, and a local television personality who was Director of a local research institute. We also had several local businessmen.

It was a representative group. To begin with we lacked a senior representative of the Anglican church as the new Bishop was, at first, hesitant about joining us as he had been advised not to get involved in a controversial situation. But he came on board a few months later as did the Roman Catholic Bishop. In addition we had the Gang of Nine and representatives of our Group Leaders.

Our solicitor and I spent many hours going through the trust deed for the new charity – the Memorandum of Agreement and the Articles of Association. There were several anomalies in the way it was worded which we tried to sort out at the time, but which were later to cause minor problems. For what in fact we were doing was providing a basis not only for the fund raising but also for managing the Hospice once it was up and running.

Most of the summer holiday was taken up with preparing the new organisation and Bill and I didn't get away until the end of October when the new charity was formally set up.

There were numerous administrative matters to sort out as well as getting on with the fund raising which really began to take off again. One of the more exciting events was an auction arranged by local radio for all the hospices in the county. Each hospice was given an opportunity to talk about its work and its needs during the week beforehand, and on the Sunday morning at the end of the week, there was a Phone-in Auction. Each hospice had to provide an item to auction. We were particularly fortunate, thanks to the efforts of one of our fund raisers, Brenda Smith who in the early days had been responsible for raising £3,000 in one month in memory of her cousin. For the Radio Medway Auction she managed to persuade Paul Macartney to part with one of his teddy bears. It was the star item in the auction and to our great delight it went for £3,200.

As our Appeal office at Linton Hospital was manned by a man who had been seconded from the National Westminster Bank, we now had to negotiate with the bank for his continued secondment to the Appeal under its new name. Our two volunteer ladies who had manned the office for a whole year without ever meeting the Chairman, had been 'dismissed' during the final stages of the dispute, having been informed that 'paid staff were more reliable than volunteers'. They were affronted by this remark. From the day they had started work as volunteers, not one Thursday or Friday had the office been left unmanned by one or other of them, such was their dedication!

The remark, of course, highlights an unfortunate attitude by some professionals who regard volunteers as a different species with neither the same abilities or commitment as a paid person. It is one of the many problems that arise when mixing volunteers and professionals in an organisation. Very much, of course, depends on the people involved. Some professionals have the sensitivity and understanding needed. Other are too arrogant, and some too insecure, to recognise the competence and professionalism of the volunteer. This was something I was to observe again once the Hospice was opened.

Using volunteers is, of course, not without some problems. One cannot use sanctions. There are seldom any written contracts, and if volunteers are not well treated and valued, they can get up and depart at a moment's notice. Nor can volunteers be forced to do something they don't want to do. But, when the relationship is right, there is no more loyal or dedicated person than a volunteer. They are as professional in their approach to their work as a paid person. Of such calibre were the two Office volunteers. We asked them to stay with the Appeal, and I gave them a warm invitation to our Barbecue at The Oast where they met for the first time all our other supporters, and thus became part of our happy Appeal family.

With the change of management, we had to negotiate with the Health Authority for the transfer of the office to the new charity. But the room we had been given was really far too small and I went to see the Administrative Officer at the hospital to beg him to find us a larger room. He promised to let us have one as soon as one became vacant.

Complicated preparations had to be made for the formal meeting at which the new charity was to be adopted. Our fifty subscribers were required to sign three copies of the Memoranda and Articles of Association before the formal meeting adopting the new set up, and we had to arrange for them all to go into town for their signing. We had to arrange a new bank account – and decided to use a different bank for the time being in order that there would be no confusion with the original Hospice account.

During the protracted period of negotiations when we were uncertain of the outcome, we had instructed all our group leaders to retain what they had raised in their group accounts until the new charity was formally set up. Once the new charity was established the money poured into the bank.

One of our urgent jobs was to find a Treasurer and a Book Keeper or Assistant Treasurer. A local bank manager agreed to become our Treasurer and a lady recently retired (and also widowed) who had worked in an accounts department, took on the job of Assistant Treasurer. Ron and I had met her at a group fund raising evening. She became a stalwart of the Appeal, spending every Wednesday morning in the Appeal Office, not only keeping all the books up to date but also taking on total responsibility for them when we were without a Treasurer.

Our accountant offered to be our financial adviser, and I had a lunch party at The Oast for the group who were to look after our finances over the coming years. They formed a happy little team – but there were soon changes owing to job moves – and we had three different Treasurers in our first year.

All was now in place, ready for the formal Subscribers Meeting to adopt the new charity. This was held at a restaurant in Maidstone on the 28th of September 1987 – almost two years from our first sight of the Trust Deed!

It was, for those of us who had worked so hard to get the hospice project put on a proper footing, an emotional occasion and we felt it warranted a celebratory supper after the formalities of the meeting were over. Many of our subscribers were meeting up for the first time, and it was a very happy occasion as well as being a proud moment for the Gang of Nine who had worked so hard to get to this stage.

We planned to make a formal announcement of the change at a Public Meeting to which we invited all our group leaders and supporters, and all the 'Members' who had previously met twice a year at Easter and Christmas. We hoped to persuade everyone to transfer their support to the new charity. But had it not been for my archival instincts, which makes me meticulous in keeping copies of everything, we would have had considerable difficulty in setting up this meeting. For when the Appeal Office was handed over, we discovered to our dismay that all the hospice papers, records and equipment had been removed, and but for my personal records and indexes of names, we should have had to start our records from scratch. As it was, we were able to contact most of the people who had been involved with the Appeal and invite them to the meeting.

This was held in October in a large church hall in the town. I was once again in the Chair and read a prepared speech, outlining what had taken place and why. I then introduced the new members of the committee and our new chairman who got up and said a few words. There were a number of questions, particularly about the transfer of money, and one or two people who felt they had not been kept sufficiently informed of the problems. But at the end of the meeting everyone gave wholehearted endorsement to all that had taken place.

That was the end of a very long chapter. I arrived home from the meeting just before midnight, and Bill and I went to bed with the alarm set for 5am ready to fly to Crete the next morning. It was our first real holiday for a very long time – and my first aeroplane flight ever. I slept very little that night!

We had a wonderful holiday in Crete visiting Knossos and other archaeological sites, seeing ancient monasteries, taking a boat trip to a leper islands, and enjoying romantic evenings high up in the mountains organised by the local 'peasants'. The scenery was spectacular, the roads terrifying with their precipitous drops, and the food appalling. We went on spec and moved round the island – spending our last five days in a tiny cove with no roads, fifteen houses, and three tavernas, where the only means of access was a boat which arrived and departed twice a day.

The sea was warm and clear and we spent these last five days lazing on the beach and wandering along the footpaths through ancient ruins which lay unnoticed and unexcavated under the sun dried scrub.

One memorable night we witnessed a Cretan Christening. The taverna where we usually ate was closed for the day. Walking past, we saw on the kitchen tables enormous sides of beef, huge fish, mounds of food, and women rushing round in a hive of activity. A priest, hatted and in a long black soutane, arrived on the morning boat, and later, the four o'clock boat disgorged a large crowd of relatives – dressed in their Sunday best. (Though, even on this festive occasion, the older women and widows were still in sombre black apparel). At about five o'clock we witnessed a procession of people going to the tiny chapel for the christening. On their return, the party started.

To begin with it was fairly quiet with pleasant music wafting across the bay. But as the evening progressed the music got louder and the voices and laughter more and more intrusive. We went to bed at about eleven, hoping that things might quieten down a bit. But it was then that the high jinks really started. Our ears were assailed by a sudden loud explosion. We leapt out of bed – but there was nothing to be seen. But it heralded a series of explosions that went on through the night until five o'clock in the morning. Looking out of our window, we discovered to our amazement that sticks of dynamite were being thrown into the water and up onto the mountain behind, setting light to the dry scrub. Machine guns rattled out volley after volley, fireworks and rockets exploded into the sky, adding to a din that was frighteningly reminiscent of the War. By three o'clock in the night we abandoned all hope of sleep and resigned ourselves to reading.

The Cretans in this part of the island were small, dark and stocky. Most of the men had black moustaches and they looked very fierce. One would not have liked to cross them. The dynamite, we were informed, was a legacy from the Second World War as it was from this part of the island that the Germans were harried and driven out with help from the very active Cretan underground organisation. We sensed that the real control in the island lay in the hands of a Mafia type element and I do not imagine that anyone in that tiny paradisal settlement of Loutro would have dared complain about the pandemonium. Reading *Zorba the Greek* at the time, I was mindful of the vengefulness of the peasant population in that part of the world!

At about five o'clock in the morning the party calmed down a little for a couple of hours, and we managed to snatch a little sleep. But then the gathering, which must almost certainly have fallen into a drunken stupor, woke up sufficiently to partake of breakfast before departing on the morning boat. As the boat glided into the harbour, the singing and noise recommenced, and the whole gathering marched in procession down to the boat. There were loud and emotional farewells, and as the boat moved slowly out of the bay, dynamite was thrown into the water, exploding perilously close to the sides of the departing boat. And from the taverna where the party had taken place, volleys of machine gun fire exploded overhead. It was a memorable occasion!

I think it must have been a couple of days later that we heard the first English voice we had encountered for many days. The words 'hurricane in England' assailed our unbelieving ears. But, passing the woman on the beach later, we heard the word 'hurricane' mentioned again, and despite our reluctance to get involved with our fellow Englishmen, asked her what she was talking about. She told us she had heard the news in Greece – that all she knew was that there had been a hurricane in the south of England – and thought that Brighton and Lewisham had been mentioned. She knew no more.

We realised that if this indeed was the area hit by a hurricane, Ulcombe would be right in the path of it – and it was with some anxiety that we got on the plane from Heraklion two days later for our return to England, wondering what would be awaiting us. The newspapers which we rushed to buy at the airport gave us some indication of the devastation, but it was by then old news so we weren't able to glean much information. We did get a little enlightenment from our pilot who, just before we landed, warned us to be careful driving as there was still a lot of debris on the roads.

Our anxiety was increased when waiting for us at the airport was not the friend who had promised to meet us but another friend – our near neighbour. We thought something dire must have happened to either The Oast or the family – and felt very relieved when he assured us that all was well at home. He explained that he had come because our other friend was ill. He then filled us in with the details.

Most of the tiles on the top of The Oast on the outer side had been blown off and our swimming pool was almost filled with leaves and debris. Otherwise we had escaped major damage. Our neighbour had lost a huge and beautiful beech tree on the boundary between his garden and ours in which owls used to sit and hoot at us, but it had fortunately fallen away from both our houses so no damage was done.

When we got home we discovered that the only memorable thing about the hurricane as far as our family was concerned was that our son, Justin, had slept right through it. He had got up the next morning and switched the iron on ready to iron his shirt before going to work, and it was not until the iron failed to warm up, and his friend came over to see him, that he realised anything was wrong! Because of a three day power cut we had also lost the entire contents of our deep freeze.

We were naturally keen to hear all about the hurricane. It seemed such an extraordinary occurrence in our peaceful country. I think we both had a secret feeling of regret that we had missed something so very dramatic and unusual. Friends and relatives from all over the country had telephoned to see if we were all right. We were touched by their concern. The tales we heard differed widely. Our neighbour, living in a seventeenth century house, said that the whole house was shaking so badly she thought it would fall down and had been absolutely terrified. Another friend said she had crouched under the heavy farmhouse kitchen table all night praying for the first time in her life, but another friend said she went back to sleep and forgot all about it!

Our daughter and her husband, living in Abingdon at the time, came down at the weekend to help our son clear up the mess. They had to put polythene sheeting down in the attic under the oast to stop the rain pouring into our bedroom. Bill's first job on our return was to get Ron the Roofer in to replace the tiles. The youngsters had started clearing the debris from the swimming pool, but it took many days of hard work before it was finally clear.

Our return from Crete saw the beginning of a pattern of work for the Hospice Appeal which was to become more and more intrusive as far as my personal life and that of my family was concerned. Within a very short time I found myself out on average three nights a week, and, during the long summer months from May to September, at least once every weekend.

It was, of course, a measure of the success of the changes we had insisted on.

Support started coming in from all directions, and I received requests to go out and meet people, help with fund raising ventures, and give talks to a whole variety of groups and organisations. I think during the next four years I must have addressed most of the Women's Institutes, Rotary Clubs, Mothers Unions and Round Tables in the area, and many clergy groups, schools and clubs. And the numbers of meetings I attended to set up new support groups and organise events were more numerous than I care to remember.

Many organisations that had held back now came forward in support. The Health Authority area, which we planned to serve, straddled two boroughs, and both Mayors took us on as their charity as did many of their successors. A number of Masonic Lodges gave donations, and in 1989 the Women of Kent Lunch Committee decided we were respectable enough to be included among the hospices to benefit from their annual lunch.

It was a frantic but hugely enjoyable time. My motto was "Fund Raising is Fun" and we certainly all had a lot of fun as well as an immense amount of hard work. Ron and I found ourselves attending a number of social events such as the Mayor's Banquet, Rotary Club dinners, Masonic Ladies Nights, Dances, pub evenings, and social gatherings in private houses. Although we tried to spread the work around, it was Ron and I, as the Appeal's main fundraisers, who were wanted at these gatherings. Very often there were formal cheque presentations, and photographs were taken for the local press. I think over the years we received enough large presentation cheques to paper the whole of a community centre! It was all valuable publicity and we were grateful to Peter for all the help he gave in promoting the Appeal in the press, and to a professional photographer, Barry, who took us under his wing and never charged for any of the many photographs he took for the newspapers and for our publications and exhibitions.

This was the time when our groups really began to develop in a wonderful way. One Group Leader who lived on the border, decided to transfer her support from the Hospice she had been helping for years to us, and embarked on an annual series of Christmas Fairs. She worked hard throughout the year, making wonderful craft items, jams and knitted dolls, and the Fair brought in more than £1,500 each time. This was just one of the ways in which her Group raised money. Another group, in a wealthy catchments area, put on a series of very enjoyable 'up market' social events which brought in considerable sums, as did two new and very energetic groups, formed in 1988, which raised money in a number of enterprising ways. One of our earliest groups, inspired because of Cynthia's illness, flourished under the guidance of her friends. By the time I retired, there were twenty-six local support groups, each raising money in their own very special way and giving support to those events which I organised from the centre. Many of the groups, as with Cynthia's friends, found their inspiration and motivation from their personal contact with terminal illness, which, of course, gave them added incentive.

I found myself involved in organising a huge variety of fund raising events such as antique road shows, art exhibitions, fashion shows, flower festivals, silent auctions, boot fairs, darts evenings, sponsored walks, swims and knits-in, cheese and wine parties, snowball lunches, coffee mornings, fetes and fairs. This was an area where my previous experience with community fund raising came in useful. I had already organised many similar events – some of course on a smaller scale – so knew some of the pitfalls, and had already made a number of useful contacts.

The one thing I absolutely refused to get involved with was jumble sales. My first jumble sale ever, when we were raising money for our playgroup, had been an instructive experience and one I shall never forget. I can still feel the discomfort in the nostrils from the dust that came out of all the old bags of clothes, the mad rush of people to get at the bargains as the doors opened, and the sight of a very dirty looking man grabbing handfuls of bras and underwear and demanding loudly of the lady behind the counter whether she thought the bras would fit his wife. To make sure she understood what his wife was like, said 'she is the same size as you' – and graphically demonstrated to the astonished helper the size and shape of his wife's breasts!

I've always suspected that the most valuable aspect of a jumble sale is providing housewives with an easy outlet for the disposal of their unwanted goods. But that is not fair comment. There are always bargains to be found – and some people even enjoy them. That first and only jumble sale came at a time when I couldn't afford to buy any new clothes. The night before the sale, when we were sorting the clothes into piles, we decided that the helpers could have first pick and buy in advance anything that took their fancy. I took away five items and after washing and ironing them, tried them on and decided to buy them. I was in fact rather delighted with my acquisitions and showed them to my friend Clare with a certain feeling of achievement. She took one look at the clothes I had purchased and burst out laughing. All five items had come from either Clare, her mother or her sister!

I am somewhat ashamed to say that from that time on I never helped at a jumble sale – even though I recognised they were quite a good source of revenue for the smaller groups. But in avoiding them, I missed one moment of excitement when someone unearthed a nightdress belonging to Queen Victoria. It was at the end of the jumble sale when the leftovers were being packed up ready to go with the 'jumble man'. One of our Hospice flower ladies, who was helping, picked up a very large, very square, long sleeved garment which she identified as a chemise. Something made her look at it more closely – and in the bottom right hand corner she found a tiny embroidered VR and the number 18. In great excitement she took it home and started phoning round museums including the Victoria and Albert Museum. To her great delight they confirmed that it was almost certainly a nightdress belonging to Queen Victoria, and it was later authenticated. The search was then on for a purchaser. Peter, our PR friend, was about to go to America on business and offered to make mention of it in various quarters. Some months later, we received a firm offer of £650 from an American Museum. We were all thrilled and our only regret

Hospice Ball at Leeds Castle

was that there had not been time to search through the jumble to see if there was any more Victoriana among the leftovers. Nor were we able to identify who had given the chemise to the jumble sale – despite articles in the press.

A year into our new charity our new Patron, Lady Monckton, helped us to organise a Ball. It was a wonderfully successful evening and for the first time, brought within the orbit of the Appeal what one might call the 'county set'. The evening raised about £7,500. Part of that success was due to a splendid tombola at which we collected £1,500. Owing to a slight mix up with tickets, the odds were very high – and one friend of ours came away with a pair of socks which he reckoned had cost him £70 – such was the enthusiasm of all our friends.

I found myself doing all sorts of things I had never done before and never really wanted to – attending charity football matches, race evenings and darts competitions; sitting in smoke laden pubs and drinking all evening; and standing in the cold manning stalls at fetes and fairs.

Not long before the split with the original charity, we had our first stand at the County Show. The wife of one of our Rotary Club friends took on the chairmanship of the committee and we had many hilarious evenings planning the event. I think the County Show Committee was one of the most enjoyable of all our committees. Our Rotary friends had a good cellar and they always produced delicious platefuls of food to help our thinking processes, while there was a wonderful spirit of camaraderie which was in part engendered by our links with the past. For the members of the committee include, among others, Cynthia's husband, and daughter, and one of her old friends.

We sorted out what we would sell, the publicity needed, the helpers on the day, and how we would finance it. To take a stand at the County Show one needs at least £500 to cover the basic costs. We were fortunate for several years in that the National Westminster Bank very generously sponsored it.

Cynthia's daughter worked in the exhibition business so she took on the planning of the stand with help from her father. Come the opening day, our stand looked very professional indeed. The Appeal had adopted as its new logo a stylised primrose designed by one of our artist friends who was one of our Subscribers. It had yellow petals and a green centre. We endeavoured to keep this colour theme in all that we did. Cynthia's friend had managed to obtain for us some thirty huge linen yellow tablecloths – extracted in somewhat dubious circumstances from a Kuwaiti sheikh – we never enquired too closely about the details! These were used to drape the stand and the tables to great effect.

Our presence at the County Show proved very beneficial. We didn't make a great deal of money, but it did give us the opportunity to make a lot of useful contacts which we were able to follow up afterwards. There were times when we got into a bit of trouble by being too 'pushy' – stepping out beyond the invisible line in front of our stand with our collecting boxes, and calling out the odds. But over the years, we seem to have been looked on kindly by the Show authorities – and in 1991 actually won Second Prize for the 'Best Small Traders Stand' in the Show. This gave great delight to the Chairman of that year's committee.

The County Show was something we all very much enjoyed. For me, it was a new experience. Although we had lived in Ulcombe for more than twenty years, we had never been there – mainly because I had, for the previous eleven years, been teaching – and it never fell to my lot to accompany the school parties to the County Show. That was always the prerogative of the Geography Department. I seem to remember that trips to the County Show betokened gum boots and bedraggled and wet pupils returning to the school at the end of the day. But that was not to be our experience. The sun seemed to shine brightly and rain, if there was any, came in brief showers which scarcely wet our heads.

For me the County Show spelt cherries, and crab sticks, wonderful smells in the food tent, beautiful displays of flowers, and exquisite craft exhibits. It also spelt visits to the trade stands of our various Appeal friends for cups of coffee, lunch, and afternoon tea. We never took any food to the Show but always made our way to one or other of the hospitality tents for our refreshments – carefully selecting those that had the most delectable food and wine on offer. It was a wonderful time – alternating between standing at our stand chatting to passers by and relieving them of their pound coins, and wandering round the Show making new converts. We were there for five days – two putting up the stand and preparing it, and three days manning it. I didn't get too involved in putting the stand together as there was always too much work to do in the Appeal office, but I usually stayed there at least two of the days as there were such valuable contacts to be made.

Hospice supporters wearing tea shirts with Hospice logo: Sheila, Norma Bennett, Pam Bland and Margaret Beesley

But come Saturday evening we wished we had never heard of the County Show! Our feet ached, and we felt utterly exhausted! And we knew we had several hours work ahead dismantling the stall and loading up our cars to the gunnels with all the equipment and sales items we had brought in. Round about nine o'clock in the evening, the helpers remaining would assemble in one or other home for a Chinese take-away – far too exhausted to do any cooking, and determined never to embark on such a crazy enterprise again. But, such was the dedication of our helpers that, year in and year out, the County Show Committee resumed the burden and started preparing for the next Show.

One of the things that people do not realise is that fund raising involves an incredible amount of lifting and carrying. One is always loading up one's car to take items to a fair or a meeting; or transporting an exhibition about the hospice, or delivering boxes of Christmas cards, or collecting donated items, or transporting tables and chairs, or setting up stands or tents or awnings. My car was for years a travelling office – and on the rare occasions when I used it for private motoring, I had to empty the boot before I could put anything into it. Let not the Insurance Companies read this – but there really should be a government health warning saying 'Charity Fund Raising damages your back!'

It was in 1988 that we decided we ought to purchase our own caravan. It was all very well going to the many fairs and fetes that took place during the summer months, but if it rained we were in trouble. So we advertised for a caravan in the press. We had several responses, but the most promising was that of a lady who had been recently widowed and as she couldn't drive, was unable to use her caravan any longer. She had advertised the caravan in the *For Sale* column for £400 – but when we went to see her, she was so interested in hearing about the Hospice Appeal that she not only insisted we should have it for £100 but also offered to help fund raise! Thus it was that when we proudly took our caravan out on its first appeal excursion, she was one of the helpers, and she was with us on many subsequent occasion

It was at the first excursion of the Hospice caravan that I met the Treasurer of the Lions Club who was later to become Treasurer of the Hospice Appeal. The Lions had a stall on the site adjacent to ours and we started chatting. I had already written to them asking for their support – and this provided a good opportunity to get to know them. The Lions at the time organised the annual Marathon in the area. They had, three years before, given the proceeds to the Hospice Appeal but had been very unhappy about the amount of support they'd received. Meeting them gave me an opportunity to try and redeem the situation, and they said they would give the Hospice the proceeds provided we gave them a lot of assistance. This I promised, and for the next few years found myself working closely with them on their Marathon Committee. They proved wonderful friends to the Hospice Appeal, not only through the Marathon but also through a number of generous donations over the years.

Hospice Caravan

To go back to the caravan. We managed to get it sprayed in green, one of our hospice colours, and sign written with our name and logo – all without cost. For the next four years the caravan was out most weekends during the summer with different teams of helpers. That first year, the job of getting the caravan on the road each weekend, stocked with items to sell, a team of helpers lined up, and towed to the site by a volunteer, was all down to me. But it took up a lot of my time which I felt could more usefully be occupied elsewhere. So in 1989 I persuaded three of our volunteers to take on responsibility for the caravan.

We first met one of them, Doreen, when she came to our Antiques Road Show in the autumn of 1988. As she walked with a stick and couldn't get about easily, she was not sure she could do much, but offered her services despite the fact that she was warned not to volunteer in my hearing unless she really meant it! It was not long before I found her a job! One week, even busier than usual and very short of time, I was asked at short notice to line up a team of people to help with an event, and to find enough prizes to run a tombola. I had so little time to spare that I felt desperate – for organising a group of people over the telephone always took an inordinate amount of time.

So, on this occasion, being busy, I asked this volunteer if she could help me by telephoning round to get together a team for the weekend. I also suggested tentatively that she might also try and get some tombola prizes for the event. The task was taken on willingly – and from that moment on, she was hooked. A few weeks later, she came to a Group Leader meeting, bringing her husband, John, with her. He was newly retired. They joined us after the meeting for a drink in the pub and he too was very quickly 'hooked'. They became some of our most valuable supporters. Between them they took on responsibility for all our tombolas, and I nicknamed them *the Tombolah Wallahs*. But that was only a small part of their contribution. John helped in a tremendous variety of ways with House to House and Street collections, fetching and carrying, helping with the caravan, and running a very useful enterprise with a huge stock of 'seconds' clothing. As an ex naval lieutenant and purser, we always got him to look after the money at the end of an event – a job he did without fuss but with great efficiency. His untimely death in December 1991 created a very big gap in our happy Appeal family.

The other volunteer, Margaret, was one of those 'unsung heroes' that no charity organisation can do without. Not only did she take on the onerous task of looking after the caravan for us and finding teams week in and week out during the summer months to man it, she was always ready to assist with our many events – washing up, serving food, manning stalls. It's the people in the forefront who get the recognition, but it's the people behind the scenes who are the backbone of a charity. And this is not always recognised – especially by the professionals.

Another group of people who made a major contribution to the Appeal were our Flower Ladies, a group of ladies whose passion for flower arranging brought them

Bill Butler and his wife

together as an informal club. The group was organised by a very gentle lady and it was through them that I first became involved with the Hospice Appeal. Their dedication was enormous and over the years, they raised thousands of pounds for the Hospice through a great variety of activities. One of their number, ran flower arranging classes at the Adult Education Centre, and had regular raffles and competitions for the Hospice; the group organised a number of Flower Festivals in churches throughout the area – one of which coincided with the Dedication Service we arranged in the town's main church. For any Hospice event, we called on the Flower Ladies to do the table decorations and any arrangements needed in the hall. At our Christmas Bazaar and our Summer Fete they always had a stall with appropriate flower arrangements and baskets for the season. And they also did the flowers at a great number of weddings – providing their services for free but asking for a donation for the Hospice. Our family had reason to be very grateful to them for they decorated our church beautifully for the wedding of both our daughter and our son, and the flower arranging tutor made all the wedding bouquets. They have been very dear friends over the years.

    An annual event that developed into a major fund raising event was the Sponsored ten-mile Bluebell Walk organised by a member of a local Lions Club. It started as a comparatively small event, bringing in some £5,000, but over the years, while I was still with the Appeal, we extended it to the point where it raised over £16,000 each year. Still going, it has now topped £50,000. The organiser, Bill Butler, was, without doubt, the individual responsible for the largest donation to the Appeal. The success of sponsored events depends on numbers – and with an event like a walk, it takes almost the same amount of organisation for a hundred walkers as for five hundred – apart, that is, from the amount of food to be provided and the number of letters to be written! After the first two years, I helped by extending information about the walk to all the groups and people I met and gave talks to, and I sent out forms and posters with our monthly Information Sheet. In this way the number of our walkers was increased so that now nearly a thousand walkers take part.

Behind the scenes was a dedicated team of people who provided an excellent ploughman's lunch each year, raising the money for the food through a series of jumble sales earlier in the year.

The Bluebell Walk was one of the highlights of the fund raising year. The walkers set out at about ten in the morning from a beautiful manor house, and walked across some of the most beautiful Kent countryside. The first half was a strenuous uphill climb, but the walkers stopped halfway for refreshment at one of the areas most notorious pubs. It has been run by two eccentric French ladies who had a reputation for being choosy about their customers. They were reputed to be in the habit of standing at the window with shotguns, and refusing to let into the pub anyone they didn't like the look of! As the pub was isolated and miles from other habitation, the story, repeated time and again, sounds quite credible. The pub is still one of the more interesting pubs that abound in our area, providing good food at reasonable prices in pleasant surroundings. The gardens are spacious and well laid out, and it was quite a sight to see hundreds of walkers sprawling exhausted in the pub gardens enjoying a half way break and refreshment, cheerful in the knowledge that the rest of the journey was downhill all the way!

From about midday onwards, the returning walkers began to fill the gardens of the manor house where they collected an excellent ploughman's lunch from the kitchen window together with a glass of very potent home-made cider. Not a year went by but that the walkers were overwhelmed by the beauty of the bluebell woods through which they passed, where the bluebells are so abundant they are like a gently rippling carpet of blue as far as the eye can see.

The walks have not been without incident. One year, much to the distress of the walkers, vandals altered the signposts – thereby adding an extra mile to the walk. Had the perpetrators been caught, I doubt their lives would have been safe, so indignant were the walkers!

Another year, the walk was moved to July as Bill was in New Zealand during May. That had two very serious disadvantages. Not only were the bluebells finished, much to everyone's disappointment, but the summer, having been very wet, all the paths were overgrown and almost impassable. Despite a seriously arthritic hip, Bill spent a hectic week beforehand, brishing down ten miles of overgrown footpaths. I sometimes suspect that those who are now working in the Hospice and those families

Norma, Doreen, Pam, John, Margaret B, Joan, Margaret H

who benefit from its care, have little idea of the effort and dedication that went into the fund raising for the Hospice over the years – and still continues.

As with so much that took place, once the basic structure was in place, I tried to hand it over to someone to continue and develop, and we were very fortunate in the volunteer who took over the House to House Collection. For organising a collection on the scale we did involves weeks of work beforehand, putting fresh labels on all the boxes, finding collectors, recording the box numbers for each area, writing out badges of authorisation, organising the distribution of boxes and leaflets, making arrangements for getting the boxes back and the money counted and banked, and finding new people to cover areas which had not been developed. The Hospice Appeal always had the whole month of August for its House to House Collection – a month that most charities avoided because of the long school holidays. Because of this we were able to have the whole month which gave us enormous flexibility, although it did mean that the task dragged on for many weeks before it was finally put to bed. Late in September we were able to send out the letters of thanks, telling each collector the grand total, and how much they themselves had collected.

Thank you letters are, in my opinion, absolutely vital to the success of a charity. It is my belief that one of the main reasons for the continued support of all our fund raisers was that we were meticulous in sending out thank you letters, and equally meticulous in keeping our supporters informed about what was going on. From time to time I was criticised for sending out too much information. But, over the years, I have been told so many times of people who have stopped supporting other charities because their support has not been acknowledged. So I was unrepentant, convinced that it is the small donors who are the lifeblood of an appeal, and they have to be treasured.

Fund raising is a curious business. There are people who are very happy to do house to house collecting, but hate doing anything else, while there are others who are prepared to do anything except knock on doors. Such is also the case with street collections – some love it, others detest it. After years of involvement with both, I now have far more sympathy with other charities which come knocking at the door, and I find it almost impossible to pass a street collector by without putting something in his box. One of the most soul destroying occupations is to stand on a busy street corner on a cold December morning and see person after person taking evading action and walking past without putting money in your box.

Taking part in a street collection does, in fact, provide a real study in human nature. As one stands hopefully, rattling one's box with an attempt at a cheerful smile on one's face, one begins to learn who will pass by on the other side and who will stop and put money in. There are the men who see your box, hesitate, put their hands in their trouser pocket, rattle their money – and then walk on. There are the little old ladies, often down at heel, who, the minute they see your box, start feeling for their purses and give more generously than they can afford. There are the women with babies in pushchairs, and women with heavy shopping bags, who will stop and relinquish their burdens while they try and find their purses. There are, on the other hand, the elegant and well heeled ladies who pass by without a glance in your direction. There are the young men who stop and give generously to impress the girl on their arm, while there are others who mock as they pass. There are the most unexpected and generous donations from young men who look as though they are thugs and troublemakers, and there are those who look so down at heel that, out of compassion, one hides away the collecting box rather than embarrass them. There are the surly men who shake their heads aggressively, and those who say they will come back later – and do. Over the years, I have found that the surest donors are the grey haired elderly ladies and the middle aged gentlemen who respond to your flirtatious smile with an 'I surrender' shrug of the shoulders and give generously.

There is no doubt at all that there is a special technique for collecting. You can have two people standing in identical spots – and one will fill a box in an hour while the other will have collected just a few coins. It is, in effect, a two-way enterprise – you have somehow to connect with the passer by without breaking the law and thrusting a box under their noses. It has much to do with body language and facial expression.

Street and house to house collections were not the only outlets for our collecting boxes. Several hundred were placed in shops, pubs, doctors and dentist's surgeries, and in individual homes, and it was a major exercise looking after them all. This proved one of our more difficult areas. In the early days, boxes had not been monitored as carefully as they should have been. Moreover, as the recession began to bite, boxes were stolen – a problem faced by all the local charities. An unattended box on a shop or pub counter was easy prey for someone out of work desperate to make ends meet, or for the unemployed youngster roaming round bent on trouble. And it is not easy to tie a collecting box down securely – the strings can easily be snipped, and the shape and the hard material from which they are made, make others methods of securing them almost impossible. Although such thefts are reported to the police, there is little they can do. It places a burden on manpower resources because it makes it even more important that the boxes are emptied frequently before they get too temptingly full.

I passed this particular burden to two retired businessmen who offered their services. For many years they worked every Monday morning in the Appeal Office, counting the contents of boxes that had come in, and entering the details on the data base – not to mention a dozen other tasks they took on over the years. They were valued supporters, but I sometimes wondered how I continued to be accepted as a friend after all the things I asked them to do, and the nickname I gave them. Two very different people in appearance and temperament, they struck up a close friendship from the beginning and I laughingly referred to them as Bill and Ben. The name stuck. But one day, forgetting who I was talking to, I addressed them as Bill and Ben to their faces. It says much for the warmth and family feeling that had grown up over the years that they not only laughed, but accepted the nickname from that time on!

It was such a very exciting time as we got involved in more and more enterprises, but as the pressure increased I had to develop a strategy that eased the burden. One of these was, while retaining overall control, to assign responsibility to a committee or a group of people for particular events or enterprises. This was not always successful. It depended very much on the ability and calibre of the people available. But I was fairly successful in assessing people's potential and assigning them a task within their capabilities. I was also fortunate in that, although I am not an original thinker, I seemed to have the ability to develop an idea. Many of our most exciting endeavours grew out of the germ of an idea sown by someone other than me.

One such was *Pledge a Ted*, dreamed up by two of our most enthusiastic helpers. They wrote to everyone they could think of, and asked them to donate a teddy bear to the Appeal. When they had assembled some four hundred teddy bears of assorted shapes and sizes, they persuaded a local public house to host the event. Come the evening of the Teddy Bear Auction, there was what must have been one of the most colourful displays of teddy bears ever. There were rows of teddy bears, from floor to ceiling, dressed in every conceivable kind of uniform or garb – policemen teddies, firemen teddies, nurse teddies, doctor teddies, soldier and sailor teddies, baby teddies, teddy families, ballet dancers, clowns, usherettes – representing every aspect of life imaginable.

The evening brought in several thousand pounds and indissolubly linked teddy bears in people's minds with the Appeal. From then on, there was never a Hospice tombola without at least two beautifully dressed teddy bears in the centre, and when a few months later a large local firm gave me five hundred beautifully packaged teddy bears in assorted colours to use in any way we wanted, we always had teddy bears to use as raffle prizes. I made sure I always had half a dozen of these teddies in my car boot, ready to produce at a moment's notice if any one wanted a last minute raffle prize.

The Hospice Appeal owes much to my car boot for it was like a travelling office and contained instant promotional material. I never knew quite where I would find myself nor what opportunities would present themselves, and having been a Queens Guide with the motto, *Be Prepared*, I made sure I was always ready for any eventuality with a supply of exhibition material and leaflets, items to sell, money bags, drawing pins and blue tack, and of course, a bottle of wine and a bottle opener to lubricate and soften up potential donors.

Another chance remark by one of our helpers led to the establishment of our Hospice Tea Dances. She told me that the Tea Dances in the town were having to close down because the local Corn Exchange where the dances were held each week was to be renovated. I decided this was a good opportunity to step in, and both rescue the Tea Dances and raise money for the Appeal. I went to the last two sessions to see what went on – and managed to persuade the man who organised the dances and provided the music to transfer his allegiance to the Hospice Appeal. We found a nice church hall on the outskirts of town which had a good floor, and we were in business.

Tea Dances were a new world to me. I discovered that those who attended were really keen ballroom dancers and ranged in age from the mid forties to the nineties! A number of people who went along were married couples, but there were many single people – some widowed and some who left their partners at home while they came dancing. There was, inevitably, a preponderance of women, and as a result the dances were secretly called 'Grab a Granny Dances'!

I was amazed at some of the people there – especially the very old who came dressed for the occasion with lovely flowing skirts and special dancing pumps. The old men were all very light on their feet and were beautiful dancers and it was a pleasure to dance with them.

The dance I found particularly amusing was the Taxi Dance which was devised to give all the ladies a chance to dance. They had to form a 'taxi' queue, and the gentlemen picked off the ladies to partner as they reached the head of the queue. But the pleasure for the ladies was short lived, for once round the dance floor, the ladies were dumped at the back of the queue and the gentlemen went off in search of a new lady. I used to go along to the dances from time to time to support the volunteers whom I'd persuaded to look after the Tea Dances – and on those occasions I was always told I must take part. I can't say that it exactly boosted one's ego to have to stand in a queue and wait to be picked up – and then be dumped after just one short waltz round the floor!

When I first took over the dances, the atmosphere was rather formal and people didn't seem to talk to each other. At the same time it wasn't always easy to find five volunteers every week to help run the dances so I decided to enlist the help of the dancers themselves. I persuaded them to take over the making of the afternoon tea on a rota basis – and also to take it in turns to produce raffle prizes. Within a short time, the atmosphere was transformed. The Tea Dancers felt themselves to be integral part of the Hospice Appeal and started helping in many other ways as well.

We ran the dances for many years and although we never raised huge sums for the Appeal, I really felt we were providing a very valuable service. Sadly, I was never able to persuade any of our senior gentlemen on the committee to come along and take part – it was below their dignity!

One especially exciting endeavour came from a seed sewn by my nephew one Christmas Day. He was a keen mountaineer. As a child, his visits had been a nightmare. He would never enter the house through the front door – always through a window. And if one took one's eyes off him for a moment one would see him at the top of a tall tree or in some desperately hazardous place. My sister seems to have taken all this in her stride, but I get dizzy and have pains in the calves of my legs whenever I even think of a precipitous drop. His visits were a constant anxiety. On one never to be forgotten occasion, at the eightieth birthday party of the aunt who was my godmother, my nephew, aged two, climbed the open doors of my father's cocktail cabinet in which resided a precious collection of glasses he had built up over many years. In a moment to be etched forever on the memory of those present, the whole cabinet toppled over and only one glass in the collection remained intact. How my nephew escaped injury we shall never know, and how my father refrained from murdering him on the spot was a miracle!

However, I loved my nephew dearly, even though he was always outrageously rude to me, and that Christmas Day, after a rather hectic water pistol fight in which both families indulged, he offered to do a sponsored abseil for the Hospice Appeal. It seemed a good idea, and when a few weeks later I received a letter from Telethon suggesting we took part, I recalled his offer.

What then happened was what I called a typical example of 'osmosis'. I am informed that I misuse the term – but for me the word osmosis means a spreading out of an idea in verious directions. My son-in-law, a scientist, is derisory about this definition but I know what I mean!

I decided to adopt Charles' idea and looked round to find the tallest building in the town from which to make the descent. It proved to be the Royal Insurance building – twelve stories high, in the centre of the town. We already had friends at the Royal Insurance and I telephoned them to see if they would let us use the building. We were referred to the Head Office in Liverpool which eventually gave consent for the enterprise.

Telling Charles the good news, I discovered that he had mentioned it to his climbing club friends and they all wanted to join in. But it was no longer to be a straight abseil. Instead, it was to be an endurance test, a mock mountaineering expedition, with the club members doing a number of descents equivalent to climbing Mount Everest!

It seemed a great idea, but, thinking about the height of the building, I began to worry about accidents. What would my sister say if her youngest son was injured? I felt urgently in need of help. One of my colleagues suggested I contact the army. The Royal Engineers were based in barracks in the town, and I got on the phone to the Colonel. He sounded interested in the venture and invited me over to discuss it the next day.

It was the first time I had ever entered an army barracks and I was amazed at the security. Halted at the checkpoint, my car was inspected and I had to open the boot and reveal all its untidy contents. I was then escorted to a control room where I had to sign in, was given a pass for the car, and a personal pass for myself, and was then escorted to the office of the Colonel.

Sitting at the desk was one of the most gorgeous looking men I had ever met – and he proved charming with it. I somehow knew he would help the moment I entered the room. He had with him his sergeant major and a young corporal, and after the preliminary courtesies, put a proposition to me. The army would organise all the logistics of the event provided they could enter a team of soldiers in competition with my nephew's mountaineering club! To make it more interesting, they would bring along a helicopter and let some of the troops abseil from the helicopter onto the roof. Moreover, the Colonel himself would do an upside-down abseil to add to the fun. It seemed almost too good to be true.

Although only twenty-four hours had passed since my phone call to the Colonel, the sergeant major and corporal had already done a lot of homework. They had been over to measure the height of the Royal Insurance building, had done some mathematical calculations and had worked out that 26 descents per members of the eight-man team would be needed to achieve the height of Mount Everest. They calculated that ten ropes at a cost of £70 each would be needed. They also suggested that, as it was an endurance test, each member of the team should carry a ten pound pack – an idea that was not greeted with any enthusiasm by my nephew's team when they considered the number of stairs that would have to be climbed to the twelfth floor between each descent.

But there was no doubt about my response to the Colonel's offer. I accepted with alacrity – and felt even more excited when he suggested that the TVS camera crew might like to go up in the helicopter to film the event. I felt we were all set for a splendid fund raising enterprise, but had no idea at that stage how much it was to escalate.

My first job was to get the rope at as little cost as possible – preferably sponsored. Talking to our photographer friend I discovered not only that he had done a lot of abseiling, but that he had friends in Chatham Dockyard who might be able to get me ropes at cost. A telephone call by our friend put me in touch with Steve, a man who ran the Fairbridge Drake Trust, a charity that worked with disadvantaged youngsters. Yes, he used lots of ropes. Yes, he could get them cheap – and could his youngsters take part? Who could say no?

Back to the Royal Insurance to report progress, they promised to put up money to help pay for the ropes. They also promised to look after the catering for those taking part, and to help with the marshalling of the public. We were making good progress.

But 'osmosis' was still at work! I decided it was time to inform the police. The event was clearly going to attract a lot of attention and as the Royal Insurance building was on the corner of a busy road I felt police supervision was important. The response was immediate and, as always, very helpful. But it didn't stop there. A few days later I received a call from the Superintendent asking if the police could take part in the abseiling. He told me there were a lot of them clamouring to be involved. It was clear our event was going to be very exciting and we decided it should be called *The Hospice Everest Expedition.*

Publicity is all important in any fund raising event. Although the local press and radio were very generous in their coverage of Hospice Appeal events, it was always difficult to get television coverage. I learnt over the years that it was only the more spectacular events such as the Graham Chapman (of Monty Python fame) crane jump in aid of the Hospice Appeal that would attract their attention. But I knew the Everest Expedition was a winner and would get good coverage – especially with the offer of the army helicopter from which to film.

We determined to make the event as money spinning as possible. A business friend persuaded a number of her business acquaintances to purchase huge posters at a cost of £250 each which were to be put up on the Royal Insurance building. She also arranged for the posters to be sign written, gratis, by Safeways.

The day dawned bright and sunny. The army had erected all the staging needed for the abseil the day before and we had made detailed plans for the four teams. The army and my nephew's club were to abseil down one wall of the building – in an endurance test of twenty-six descents each, while on the other wall, the police (about twenty-nine of them) and the twelve youngsters from the Fairbridge Drake charity would make their descents.

As the morning progressed, we had more and more spectators, and it seemed the whole of the local police force was there to watch the event. Our Superintendent friend had been persuaded to take part, much against his will, and his colleagues were there in force to cheer him on. I persuaded all the police to wear our yellow Hospice sashes and, such was the atmosphere of the occasion that the police helped us accost traffic when the lights were red and demand donations from drivers as they waited for the lights to change to green! One reluctant driver soon changed his mind when one of our police friends pointed out he hadn't got his seat belt fastened! A five pound note was quickly popped into the box!

At the end of the day we added nearly ten thousand pounds to our funds, as well as having a lot of press and television publicity. Such was the plant that had grown from the seed planted by my nephew six months earlier.

That was a very busy weekend for, at the other end of our area, our Chairman saw the development of another seed. Near his house was an area of woodland where an enterprising friend had developed a 'skirmish' area. He offered help – and we organised a day which involved eight teams from nearby firms. Each team came arrayed in fancy dress – we had the *Naughty Nurses* (a team of my son and his reprobate friends who represented the Hospice Appeal), while the *Kleenex Tissue Tots* in nappies, represented a local paper firm, Kimberley Clerk, and the *Bash Street Kids* and their teachers were aggressive representatives of the Royal Bank of Scotland. All entered into the spirit of the occasion, and my photograph album with pictures of each team spectacularly attired is evidence of their enterprise. Sadly, it was too far out from the centre of town for us to persuade the camera teams to come out – something that was a great disappointment to our Chairman.

We were always on the look out for ways of attracting television. One of our most successful times was the arrival of Granny Vera – a lady in her sixties who spent a year walking the length and breadth of Great Britain raising money for the hospice movement by visiting every hospice and hospice project in the country. She was to arrive in our town in the evening when it was dark, and depart at 8 o'clock the next morning. I decided we should make as much as we could of this event in order to attract the media. The Railway Hotel where she was staying laid on a social gathering in the evening, and next morning I organised a spectacular departure through the town. We persuaded a Scottish piper friend to pipe her through the town, and gathered together a large number of our volunteers to accompany her. We set out from the Railway Hotel at 8am carrying a 70 foot banner bearing our name and logo and walked through the town which was busy with people on their way to work. The Mayor met us at the Town Hall and then joined the march. We all carried collecting boxes, and once again, accosted passers by and any cars that had to slow down at traffic lights or pedestrian crossings. It was all strictly illegal, but as we were accompanied by both the local police and television cameras,we were not worried. TVS gave us good coverage that evening – and once again we felt we had heightened public awareness of the Hospice Appeal.

It was a family event that triggered off a succession of similar social occasions which brought in some very valuable funds. Our daughter, Alex, was married in the summer to Paddy, and we had a marquee in the garden for the wedding reception. Someone suggested that we should have a Champagne Lunch in the marquee for the Hospice the day after the wedding. Bill was not exactly enthusiastic about the idea, but when a group of people, including the caterer, offered to take it on and promised I would not be involved, he couldn't refuse.

It was a great idea and, although I was up at seven the morning after the wedding to help get the marquee tidied up after the festivities of the previous night, it proved to be a wonderful finish to the wedding weekend. A number of our friends who had stayed on came to the lunch, and we were able to sit back and enjoy ourselves (that is, until the water main sprung a huge leak during the lunch. Water poured down the village street, and a man from the water board arrived at 2 o'clock, while lunch was still being served, and threatened to cut off the water on the instant. I had to leave the marquee and ply the water board man with champagne before he relented and agreed to delay cutting off the water till after the lunch was over. This little drama apart, we had a wonderful lunch and added some £2,400 to funds.

That was the start of a series of marquee events following eighteenth and twenty-first birthday parties as well as weddings. We had musical evenings, garden parties, and more champagne lunches. These proved the highlight of the Appeal's social calendar and they were always over-subscribed.

When I look back over my diary I am amazed at the many different fund raising events I was involved with both prior to the opening of the hospice and since. In the early days I coupled all this activity with supply teaching and with looking after our overseas guests. But it became increasingly difficult to fit everything in. The guest house venture ground to a halt as Bill became increasingly irritated by my constant absence from home on Appeal business which meant I was never available to help look after the guests. It was the breakfasts in particular which bugged him – and I always say that it was fried eggs that brought our guest house venture to an end. For the one thing guaranteed to send Bill into a tizzy was frying eggs. He could never get them out of the pan in one piece – but being a perfectionist, was not prepared to serve a broken egg to our guests. Hence, during any breakfast operation in which Bill was involved, there would be an array of imperfectly cooked eggs littering the kitchen. The atmosphere would get more and more explosive until I came to the rescue. As the Hospice work often meant that I had left the house well before our guests were ready for their breakfast, Bill decided enough was enough and refused to take in any more guests!

As for the teaching, that too soon ground to a halt for it was not long before the Hospice work had so taken over my time that I was never available when schools rang me up to ask me to go in. Unless you have a fixed contract, as I had had during my first year of retirement, supply teachers are usually called in at short notice. If you prove reliable and available, you become part of their regular supply team and will find yourself called in very frequently. But if you proved elusive, as I began to be, you are last on the list to be telephoned.

It was sadly detrimental to our financial well being and I think our chairman, being sensitive, must have noticed what was happening because he called me aside one day and asked whether I would consider being paid for some of the work I was doing on a consultancy basis.

I thought about it long and hard. I felt that for the Appeal it would be advantageous as I would be able to devote all my time to fund raising without having to divert in other directions to supplement our income. On the other hand, I realised it would subtly alter my relationship with the other members of the team. I spoke to a lot of our group leaders and grass roots supporters to see how they felt about it. They all were in favour. The one person who advised me against was my friend Ron, our Fund Raising Chairman. He pointed out that it would change my status and my relationships, and could lead to difficulty. It is interesting, looking back, that the relationship into which my decision to accept the offer most intruded was that with Ron. It seemed that he was increasingly unhappy about my role and gradually distanced himself from what had been a very close and valued friendship. Happily, with none of our group leaders and supporters was our relationship affected at all.

Other areas of difficulty arose which caused considerable hurt and stress, but this came much later and with only a very small group of people.

It was during this period of hectic fund raising that I forged so many new and valuable friendships, meeting people from all walks of life and from all age groups. We seemed united in a common purpose and the sense of family, as I have said before, was very strong indeed.

I felt at home in the town among many different groups and organisations, and was constantly amazed at the generous way in which people responded to my many and often bizarre or cheeky requests for help. It seemed that the social barriers came down in all directions and where people were valued for what they were rather than for what they possessed and what they did, friendship was offered in full measure.

One learnt to work with all the other charities in the area and one had a great sense of pride in what the charity field was doing to help fill in the gaps in our social fabric, and put pressure in areas where nothing was being done. I found it fascinating to meet up with people whom I had known in my earlier playgroup days and lost touch with. It somehow seemed a natural progression. It was good being able to meet with clergy and parishioners from a wide variety of churches and to feel at home everywhere, and to enter schools and clubs and know a warm welcome would be extended. It felt good to be part of such a worthwhile enterprise and I felt that my whole life had been directed to the work of providing a hospice for the people of the area.

CHAPTER 26
The Hospice is Built, October 1991

During those four hectic years, my activities were not confined to fund raising, as I was keen to be involved in the whole enterprise. We had, first of all, to forge a new team of people to move the project forward. The fifty subscribers we had recruited, once the charitable company was incorporated, became the Council of the Company. But that was far too big a body to manage the Appeal. So a Management Committee was appointed of some seventeen members to forward the work.

I soon became aware that, despite the infinite good will that existed, there would still be problems. Aids had not long hit the headlines, and was a controversial issue – most of the cases at that time being confined to the homosexual element in society. The question came up at our very first meeting. Would we take Aids patients in our hospice? I was distressed to see a polarisation of views. I knew that some hospices refused to take other than cancer patients, but our trust deed was deliberately worded to embrace all terminally ill patients. Whether we would take Aids patients in our hospice was a question that I had had to answer a number of times when I addressed new groups of supporters. Knowing what an emotive subject it was, and not wishing to alienate support I had always been slightly evasive – suggesting that as Aids threatened to be such a pandemic, it was something the government would have to take on board and it was not really a problem for a voluntary body. But I added that hospice care was for the terminally ill, that many hospices were already admitting Aids patients, and that, if it seemed needful and practical, our hospice would almost certainly take in Aids patients. This qualified answer always seemed to satisfy even the most vociferous opponents of accepting Aids patients, and though it may have seemed to some that I was sitting on the fence, I have always believed that just a little 'trimming', provided it is not dishonest, is the best way to deal with controversial issues. For there is always the element of time that changes any situation.

But at that first Management Meeting it was clear that people had very strong views on the subject – and not the least strong were the views of our new Chairman who felt passionately that we should take Aids patients when the hospice was built. He said he would not be prepared to continue were that policy not adopted – and wanted the group to make a firm statement to that effect. After heated discussions we managed to come up with a formula of 'at the Medical Director's discretion' which temporarily satisfied everyone. But ruffled feathers had to be smoothed down, and it was an intimation that future discussions would not be without heat.

One of the things that soon became very apparent was the need to develop our office facilities. I had negotiated a new room with the hospital administrator but that was not to be available till after Christmas. And just after Christmas we learnt that Bob, seconded from the National Westminster Bank, was soon to retire and would not be replaced.

We little realised what a lucky chance it was that an elderly retired bank manager in his eighties, Leslie, had recently started helping Bob in the office. Leslie's daughter was a Friend of the Hospice and she had shown him a little notice we had put in our Information Sheet asking for more volunteers in the office. Leslie, not long widowed and at a loss for occupation after nursing his wife for many months until her death, had started coming in to help Bob. On Bob's retirement at the age of sixty, Leslie at the age of eighty took over!

Leslie

It was a most happy development. It would be difficult to find anyone who had his wits about him more than Leslie. His brain was sharp as a razor, and his figure work quick and accurate. I am one of those impatient people who hate, above all things, proof reading. I always miss the most obvious errors, and over the years, I always relied on Leslie's accurate eye to pick up my many mistakes. His quick sense of humour helped keep the Appeal office light hearted and happy over many years, and the Hospice owes him a great debt of gratitude. While we were at the Hospital he worked three days a week – arriving at the Appeal office on the dot of nine and departing on the dot of five. He had an hour and a half for lunch. But that was not the end of his commitment. If anything needed urgent attention on the other two days, he would quietly go into the office and get on with it. We laughingly referred to him as our 'office boy' and people were always amazed when they met Leslie and realised how fortunate we were in having his services.

It was soon after the new charity was set up that we were joined by a much respected former Assistant Chief Constable of Kent who had been the Deputy Commandant at the Police Staff College. He was a formidable character. I remember on first meeting him with our Chairman, that I was very impressed with his abilities – and felt he would be a valuable addition to our Appeal team. But I was reminded by a friend some years later that, in describing him, I expressed enthusiasm about his abilities but anxiety that he might be the sort of person who would want to take over the Appeal! Little did I realise I was making a prophetic remark!

He agreed to become the Appeal's Administrator and take on the oversight of the office. He joined us just as a new and larger room was made available to us at the Hospital with, joy of joys, an adjacent toilet. Up to that time, a visit to the loo had necessitated a long march across the hospital grounds. Our new recruit took on the task of preparing the new office. He involved the probationary services in cleaning and decorating the room, and scrounged an assortment of office furniture to equip it. I had meanwhile obtained a donation of £1,200 from a local Trust to purchase a computer, and had also obtained the loan of a photocopier from a firm owned by friends of mine, who gave us incredibly generous rates for photocopying and maintenance. Various typewriters appeared by magic – and we had an Appeal Office that was well equipped and pleasant to work in.

For some reason no provision was made for me to work in the Office so my base remained at home. Fortunately we had a room downstairs in our Oast which we had designated as a study. It became for the next four years a second Appeal office – equipped with desk, filing cabinet, telephone, and my own Amstrad computer. Not long after we set up the new charity our solicitor friend gave me an old Philips computer, huge but with an excellent printer. That served the Appeal well for many years and was still in good working order when I left in 1991.

Having an office at home had its advantages – but it was also quite a burden on the family. The phone started ringing soon after eight o'clock in the morning and continued late into the evening. If I was out on Appeal business, Bill had to take the calls, and I would arrive home to find five or six pieces of paper containing messages and telephone numbers spread across the living room floor. Although not an official participant, the Hospice owed Bill more than anyone realised. He helped me and my Appeal friends talk through problems, assisted in drafting letters and memoranda, took messages, answered queries, and supported me at I know not how many events. He also acted as host to many Appeal events in our house – and extended warm and kindly hospitality to some of the Appeal friends I took under my wing and brought home. Moreover, he put up with two or three evenings a week on his own while I was out on Appeal business, not to mention the numerous Saturday and Sundays involved in Appeal events throughout the year. Knowing how much he had contributed to the Hospice Appeal over the years, I felt deeply upset when the Hospice was built when one of the senior staff said sharply, when I suggested that Bill's presence would be useful at a particular discussion, that Bill 'was nothing to do with the Appeal!' Such insensitivity enraged me and made me want to weep.

In fact, the next few years were for me a real study in human nature. I am gregarious by nature and like people. I have always tended to enter quickly into new relationships and Bill said I was always far too trusting, with high expectations of people's abilities and virtues. As a result I have often been sadly disappointed. Having done some studies in management for my master's degree, I should not have been surprised. For typical group dynamics were very much in evidence as the new team began to settle down.

Management Committee meetings were not called very frequently and about six months into the new structure, I felt we were all working in isolation. This was something our Vice Chairman picked up, and he set up a Finance and General Purposes Committee which, to begin with, comprised the Vice Chairman, the Administrator, the Treasurer and me. The Treasurer was a close friend of our Administrator, who, like him, had been an Assistant Chief Constable, so they made a happy pair. We had some very positive and fruitful meetings and things began to pull together.

Meanwhile, our Chairman was making tentative progress on the building side – entering into discussions with the Health Authority about possible sites and possible help. As progress began to be made on that front, he started coming to our meetings as did a retired headmaster who, at my suggestion, had taken on responsibility for getting money from charitable trusts. Ron had come back into action again after his major operation, and as the Appeal Chairman we felt he should also be present.

This Finance and General Purposes Committee became the effective working group of the Appeal and within a short time was making most of the major decisions – with only occasional reference to the Management Committee, and even fewer referrals to the Council. I found myself the only woman working with six men. It was an instructive experience! The six men came from very different professions – the police, civil service, teaching, trade, and big business – each of them with experience of widely different working methods and ethos. Only one member of the group had quite reached the top in his profession. The others had advanced nearly to the top, holding the number two or three position. I did not at first realise how significant this was. They had all recently retired. Again, the significance of this did not hit me. But that first year, there seemed to be constant jockeying for position and muttered comments about the other members of the group, as well as occasional threats of resignation. I felt like a coach driver with a team of unruly horses whom I had somehow to tame and get to work in harness. It was tough going. But even tougher when they at last began to work as a team and suddenly realised they had been schooled by a woman! For then, male pride and male camaraderie came much into evidence. How often this occurs is an issue often raised in female circles.

What I did not fully appreciate was the feeling of insecurity and loss of identity that assails a person when they first retire. From being someone in a very senior position, one is suddenly a nobody, and one has to create a new identity. In fact, for the first time, many people come face to face with their real selves – 'Who am I?' For those with ambition, who have not made it quite to the top, association with a charity seems to promise a way of establishing a new and worthwhile identity. And this, I think, is what, in some measure, was happening in that first year.

I was also interested to observe the pairing that goes on, and the male need for a personal ally. We had two sets of pairs within the group – and much to my amusement each pair had secretly nicknamed the other pair 'Tweedledum and Tweedledee.' While this pairing lasted, I was safe. But with the departure of our new Treasurer, the whole alignment of the group changed. There was only one person available to fill the gap for our Administrator, and that was Ron. I suddenly found myself without support. It was a hurtful experience for I was now isolated, and I was made more aware than ever that I was the only female in the group.

Looking back, I think one of the problems was that I did not then, nor do I now, find it easy to accept that men and women are different. Although I accept our different sexuality I always expect men and women to react in the same way. As a consequence, whether I am working with a man or a woman, I tend to react to them according to their ability and competence rather than to their gender. Perhaps this is due to my own poor self image. I have never thought of myself as particularly attractive sexually, and therefore, working with men in a professional capacity, the element of sex does not intrude for me as a factor. I treat men in the same way as I would a woman, as equals, and expect to be treated myself as an equal. What I did not realise, and what caused me a lot of hurt, was that men on the whole find it very difficult indeed to accept women on equal terms. There is always that element of sexuality, that unconscious belief that women are inferior. Moreover, because I did not pander to their masculinity, because I did not flirt with them or indicate that I thought them sexually desirable, I have a feeling, looking back, that their male egos were dented. They felt threatened by my outspokenness, jealous of my success, and hurt by my lack of response to their masculinity.

Me

Had I been aware of this 'hidden agenda', and perhaps been more sensitive, I might have been able to handle the situation in a more adroit fashion.

Despite the misunderstanding I liked the members of the group very much and I believe they liked me. They all had excellent qualities – humanity, humour, intelligence – and were very good companions. I enjoyed their company and I think they enjoyed mine. The difficulties I encountered with the group, fortunately, remained hidden from general view, and only Bill and one or two of our close friends knew what was going on.

But things were moving apace. The Health Authority offered to give us a site for the Hospice. This was a considerable move forward, and was an offer we were pleased to accept. The first offer was of a site adjacent to the new hospital – but after about nine months, the offer was withdrawn and we were offered a different site at the home of the Royal British Legion. The site was small, about half an acre, but it had beautiful grounds, and we decided to accept it, though we did have some reservations about its size and the noise from the motor way.

I personally began to have reservations about building from scratch. I suggested, rather at the last minute, that as the site was so small, we should explore the possibility of purchasing a house in large grounds – an idea we had talked about tentatively in the early days. The sharp reaction from the medical representative on the Management Committee made me realise that such a decision would not be a good political move, so I did not push it. But once the Hospice was up and running and I'd had an opportunity to visit some of the hospices built at about the same time as ours, I believe my instincts were correct, and that we would have been better off with larger grounds. Expansion would have been easier and we would have had immediate facilities for an office and for day care. But we were handicapped by the constraints of finance and of Health Authority politics, and did not have the courage to explore further.

Because negotiations with the Health Authority proceeded so slowly, a number of people, including our Administrator, began to question the wisdom of having two men who were Members of the Health Authority as our Chairman and Vice Chairman. It was suggested that their dual role might be making it very difficult for them to put the necessary pressure on the Health Authority for financial support. It was a debatable point. Certainly our Chairman and Vice Chairman worked immensely hard to forward the cause of the Hospice, and it cannot have been without personal difficulties for them.

It was in 1989 that our Chairman suggested I met the Nurse Manager in charge of the Macmillan Nurses. He thought it would be a good idea to make contact as we wanted to involve the Macmillan Nurses in the Hospice once it was open. I telephoned her and invited her to lunch. She asked if she could bring along the Nurse Manager of the Night Shared Care service who was very interested in the Hospice.

So, one day in early March, the two came to lunch at The Oast. They talked about what they perceived, from their own experience, to be the needs of the terminally ill, and said there was a serious gap in the service for those nursing terminal patients at home. They said that carers were desperately in need of relief during the day. Knowing that it would take some years to raise the necessary funds to build the Hospice I had long felt the desire to offer some sort of service to the terminally ill before the Hospice opened. I'd toyed with the idea of suggesting day care – but we did not really have the manpower to seek out and develop suitable premises. But a service involving people rather than a building was something that hit me as immediately possible. Such was the rapport between us, that, by the end of lunch, our two nurse managers and I had planned in outline a Volunteer Sitting Service!

Our combined enthusiasm had the strength of a juggernaut – nothing could stop us. We decided that our first priority was to organise a day seminar to which we would invite all those who, over the years, had expressed an interest in working in the Hospice – as well as extending an open invitation to our other supporters. We did a lot of research and wrote to a number of hospices which were running sitting services of one kind and another, and invited them to come and speak at the seminar and tell us how their services were organised, and about the pain and the joy involved in sitting.

We decided to invite the Volunteer Co-ordinator from the local Hospital, and a counsellor who had expressed an interest in helping with the service, to help us plan the Seminar – and we had a number of valuable and interesting meetings getting everything ready for the big day.

Through the efforts of our Chairman, we obtained the use of the Postgraduate Medical Centre at the local Hospital for the Seminar and on the 10th of July 1989 (a week after our daughter's wedding) over a hundred people turned up for an all-day Seminar. Our Chairman's wife organised the catering for us, providing a splendid ploughman's lunch.

It was an exciting day with some excellent speakers, a lot of questions, and a tremendous amount of enthusiasm. Our speakers outlined the way their services were run, talked about the qualities needed in a sitter, explained the pitfalls and the problems, and enthused about the blessings such a service conferred on the carers. I was in the chair and opened the seminar by giving a brief outline of how far we had progressed with our Hospice Appeal, and what we planned to provide. At the end of the day I had the unenviable task of summing up what had been said.

Before the participants left, we presented them with a questionnaire to fill in, and a form on which to indicate whether, after what they had heard, they still wished to become sitters. Some, wisely, decided it was not the sort of thing they really wanted to do – but a large number volunteered.

The next step was to try and get some financial support. It was here that we had a most fortunate break. We saw an advertisement inviting applications for a grant from a special Post Office fund set up from the sale of stamps. The advert invited applications from new charitable ventures. Our Nurse Manager wrote an application, I vetted it, and our Chairman signed it, and a few months later, to our immense delight, we learnt the Post Office was to give us £19,000 – enough to put the Volunteer Sitting Service on its feet for the first two years.

As was to happen on a number of occasions during the next few years, our joy was tempered with 'aggro'. Our Administrator, without telling me, had also put in an application to the Post Office for funding. With two different applications before them, the Post Office, not unnaturally, started asking questions. The consequent investigation led to a certain amount of bad feeling and it was quite clear that the roles, responsibilities and functions of Appeal Organiser and Administrator were interpreted in different ways. As the Appeal Organiser, I felt I should, at the very least, know about all applications for funds, otherwise wires would be crossed – as on this occasion. The Administrator saw it differently. What was needed at that stage was a strong person to sit down and sort out the problem and define the roles, but, sadly, that did not happen and was in time to cause further problems, and a considerable amount of difficulty and unhappiness.

It brought home to me very strongly the vital importance of having a good organisational structure with clearly defined roles and responsibilities. Sadly, again, it was a lesson that was not learnt properly, and when the Hospice had been up and running for a year, a number of quite serious administrative and relational difficulties arose which meant that the whole structure had to be revised and roles redefined. Our Hospice was not alone in this. When discussing our structure at one of the Help the Hospices Conferences a year before we opened, I learnt not only that hospices all seemed to adopt different administrative structures but that most of them had to amend their structure and redefine roles within a year. So much depends on the personality and the character of the people at the top.

A poor organisational structure can work if there are exceptionally tolerant and sensitive people in post. But people being what they are, there are very few with sufficient wisdom and maturity to be able to cope for long with a muddled and poorly defined structure. Over the years I have come to the conclusion that one of the strongest motivating factors in life is the desire for power. It is my belief that it is a far more powerful factor than sex. And coupled with the desire for power is jealousy. The presence of these two elements was very apparent at certain levels in the charity – and it was very sad.

But, by contrast, at the grass roots level there was a marvellous sense of family unity and everyone worked together as a team. Close friendships were formed and that wonderful spirit of love and care, which we were all working towards providing in the Hospice when it was built, seemed to pervade everything we did.

To go back to our Sitting Service. It was clear that neither of the nurse managers nor I could administer the new service as we were all fully occupied with our own jobs. The great value of the Post Office grant was that we were able to appoint immediately a part time Sitting Service Co-ordinator and give her a small salary. Our counsellor friend took on this job and, with enormous help and support from the two nurses, got the service under way. She started by interviewing all our potential volunteers, and making contact with the families who needed help with sitting.

We realised right from the beginning that the service would need a manned telephone if it was to be of any value to the carers. The Night Shared Care Service had full time secretarial help – a post that was manned on a part time basis by three ladies. They all agreed to work an extra two hours each day between the hours of one and three, and we sent out letters to all the relevant caring agencies telling them that was the time when the Sitting Service Office would be manned. But we gave as an alternative number our Appeal Office which was always manned during the morning. The need for office accommodation was easily met for we'd still retained the use of our original tiny office which we'd been using for storage. With judicious sorting, we were able to make the room into a comfortable office for the Sitting Service. It was adjacent to our new Appeal Office and thus, right from the beginning, very close links were established between the Sitting Service and the Appeal.

The volunteers who emerged from our Day Seminar needed some basic training. Their role was not a nursing one – but we knew they would be called upon to do some basic nursing duties like lifting, helping patients to the toilet, and making them comfortable. There was the problem of confidentiality, the need for emotional support as they were dealing with the dying and their relatives, and the need to know who to call upon in an emergency. Insurance, expenses, and the responsibilities of sitters and the service were also problems that had to be addressed.

A six session basic training course was therefore devised for the sitters, and arrangements were made for them to do a Cruse Counselling course. We planned that the volunteers should sit with patients for three hour sessions during a morning, afternoon or evening. During that time carers were free to do anything they liked. Some used it to shop or have their hair done, others to garden, visit family or friends, or just relax or have a sleep. The Volunteer Co-ordinator, always made a preliminary visit to the family to assess the situation, and then assigned a carer to the family. Where possible, she tried to assign the same sitter to the family throughout the period they needed help – but this was not always easy to arrange when the carers were in need of several sittings during a week.

Among our first group of Sitters were a number of our fund raising volunteers including the man who had been our Covenant Secretary for two years. The dedication of the Sitters was wonderful – and the service they offered greatly valued by the terminally ill and their carers. After the first year, we appointed a new Volunteer Co-ordinator and when the hospice opened in October 1991 she and the secretaries moved into an office in the hospice building. The Sitting Service then became an integral part of the service offered by the hospice, and at the end of the first year its name was changed to Volunteer Community Service.

The Sitting Service was only one of my departures from fund raising. Once our new charity was established in 1987 we began to make more contacts with other hospices. We attended the annual Help the Hospices Conference in London at the Royal College of Surgeons. This was the charity founded by the Duchess of Norfolk to bring together under one umbrella the hospices throughout the country. It provided an information service and training, and was largely responsible for bringing the hospice movement to the attention of the government, and persuading it to make a commitment to fifty-fifty funding. It is a commitment that has, so far, only been honoured in certain parts of the country, notably Scotland, but it is one to which the government still stands publicly committed.

One area where we were dogged by disappointment was over a hospice shop. From the very beginning we had wanted a charity shop and started looking for one way back in 1986. But nothing suitable or within our price range emerged during those early years when funds were limited. We then took on as a shop consultant a man who had set up some seven hospice charity shops for our neighbouring hospice, and another two hundred for other charities throughout the country. He was confident he would get one for us, but time dragged on, and none of the shops we were offered did he think suitable. One of the problems was the very high rents charged in the town – among the highest in the country.

In 1989 I found a shop which I felt was very suitable – two stories with a rent of £12,000 a year and no premium. But our shop consultant advised against it as it was not large enough to generate the sort of annual income he felt a hospice shop should bring in. His advice was based on the net income from some of the neighbouring hospice shops, many of which had been purchased outright before inflation really took off. To my great regret we let it go. I always felt very sad about this. It would not only have provided us with a nice little shop and a base in the town, there was also accommodation over the shop which could have been used for an Appeal Office. Four years on, we could easily have generated at least £80,000 net which could have gone a long way towards renting or purchasing a better shop, as well as bringing the Appeal to the attention of a whole new group of people. But the Appeal worked as a group through committees and one had to bow to majority decisions. On the matter of this particular shop I was a lone voice, and as I was not in a position to run the shop, I felt I was in a weak position, and was unable to persuade the rest of the committee to my point of view. Nothing so suitable came up again until after I retired, and I always felt we lost a great opportunity.

However, at the end of 1991, thanks to the generosity of one of our supporters we had some shop premises for two months at a very low rent in which we ran an on-going Christmas Bazaar. An old friend took on the responsibility for organising this, ably assisted by two of our most stalwart volunteers, David and Norma, who both devoted several days each week to the Hospice. One of them had just taken over as Administrator as our former Administrator had had to resign because of eye trouble. Norma, his wife, was one of the real stalwarts of the Appeal providing cakes and refreshments whenever needed, and running an annual Garden Party at their home.

The Bazaar flourished and added several thousand pounds to funds. It also provided a sort of training ground for our shop volunteers who had been champing at the bit ever since our shop consultant and I had organised a Day Seminar for our potential shop volunteers way back in 1989.

At the end of 1992 we obtained, at a very low rent, a delightful but tiny shop in a little square which generated a steady income of around £500 a week. Its small size and off centre location made it far from ideal, but the steady income and the enthusiasm of the team of helpers made it a worthwhile enterprise while the search for more suitable premises continued.

That there is money to be made from charity shops has been proved time and again, but to take on expensive long term leases is not something a small charity can do lightly. There are numerous charity shops in the town, but they all belong to national charities which have capital and a strong organisation behind them. For small local charities the situation is much more difficult. But the importance of shops has now been recognised and there are now many Hospice shops in and around Maidstone.

The offer of a site by the Health Authority saved the Appeal the considerable expense of purchasing land on which to build. But we were unable to make progress with obtaining any promise of help with the funding of the running costs. Because of this, whenever I gave a talk or tried to persuade someone to donate, I was at pains to make people aware that once the Hospice was built we should have to continue fund raising for running costs. Although that message was not taken on board by everyone, the majority of our fund raising supporters from very early on realised that they were involved in a long term commitment to the Hospice – and over the years there was very little falling off of support.

It was during this period that we visited a number of hospices throughout the country to look both at the building and at the services on offer. We were also keen to find out more about the way they went about fund raising, and the implications of revenue fund raising as opposed to capital fund raising which, we guessed, would be more difficult.

The Chairman took on the responsibility for getting the Hospice building plans under way. He and one of our Council members, a former Mayor who was an architect, visited a number of hospices throughout the country, looking carefully at the designs and making enquiries about the architects who had been responsible for designing them. They narrowed down a list of four architects and in 1990 they were invited to submit designs to a Planning Committee comprising the members of the Finance and General Purposes Committee – our consultant friend; our G.P. representative; the Macmillan Nurse Manager; and a doctor who worked in a hospice. The former Matron of the neighbouring hospice whose experience we felt would be invaluable, also joined the Committee.

After the presentations we chose a firm of young architects who had designed the Plymouth Hospice where Dr Sheila Cassidy was the Medical Director. We were taken by their enthusiasm and their unusual design, as well as by the technology used in their presentation. For their computer aided design enabled us to see the sort of building we would get. The building that emerged is a very beautiful one with an excellent finish, but it has a number of weaknesses, and has been called 'an architect's building'. Looking back I think we should have opted for a more practical design which would have utilised more effectively what was a very limited site – but it is easy to be wise after the event!

Some of the impracticalities that emerged can perhaps be attributed to the fact that, at the more detailed planning stage, no medical or nursing staff were involved. Their input would have been very valuable but, sadly, it was not sought. When appointed, the Matron and the Chairman of the Board of Governors who took on the running of the Hospice, both felt deeply regretful that they had not been around at the planning stage when changes could more easily have been made.

But, whatever the weakness in the design, we could not have had a more helpful and co-operative group of architects. They threw themselves into the project, and also involved themselves with the whole enterprise, joining in with some of our fund raising events. That support continued once the Hospice was up and running. One of the architects was so enthusiastic about the Hospice that it was not long before he persuaded his father, an artist of international repute, to support the fund raising. Together we organised a very successful Art Exhibition and he donated a number of Christmas card designs which brought in several thousand pounds for the Hospice.

He was not the only artist friend to whom we were indebted. One well known local artist, Graham Clarke, organised several exhibitions of paintings by local artists, and designed Christmas cards for the Appeal for four consecutive years. And another artist, one of our Subscribers, Brian Higbee, who was an entertainer as well as a painter, designed our logo and made a popular tape which brought in £3,000. He also entertained at several fund raising events. Another artist supporter was Mike Chaplin.

To go back to the building. Equally co-operative were the builders, while their foreman was a wonderful help to the Appeal as the building neared completion. Once the Hospice opened, his wife became involved as one of the Hospice volunteers. It demonstrated yet again the wonderful family spirit that had developed over the years.

During the later stages of building, I was much occupied in converting into habitable office accommodation an old bungalow which had been used for many years by the Health Authority's transport department. We were initially told by the Health Authority that we could have the whole building, but when the old plans were dug out, it was discovered that the boundary line ran the opposite side of the building to the one believed, and that the building belonged to the British Legion. It was a sad blow. The Legion did, however, offer to let us have half the building on a gentleman's agreement, and I set to to make it habitable at the least possible cost.

I arranged with British Legion Kent, who were to occupy the other half of the building, that they would provide the materials and I would find the labour. It was a happy arrangement. I persuaded the local Prison to let me have two prisoners to work on the building. They stripped it out – removing smelly carpets, disintegrating furniture and rotting wood – and painted the building inside and out. I then found a friend to re-wire it for us at cost, and another friend who carpeted the whole building for nothing. Finally, one of our Hospice supporters, recently retired, discovered that her old firm had been taken over by Robert Maxwell. He announced that the office was to be moved out of its lovely London Queen Anne house to a warehouse down river. All the office furniture was to be disposed of. Our friend moved in quickly and obtained a lot of it for our Appeal office. So, at no cost at all to the Appeal, we had managed to provide clean and comfortable office accommodation.

Our only expenditure came later when the Gas Board informed us the boiler was dangerous and had to be replaced. And later still, we were so short of space, we converted a shower room into an extra tiny office. But we were very snug and comfortable and ready to bring over everything from our hospital Office which was about to pulled down when, to our consternation, the British Legion announced that it was going to renege on the gentleman's agreement and take back the building! The situation was eventually resolved by the British Legion having one of the rooms we had refurbished – but it was a nail biting time while we waited for a resolution of the problem.

Another area in which I became much involved was the chapel. There was a small Roman Catholic chapel on the Hospice site which, we learnt, belonged to the Health Authority, and we were told could be part of the Hospice. Our Roman Catholic friends had been wonderfully supportive over the years, and we were all anxious to work together for the benefit of the Hospice and the Roman Catholic community. So our Chairman, got together a committee which comprised the Roman Catholic Monsignor, the Anglican Bishop, our free church council member, and myself. We had a number of meetings to discuss the Chaplaincy of the Hospice and the chapel itself. As it stood, the Chapel was not suitable as a Hospice Chapel – for access was impossible for the patients. Very generously, the Roman Catholic congregation agreed to major alterations to the chapel, moving the altar from east to west, knocking down an arch, and levelling the floor where the altar had been in order to create access for wheelchairs. They also helped raise money for the conversion which amounted to well over £20,000.

It was agreed there would be a joint chaplaincy, with an Anglican priest as the 'secretary' to the chaplaincy. There was an interregnum in the nearby parish, and the Bishop agreed to appoint someone who was interested in hospice work. In the first year, the chaplaincy developed according to plan. A young clergyman was appointed to the nearby parish and came in regularly to the Hospice. But he soon found he couldn't give the amount of time he felt the Hospice needed, and he asked the Bishop to find a replacement. This he did by asking a recently retired clergyman to take on the task. It was an inspired choice – the Rev. Donald Bish. He worked hard to develop a real Christian life in the hospice.

During the period leading up to the opening of the Hospice I became involved in the garden – and managed to save the Appeal thousands of pounds by getting goods and labour donated. One good friend, owner of a large construction firm, gave us lorry loads of first class top soil, while a garden centre friend and his son gave hours of their time in getting the whole garden levelled and seeded – a mammoth task. We were also fortunate in that our first Bursar had a wife who was a keen gardener, and she managed to get hundreds of lovely plants and bulbs donated, and planted them out in such a way that the patients and their families had beautiful gardens to look out on.

The Bursar's wife was also much involved with the 'Hanging Committee' which, with the help of local artists, begged and borrowed a wonderful selection of paintings to hang on the walls of the Hospice.

I spent a lot of time trying to get help with constructing a pond. The architects had pencilled into their plans quite a large area for a pond, but we felt we couldn't afford to pay the cost involved. But it was an unsightly area just below the Day Care windows and I determined we would somehow get the pond built as quickly as possible without cost. I contacted our old friends, the Royal Engineers, who came and dug out the pond for us, while our architects decided they would make a personal contribution to the Hospice, and come and help build the pond. They in turn enlisted the help of the site foreman – and between them provided a lovely pond without major expense. As a final touch, a beautiful fountain was donated by one of our Group Leaders in memory of her husband who had died suddenly at an early age the previous year.

One of our roadside boards

Looking back, the year leading up the opening of the Hospice and the year following were years of frenetic activity. The need for money was urgent. We had to raise £1.3 million to build and equip the building, and from April 1991 we were paying the salaries of senior staff – first of all, the Matron, then the Bursar, followed closely by a Secretary and the Medical Director. This meant additional funds were needed. We calculated that the first year's running costs would be around £600,000 – towards which we were promised a grant of £150,000 from the Health Authority. This left us with nearly £half a million to raise from the community – a formidable task. We had raised over £500,000 the previous year, and managed to do the same again in 1991 which we felt was quite an achievement as the recession was beginning to bite.

While all the frenetic activity was going on with fund raising and building, there was equally hectic work going on preparing the Hospice for opening. After many lengthy and agonised discussions it was decided to set up a Board of Governors to run the Hospice while keeping a separate Appeal Committee to manage the Appeal. Both would be answerable to the Council. Our Chairman in particular felt that the Appeal should be kept entirely separate from the Hospice, and was determined that the fund raisers should be kept out of the Hospice altogether. His ideas were based on comments made by other hospices about fund raisers interfering in medical matters, and we were able to see some of the dangers. But the separation was taken to extremes and the Hospice had not been long in operation before we began to reap the problems of such a structure. Within a few months, the new Governors, many of whom had had little connection with the Appeal, were asking why there was no contact with the Appeal Organiser or the fund raisers who had built the Hospice.

There was a determination to change the organisational structure, but not before a lot of problems had built up and a lot of unhappiness caused.

We were all asked to put forward names of people to be approached to serve on the Board of Governors and at about this time I received a letter from a lady I knew slightly offering her services to the Hospice when it opened. She was a member of the Regional Health Authority and much involved with the Cheshire homes. I passed her letter to our Chairman who knew her, and he immediately identified her as a possible Chairman of the Board of Governors. Approached, Rosanne agreed to serve, and took on the onerous task of setting up appointment committees to find the senior staff. She identified herself fully with the Hospice and worked hard to get it open and functioning well.

In April 1991 a Matron was appointed followed soon after by a Bursar, a former High Sheriff. It would be difficult to find two more contrasting characters – from very different backgrounds and with totally different approaches to their work and to people. But they quickly settled down to equipping the Hospice and preparing it for the arrival of the first patients. It was a time consuming task, and as the weeks went by, our Assistant Treasurer watched with dismay as accounts for beds, furniture, curtains, chairs and tables, bed linen, towels, medical equipment, cutlery and crockery, kitchen equipment, and a host of other items poured into the Appeal Office, and the funds we had accumulated over the years rapidly dwindled.

The Matron and Bursar were soon joined by a secretary and a Medical Director, and by the beginning of September there was a full complement of staff ready to be trained before the opening on the 28th of October 1991.

The imperative need to raise sufficient funds to be able to open without debt, and with sufficient money in the bank to keep going for several months ahead, put enormous pressure on me and my volunteer fund raisers. We looked in every possible direction for financial support and had two or three large scale fund raising events planned, it seemed, every month. We held our first Hospice Fete in 1990 in the grounds where the Hospice was being built, and it carried on for several years. It provided an opportunity for people to see where the Hospice was being built. It was a mammoth effort, and as I was unable to find anyone to organise it, I found myself involved in a lot of additional work. In fact, during this period the pressure of work was enormous and I found myself working longer and longer hours – often totting up well over seventy hours in a week.

As opening day approached, we felt it was important that all those who had helped raise money for the Hospice over the years should have an opportunity to visit the hospice and see where their money had gone. I also knew it would be a way of engendering further financial support. Over the years I had kept a card index of the names of anyone who had shown the slightest interest in, or support for, the Hospice. Because of problems with our computer, we had only managed to put a small number of them on a Data Base before the date of the Opening. So when we decided to send

The Hospice

out invitations to all our supporters, three thousand of them, much of the work had to be done by hand and I spent most of a holiday in Derbyshire sorting out the names on my card index into appropriate groups. On my return, we had two Saturdays working on addressing envelopes and at the same time, noting down the details ready to go on the computer. It was a mammoth task and said much for the loyalty and devotion of our fund raisers that they were prepared to give up their weekends for such a tedious task

Once the Hospice was open, one of my major enterprises was to get all the names of our contacts computerised. We had considerable difficulty with the computer purchased by our Administrator, and it was only thanks to the kind offices of one of our volunteers that we were able to get it working properly. I had no regular paid secretarial help until nine months after the Hospice was opened and had to rely on volunteers. Their help was invaluable – but it was often only for half a day a week and it was very frustrating trying to get anything large scale done quickly. For a year or two I was able to call on a young friend of my daughter, Bridget, when I had a particularly large and difficult job to do. And when it came to computerising our mailing list, I enlisted Bridget's help and she spent tedious hours putting the three thousand names and addresses on the computer – a real labour of love.

In the year coming up to the opening, our Patron and I recruited a new group of supporters called Benefactors – people who covenanted £75 or more a year to the Hospice. We had a special social gathering for them at the Hospice so they could see what they were supporting.

It was a period of frenetic activity as we organised concerts, wine wit and wisdom evenings, silent auctions, auctions of promises, antique road shows, gala concerts, garden safaris, plant sales, tea dances, jumble sales, and coffee mornings. Our Hospice Caravan was out most weekends during the summer at various fairs and festivals around the town. We ran sponsored events, got involved in marathons, chased up charitable trusts and businesses, circulated solicitors in the hopes of obtaining legacies, and funeral directors in the hopes of donations. I had numerous speaking engagements, addressing the Chamber of Commerce, Rotary Clubs, Round Tables, W.I.s, Townswomen's Guilds, Mothers Unions, and Schools. I preached in morning services in a number of churches, addressed the Deanery Synod – and never seemed to be at home.

During the two weeks before the opening of the Hospice, we had nearly three thousand people through our doors. I organised teams of volunteers to take them round, provide tea and coffee, and sell an assortment of Hospice goods to raise funds.

On Monday the 28th of October 1991, our first three patients were received in the Hospice – one of whom had hung on to life because she was determined to get to the Hospice before she died. On the Saturday before, her husband and family had organised a coffee morning for her in her bungalow and all her relatives and friends had come along to say goodbye – knowing she had only a short while to live. Beside her bed was a Hospice Appeal collecting box which she encouraged her visitors to fill. On the Monday morning she arrived at the Hospice clutching the box with well over £400 in it – happy at being the first patient to come into the Hospice. That night she died peacefully, and a week later her funeral took place in the little Hospice Chapel where she had worshipped before she became ill. Somehow she symbolised what we had all been working so hard for over so many years.

On the 27th of November we gave thanks to God for the opening of the Hospice in a service of Thanksgiving at All Saints, the civic church. It was for me a great joy that I was asked to be part of the group that planned the service – a group that included our Chairman, the Monsignor, our free church friend, and the priest in charge of All Saints. The church was crowded with supporters, and the Bishop preached the sermon. It was a very special service, and what was so memorable for me was the wonderful spirit of Christian unity and love that pervaded.

All that remained was to plan the formal opening of the Hospice. Everyone wanted a 'Royal'. Our Foundation Stone had been laid by the Countess Mountbatten of Burma. It had been a very happy day and we hoped for a similar occasion with the formal opening. Six months after the Hospice opened we were delighted to learn from our Patron that Her Royal Highness the Princess of Wales had agreed to open the Hospice on the 28th of October 1992. The planning of the day was organised by the Patron, the Matron, the Bursar and the Chairman of the Board. None of the Appeal staff were involved. It was a mark that we had moved into a new era – the old giving way to the new. But it was a day that gave great delight to everyone – to all the Hospice staff and the six Appeal supporters who were introduced to her, to the patients with whom she talked with great care and understanding, and to the rest of the Appeal supporters who waited patiently in the gardens while she went round the Hospice, and who were thrilled when, in an unscheduled walkabout, she stopped to talk to them and congratulated them on their efforts. It was for our fundraisers a memorable day which made all their efforts over so many years seem worthwhile.

I stayed on for a year after the Hospice was opened but when I reached sixty I felt the time had come to retire, so I left the Hospice in August 1993.

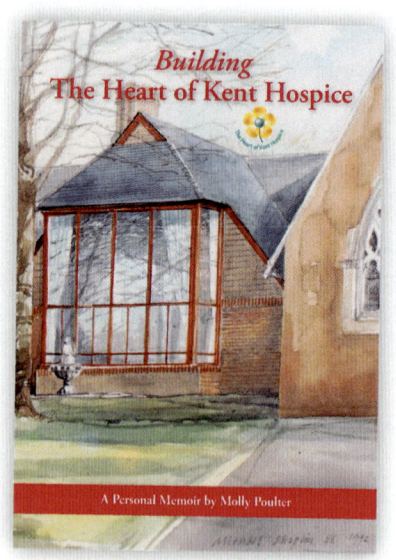

The Hospice story by Molly

Lady Diana opens the Hospice, October 1992

CHAPTER 27
My Christian Journey

Now in my 83rd year, I realise, looking back, that one of the most significant happenings in my life was becoming a Christian in 1981.

As I said earlier, neither Bill nor I were believers, but when our son was born, we had planned to have him christened. The moral scruples of the Godmother designate, who declined the invitation, had stopped us in our tracks. We had left the whole matter in abeyance, when terror struck and Justin developed the gastro-enteritis from which he nearly died. On the urging of the hospital matron, Justin was christened at the bedside by the hospital chaplain.

So it was that, a year later, when we moved to Ulcombe with Alex aged three months and Justin aged two and a half, we decided to have Alex christened – and I resolved to start going to church.

We were delighted to find we had such a beautiful mediaeval church in the village. With a simplicity and austerity which speaks of centuries of prayer, it has a

Ulcombe Church

dominating position at the top of Ulcombe Hill where it looks out across the valley and the village. When the Church is floodlit, its glow can be seen for miles around.

As I learnt later, the Church was built on Saxon foundations. The nave was built, soon after the Norman Conquest, by William St Leger who accompanied the invasion. Later, in 1213, a College of Priests was established there by Archbishop Simon Langton – a college for three priest, which was later was increased to five.

It had clearly been a religious site long before Christianity reached these shores. Two ancient yew trees in the churchyard, known to be over two thousand years old, are testament to pre-Christian rituals.

It's other claim to fame is that Cardinal Newman officiated there from time to time in the nineteenth century when he was staying as a guest in the Rectory at Ulcombe. The living was in the gift of the Marquis of Ormonde and was reputed to be one of the richest livings in Kent. At the turn of the century, the Rector was Lord Butler, a son of the Marquis of Ormonde. He lived in the huge Victorian rectory with seventeenth century outbuildings, attended by a retinue of retainers. Contemporary photographs show him as a tall, portly and imposing gentleman, with the bearing and confidence of an eighteenth century magnate.

Times changed. A new rectory was built in the 1970s – only to be sold by the Diocese a few years later, and replaced with a modern bungalow. That in its turn was sold in the 1980s and the parish amalgamated with nearby Harrietsham – much to the regret of the village which valued the presence of its own Rector, even though few ever worshipped at the Church.

My Godparents, Auntie Marie and Uncle Per, with our son, Justin

The village had a succession of what might be called eccentric Rectors. One, who had only one arm, used to ride vigorously round the countryside in a 'hail fellow well met' style which some people found intimidating. Another was twenty-nine years in the parish, spending as much time in the local pub, it seemed, as in the Church. He was regarded as a saint by a few devoted parishioners, but as a rogue by the villagers. Perhaps in despair of converting the village, he introduced high church practices and collected round him a group of worshippers who liked the incense and the elaborate ritual of Anglo-Catholicism – but who had little time for outreach and pastoral work. The congregation was small and eclectic, and the villagers distanced themselves more and more from the Church. The fabric was neglected, the Church rarely cleaned, and it was not until 1981 that the Rector finally departed under a cloud, and the Diocesan authorities grasped the problem and appointed, as priest in Charge, the Rector of a neighbouring parish. It was at this stage that my real Christian journey began.

Though my grandmother, and my aunt and uncle (who were my Godparents) had been church goers, my parents never went to church other than for weddings and funerals. If asked, they would have said they were C. of E. My father, with his strong sense of history, was a staunch upholder of the Church of England as an intrinsic part of the establishment. He was, at the time, Chairman of the Conservative Association in Bromley, and Harold Macmillan was our MP!

Although I was brought up in a non-Christian household, very good foundations were laid down from the age of twelve when, as I said earlier, I was taken to a Baptist Sunday school. From then onwards, the Baptist Church was, together with our very active Girl Guide Company, the centre of my social life. I attended Guides every Friday and the Young People's Fellowship with great regularity every Sunday afternoon, and again for the evening service at 6 o'clock.

Although the Baptists put strong pressure on us to commit ourselves and be baptised, I resisted. I was not helped by my father's attitude who, because of his historical interests, would have preferred to see me a part of the local Anglican church. When I suggested I should be baptised, my father was horrified. He believed that one got on in life better if one were part of the established church rather than a member of a non-conformist group. His opposition was total. And when I brought home *The Pledge* to sign, never to touch alcoholic drink, his horror was intense, and he tore it up in front of me. Suffering as I do from feelings of guilt about so many areas of my life, I shall ever remain grateful to him because alcohol, in moderate quantities, has been for Bill and me one of the pleasures of our social life! Had I signed *The Pledge* at the age of fifteen, I would, even now, feel guilty whenever I drank a glass of wine or my evening sherry!

It thus happened that when I left home to go to university, I'd made no commitment as a Christian. Arriving at the Hall of Residence at Bedford College to read History, I was soon pounced on by members of LIFCU – the London University Christian Union – and asked to join. The people canvassing me seemed far less interesting than some of the others I met – and I declined their invitation. I did go to church very occasionally but found the churches near the Hall of Residence in Swiss Cottage poorly attended by a handful of geriatric ladies, and soon stopped going to church altogether.

My degree completed, church figured in our lives through our wedding in church, and through attendance at the weddings of our friends – all of whom opted for church weddings, though few of them were church goers.

But Bill and I did enjoy visiting old churches and abbeys – Ely Cathedral with its massive Norman columns and Lantern Tower; Fountains Abbey in its serene setting with the beautiful remaining walls standing stark against the skyline; the nave of Canterbury Cathedral towering up and up; the beautiful fan vaulting of Westminster Abbey; the curious inverted arches of Wells Cathedral; the openness and light of York Minster; the massive remains of Rievaulx Abbey; and the simple Saxon churches we occasionally lit upon in our travels. The fascination of such a tremendous variety of architectural styles – the elaborate but very different cathedral façades, the arches ranging from solid Norman to graceful Perpendicular, the carving on the doorways, the different shaped windows, the stained glass, the complex and simple roof structures, and the very varied layouts – all so different and yet all designed to one end – the worship and glorification of God – provided endless interest – but nothing more.

So it was that when we moved to Ulcombe, we resolved to have Alex christened. That resolve soon foundered when we met up with the Rector who proved not only eccentric, but also very difficult. Because we weren't regular members of his congregation, the Rector was not over eager to fix a date. But we eventually pinned him down, and he said Alex could be christened during the morning service – not then the normal practice.

Our two families assembled at the Church in vast numbers for the christening, and sat through what was for them a very unfamiliar Anglo-Catholic service. The service over, and Alex not yet christened, everyone expected the christening to take place straight away. But the Rector decided otherwise. Completely ignoring the assembled company, he and his friends moved a grand piano from one side of the Church to the other, then stood putting the world to rights for ten minute, before at last acknowledging our presence

Our respective families were not impressed with his attitude, and my resolve to attend church regularly quickly waned. This was confirmed a few weeks later when the Rector proved obstructive about our desire to get a playgroup under way in his church hall. I felt that if this was how the Church treated aspiring Christians, rejecting the opportunity to bring our pre-school children within the ambience of the Church, I was not too sure I wanted to become part of the Christian community!

The final disillusionment came a year later when I took both Justin and Alex to the Mothering Sunday service and heard the Rector thundering from the pulpit

Alex at her christening with Bill's mother, 1967

that Mothering Sunday was not about mothers and children but about the Motherhood of the Church. That, coupled with the fact that it was a communion service, and everyone but me went up to the altar to receive communion, left me feeling a complete outcast, and I didn't enter the Church again, apart from school services, until we had a new Rector in 1981.

In fact, from this point on, both Bill and I became very cynical about religion – a cynicism that was already endemic for Bill who still found it difficult to reconcile with Christian belief his memory of army chaplains blessing guns during the War.

Unlike a town church, a village church, especially a mediaeval church, plays an integral part in the life of a village. For though the regular worshipping congregation is often very small, and regular services are attended by only a few of the parishioners, most villagers regard the Church as theirs of right to use for the *Rites of Passage* – baptisms, marriages and funerals. They practise a sort of folk Christianity which provides a base from which true Christian belief can either grow or wither. And those involved with the village school would be affronted were the pupils not able to perform their Harvest and Christmas Nativity rituals in the Church, observed by their doting parents and grandparents.

Then there are the parishioners who value their mediaeval church for its historic interest, and who work hard to preserve the fabric of the buildings, though they rarely attend any of the services of the Church.

Returning a few years ago, after forty years absence, to the Baptist Church where I spent my youth, I realise what wonderful Christian foundations were then laid. We had excellent Bible Study sessions, culminating in annual Bible Study Exams (at which, being of an academic turn of mind, I excelled and usually obtained top marks) and we all knew the main Bible stories by heart. We were given beautifully illustrated little texts – the first I ever received, which I still have in my Bible, was John 3:13: 'For God so loved the world that he gave His only Begotten Son whosoever believeth in Him should not perish but have everlasting life'.

It is a text that is often with me. One of my first memories of the Baptist Sunday School was learning by heart the 23rd Psalm, and not long after, we had to commit to memory 1 Corinthians 13: 'Though I speak with the tongues of men and of angels and have not charity I am become as a sounding brass or a clashing symbol.'

How often has that text in recent years come to mind! What the Baptist Sunday School did for me was to imbue a theoretical knowledge of Christianity. But it had no personal relevance. It was theory in a vacuum. Like so many others, I subscribed to Christian values and, to a certain extent, to Christian moral concepts. But the joy and the pain, the certainty, and the God given strength that comes from true belief was totally lacking.

Looking back, I realise that God had been nudging me over the years and I was not hearing. I think of the poem, *The Hound of Heaven*, by Francis Thompson

> *'I fled Him, down the nights and down the days,*
> *I fled Him down the arches of the years*
> *I fled Him down the labyrinthine ways*
> *Of my own mind; and in the midst of tears*
> *I hid from Him'*

But I little expected to be caught as totally as I was on one particular morning in September 1981.

Our eccentric Rector finally departed under a cloud, though I had, in the last years, seen a different side to him when we found ourselves looking after two young boys whose father had had a stroke and quickly died. Aged only ten and twelve, they had already suffered the trauma of their mother's death from cancer less than a year before, and it was a desperately painful time for us, and devastating for the boys. The only relative they had, on either side of the family, was an aunt in Derbyshire, so the boys stayed with us while we sorted out their father's funeral and their own future.

I asked the Rector to conduct the funeral service and to talk to the boys beforehand as, in their grief, they had developed all sorts of bizarre ideas about death and funerals – having been denied the opportunity of going to their mother's funeral. I was impressed, and touched, by the delicate way in which the Rector dealt with the boys, and realised that, though he had gone astray in so many ways, there was an underlying faith which made his Christianity real.

With the Rector's departure, the Diocese decided to place the parish under the care of the incumbent of a neighbouring parish as Priest-in-Charge. One of our local farmers, the Chairman of the Parish Council, who had a strong social conscience, urged everyone to go to church 'to support the new man', and Bill and I dutifully attended once or twice. At that point, had anyone asked us about our religious beliefs, we would both have said we were agnostics. It was something we had discussed in depth in our younger days, but over the years, we had both accepted that we 'didn't know whether there was a God or not' and we left it at that – a sort of sublime indifference.

Most of our friends seemed to share the same indifference and uncertainty, but there was one particular friend who had very definite views. He was a confirmed atheist. Having been brought up by a very strict sect of Plymouth Brethren, he had a comprehensive knowledge of the Bible, and a full understanding of what 'conversion' meant, and was in headlong flight from all the beliefs that his parents had tried to inculcate.

So it was on that fateful weekend, pursuing my life in the normal humdrum manner, that I entered, unsuspecting, into a conversation and a visit to church that was to change my inner life in a most dramatic fashion.

For those without Christian belief, the description and explanation of religious experience both embarrasses and affronts. I experienced that embarrassment as a teenager when confronted by the Billy Graham Crusade, and later when meeting up with 'born again' Christians. And I am aware that for those with a scientific approach to life, who want 'scientific proof' of the existence of God, descriptions of religious experience appear as hysteria or emotionalism.

It is, therefore, not easy to explain in terms which the non believer can understand what happened that day in September 1981. Nor, perhaps, should I even attempt to. But none of my family and friends will deny the impact it had on my own life, and on the lives of those around me.

One Friday afternoon, returning from school, I found the new rector had called. I made a pot of tea and we sat down and talked. I told him I had been in the wilderness for years, and that Bill and I were 'very hard nuts to crack.' I explained a little of our religious background, and also expressed my lack of ease on those rare occasions when I went to church and it was a communion service. I said I felt embarrassed and isolated sitting alone in the pew, while everyone else went up to the altar to receive communion. He expressed surprise that no one had ever suggested going up to the communion rail for a blessing, and suggested I might do that the next time I went to church.

It happened that the next Sunday was Harvest Festival. Bill, Alex and I had already decided to go to church. Village Harvest Festival Services are always rather special and we had, over the years, gone from time to time because the local primary school was involved in the service. I resolved I would accept the Rector's suggestion and go up and receive a blessing, and suggested to Alex and Bill that they accompany me. They declined.

How can one describe an experience of such profound significance that it has coloured my whole life since? At one moment I was a sceptic, and at the next I had an overwhelming awareness of the presence of God, and of His love and power. He seized me and entered my life in a very real sense. Yet I am aware that there is no way I can describe what happened which a non-believer would find credible. All I can say is that at the moment the invitation to the communion came, I started quaking, and a few minutes later, as I knelt at the altar rail and received a blessing, I knew with a certainty that I cannot explain in a tangible or scientific way, that God existed and that His son, Jesus Christ died for me, that I was loved, and that in accepting Him as my Saviour my sins were forgiven.

Such words, the day before, even the hour before, would have sounded to me trite and pious. But from that moment on, I was aware of their reality.

For the next weeks I lived in a daze. Everything I was involved in seemed to have a different feel about it. I remember the next day, immediately school was over, going into town to buy a Bible, which from then on I started reading each day. I also went to see the Rector to discuss what had happened – but it was some days before I was able to share it with Bill who, as I had feared, was deeply sceptical.

I remember, too, that the following Saturday we all went to a twenty-first birthday party. It was a typical party with a lot of drink, and a lot of loud music and laughter. I somehow felt distanced from my fellow guests during the evening in a way difficult to explain. And the following weekend we celebrated my father's eightieth birthday at The Oast. Again, everything felt different, and I looked at my family with new eyes.

Since that Harvest Festival, I have never willingly missed a Sunday service. Church services, instead of being routine and meaningless, suddenly became alive and joyous. The prayers, which had before seemed endless, now took on life and became real conversations with God. My first waking thought was an awareness of God's presence, and I started on a regular prayer life and Bible reading. I soon realised that though I was very familiar with the Old Testament and Gospel stories, I had never read the Acts of the Apostles in a coherent fashion, nor understood the story of the early church, the real significance of Pentecost, and the coming of the Holy Spirit.

I had much to learn and discover, and started on a course of avid religious reading – with books regularly supplied by the new rector who was delighted to find such a keen student. Looking back, I think I was fed solids when I should have been given milk. The Christian life is not easy, and there are many pitfalls as C.S. Lewis so vividly portrays in his *Screwtape Letters* with the devil doing his best to recapture the soul of the newly-converted Christian.

I smile when I think of those who say that Christianity is an escape, an easy option, or a 'cop out' from reality. I found the Christian life far from easy. I discovered slowly that the Christian life is not about doing, but about being, about forgiving, about giving, and above all, about love.

Entering into the Christian life as suddenly as I did was not, after the honeymoon period was over, as easy as it might be perhaps for those who have come to faith gradually over a long period. One is forced into self examination, into an admission of all the failures, the omissions and neglect, the self seeking, the censorious attitudes, the pride, of one's former life. It was, and remains, a time of self evaluation and self revelation. The use of the Confessional is something many Anglicans find anathema, and I am not sure of its place, for me, in my everyday Christian life. But that first confession I was encouraged to make, had a cathartic effect, and though very difficult, I believe helped me in those early heady days of belief.

If asked what was the aspect of Christianity that had the most impact on me on first becoming a Christian, I would say that it was a realisation, which had eluded me in my early Baptist days, that the central theme of the Gospel is love. But it was something that came through with startling power as I embarked on my Christian journey. Love is a word that appears time and time again, and it is about a love that is total – 'Thou shalt love the Lord thy God with all thy soul and with all thy might. And the second commandment is like unto the first, Thou shalt love thy neighbour as thyself.'

I realised how easy it is to love those one likes and who like you, and to be kind and helpful to your friends, or even to the needy. But how very difficult to love those one doesn't like, and those who have done you harm! But that is the Christian gospel.

And, in some ways, as I explored further, I realised that that simple injunction included the loving of oneself. And for me, that has been almost more difficult. We are all complex beings, the products of our environment as well as of our heredity. I had a very happy childhood despite the trauma of being brought up during the War years with all the fears and anxieties of the bombing. But my parents, though caring, were not demonstrative, and my father was one of the old school, who never believed in giving praise in case it made one 'big headed'! So, although he would boast to his friends of my academic achievements, he would never give me any praise. And, moreover, he would indicate that he thought I was difficult and no beauty, and that I would not find it easy to get myself a husband! Although I was well aware of my abilities, it made me feel unattractive, and led to a lack of confidence in my relationships. My sister, on the other hand, who was vivacious and very attractive, he made to feel intellectually inferior to her clever sister, and she was thwarted in her ambitions to pursue a worthwhile career. But she had no self doubts in her relationships with the other sex. I am sure this sort of parenting is not unique, and that the hang-ups we both suffered from over the years is fairly widespread. But this sort of upbringing makes it difficult to love oneself, and to have that inner confidence which is so important if one is to relate easily to other people.

That is what becoming a Christian did for me. It was as though, in accepting Christ, a well spring of love was released. I felt a love and a warmth to the people around me. I was aware that in the past I had been far more concerned with what people thought of me, than in what sort of people they really were. I began, in a very tentative way, to empathise with people, and feel their sorrows and their joys. I no longer felt inhibited about touching people, and was happy with the spontaneous touch or embrace which previously had made me withdraw like a frightened kitten. And I realised what I had missed in not having demonstrative parents. I envied those who had been brought up in hugging families – and realised for the first time how important touch is to human well-being. I was grateful to the Christians I began to meet with who were spontaneous in this way, and I found myself able to give that sympathetic squeeze of the hand, that embrace, even that simple kiss, that is so helpful to people in times of distress.

But, of course, there are pitfalls. That overflowing of love which becoming a Christian releases, can overflow in the wrong direction – and it is the sort of temptation which C.S. Lewis so aptly describes in his *Screwtape Letters*.

I was fortunate in my marriage, having found a husband who was consistently true to the married state, and incredibly supportive of all my enthusiasms over the years. We always shared everything – opening a joint account before we were married, sharing domestic duties and responsibilities, and sharing ideas and beliefs. A great believer in the equality of the sexes, and the innate right of a woman to work and use her talents and abilities, he provided the steady base, the rock, from which I launched myself into new work and experiences. But we are not always analytical or aware of the source of our strength. And being of a dilettante nature, there were times when I found the sameness of marriage irksome. It seems to me not an entirely natural state. One enjoys variety in one's activities, in one's food, in one's work. As someone who is very gregarious, I enjoy meeting new people and developing new friendships – and this cuts across the barriers of sex. But when one is overflowing with a love that has been liberated, there are dangers and temptations – and these can and did cause sadness and confusion as I moved into the new life of a Christian.

The problems were exacerbated by the fact that Bill and the children, instead of following me into the Christian life, reacted violently against it. Again, this was probably inevitable, judging by the enthusiasm and conviction with which I proclaimed the Gospel. But had I joined a church that was united, where people worked together in true Christian harmony, their reaction may not have been so extreme. But as it was, I had entered the Christian life in a church which was rent in half by controversy – a conflict between the 'high church' outsiders who had worshipped there for the past ten years, and the 'low church' villagers who wanted to reclaim their inheritance. With a rector who was, as he said himself, a 'Christian cocktail', enjoying both the charismatic and the orthodox forms of worship, as well as being drawn by the high church ritual of Anglo-Catholicism, which he now found himself surrounded by, he was in no position to give a firm lead in any particular direction. And with a nature that preferred compromise to confrontation, he followed a policy of going along with the views of whichever group he happened to be with, and resolutely refused to be drawn into an open debate or confrontation. Since not all the groups were totally loving in the way they promoted their own views, and the way they fought those who threatened them, they were not very good representatives of the Christian faith.

As Bill and I had always been open and shared thoughts and ideas, I could not refrain from telling him what was happening in the Church. And this, of course, convinced him that Christianity was a sham and that my belief was misguided and based on an emotional mid-life crisis. He demanded scientific proof whenever we discussed Christianity – and though I tried using the contrary argument that there was no scientific proof that God did *not* exist, he was not to be moved. And this, for a time, put a divide between us which made other pastures look even greener. It was a difficult time, and it was only through the support of prayer and some wonderful Christian friends and counsellors that I was able to work through it, and not only accept the divide within our marriage but also find it enriched.

The years that followed my conversion were difficult and sad in other ways. We seemed to be surrounded by illness and death. My mother had died six years earlier and looking back, I am not sure I ever grieved properly for her. Her death in hospital, as I have said, was far more sudden than we had expected, and we were unsupported and found it difficult to grieve openly. Later, leading the local Appeal for a hospice, from time to time I gave the Address in a morning service, and told the parishioners about the way she died in hospital and how, unlike in a hospice, we were neither supported nor helped, I was stopped by many after the service, who came up to me and said how closely my words had touched them as I had spoken to them of their own experiences.

Around the time of my conversion, we lost our neighbours, both husband and wife, within a year of each other. They left behind the two sons aged nine and ten whom I mentioned earlier. We looked after them for six weeks while we tried to sort out their future. Their only remaining relative was an elderly cousin, who had agreed to be their guardian some months before their mother died. She was willing to do her duty, but felt she could not take on total responsibility for them unless they went to boarding school during term time. As a result their secondary school headmaster and I spent a lot of time in consultation with the Education and Social Services departments of both Kent and Derbyshire, between which counties their lives had been divided, trying to persuade them to pay for boarding school for the boys – though I knew in my heart of hearts that this was not the best solution for them and that, were we truly Christian in our giving, we would have made a home for them ourselves.

Two uncles of whom I was very fond, and an aunt, died in quick succession, and we had both Bill's mother and my aunt in hospital in opposite directions – one in Morden, Essex, and one in Eastbourne – both suffering from Alzheimer's disease. For two years we spent two evenings each month on a five hour round trek, visiting Essex one week and Sussex the next. That was a deeply distressing time. Neither my mother-in-law nor my aunt recognised us, and it was heartbreaking to see them lingering on in a cabbage-like state year after year – well looked after but with seemingly no quality of life at all. Bill would ask, 'And where is God in all this suffering' – a question that all Christians are confronted with and one which they cannot, in truth answer except through faith. But that leap of faith is something the person who has not made it cannot comprehend.

My mother-in-law's death was the real ending of a chapter. Before going into hospital, she had lived for many years with Bill's eldest sister and her husband. All three died within a five month period, and we found ourselves visiting the same crematorium in Brentwood on three occasions between the April and August. It was a desolate period.

Looking back, I think it was a major cause of the depression that hung over the family for many months. And not long after that we lost one of our oldest and dearest friends, Bish Pandey, a historian and author of a biography of *Nehru*, who, over the years, had become one of the family, and had spent many holidays with us and our children. It was his daughters whom Alex chose to be her bridesmaids when she married some ten years later.

My mother's death, which I have already written about, occurred during this same period. Looking back, it is perhaps not altogether surprising that I found myself a few years later involved with the hospice movement

It was probably inevitable that soon after I was confirmed, I became involved in the administrative life of the Church. I was elected onto the Parochial Church Council, and was persuaded to unlock the Church each morning on my way to school. The Rector presented me with an enormous and heavy key which I carried round in my handbag for years. I unlocked the Church every morning from then on until long after I'd retired from school and the Hospice Appeal – and it was only my bad back which led me to pass on the key in 2011.

I soon found myself as a representative on the Deanery Synod – and from there was elected to the Diocesan Synod where, a few years' later, I missed out, by just one vote, being elected as its Lay Chairman.

I then served as a Church Warden for eleven years, and finally became the Lay Chair of the North Downs Deanery Synod.

Some years into my Christian life, not long before the ordination of women to the priesthood was accepted, I very tentatively explored priestly ministry at the suggestion of two very different local clerics. But the then Archdeacon, not having a very high regard for women priests, said he thought I would have a more useful role as a lay person, so I dropped the idea.

My new found belief led to the holiday fostering of an eleven year old boy from the Caldecott Community. He had had a horrendous childhood, and although his mother was still in contact with him, the Caldecott Community felt it would be good for him if he could spend time with a 'normal' family during the summer holidays. He spent part of every holiday and half term with us, and became a real part of the family. Now living in Canada, he is married with a beautiful baby daughter. But there were long periods when we didn't hear from him at all. But he was always totally confident of his welcome, and now, twenty years on, with his real and very difficult mother dead, he insists on calling me his foster mother and I am 'grannie fos' to his daughter. He was a very bright lad and should have gone on to higher education, but it was the necessary sorting out of who he was, and of his roots, that prevented him for some years from developing his potential. But, as he often says, the contact he had over the years with our son and daughter, helped to provide him with a stable pattern on which to model himself. He achieved academic success and held a senior post in the computing world before setting up his own very successful computing business. He is now a minister in the Centre for Spiritual Living.

Carmien and Molly

In 1993, at the age of 60, I felt the time had come to leave the Hospice. But I was not ready for real retirement, and got involved with a group of people in Guildford who wanted to raise money for their own hospice. I spent nearly a year laying the foundations for an appeal, when it was discovered there was a semi-official group which wanted to take over – so I left.

But I was not meant to retire. Within a short time, the new rector, knowing I had raised a lot of money for our own mediaeval church at Ulcombe, asked me to head up the fund raising appeal at his other church in Harrietsham.

The money successfully raised, our church architect then asked me to organise the fund raising at Brookland Church on the marshes, and this was followed by a request, through the Diocese, that I help St George's in Ramsgate – a huge Victorian church which Queen Victoria used to attend, and which, originally, could seat 2,000 people.

In this way, my circle of friends and acquaintances increased rapidly. I was also, during this period, a member of the Church organisation called FLAME – Family Life and Marriage Education. My reputation for successful fund raising led the Bishop's wife, Jennifer Llewellin, to ask me to try and raise funds for the organisation so we could appoint a full worker. This we did. I was also involved in fund raising for MOD – the Maidstone Organisation for the disabled.

Now, at the beginning of 2016, my only 'official' involvement is with the Diocesan Synod, the PCC, and the Chairmanship of the Friends of Ulcombe Church.

But it is, of course, the Christian life itself that is the more important. Ten years ago I wrote, 'But the journey to this present plateau has not been easy nor without some pain and difficulties, and I am deeply conscious that the plateau we are now on is but a stage in the journey. For life is a pilgrimage and no one knows what the next stage will bring. Over the years I have felt God's guiding hand. He has broken me at times and moulded me at others, and little by little I have begun to trust and wait on the Holy Spirit. I have learnt that when one door shuts it is because another is waiting to open. I have tried to 'wait patiently on the Lord.' What perhaps has been the most important thing is to know the power of love and that I am loved.

CHAPTER 28
Of Such Things

It was in 1996 that Bill and I decided the time had come to downsize. We started exploring the possibility of converting the broken down dairy in the garden into a house, dividing the garden and keeping the swimming pool. It took us two years to get planning permission, and when we finally succeeded, we put The Oast on the market in 1997.

Our first buyers fell through, so it took eighteen months to sell. What we had purchased for £5,000 in 1966, we sold for £376,000 in 1999! It cost us about £230,000 to convert The Old Dairy, and for a while we felt we were financially secure.

While the dairy was being converted, the farmer, who owned the farm buildings opposite, got permission to convert them into dwellings, so, by the time we moved into The Old Dairy, we had three attractive houses opposite instead of derelict farm buildings.

Because we had no capital behind us, we knew we would have to live in rented accommodation while the old dairy was being converted. We were very lucky indeed when friends in the lovely old house by the Church, Ulcombe Place, offered their flat to us. We were very happy there, and, apart from three months just after Christmas, we spent the whole of the fifteen months at Ulcombe Place – moving out of The Oast in October 1999, and into The Old Dairy in December 2000.

It had been a great wrench leaving The Oast and I wept all day. We'd lavished so many hours of work, money and care over the thirty-three years we'd lived there. But once we moved into The Old Dairy, we realised it had been a wise decision. The new house was well insulated, had all the modern conveniences, was spacious, easier to maintain, and had even better views than we had at The Oast. Moreover, we still had the swimming pool!

Above The Old Dairy as it was in 1966,

Above and below: The Old Dairy before conversion

Of Such Things

Above: The Old Dairy converted. Below: One 'room' in the Old Dairy garden

343

Bill and Molly on the Baltric Cruise in 2000

    We were very happy. In 2002 we went to Prague and then cruised down the Elbe, and in the July had a wonderful cruise through the Baltic to St. Petersburg.

    Bill and I had four years together at The Old Dairy. We spent a lot of time creating the new garden. Bill built stone walls and iron railings round the swimming pool while I landscaped the garden.

    In that summer Alex and Paddy moved up to York when Paddy got a new job. We were very sad to see them go and it hit home in the November when drama struck and I was diagnosed with breast cancer. It was just a month before their third baby was due. We'd promised to go up to York for the birth to look after the children. Though the surgeon was very helpful and did the operation almost immediately, I was not well enough to go until the New Year, so Paddy's parents stepped in. We arrived on New Year's Eve to see our latest grandchild, Oscar.

    2003 was spent coping with chemotherapy and radiotherapy which lasted for ten months, but by the end of the year all this was behind us and we were hoping to get back to a normal life when drama struck again – this time much more serious. Bill was diagnosed with mesothelioma – a fatal malignant disease for which there is no treatment.

    Bill was born during the General Strike in 1926 in relative poverty in East Ham. He passed the exam to go to the grammar school but his parents couldn't afford the uniform and books, so he went to the local elementary school. The school closed down because of the bombing, and he had little education after the age of thirteen.

He undertook a number of jobs, including working in the office of an asbestos factory, before joining the Royal Corps of Signals in 1944. He was posted to the Far East and spent the latter part of the Second World War in India, Malaya and Java in the Royal Signals as a Signalman, using morse code as a wireless operator. Towards the end of the war, there was an opportunity for service men to study and take exams which would enable them to go to university when demobbed. Bill did well and enjoyed the study but sadly, just before the day of the exams, he was needed as a wireless operator and was posted away. The opportunity did not come again.

After the war, Bill worked for the United Scottish Insurance Company. We met at a Workers Travel Association hotel at Southbourne where I was working during the summer after getting my degree. I encouraged him to resume the studies which had been interrupted while in the army. He went to a college of further education and sat 'O' and 'A' levels in a year. He then went on to Goldsmiths' College where he obtained a diploma in education and went on to teach, firstly at Raglan Hayesford School and then as a lecturer at the Mid Kent College of Technology. He retired in 1982.

He lived all his married life in Kent, and in his spare time he converted the Oast, restored furniture, and indulged his passion for fishing and writing poetry and prose. He was a great family man and adored by his children.

Bill was ill for just three months. He died at home surrounded by the family. On the morning of his death, his book *Wisps*, was published, and he died holding it in his hand.

"See those little wispy clouds, they have to go wherever the wind takes them. Sometimes they meet and join together. Sometimes they're big enough to make rain, and then the wind and the Sun changes them again – but in the end they become nothing! That's just what we are, Jason, just wisps!"

Set during the Second World War, Wisps tells the story of artist Jason Bridge, born in poverty in Rotherhithe, and privileged Elizabeth Westfield, heir to the Trepplestone Estate. Their relationship begins when Jason and his sister are evacuated to Elizabeth's country house. Wisps takes us on their personal journeys of war and class prejudice, through bombed-out London, a troopship to India, Calcutta and Burma, and then back to post war Britain. Their journeys weave in and out like wisps of cloud.

For Bill's funeral service we chose the crematorium at Charing for the funeral – a beautiful and tranquil place. Over a hundred people came to the service, and in the afternoon we had a Memorial Service in Ulcombe Church where two hundred people arrived to say farewell.

One of my paintings

    Services such as Memorial services can be a great consolation to the family. No less than eight people – family and friends – got up and paid tribute to a lovely, gentle and humorous man. I am sure it was a help to me, and to Justin and Alex, and our son-in-law, Paddy, who all grieved deeply for him.

    What can one say about widowhood? It's something every couple has to face – that one or other of you will die first, leaving the other behind to face life alone. We all deal with it differently. Some let grief take over so that they find it difficult to cope with life. Queen Victoria was a prime example of this. But others try to get on and rebuild their lives. I'm very fortunate in that I have many interests and continue to have a significant role in three local societies – the History Society, the Roundabout Lunch Club, and the Friendship Club for old people! A new involvement has been the setting up of a Friends organisation to help raise money for the improvement of our mediaeval church. I also continue my involvement with the Diocese, although I have recently resigned as Lay Chair of the Deanery Synod.

    I spend a lot of my time writing – novels, short stories and these Memoirs. Painting is another hobby – though I don't seem to find much time to settle down and paint. Evenings are often the lonelier times – but television is a great comfort! I'm surrounded by friends and very good neighbours – so I feel blessed – and it is only when I feel unwell that the loneliness becomes most difficult to cope with.

Looking back, I realise that since Bill died I have had a trip abroad almost every year. The first was to India with NADFAS when my childhood friend, Pam, came with me. Then I went to South Africa with *Habitat for Humanity* to help build houses in the township of Mutelani. My foster son sent me a ticket to visit Canada, so I had a lovely time getting to know his baby daughter and wife, sharing for a fortnight his life out there. I went alone to Egypt on a cruise up the Nile, and then spent a week exploring Luxor. I visited Pompeii and Herculaneum with a hospice friend, and the Isle of Wight with another. I had a second visit to Canada, went to Oberammagau with a Christian group to see the Passion play, went on a pilgrimage *In the steps of St Paul,* where sadly I contracted a noro virus and missed seeing Ephesus. The following year I went on a pilgrimage to Israel where I ended up in hospital in Jerusalem and Alex had to fly out to rescue me! That, I think, has put an end to flying as I don't think the insurance companies will cover me again!

But there is still much to do and see in England. I visit York regularly to see Alex and family, and have lovely friends in Scotland whom I visit each year. I used to visit my sister and her husband often when they lived in Sussex but sadly they have now moved to Cumbria so I see them less frequently.

Though my body is not as robust as it was, and the advancing years are causing deterioration, I still manage to lead a very active life. The breast cancer, which I had in 2002, is now, hopefully, behind me (though there is always the niggle that it might return), a small heart problem, recently diagnosed, thanks to the miracles of modern medicine, seems to be under control. What is most troublesome is the back problem that originated from making The Oast garden way back in 1967. I can no longer wander the fields and footpaths as I used to, which is sad. But I still retain all my mental faculties – for which I thank God.

My main worry now is that my pension is scarcely keeping up with the rise in the cost of living. I am one of the many pensioners who is 'asset rich and income poor'. The solution would be to sell up and move to a smaller house and garden, but that is something I am reluctant to do as I have so many friends who live locally and as I said above, I have a very full work and social life.

MY FAMILY
Though my children, Justin and Alex, have featured often throughout my Memoirs, I don't think I have expressed fully how much they mean to me. Without the love and care they have showered on me I would not be as content as I am. They are my pride and joy and I love them dearly. I have also been fortunate in having a lovely daughter-in law, Eve, and a very caring son-in-law, Paddy, as well as six grandchildren whom I adore.

Wedding of Justin and Eve, October 1992

Looking back, I think Bill and I were blessed with our children. We never had any real problems with them other than anxieties when illness struck or exams loomed. I know they both look back to happy childhoods and both have fond memories of The Oast which was the venue for many happy parties and social gatherings.

In their early years we made every effort to introduce them to a variety of activities to widen their horizons. Justin in his early teens discovered *Dungeons and Dragons*, and then *Napoleonic War Gaming* – and his hobby was set for life! He has a group of friends whom he has 'war gamed' with weekly over the years, and has a large wooden shed furnished specially for their gatherings.

Both Alex and Justin started learning to play the piano but Justin gave up fairly quickly (though now regrets it). Alex also plays the flute – the result of hearing James Galway playing at a local concert. She is an accomplished musician and has passed on her love of music to her three children.

Harriet, Angus and Felicity Poulter, 2007

Both Justin and Alex were part of the short-lived Thameside system of education, and went to the local grammar schools at the age of thirteen. Justin, whose interest in computing started early, did a degree in mathematical sciences at Portsmouth Polytechnic, while Alex went to Oxford Polytechnic (now Oxford Brooks University) and did a degree in English and Publishing.

Justin came home to live after graduating. He first got a computing job with Kent County Council computerising all the lampposts in and around Maidstone! He then joined a large London firm, and after a few years moved on and is working for a large American insurance company in charge of an international computing network. It involves travelling regularly to the USA and to many other countries.

He met Eve through one of my hospice friends and they married in 1992. They first bought a house in Maidstone and then purchased a large house in Sutton Valence which they moved to at about the same time we purchased The Old Dairy. For me, this is a blessing as they are only four miles away and I see them frequently.

They have three children who are a delight. Harriet, the eldest, is artistic and is now doing a Fine Arts degree at Bath Spa University, Angus, mathematical like his father, is at the University of Bath reading maths, while Felicity wants to be an actress. She has a natural talent and I am hopeful she will succeed. All three have taken part in local drama and played leading roles in local pantomime.

Eve has been very involved with the local community. Then a few years ago decided to do a degree in History as a mature student at Christchurch University in

Of Such Things

Wedding of Alex and Paddy, July 1989

Canterbury. We were all very proud of her as it was a big commitment with three children still at school, all needing transport for the usual after-school activities – drama, music lessons, scouts, ballet and homework!

Alex first got a job in Oxford working for Blackwells Bookshop where she met her first Apple Macintosh computer. No one was very keen on using it so she set to and learnt how to master it. It was not long before she was head hunted by a private graphic designer who wanted her to teach him how to use his Apple Mac and in return he taught her how to design – a sort of apprenticeship. Their main client was Oxford University so it was a fantastic learning experience for her. After a couple of years, in 1992, she decided that she would set up her own graphic design business in Kent called Ampersand. She ran it from the large bedroom in the Oast and Bill helped her with the accounts, proof reading and day-to-day running which he thoroughly enjoyed. It was lovely for Alex to work so closely with her father,

Toby, Genevieve and Oscar Hawes, 2007

something she is eternally grateful for. The business was very successful and at one point they were designing seven glossy magazines. Once Alex moved to Yorkshire it became difficult to keep running the business on a large scale so she went freelance. She now works for a subsidiary of The University of York as their senior designer

Alex met Paddy when she was just sixteen and had gone to Portsmouth to visit her brother. Paddy was studying Biological Sciences and was very musical. I think it was love at first sight because she never went out with anyone else after that.

Paddy now works in a niche market designing constructed wetlands, or reed beds, to treat both municipal and industrial waste waters, allowing them to be discharged back, harmlessly, into the environment. He travels a great deal around the country and often overseas.

They married in 1987 and moved to Abingdon for a few years before moving back to Kent where their first two children, Toby and Genevieve were born. Then, when their third child, Oscar, was on the way, they moved up to York. Though they live what seems a long way away to me, we manage to get together about six times a year.

Their three children are very musical like their parents and have all been choristers at York Minster which has been a great joy. Oscar left in July 2016. It was a real bereavement for them all when he left as the children have been part of the Minster choir since 2007. I don't think people realise quite how much time choristers (and their families) spend in a place like York Minster. None of the choristers are boarders, so parents have to get them to school by 8am every morning for choir practice. After

My six grandchildren in the Summer of 2015 – Top from left: Felicity, Genevieve and Harriet. Bottom from left: Toby, Oscar and Angus

Evensong, parents don't collect them until after 6pm. Weekends are as busy – although, as York Minster has girls as well as boys they share all the services out. This does not touch on all the extra services that take place during the year which involve more practices and visits to the Minster. One of the highlights of my grandchildren's time at the Minster was the Queen's visit in 2012 when she distributed Maundy Money.

It is almost a full-time commitment. Parents spend a lot of time waiting around, and as a result a real sense of family develops. When the choristers finally leave, parents feel bereaved as Alex and Paddy did when their long association with the Minster and its community came to an end. But it doesn't really finish, because ex choristers are invited to sing with the St. William's Singers – a choir which sings at Midnight Mass on Christmas Eve and at the Easter Vigil. Toby, Genevieve and Oscar will sing together with this choir for the first time at Christmas 2016.

Toby is now training to be a doctor and Genevieve wants to follow a singing career – a result of her years as a chorister. She has a very beautiful voice and has already taken part in productions of *Les Miserables* and *The Phantom of the Opera* in York, and has been down to Ulcombe on two occasions to sing where she greatly

Bill

impressed her audiences. But I know it will be a difficult career to follow. Oscar, at 13, is still uncertain what he wants to do.

    I sometimes wonder from whom the musical and acting talent of my grandchildren has been inherited. It certainly wasn't from me! They are all a great joy to me and I love them dearly. What gives me great happiness is that the six grandchildren, though living at such a distance from each other, love getting together.

    In September 2015 both Toby and Harriet 'fled the nest' and went off to university – Toby to Leicester and Harriet to Bath. I am not sure that many parents realise the significance of this departure – the fact that their children may never come home again to live and the whole family structure is changed for ever.

I was very happy that both Justin and Alex and their spouses felt confident enough to come back and live at home again. When Alex and Paddy had been married for several years they wanted to sell their house, get new jobs and move back to Kent. It was the time of the slump and things were not easy so they moved in with us and stayed for two happy years. It was during this time that Alex set up her very successful business, Ampersand. Then, some years after Bill died, Justin, Eve and family moved in for six months while their house was extended and completely re-modelled.

I now look back over the years and feel that I have been blessed even though I have lost Bill. I had a very happy marriage and a husband who was caring and very supportive of my many interests and ventures, and he was a father who was respected and greatly loved by Justin and Alex

Now, with all the love and care showered on me by Justin and Alex and their families, I feel content and thank God for my life.

Molly 2015